The Protectors of Indians in the Royal Audience of Lima

Studies in the History of Private Law

VOLUME 19–10

The titles published in this series are listed at *brill.com/lhl*

The Protectors of Indians in the Royal Audience of Lima

History, Careers and Legal Culture, 1575–1775

By

Mauricio Novoa

BRILL
NIJHOFF

LEIDEN | BOSTON

Library of Congress Cataloging-in-Publication Data

Names: Novoa, Mauricio, author.
Title: The protectors of Indians in the Royal Audience of Lima : history, careers and legal culture, 1575-1775 / By Mauricio Novoa.
Description: Leiden : Brill, 2016. | Series: Legal history library ; 19 | Series: Studies in the history of private law ; 10 | Includes bibliographical references and index. | Description based on print version record and CIP data provided by publisher; resource not viewed.
Identifiers: LCCN 2015045121 (print) | LCCN 2015044039 (ebook) | ISBN 9789004305175 (E-book) | ISBN 9789004305168 (hardback : alk. paper)
Subjects: LCSH: Indians of South America--Legal status, laws, etc.--Peru--History. | Lima (Audiencia)--History. | Ombudspersons--Peru--History. | Appellate courts--Peru--History. | Justice, Administration of--Peru--History.
Classification: LCC KHQ2202 (print) | LCC KHQ2202 .N68 2016 (ebook) | DDC 342.8508/720903--dc23
LC record available at http://lccn.loc.gov/2015045121

Typeface for the Latin, Greek, and Cyrillic scripts: "Brill". See and download: brill.com/brill-typeface.

ISSN 1874-1793
ISBN 978-90-04-30516-8 (hardback)
ISBN 978-90-04-30517-5 (e-book)

This book is printed on acid-free paper and produced in a sustainable manner.

A Marina

Contents

Acknowledgements

Many people supported my work in my sojours in Cambridge, Lima, London, Santiago, Berlin, Gerona, Bloomington (Indiana) and Quito. I am particularly grateful to individual scholars and friends who provided me with critical comments and advice at many times: Ana María Stahl de Montoya, Maricarmen Barbabosa, Rosemarie Terán, Guillermo Bustos, Ricardo Cubas, Eduardo Dargent, Carlos Gálvez, Renzo Honores, José de la Puente, Paul Rizo-Patrón and Sandro Patrucco. From the very beginning of this project, which started as a doctoral dissertation, I have been very fortunate to count with the friendship of Carmen McEvoy, Natalia Sobrevilla, Mantas Adomenas, Sebastián Herraiz, Pablo Gil de Montes, José Medina, Alfonso Montoya, and Rafael Pastor. I owe enormous gratitude to the spiritual support of Fr. Alban McCoy. Their help has made possible, in many different ways, the completion of this book.

I am grateful to Professor David A. Brading, with who I have a great intellectual debt, for his generosity. Both he and his wife, Celia, made Marina, the girls and myself feel at home in Cambridge with their wonderful hospitality.

I would like to give special thanks to Professor Neil H. Andrews and Clare College for their generous support through the William Senior Studentship in Comparative Law and Legal History. I thank Dr. Charles Jones, as well as Clare Hariri and Julie Coimbra, at the Centre for Latin American Studies. I am particularly indebted to Professor David Ibbetson for his unfailing patience and dedication during these years, as well as for his wise suggestions. I owe gratitude to the examiners of my dissertation professors David Brading and Matthew Mirow for their careful reading and insightful comments on that work. I also wish to thank my editor at Brill-Nijhoff, Jennifer Obdam, for her interest and support in this project.

This work had the support of the Bernardo Mendel Fellowship of the Lilly Library at the University of Indiana (Bloomington), the Albin Salton Fellowship of the Warburg Institute London, the Faculty of Law of the University of Gerona, and the University of Cambridge's Antofagasta Travel fund of the Centre of Latin American Studies and Maitland Fund. I am grateful to professors Breon Mitchell, Charles Hope, José María Pérez Collados and Aniceto Masferrer. Fr. Terry Phipps in London and Carlos and Ana María Herraiz in Santiago provided me a home during the arid months of research in these cities. Gonzalo de Aliaga generously allowed me to use the wonderful painting of his ancestor, Pedro Bravo de Lagunas, for the cover of this book.

My personal thanks go to my parents, Alfredo and Patricia, for their unfailing support and prayers, Thanks be also given to Lucila and Victor Andrés for their hospitality and encouragement.

My heartfelt gratitude goes out to Marina and my daughters Marina, Aurelia, Emilia and Sabina, who made life enjoyable even in the most difficult moments of this work. Thanks are not enough.

Lima, September 2015

List of Illustrations, Charts and Tables

Illustrations

Charts

Tables

List of Abbreviations

AGN	Archivo General de la Nación (Peru)
AGI	Archivo General de Indias
AHN	Archivo Histórico Nacional (Spain)
AI	Advocate of Indians
BAE	Biblioteca de Autores Españoles
BNP	Biblioteca Nacional del Perú
C	Codex Iustinianus
DGI	Defensor General of Indians
D	Digesta (*Pandekta*)
Lilly	Lilly Library
P	*Las siete partidas del Sabio rey Don Alfonso el Nono*, glosadas por el licenciado Gregorio López 3 vols. (Salamanca: Andrea de Portonaris, 1555).
Recop.	*Recopilación de leyes de los reynos de Indias*, 4 vols (Madrid: Iulian de Paredes, 1681)

Introduction

In 1671 a memorial was published in Madrid with the purpose of explaining the origins and importance of the office of Protector of Indians in the vice-royalty of Peru to the Court of the Spanish Habsburgs. Its author, a Lima-born creole, affirmed that noble Peruvians were bound to undertake the protection of Indians for two reasons: love for their *patria* and compassion towards the miseries of Indians. The memorial gives an account of how the protectors came into existence during the reign of Manco Cápac, the first Inca ruler, and were considered one of the most 'secure foundations' of the monarchy during this period. Upon the arrival of the Spaniards, Emperor Charles V (1500–58) had 'acknowledged' the positive effects of this office and, 'not wishing to change such a just law', resolved to maintain the institution appointing the first bishops as protectors of Indians.[1] In other words, by the time the memorial came off the presses, its author, Nicolás Matías del Campo, estimated that Protectors of Indians had been around in Peru for the last 700 years.

Including speculation about the Inca origins of the protectors or otherwise, the title of Protector of Indians has enjoyed widespread use in Spanish America. Bartolomé de las Casas (1474–1566), the prolific Dominican friar, was appointed Procurator and Universal Protector of Indians in 1516. A number of sixteenth century prelates, such as Hernando de Luque (Bishop of Tumbes), Vasco de Quiroga (Bishop of Michoacán), Antonio de Valdivieso (Bishop of Nicaragua) and Juan del Valle (Bishop of Popayán), were also named protectors in their own dioceses. Almost a century later, another ecclesiastic, Bishop Juan de Palafox y Mendoza (1600–59) of Puebla (Mexico), called himself the Protector of the Indians of New Spain. In the late seventeenth century, the Spanish Crown started appointing professional lawyers to defend Indians at the local courts and the royal audiences. Between 1864 and 1867, Emperor Maximilian of Mexico appointed a number of advocate-defensors in rural areas to defend Indian interests. Nicolás de Piérola (1839–1913), President of Peru, restored the title by appointing himself Protector of the Indigenous Race during the Peru-Chile war of 1879–84. As late as 1922, Emilo Lissón (1872–1961), Archbishop of Lima, presided over the Patronage of the Indigenous Race, a state sponsored institution created to improve the living conditions of Andean communities.

1 Nicolás Matías del Campo y de la Rynaga, *Memorial historico y ivridico, que refiere: El origen del Oficio de Protector general de los Indios del Perú* (Madrid, 1671), 1–2v.

 | DOI 10.1163/9789004305175_002

The legal nature of these institutions, however, varied considerably. The fact that modern historiography considers the appointment of Las Casas as the direct antecedent of all other modern protectorships of Indians, hides the fact that he never possessed the attributions granted to the men of letters who, either as magistrates or officials, pleaded on behalf of indigenous communities before the high courts of justice until the end of colonial rule.[2] Similarly, despite his formidable efforts in favour of the Indian cause, Las Casas lacked the civil and criminal jurisdiction in Indian matters exercised by the Bishop of Mexico between 1527–28—as indeed did every other prelate appointed to Spanish American bishoprics after this period. Even if the advocates-defensors of the Mexican Empire drew upon the experience regarding the representation of Indians before colonial law tribunals, their role went far beyond the courts of justice. In turn, the nineteenth and twentieth century Peruvian protectors lacked any of the effective powers of their namesakes during the vice-royalty.

The subject of this book is the study of the defensors, advocates and protectors-*fiscales* of Indians, a group of royal offices commonly referred to as Protectors of Indians that developed in the audience of Lima during the vice-regal period. These officials were the product of a series of measures passed by the viceroys of Peru and the Council of the Indies between 1575 and 1775; hence the chronological boundaries of this book. As a result, the Protectors of Indians were defined as the crown representatives charged with the protection of the indigenous population before the courts of justice. The book examines the institutional and legal foundations of the Protectorship of Indians in the audience of Lima and provides an account of the background, legal culture and work of the men who served in these posts. The study thus surveys one the most emblematic institutions of Spanish American Law and examines the formation of a learned elite that helped to consolidate the vice-regal legal order. It argues that the characteristics of the professionals who staffed the Protectorship of Indians allowed them to be successful in their court disputes, as well as to develop legal strategies which, in some cases, translated into the juristic doctrine that defined indigenous status throughout the Colonial period.

The present book could not have been so much as thought of without the path-breaking research of other legal historians, both past and present, who

2 Cf. Constantino Bayle, *El protector de indios* (Sevilla, 1945), 14–15; Enrique Dussel, *El espicopado latinoamericano y la liberación de los pobres, 1504–1620* (Mexico, 1979), 11ff; Manuel González Calzada, *Las Casas, el Procurador de los Indios* (Mexico, 1981) and Carmen Ruigómez Gómez, *Una política indigenista de los Habsburgo: El Protector de Indios en el Perú* (Sevilla, 1988), 47–50.

have addressed the institution of the Protectors of Indians.[3] A good part of the studies have focused on Bartolomé de las Casas and the prelates who followed him as Protectors of Indians until the first half of the sixteenth century. In most cases, however, these works deal with the pastoral action of the bishops in favour of Indians rather than their protection before the courts of justice.[4] Since the 1945 publication of Constantino Bayle's *El Protector de Indios*, there have been a number of historical studies highlighting the institutional framework and role of the protectors both at the level of royal audiences and provincial courts. These have provided straightforward narratives of the history of the protectorship in certain audience jurisdictions and insights into aspects such as changes in legislation, appointments and participation in judicial matters.[5] Scholars have also become interested in the manner in which the protectorship worked at a local level.[6] Beginning in the 1980s, these studies probed the role

3 Bayle, *El protector de indios*; Charles R. Cutter, *The protector de indios in colonial New Mexico, 1659–1821* (Albuquerque, 1986); Ruigómez Gómez, *El Protector de Indios*; Diana Bonnett, *El Protector de Naturales en la Audiencia de Quito, siglos XVII y XVIII* (Quito, 1992); Francisco Cuena Boy, "El *Defensor Civitatis* y el Protector de Indios: Breve ilustración en paralelo," *Ivs Fvgit* 7 (1998), 179–95; and "Utilización pragmática del derecho romano en dos memoriales indianos del siglo XVII sobre el protector de indios," *Revista de Estudios Histórico Jurídicos* 20 (Valparaíso) (1988), 107–142.

4 Chauvet, Fidel de. "Fray Juan de Zumárraga, Protector of the Indians." *The Americas* 5 (1948–49): 283–310; Julio Santiesteban Ochoa, "Fray Vicente Valverde, protector de los indios, y su obra," *Revista de Letras* 1(2) (Cuzco, 1948), 117–182; Juan Friede and Benjamin Keen, eds. *Bartolomé de las Casas in History: Toward an Understanding of the Man and His Work* (DeKalb, 1971); Enrique Dussel, *El episcopado latinoamericano y la liberación de los pobres, 1504–1620* (Mexico, 1979), 11ff; González Calzada, *Las Casas, el Procurador de los Indios*; Ramón Ramírez, *Gil Gonzalez de S. Nicolas, Dominico: el primer defensor del los indios en Chile*, Colección Cuarto Centenario Dominico 1 (Santiago, 1986); Manuel Olmedo Jiménez, *Jerónimo de Loayza, O.P.: Pacificador de españoles y protector de indios*, Los Dominicos y América 7 (Granada, 1990); Francisco Martín Hernández, *Don Vasco de Quiroga (Protector de Indios)* (Salamanca,1993).

5 Edberto Óscar Acevedo, "El protector de indios en el Perú: (hacia fines del régimen español)", *Congreso del Instituto Internacional de Historia del Derecho Indiano. IX. 1990. Madrid. Actas y estudios* vol. 2 (Madrid, 1991), 29–54; Ruigómez Gómez, *El Protector de Indios en el Perú*; Bonnett, *El Protector de Naturales en la Audiencia de Quito*; Cuena Boy, "El *Defensor Civitatis* y el Protector de Indios" and "Utilización pragmática del derecho romano en dos memoriales indianos del siglo XVII;" and Javier Saravia, "Los Miserables y el Protector. Evolución de la protectoría de indios en el Virreinato peruano. Siglos XVI–XVIII" (Licentiate thesis, Universidad Nacional Mayor de San Marcos, 2012). A recent bibliographical revision on this subject is found in Javier Saravia Salazar, "El fiscal protector de indios en el siglo XVII: Espacios de poder y arbitrismo," *Nueva Crónica* 1 (2013), 1–22.

6 Cutter, *The protector de indios in colonial New Mexico*; Bernard Lavallé, "Presión colonial y reivindicación indígena en Cajamarca (1785–1820), según el archivo del protector de naturales,"

played by what were mostly non-university trained protectorship officials within the provincial legal structure of the Vice-royalties. The historiography of the Protectors of Indians, rich as it is, leaves unexamined certain basic historical questions about the legal nature of the institution and about the men appointed to this position.

This study addresses important questions thus far overlooked in these works. The first, as pointed out earlier, is to define the Protectorship of Indians as a secular office whose central objective was the defence of Indians in court. The second is to consider the legal ideas used to create and justify the institution itself, and to defend Indian lawsuits. For this reason, it considers litigation primarily as a legal phenomenon, and thus it departs from the sociological perspective that characterised the previous studies in this subject in the Spanish Monarchy.[7] In litigation, as in the study of legal doctrine, the book pays particular attention to the influence of the *ius commune*. As David Ibbetson has pointed out, legal ideas are "indeterminable and flexible" and lawyers will "commonly disagree about them."[8]

More importantly, the book also examines the lives of the men who served as Protectors of Indians. Given the fact that many protectors ended their careers as *oidors* or high court judges, its collective assessment of family backgrounds and careers will broaden our understanding of the upper echelons of Peruvian colonial legal bureaucracy. On the other hand, its account of the protectors' material and legal culture, fills some important gaps in the existing works of high court magistrates.[9] In addition, the book examines a segment of the learned elite who did not achieve audience-rank, made up of lawyers who combined academic positions, legal practice and minor bureaucratic posts,

---

Allpanchis 12 (35–36) (Cuzco, 1990),105–137; Beatriz Suñe Blanco, "Evolución de la figura del protector de indios e la frontera norte de Nueva España," in Antonio Gutierrez Escudero and María Luisa Laviana Cuetos, eds. *Estudios sobre América: Siglos XVI–XX* (Sevilla, 2005), 727–743; Ascensión Baeza Martín, "Presión e intereses en torno al cargo de protector general de indios del Nuevo Reino de León: el caso de Nicolás de Villalobos, 1714–1734," *Anuario de Estudios Americanos* 67 (1) (2010), 209–237; Marcela Echeverri, "Los derechos de indios y esclavos realistas y la transformación política en Popayán, Nueva Granada (1808–1820)," *Revista de Indias* 69 (246) (2009), 45–72.

7 Richard Kagan, *Lawsuits and Litigants in Castile, 1500–1700* (Chapel Hill, 1981).

8 David Ibbetson, *A Historical Introduction to the Law of Obligations* (Oxford, 1999), v.

9 Guillermo Lohmann Villena, *Los ministros de la Audiencia de Lima en el reinado de los borbones (1700–1821)* (Sevilla, 1974); Mark Burkholder y D.S. Chandler, *From Impotence to Authority: The Spanish Crown and the American Audiencias, 1687–1808* (Missouri, 1977); Mark A. Burkholder, *Politics of a Colonial Career: José Baquíjano and the Audiencia of Lima* (Albuquerque, 1980).

that has remained thus far unstudied, despite the numerous contributions regarding the lives and careers of magistrates and lawyers in the vice-royalty.[10] By studying the Protectors of Indians, the book will provide valuable insights into the lives of legal professionals and will thus offer a new perspective on the colonial bureaucracy of the Spanish Monarchy.

The institution of the Protectors of Indians rested on the idea that just rulers should appoint officials to defend, both within and outside the courts of justice, persons who were less favoured. The first issue that needed to be examined was the nature of Indian personal status. That Nicolás Matías del Campo y de la Rynaga opened his 1671 *Memorial* by stating that Indians 'were, and should be reputed among the persons that the Law calls *miserables,*' evidences the importance of this issue to those involved in the protectorship.[11] As the discussion of Indian status appears in many parts of this book it is important to review beforehand its main characteristics, as well as its antecedents in Spanish Law.

The concept of *miserabiles personae* in law derives from the *lex unica* of the title *Quando Imperator inter pupillos vel viduas vel miserabiles personas cognoscat et ne exhibeantu*, a constitution enacted by Emperor Constantine (*c*.272–337) in 334 which provided that pupils, widows, the incurably ill, invalids, and those affected by 'injuries of fortune' could not be compelled to litigate outside their provinces. It was thus established that, by virtue of their personal condition, certain defendants were granted a special protection

10 Guillermo Lohmann Villena, "El licenciado Francisco Falcón (1521–1587): Vida, escritos y actuación en el Perú de un procurador de indios," *Anuario de Estudios Americanos* 27 (1970), 131–194, and "El jurista Francisco Carrasco del Saz," *Anuario Mexicano de Historia del Derecho* 11–12 (1999–2000), 339–59; Rafael Jaeguer Requejo, "Notas para la biografía del jurista peruano don García Francisco Carrillo Alderete," *Revista del Archivo General de la Nación* (Lima) 8 (1985), 237–268; Oswaldo Holguín Callo, "El doctor Diego Salinas (1558–1595): Primero lances de un limeño ambicioso," *Boletín del Instituto Riva Agüero* 14 (1986–87), 9–63; José de la Puente Brunke, "La burocracia en el virreinato del Perú: (Apuntes sobre los siglos XVI y XVII)," *Mercurio Peruano* no. 501 (1991), 49–62 and "Los jueces en la vida limeña del siglo XVII," *Derecho y Sociedad* 12 (1997–1998), 196–202; Teodoro Hampe Martínez and Renzo Honores, "Los abogados de Lima colonial, 1550–1650: (Formación, vinculaciones y carrera profesional)," *Revista del Foro*, no. 2 (2002), 365–386.

11 "Los Indios del Perú, como los demás de Occidente, son, y deben ser reputados entre las personas que el Derecho llama *miserables*." Campo, *Memorial*, 1. By far the most complete study on the subject of miserability is Thomas Duve, *Sonderrecht in der Frühen Neuzeit: Studien sum ius singlare und den privilegia miserabilium personarum, senum und indorum in Alter und Neuer Welt* (Frankfurt am Main, 2008), which includes a comprehensive bibliography.

against forceful summoning in imperial courts outside their province of residence.[12]

There is considerable evidence of the reception of this constitution in both Castilian and Spanish American Law. The *Siete Partidas*, for example, established that orphans and widows, the very old and very ill, and those in 'great poverty' should be protected against lawsuits or rulings originating outside their place of residence.[13] Similarly, Gregorio López (1496–1569) cites Constantine's norm in his gloss of the *Partidas* to explain the relationship between *miserables* and Ecclesiastical jurisdiction in the *ius commune*,[14] and how women, widows and minors were, in fact, under the direct jurisdiction of the King's Court.[15]

From a scholarly perspective, the influence of the *Quando Imperator* constitution is also found in the treatise of Antonio de Escalante, an advocate in the Royal Council of Castile, on the protection of the poor and wretched.[16] Escalante observed that the poor and *miserables* should be the chief beneficiaries

---

12 "*Imp. Constantinus A. ad Andronicum.* Si contra pupillos viduas vel diutino morbo fatigatos et debiles impetratum fuerit lenitatis nostrae iudicium, memorati a nullo nostrorum iudicum compellantur comitatui nostro sui copiam facere. quin immo intra provinciam, in qua litigator et testes vel instrumenta sunt, experiantur iurgandi fortunam atque omni cautela servetur, ne terminos provinciarum suarum cogantur excedere. 1. Quod si pupilli vel viduae aliique fortunae iniuria miserabiles iudicium nostrae serenitatis oraverint, praesertim cum alicuius potentiam perhorrescunt, cogantur eorum adversarii examini nostro sui copiam facere." Code 3.14.1 = CTh. 1.22.2 = Breviary 1.9.2.

13 "Muevense a las vengadas maliciosamente omes ya, a ganar cartas contra los huérfanos, ellas viudas o los omes muy viejos, o cuytados de grandes enfermedades, o de muy gran pobreza, para aducir los pleitos ante el Rey, o ante los Adelantados, o ante otros, que no son moradores en la tierra do viven estos sobredichos contra quien las ganan. E porque esto no tenemos por guisada cosa, nin por derecha; mandamos que la carta que fuere ganada contra cualquier destos sobredichos, o contra persona semejante dellos, de quien ome debiase aver merced o piedad, o responder por ella, a ninguna parte , sino ante aquel juez de su lugar do vive. Mas las otras que cualquiera destas personas cuytadas contra otri ganasse , para aduzirlo ante el Rey, o ante otro juez que lo oyesse, e le fiziesse aver derecho; mandamos que vala." P.1.41.18.

14 P.1.41.18, gloss 8.

15 P.3.3.5, gloss 3.

16 Antonio de Escalante, *Discurso breve a la Magestad Católica del Rey nuestro señor don Felipe quarto el gran rey de las Españas. Dividise en dos partes. En la primera se trata del auxilio y proteccion real a favor de los pobres y miserables personas. Y hazense alguna provisiones para que su Magestad mande por su Real Prematica, y ley se les guarden sus privilegios y favores. En la segunda se trata de la obligacion correspectiva de todos los vasallos al socorro de las necessidades del Patrimonio y Magestad Real…*(Madrid, [1638]).

of royal protection because, within the body politic, it was those 'most hurt and ill who solicit and require the care and attention of their head.'[17] In this regard, he argued that the scope of royal protection should extend beyond the widows, orphans or very poor or ill, included either in the *lex unica* or the *Siete Partidas*, to 'people...who inspired pity or piety, by reason of the meagreness or misery in which they lived.'[18]

As for the legal nature of the protection granted to *miserables*, Escalante considered that Roman Law established that the privilege of litigating within the province was conditioned to the existence of a judicial case (*quando iudex*) and a powerful opponent (*quando potentium partes*). By contrast, Castilian Law provided that all magistrates, as representatives of the king's justice, be compelled to favour and protect the poor and helpless in their dealings before courts and tribunals regardless of the nature of their case. For Escalante, this resulted in a number of privileges for *miserables* which included not only protection from litigating outside the provinces of origin, but also trial before a royal audience or high court, brevity in lawsuits, exemption from judicial fees, or the appointment of an advocate or procurator. In other words, Escalante believed that Castilian Law not only extended the number of beneficiaries of the prince's protection, but increased the scope of its 'piety, or compassion.' It was, therefore, more than 'judicial good government.'[19]

Although early legal codes enacted by the Catholic Monarchs such as the Laws of Burgos (1513) and the New Laws (1542) were concerned with the protection of Indians, reference to native Americans as 'miserable persons' (*miserabiles personae*) in official documents can be traced to the second half of the sixteenth century.[20] Perhaps the earliest example of this usage is found in a

17 "[E]n este cuerpo vniversal viene[n] a ser los miembros mas doloridos y enfermos, y que mas solicitan y requieren del ciudado y atencion de su cabeça." Ibid. 7v.

18 "[P]ersonas semejantes dellos, de quien se deua tener lastima, ò piedad por razon de la mezquindad ó miseria en q viven." Ibid., 22. Citing P.2.10.3, earlier in the text, Escalante also refers to 'all gender of poor, and miserable people' ("todo genero de personas pobres, y miserable." Ibid., 7v–8v.

19 "[D]exó mayor ampliacion a qualquier caso de piedad, o conpasion." "[U]na forma de buen gobierno judicial." Ibid., 20–22, 33–33v, 34v–35, 38.

20 The legal condition of Indians has been studied by Carmelo Viñas y Mey, *El estatuto del obrero indígena en la colonización española* (Madrid, 1929); Lewis Hanke, "Pope Paul III and the American Indians," *The Harvard Theological Review* 30 (2) (1937), 67–102; Manuel Vicente Villarán, *Apuntes sobre la realidad social de los indígenas del Perú ante las leyes de Indias* (Lima, 1964); Martha Norma Oliveros, "Construcción del régimen tutelar del indio," *Revista del Instituto de Historia del Derecho Ricardo Levene* 13 (1967), 105–126; Paulino Castañeda, "La condición de miserable del indio y sus privilegios." *Anuario de Estudios*

1563 rescript drafted under King Philip II.[21] Soon after, a 1571 ordinance charged the *fiscal* or attorney of the Council of the Indies with the 'protection and shelter' of Indians 'as poor and miserable persons.'[22] Similarly, a 1580 rescript directed to the governor of Chucuito admonished him that Indians should not be overburdened with taxes due to their condition of "miserable" which derived from either being poor or recently converted to Christianity.[23] The term soon entered official correspondence as evidenced by a letter of Friar Juan Binero reminding the King of his royal obligation towards the 'miserable Indians' of which he was 'tutor and caretaker.'[24]

The legal nature of Indian status in Spanish American Law was soon discussed in the writings of local jurists. Gabriel Alvarez de Velasco (1595–*fl.*1658), an *oidor* in the audience of Santa Fe, for example, wrote a comprehensive treatise on the privileges of the poor and *miserables*.[25] Drawing upon the constitution

---

Americanos 28 (1971): 245–335; Lewis Hanke, *All mankind is one: a study of the disputation between Bartolomé de las Casas and Juan Ginés de Sepúlveda in 1550 on the intelectual and religious capacity of the American Indians* (DeKalb, 1974); Woodrow Borah, "El status jurídico de los indios en Nueva España," *América Indígena* 45 (2) (1985), 257–76; Rafael Sánchez-Concha Barrios, "De la miserable condición de los indios en las reducciones." *Revista Teológica Limense* 30 (1996), 95–104; Jesús María García Añoveros, "La idea, 'status' y función del Indio en Juan de Solórzano y Pereyra," in *De Indiarum Iure (Liber III: De retentione Indiarum)* by Juan de Solórzano (Madrid, 1994); Gorki González Mantilla, "La consideración del indio como persona: El Derecho Romano, factor de resistencia en el siglo XVI," in *La tradición clásica en el Perú virreinal*, ed. Teodoro Hampe (Lima, 1999); and Mauricio Novoa, "El Indio Americano Derecho Romano en Solórzano," *Boletín del Instituto Riva-Agüero* 26 (1999), 253–272. Reference to this subject can also be found in Constantino Bayle, *El protector de indios* (Madrid, 1945), ; Carmen Ruigómez 25–33; M.C. Mirow, *Latin American Law: A History of Private Law and Institutions in Spanish America* (Austin, 2004), 84–94; Bianca Premo, *Children of the Father King: Youth, Authority and Legal Minority in Colonial Lima* (Chapel Hill, 2005), 32–37.

21 See Martha Norma Oliveros, "Construcción del régimen tutelar del indio," *Revista del Instituto de Historia del Derecho Ricardo Levene* 13 (1967), 118.

22 "De cuya protección y amparo, como de personas pobres y miserables se tengan por encargado." *Memorial al Rey N.S. Don Felipe IIII. A favor de los indios del Piru. Sobre el oficio de Protector General en la ciudad de Lima, corte y cabeza del Piru* (Madrid, 1622), 3.

23 "Real Cédula para que no se imponga a los indios más tributo de lo que cómodamene pudieren pagar", Badajoz, 23 September 1580. In Richard Koneztke, ed., *Colección de documentos para la historia de la formación social de Hispanoamérica, 1492–1810* (Madrid, 1953), 1: 528.

24 Ruigómez, *Protector de Indios*, 29.

25 Gabriel Alvarez de Velasco, *Tractatus de privilegiis pauperum et miserabilium personarum*, 3 pts in 2 vols, (Matriti, 1630–1636). He married Francisco Zorrilla y Ospina (†1649). His testament is found in the Archivo General de la Nación of Colombia, notaría 3a, protocolo 1658, fs. 207–218.

quando imperator and the work of Giovanni Maria Novario,[26] Alvarez de Velasco considered that the privileges and protection of *miserables* had been understood by 'the doctors' and contemporary writers as a privilege of *fuero*, that is inherent to their condition.[27] On the other hand, Francisco de Alfaro (*c.*1551–1642), an *oidor* in Charcas, considered that the miserable condition could be equalled to that of a minor[28]; a position later cited by the 1622 Memorial.[29] Bishop Gaspar de Villarroel (1587–1665) considered that the law did not define this concept and neither could a comprehensive list of *miserable* persons be drafted.[30] In turn, Juan de la Rynaga, an *oidor* in Panama, considered that *miserables* were 'those whose nature moves [us] to feel misery…as well as newly converted.'[31] Similarly, Nicolás Matías del Campo explained that this legal status was derived from either natural compassion due to 'state, quality or works' or recent conversion to the Catholic Faith.[32]

Perhaps the most influential work on the legal nature of Indian status was developed by Juan de Solórzano Pereyra (1575–1655), a former *oidor* of the audience of Lima and councillor of the Indies. In *Política Indiana* (1648), Solórzano provides an explanation of the legal nature of the miserability of American Indians and, as a consequence of this, establishes a number of privileges in public and private law. He starts by giving an account of the sixteenth century rescripts which refer to Indians as 'miserable persons' due to their condition of either being poor or recently converted to Christianity.[33] This condition, he argued, implied that Indians were *miserabiles personae* chiefly because

26 Giovanni Maria Novario, *Praxis aurea priviligiorum miserabilium personarum* (Neapoli, 1623). Two other editions of this work were published in 1637 and 1669 under the title *Tractatus de miserabilium personarum privilegiis.*

27 Gabriel Alvarez de Velasco, *Tractatus de privilegiis pauperum et miserabilium personarum*…(Matriti, 1630–1636) 3p, 3q, 19n.

28 "Fiscus etiam minori aequiparatur…licet contra pupillu privilegiu[m] no[n] exercear." Francisco de Alfaro, *Tractatus de officio fiscalis* (Valladolid, 1606), 25.

29 *Memorial* (1622), 5v.

30 Gaspar de Villarroel, *Gobierno Eclesiastico-pacifico, y union de los dos Cuchillos Pontificio, y Regio*.... (1656–1657; Madrid, 1738), 2.14.3.5 (p. 193).

31 "[A]ssi porque son de aquellos, De cuibus natura amovetur ad miserendum…como por nuevamente convertidos." The quote is from Rynaga cited Gregorio Lopez P.1.6.48, Matienzo Glos to recop 5.1.28:. (Rebuffi de Senten pronunc 14art. 3, glos cult 14.art 3 glos cult).

32 "[A]ssi por ser de aquellas de quien naturalmente nos co[n]padecemos, por su estado, calidad, ó trabajos, como por nuevamente convertidos á la Fé." Campo, *Memorial*, 1.

33 "Real Cédula para que no se imponga a los indios más tributo de lo que cómodamene pudieren pagar", Badajoz, 23 September 1580. In Richard Koneztke, ed., *Colección de documentos para la historia de la formación social de Hispanoamérica, 1492–1810* (Madrid, 1953), 1: 528.

they fulfilled all 'the epithets of miseries, and wretchedness, which the evangelical prophet Isaiah gives to the peoples living beyond the rivers of Ethiopia.' Yet, even if these 'epithets of miseries' were not fulfilled, their condition of being newly converted to the Catholic Faith sufficed to repute them as miserable persons in the law.[34]

The broadening of the causes of miserability to include Indians was, in itself, a significant innovation of Spanish American Law: in Castile miserability was associated with a number of diverse causes such as excessive taxation, rusticity, war, crime or usury. The *Lex Visigothorum* or *Fuero Juzgo* (*c*.681), for example, contemplated protective measures against the greed of the Princes for it understood that a tyrannical government made men 'poor and miserable.'[35] On the other hand, Gonzalo de Berceo (*c*.1195–1264) associated the term with diabolical possession,[36] and ascetic Gerónimo Gracián (1545–1614) linked it with atheism.[37]

As for the legal privileges, Solórzano stated that the fact that Indians were *miserabiles* made them subject to enjoy 'all the favours and privileges to minors, poor, rustics [...] both judicially and extra-judicially.' These privileges entitled Indians to a number of procedural rights such as litigating before the royal audiences as first instance courts, enjoying summary trials, summoning any wrongdoer or law-breaker before secular or ecclesiastical judges (*mixti fori*) or presenting new evidence and witnesses after the discovery process or even at courts of appeal. In addition to this, Indians were exempt from being subject to the presumption of contempt of court if they did not appear before the judge at the first citation. Privileges also covered special provisions for the writing of wills and protection from harmful contracts – including the possibility of restoring matters to their state before the transaction or *restitutio in integrum*. As for public law, they could present claims at any stage of the Trial of Residence

34 Juan de Solórzano, *Política Indiana*, eds. Francisco Tomás y Valiente and Ana María Barrero (Madrid, 1996), 2.28.2,3.

35 "[P]obres e miseros." Fuero Juzgo 2.1.5, in *Los Códigos Españoles*. See also *Leyes de Estilo* 4.5 y el *Fuero Viejo de Castilla* (1079), Ignacio Jordán de Asso y Miguel de Manuel, eds. (Madrid, 1771). The influence of this idea in political theory is found in Rodrigo de Arévalo, "Suma de la Política" in *Prosistas castellanos del siglo XV*, Mario Penna, ed. BAE 116 (Madrid, 1959), 285.

36 "Todas estas femnas/eran demoniadas/viuen en gran miseria/eran muy lazradas," Gonzalo de Berceo, *Vida de Santo Domingo de Silos*, ed. José Antonio Fernández Flórez (Burgos, 2000), verse 638.

37 Fray Jerónimo Gracián, "Diez lamentaciones del miserable estado de los ateístas de nuestros tiempos" (1611), in *Beatus vir: carne de hoguera*, Emilia Navarro de Kelley, ed. (Madrid, 1977), 270–272.

(*juicio de residencia*) without having the need to present a cash bond for this purpose.[38]

The Protector of Indians was charged with the enforcement of these privileges, and although the institution originates in a set of ordinances issued by the Viceroy of Peru in 1575, the idea that miserable persons should enjoy the protection of a crown official when litigating before the courts of justices had a long history in Spanish Law. The earliest legal dispositions regarding the fair treatment of those less favoured dates from the *Lex Visigothorum* which stated that if a rich man went to trial with someone poor, the procurator he appointed needed to be as poor as his adversary; in turn, poor litigants could appoint procurators who could be as powerful or even more so than their adversaries.[39] More to the point, the *Siete Partidas* (1265) established that an advocate should assume the defence in court of those who were 'unprotected and more destitute of advice than others' such as widows and orphans, the blind and deformed, and diseased and old.[40] It was thought *miserabiles* were 'helpless' when facing the powerful both inside and outside courts of justice. As the right of bearing arms was a prerogative of the hidalgo class, the figure was not purely metaphorical.

The example set by the Partidas was followed consistently in the Spanish peninsula from the fourteenth until the early seventeenth centuries. Leonese fueros, for example, protected the property of widows and orphans, and established that the alcaldes acted as procurators in legal disputes of widows, women with a permanently ill husband, single maidens who lived in cities, and orphans.[41] Within the Crown of Aragon a disposition of 1343 in Mallorca ordered that a 'suitable procurator' should be appointed to advocate for the poor and *miserables* before the judicial courts.[42] The 'father of orphans' (*Fuge et Pare d'Orfens*) first created for Valencia by king Peter IV of Aragon in 1337–38 not only had the duty to represent orphans in tribunals but also to provide

38 Solórzano, *Política Indiana*, 2.28, 25–26, 47–48, 55–56; 2.29.11, 37–33.

39 Cap. 9: "E si algun omne poderoso a pleyto con algùn omne pobre, e non quiere traer el pleyto por si mismo, non puede meter por personero si non omne que sea igual del pobre, o que se amenos poderoso del que lo mete. E si el pobre quisir meter personero, puede meter por personero tal omne que sea poderoso tanto cuemo su adversario;" quoted in Miguel Cid Cebrian, *La Justicia Gratuita: Realidad y perspectivas de un Derecho Constitucional* (Pamplona, 1995), 33–37.

40 P.3.23.20; 1.23.7; 2.10.3.

41 See, for example, the fueros of Salamanca and Ledesma, Fuero de Salamanca, 256, 258, and Fuero de Ledesma 173, 175 (Ed.Pilar e Inés Carrasco, Granada).

42 "[S]ian tinguts advocar y procurar a las personas pobres y miserables." *Recopilación del Derecho de Mallorca 1622 por los doctores Pere Joan Canet, Antonio Mesquida y Jordi Zaforteza*, ed. Antonio Planas Roselló (1622; reprint Mallorca, 1996), 2.24.1.

them with an apprenticeship. As a general overseer of the city's 'police and good government', his obligations also included finding 'ruffians, thieves, renegades, and other evil people' useful employment but also the power to prosecute them in criminal courts. The institution influenced the creation of other 'fathers of orphans' in other Aragonese cities like Zaragoza (1475) and Daroca (1591) where he was procurator general for poor, widows and defenceless pupils; Tarazona (1594), where he was made a magistrate of justice; or Huesca (1631) where he was a councillor of the cabildo and given powers to flog lawbreakers.[43]

On the other hand, the idea that the poor and less favoured should enjoy preferential treatment by legal professionals is found in the *Fuero Real* (1225). This law established that the poor could not be imprisoned for debts to their lawyers. It was considered that lawyers should undertake this defence as an act of merciful help.[44] The Partidas stated that advocates should assume the defence of the poor 'by measured salary.' If, however, it was established that the litigants were so poor that they could not afford any fee, the judge could order the advocate to undertake their defence 'for the love of God.'[45] In the sixteenth century Castilian laws considered that procurators for the poor should be employed in the audiences. The ordinances for the chancellery of Valladolid (1493) stated that a procurator for the lawsuits of the poor should be elected by the high court judges and be granted a salary of 8,000 maravedis. These procurators should take 'much care and diligence' in the lawsuits of the poor and could not be negligent when dealing with these.[46] Similarly, within the Crown of Aragon dispositions dating from the *corts* or parliament of Barcelona (1503) regulated the conditions by which plaintiffs could be declared 'poor' and consequently have their judicial expenses paid by the royal treasury.[47]

---

43 See Gregorio Lasala, "Instituciones de protección y reforma en Valencia," *Surgam* 7 (73) (February, 1955), 18–24; Agustín Rubio Vela, "Infancia y marginación: En torno a las instituciones trecentistas valencianas para el socorro de los huérfanos," *Revista d'Història Medieval* 1 (1990), 111–153; T. Roca, "El Padre de los huérfanos en Zaragoza," *Surgam* 6 (60) (January, 1954), 27–32; Ricardo del Arco, "Una notable institución social: El padre de huérfanos", in *Estudios de Historia Social de España*, ed. Carmelo Viñas y Mey (Madrid, 1955), 3: 191–193, 199, 217–219.

44 *Fuero Real.* Lex 20.

45 P.3.66. "por mesurado salario"... "fuere tan modesta persona...debe mandar el juez que lo haga por amor a Dios."

46 *Recopilación de las Ordenanzas de la Real Audiencia y Chancillería de Su Magestad, que reside en la villa de Valladolid* (Valladolid, 1566), 2.3 (77v).

47 Pedro Nolasco Vives y Cebriá, trans. *Traducción al castellano de los Usages y demas derechos de Cataluña...*, ed. Joan Egea y Fernández, 4 vols in 2 (Barcelona, 1989), 1: 238.

Legal dispositions directed towards the protection of poor litigants continued in the seventeenth and eighteenth centuries. In Aragon, the compilation of laws of Mallorca (1622) continued to cite a 1343 disposition to have a salaried advocate to act as procurator for the lawsuits of 'poor and miserable persons' in the high courts.[48] In Castile, a royal *cedula* of 1637 decreed that poor litigants would be exempt from the use of *sello cuarto* paper[49] and a pragmatic of 1771 ordered the *Colegios de Abogados* to appoint six procurators to defend the poor.[50]

The protectorship of Indians provides a good example of the composite structure of Spanish American Law or *derecho indiano*.[51] On one hand, it was a creation of the Indies' 'own and particular' laws.[52] On the other, it derived important antecedents and principles from Castilian and Roman Law. All these elements were shaped by judicial practice, indigenous custom and the protectors' legal culture and antecedents. The result was one of the most distinct institutions in Latin American legal history.

The period of time considered in this study, while extensive, provides an historical perspective that includes the development of the institution of the Protectors of Indians, the characteristics of the men who served as protectors and advocates of Indians, and their work and influence at the royal audience of Lima. Covering more than two centuries proved less daunting than it may seem, since the different types of historical sources clustered around particular themes and particular decades.

The first two chapters of the book introduce the institution of the Protector of Indians. Chapter 1 examines the nature of the appointments of the early protectors by pointing out the differences between the rescripts granted to Las Casas to those of the bishops of Mexico and Peru. It aims to define the manner

48 "[S]ian tinguts advocar y procurar a las personas pobres y miserables", *Recopilación del Derecho de Mallorca 1622, por los doctores Pere Joan Camet, Antoní Mesquida y Jordi Zaforteza*, ed. Antonio Planas Roselló (Mallorca, 1996), 2.24.1 (p. 170).

49 "Cedula en que su Magestad declara por instrumento publico los conocimientos de los pleitos que se hazen por los Procuradores, Abogados, y Agentes, y otras personas…" Real Cédula, Madrid 16 May 1637 (Madrid, 1637), [1v].

50 Cid Cebrian, *La justicia gratuita*, 37.

51 See Matthew Mirow, *Latin American Law: A History of Private Law and Institutions in Spanish America* (Austin, 2004), 6–7, 15–18. The bibliography on *derecho indiano* is legion but an excellent guide is found in in Norberto Dagrossa, "Bibliografía de historia del derecho indiano," in José Andrés-Gallego, ed., *Nuevas aportaciones a la historia juridical de Iberoamérica* (Madrid: Digibus, 2000) and its more up-to-date, on-line version "Bibliografía de Historia del Derecho Indiano" (2011), 283–299; available at http://www.larramendi.es.

52 Antonio de León Pinelo, *Tratado de confirmaciones reales* (Madrid, 1630), 1.8.22.

in which the protectorship of Indians acquired its definitive form as a secular office. In turn, Chapter 2 provides a chronological history of the Protectors of Indians from the statutes enacted by Viceroy Toledo in 1575 to its decline in the decades of 1750–60. It addresses the manner in which the institution was transformed from a threefold structure comprised of a vice-regal appointee aided by a university trained advocate and a procurator; to a single, Crown-appointed magistrate of the royal audience; and finally to a locally-appointed official with the prerogatives of an audience minister. The chapter surveys the struggle for institutional prerogatives and its relationship with the royal audience, the viceroy and the metropolis. It provides a close look into the process by which the Council of the Indies abrogated the institution in the mid-eighteenth century.

The book then surveys the men that made up the institution. Chapters 3 to 6 study, respectively, the social status, economic performance, legal culture and careers of the men who served as defensors, protectors-*fiscales* and advocates of Indians. By examining *relaciones de servicios*, notarial records, diaries and travellers′ accounts this part provides a collective biography of the protectors. Together with looking into the well trodden path of characteristics and strategies of family groups found in Chapter 3, Chapter 4 also offers a glance at the material culture and consumption patterns of these officials. Chapter 5 surveys the protectors' legal education and book collections. Lastly, Chapter 6 traces their professional careers, as well as influence in public life and colonial politics. By dividing the officials in those who rose into upper audience ranks and those who became independent practitioners and university professors, it offers a comprehensive view of the upper echelons of bureaucratic, social and economic power of vice-regal Lima.

The last part (Chapter 7) examines the work of the protectors in favour of Indians before qualified judges. It focuses on the pleadings before the audience in Lima, and in particular in those cases concerning civil law. As a result, it is based on the opinions and arguments of university-trained legal experts and thus makes no attempt to discuss Indian litigation undertaken in the numerous jurisdictions staffed by non-*letrados* that functioned during the vice-royalty. The chapter surveys the performance of these legal professionals in lawsuits over Indians′ rights and gives an account of their use of legal norms, ideas and arguments. It surveys the use of the *ius commune* in Indigenous demands. The chapter concludes with an assessment of the role played by protectors of Indians in shaping the ideas on Indian personal status and Spanish American judicial practice.

The primary sources used for this book proceed primarily from the national archives and libraries of Lima and Madrid. They include administrative, judicial and notarial records, as well as correspondence, memoires, jurisprudence, laws and literature. In examining the work and lives of advocates and protectors, I scrutinized some two hundred court cases and notarial records, most of which came from the National Archive of Peru. Valuable sixteenth and seventeenth century cases were found at the Bernardo Mendel Collection of the Lilly Library. The national archives of Chile and Ecuador allowed me to fill documentary gaps in the careers of protectors, as well as evidence of the overall scarcity of Indigenous civil litigation before the royal audiences. I also profited from the valuable holdings of the British Library, the Staatsbibliothek zu Berlin, the national library of Chile, the library of the Central Bank of Ecuador, and the libraries of the universities of Cambridge, Columbia, Gerona and Indiana.

Much biographical information and other vital materials required to substantiate the book's general arguments and the claims made to specific chapters are contained in several appendices. Appendix 1 contains short biographies of the defensors, advocates and protectors-*fiscales* of Indians, drawn from the documentary evidence analysed in the relevant chapters. Appendix 2 provides a transcription of the book lists found in the extant probate records of advocate Cipriano de Medina—in its own right, possibly one of the most important libraries in seventeenth century Peru. For reader's convenience, many of the books have been identified and entries contain possible editions. Unfortunately, as none of the books owned by this official has been located in the existing libraries in Lima it is impossible to assess the particular editions, bindings, conditions, marginalia, ownership indicia and other physical characteristics of the protectors' books.

CHAPTER 1

Bishop Protectors

The institutionalisation of a protectorship of Indians in the years that followed the discovery of America is permanently linked with the role played by the Catholic Church, and in particular by the bishops appointed to the newly created dioceses. However, as in the case of Bartolomé de las Casas (1474–1566), and many others later involved in the Indian cause, the title of 'protector,' often self-assumed, constitutes a confusing element in establishing the legal nature of this institution; in particular as many religious figures were convinced, as Toribio de Motolinia in Mexico, that the protection of Indians by religious institutions was a providential matter.[1] Moreover, the difficulties in determining the nature of the first protectors of Indians were added to by the fact that bishops, as St. Augustine (354–430) understood it, should not only be judges of their brethren, but also procurators in their legal disputes.[2]

This chapter explains the legal nature of the protector of Indians. It shows how, despite the influence of Church institutions and its link with the early American prelatures, it was conceived and created as a secular office. Thus, the first section will briefly discuss the legal nature of the 1516 appointment of Las Casas as protector of Indians. The second and third sections will explain the bishop protectors' grant of civil and criminal jurisdiction in 1527–28, the manner in which this power was used, and the conflicts that followed their use.

1 Motolonia was convinced that the tenth plague that oppressed Mexico was the division of Spaniards. It had therefore been the Grace of God which had brought the friars to calm these disputes. The Spanish themselves, wrote Motolinia, had 'begged' the friars to make use of the 'power granted by the Pope' until the new bishop arrived in Mexico. Toribio de Benavente Motolinia, *Memoriales ó libros de las cosas de la Nueva España y de los naturales de ella*, ed. Edmundo O'Gorman (1541; México, 1971), 30.

2 Even if at times magistrates' offices were no place for a bishop, St. Augustine wrote, it was the needs of the brethren which obliged him to await at the doors, and beg for a grace even if many times one came back empty handed. *De opere monachorum* 29.37. "Episcopus pius rem habere cogitur, cum sæcularibus potestatibus....Sæpe de nobis dicitur, Iut ad illam potestatem: et quid quærit episcopus cum illa potestate? Et tamen omnes nostis quia vestræ necessitates nos cogunt venire quo nolomus: observare ante ostium stare, in trantibus dignis et indignis exspectare, nuntiare, uix aliquando admitti: ferre humilitatis, rogare, aliquando impetrare, aliquando tristes adscedere." Sermo 302. J.P. Migne, *Patrologia Latina* (Paris, 1844–64), vol. 38, 139. On this subject see Ana Inés Ovalle, "La Audientia Episcopalis," *Revista Chilena de Historia del Derecho* 9 (1983).

 | DOI 10.1163/9789004305175_003

In the fourth part I will discuss how the institution was established in Peru in 1529. Lastly, I will assess the elements that define the institution and will argue that the protectorship was a secular office.

Las Casas as 'Protector of Indians'

The institutionalisation of a protectorship of Indians in the years that followed the discovery of America is fundamentally linked to the endeavours of Bartolomé de las Casas (1474–1566).[3] Las Casas arrived in the Caribbean in 1502 with Nicolás de Ovando (1451–1511)'s expedition and for some time administered a modest encomienda in Hispaniola inherited from his father. Here he would be a witness to the death and exploitation suffered by Indians. A sermon by Antonio de Montesinos based on the psalm *Ego vox clamatis in deserto* in which he denounced the colonists for their exploitation and abuse of the Indians, moved him to act in favour of the Indian cause.[4] As a consequence, he returned to the Peninsula in 1515 with the support of the Dominican order both in Hispaniola and Spain, and staged a formidable campaign in favour of the American Indian.

One of the results of his endeavours at the Royal Court of Castile was his appointment, in September 1516, as Procurator and Universal Protector of Indians. The *real cedula* creating the office was signed by Cardinal Adrian Dedel (1459–1523), later Pope Hadrian VI, as ambassador to Charles V (1500–56) in Spain in matters of the Indies, and encompassed duties over an extensive territory. Las Casas was ordered to inform himself of 'all things pertaining to the liberty and good treatment and health of the souls and bodies of the… Indians' in the islands of Hispaniola, Cuba, Jamaica, San Juan, and those parts of the mainland thus far discovered. He would write an account based on his findings indicating both the situation of the Indians and measures to remedy any injustices. In other words, Las Casas's instructions were to inform both the

3 The bibliography on Las Casas is legion. For his complete works see Bartolmé de las Casas, *Obras completas*, 14 vols, ed. Paulino Castañeda (Madrid, 1989–98). General guides to his work are Juan Friede and Benjamin Keen, eds., *Bartolomé de las Casas in History* (De Kalb, 1971) and Henry Wagner and Helen Parish, *The Life and Writings of Bartolomé de las Casas* (Albuquerque, NM, 1967). A selective bibliography is also found in Friedrich Wilhelm and Traugott Bautz, eds., *Biographisch-Bibliographisches Kirchenlexicon*, vol. 4 (Herzberg, 1992), 1188–1189.

4 'Are thet not men? Do they not have rational souls? Are you not obliged to love them as yourselves?' See David Brading, *First America: The Spanish Monarchy, Creole Patriots, and the liberal state, 1492–1867* (Cambridge, 1993), 59.

Franciscan envoys of Cardinal Francisco Jiménez de Cisneros (1436–1517), archbishop of Toledo and regent, of all matters related to the 'reform of the Indies' and concerned with the health of the soul and body of the Indians. The universal protector's mandate could not be challenged by the authority of the Almirante Mayor or of any justice. Neither could any official challenge the person of Las Casas himself. A fine of 10,000 maravedíes would be imposed if any infringement of this occurred.[5]

Although Las Casas was the first instituted protector and procurator of Indians in Spanish American history, the legal nature of his office bears little, or no, relation to the protectorship of Indians studied in this book. This, however, has been the claim of modern scholarship on the subject. In his seminal work on the protector of Indians, Constantino Bayle (1882–1953), for example, stated that the institution of the 'office' of the protectorship constitutes one of the 'undisputed merits' of Las Casas.[6] More specifically, Carmen Ruigómez describes Las Casas's appointment as a procurator and inspector with 'unlimited powers and rights' regarding the well-being of the Indians and their treatment.[7] Similarly, Enrique Dussel observes that the universal protector was, in fact, an 'innate fiscal or procurator' for the Indians.[8] In other words, it is implied that Las Casas not only became an accredited observer and informant for Charles v, but also a procurator empowered to put forward suits before courts of justice in Spain and the Indies on behalf of the native inhabitants of the New World in matters concerning their good treatment and liberty.

The idea that Las Casas was not only an informant but also a procurator for Indian legal claims is supported by two interpretations. The first is that of Las Casas's own account of the events surrounding his appointment contained in his *Historia de las Indias*. In this text, the refusal of Luis Zapata and Lorenzo Galíndez de Caravajal, councillors of Castile and members of the junta created for the government of the Indies (1511), to sign the orders which facilitated his

---

5 "[V]os mandamos que paséis a aquellas partes de las dichas Indias…y déis parecer a los devotos padres Hierónimos que nos envíamos a entender en la reformación de las Indias…de todas las cosas que tocaren a la libertad y buen tractamiento e sald de las ánimas y los cuerpos de los dichos indios…y para que nos escribáis e informéis…de todas las cosas que se hicieren y convinieren hacerse en las dichas islas, y para que en todo hagáis lo que conveniere al servicio de Nuestro Señor." Bartolomé de las Casas, *Historia de las Indias*, eds. Isacio Pérez Fernandez et al., vols. 3–5 of *Obras Completas* (Madrid, 1994), 3: 2134–2135.

6 Constantino Bayle, *El protector de indios* (Sevilla, 1945), 15–16.

7 Carmen Ruigómez Gómez, *Una política indigenista de los Habsburgo: el Protector de Indios en el Perú* (Madrid, 1988), 49–50.

8 Enrique Dussel, *El espicopado latinoamericano y la liberación de los pobres, 1504–1620* (Mexico, 1979), 42.

duties in the Indies was interpreted by Las Casas as based on the 'exorbitant powers' granted due to his appointment as protector. Essentially he argued that the opposition to the newly created protectorship was rooted, on one hand, in the vested interests of the councillors and Zapata's fear that the universal protector would reduce the importance of the judges and officials already elected under the junta's influence.[9] On the other hand, he claimed that the members of the newly created audience of Hispaniola were behind the enslavement of Indians, and that his office of universal protector collided with this practice and with 'everything' which the councillors had blindly supported. Therefore, the order issued by the ageing Cardinal Cisneros, then regent of Spain (1516–17), that the councillors should sign the provision of his appointment as universal protector of Indians and the subsequent reception thereof by Alonso de Zuazo, elected residential judge in Hispaniola, was understood by Las Casas as a measure that would cause 'hurt' to many. In other words, Las Casas's perception was that his office not only gave him immense powers, but that these powers could effectively influence the course of government and administration of justice to the benefit of the Indians.[10]

The second is the idea that the immediate antecedent of Las Casas's protectorship was the protector of the Canary Islands.[11] This observation is partly supported by the fact that both Juan Frías, Bishop of Rubicón and first protector of the Canary Islands, and Las Casas were charged with the protection of the indigenous population. Like Las Casas, Frías was appointed protector and procurator of the indigenous population of the Canary Islands and was particularly concerned with the Canarians' enslavement by the Spanish authorities. Las Casas and Frías each enjoyed a wide competence over Indians. This is evidenced by the fact that Las Casas was sought to protect the liberty as well as the spiritual and physical health of the Indians, regardless of their state of conversion in the islands and mainland thus far discovered by Castile. Similarly, although Frías's jurisdiction, by virtue of rescripts of 1474–77 to the audience of Seville, initially included only those who had embraced the Catholic faith, by further rescripts of 20 and 28 September 1477 it would also include both Christians and

9 In 1516 and partly due to the influence of Cisneros, Zapata and Galíndez de Carvajal virtually monopolised the government of the Indies. On this subject and on the antecedents of the Council of Indies (1524) see Antonio Muro Orejón, "El Real y Supremo Consejo de las Indias" *Anuario de Estudios Americanos* 27 (1970), 208–209, passim.

10 Las Casas, *Historia*, 3: 2134–2142. Las Casas, however, believed that the councillors had not written their true signature but only a 'certain sign,' so that they could later claim before the King that Cisneros had forced them to do so, 3: 2136.

11 See Ruigómez, *Protector de indios*, 41.

those who were still 'in the path of conversion to the Holy Catholic Faith.'[12] Moreover, that the rights to undertake the conquest of Gran Canaria, Tenerife and La Palma (1477–85) were given by the Castilian Crown to Captains Juan Bermúdez and Juan de Rejón, and to Bishop Frías, suggests that the bishop could protect those not yet converted from any abuse by the captains. The bishop's competence would later also extend to islands which remained under seigniorial jurisdiction such as La Gomera.[13]

However, available evidence suggests that Frías used his prerogatives to take cases of abusive treatment of Spaniards towards Indians before the royal courts of justice. In 1477, for example, before the audience of Seville he opposed the unjust enslavement of some 100 Gomeros by Fernán Peraza, heir to the feudal lords of Lanzarote, Fuerteventura, Hierro and Gomera. In his plea he stated that it was his duty to 'procure that they be free' and demanded the audience to grant the indigenous people their liberty. The Canarians were declared free by the audience which ordered Peraza to pay the bishop 1200 maravedíes for legal costs. After this, several rescripts were issued by the Catholic Kings to various magistrates in the area of Andalusia, where the sale had taken place, ordering the execution of the sentence and to report and hand over all of the illegally sold Canarians to Bishop Frías.[14]

By contrast, this crucial aspect of Frías's work as protector of the Canary Island Indians is absent from the rescript which contains the appointment of Las Casas as universal protector of Indians. In fact, an overview of Las Casas's career suggests that in practice this possibility was also highly unlikely. In particular, the first five years that followed his appointment (1516–21) were spent in the Peninsula where he devoted his time to writing memoranda which reported the cruelties of the conquerors and promoted remedies to the structure of the Spanish settlements in the New World. When Las Casas returned to America he established a small colony at Cumaná on the northern coast of Venezuela, which would be an example of peaceful colonisation based on trade and agriculture. After Indian attacks drove the friars and colonists to abandon the venture, Las Casas entered the Dominican order in 1524 and thereafter devoted himself to the cause of peaceful Indian conversion and of

12 Dominik Joseph Wölfel, "La Curia Romana y la corona de España en la defensa de los aborígenes canarios," *Anthropos* 25 (1930), 1050–1052.

13 Eduardo Aznar Vallejo, *La integración de las Islas Canarias en la Corona de Castilla (1478–1426): Aspectos administrativos, sociales y económicos* (Sevilla, La Laguna, [1982]), 42–43.

14 "[P]rocurar como sean libres que nos suplicava e pedia por merçed los mandasemos poner en su libertad." Dominik Joseph Wölfel, "La Curia Romana y la corona de España en la defensa de los aborígenes canarios," *Anthropos* 25 (1930), 1020, 1054–1058.

the abolition of the encomienda. The only other appointment he enjoyed was that of bishop of Chiapa (1537).

In the light of this, it seems that the chief objective of the universal protectorship as established in the 1516 rescript was to appoint Las Casas as an authorised voice for the Indian cause in Spain, not to make him, as Bishop Frías was, a procurator for Indian legal claims. Therefore, although Las Casas would boast that his appointment would cause inconveniences to the Spanish authorities in America, there is no evidence to suggest that Las Casas himself, despite being a prolific writer, understood the protectorship of Indians as an office connected with particular claims before the courts of justice.

Las Casas would later explicitly state that Indians should be under the jurisdiction of no institution other than the Catholic Church – a possibility which was excluded under Las Casas's protectorship due to his condition of layman until 1524. Thus, in a 1545 memorandum to the audience in Guatemala, he wrote that the protection of the lawsuits of miserable persons, as the Indians were considered to be, should be the competence of the bishop and that royal proclamations should be sent in this sense to all alcaldes and justices of pueblos, cities, villas and places. This desire, Las Casas wrote, should not be interpreted as an usurpation of royal jurisdiction, which he defended and revered, but as a measure that could prevent the excommunication of many officials, and a way of ensuring the mutual help of the ecclesiastical arm to the secular and vice versa.[15]

Moreover, in the last year of his life, and after a titanic fifty-year-long struggle on behalf of the Indians, Las Casas wrote a petition to Pius V (*r.*1566–72) stating that experience had demonstrated as necessary in present times the need to 'renovate all canons' by which bishops were instructed to take care of the 'poor, captives, afflicted men and widows until the last drop of blood is shed for them,' an obligation of both natural and divine law. Las Casas therefore urged the Pope,

> to renew these sacred canons, and order all bishops of the Indies...to have all care of those naturals, which were oppressed by...works and tyrannies, ...[and] take upon their frail shoulders...a most heavy yoke and unbearable load, it is therefore necessary that Y[our] Hol[iness] orders that the

15 "V.M. declare perteneçer el conocimiento y proteçión de las causas de las myserables personas, como son estas gentes indianas, al juizio eclesiastico, y embié sus provisiones reales sobre ello a los alcaldes y justicias de los pueblos, çiudades, villas y lugares." Bartolomé de las Casas, "Representación a la Audiencia de los Confines" (20 October 1545), in *Cartas y memoriales*, vol. 13 of *Obras Completas* (Madrid, 1995), 208–209.

> said bishops should defend this cause, placing themselves as a wall for them, until they shed their blood, as obliged by divine law[16]

Despite this statement, Las Casas's concern to stress the role of the Church in the protection of Indians should not be taken as indicating that his appointment was in any way an ecclesiastical one. Unlike Bishop Frías of the Canaries, he had no permanent link with ecclesiastical institutions at the time of his appointment in 1516. Although he had the support of the Dominican order in his first campaign at court (1515–21), he himself would enter the Dominican order in 1524, and became bishop of Chiapa in 1547. Therefore, the legal nature of Las Casas's appointment as protector of Indians was secular and limited to the task of reporting the situation of the American Indians to the crown. In the same way, the lack of legal activity makes the title of 'procurator,' which the office also possessed, merely symbolic. Las Casas's concern that Indians should be under the protection of bishops would materialise in 1527–28 when the protectorship of Indians was attached to the episcopal appointments of the newly founded dioceses of America.

The Bishop Protectors, 1528–30

The Mexican Experience

The office of protector of Indians gained the jurisdictional powers that Las Casas's office lacked when it was formally attached to the episcopal appointments of Diego Alvarez de Osorio in Nicaragua (1527), Fr. Tomás Ortiz in Santa Marta (1528) and Juan de Zumárraga in Mexico (1528).[17] Overall, however, the career of Juan de Zumárraga (1468–1548), a Franciscan friar, constitutes the

16 "Porque la experiencia, maestra de todas las cosas, enseña ser necesario en estos tiempos renovar todos los cánones en que se manda que los obispos tengan cuidado de los pobres captivos, hombres afligidos y viudas, hasta derramar su sangre por ellos, según son obligados por ley natural y divina, a V.B. humildemente suplico que renovando estos sacros cánones, mande a los obispos de Indias por sancta obediencia que tenga todo cuidado de aquellos naturales, los cuales, oprimidos con sumos trabajos y tiranías (más que se puede creer) llevan sobre sus flacos hombros, contra todo Derecho divino y natural, un pesadísimo yugo y carga incomportable, por lo cual es necesario que V.Sd. mande que los dichos obispos defiendan esta causa, poniéndose por muro de ellos, hasta derramar su sangre, como por ley divina son obligados...." Las Casas, "Petición a Su Santidad Pio V" (1566), in *Cartas y memoriales*, vol. 13 of *Obras Completas* (Madrid, 1995), 370–371.

17 Osorio by *real cedula* of 2 May 1527 and Ortiz by *real cedulas* of 15 February and 17 August 1528. See Bayle, *Protector*, 34, 52–53.

best documented account in this period of the manner in which the bishop discharged his duties.[18] In addition to this, it is safe to conclude that his actions before the secular authorities in Mexico in 1528–30 shaped the definite characteristics of the bishop-protectorship until the institution ceased to exist in 1554.

The impact of Zumárraga's protectorship is reflected in the fact that even before his arrival in Mexico City in 1529, his prerogatives were already dividing secular and ecclesiastical authorities in this jurisdiction. The force behind this division was the twelve-man strong Franciscan mission charged with the evangelisation of Indians, which arrived in 1524.[19] In his chronicle of the endeavours of the Franciscans in Mexico, Toribio de Benavente Motolinia (1500?–1569), one of the twelve friars, stated that upon their official presentation before the *cabildo* of Mexico City in 1525, they declared that Martín de Valencia, leader of mission, was not only competent in spiritual matters, but also in 'civil and criminal jurisdiction.' Moreover, they informed the town council that even if this claim 'hindered…[the] justices' it was the legal consequence of the 'episcopal pre-eminence' possessed by the friars. In sum, the Franciscans not only claimed that their leader possessed episcopal authority until the arrival of the bishop, but also that this authority included secular jurisdiction.[20]

Motolinia narrates that the town councillors contested this claim by noting that there could be 'no bishop [elected] by Their Majesties' with provisions to exercise secular jurisdiction.[21] This he answered by personally delivering two *reales cédulas* and two Papal bulls which allegedly validated his claim. The two *cédulas*, dated 15 November and 12 December 1523, were, in fact, royal licenses authorising the friars to travel to the Indies and were duly transcribed by the notaries. The bulls, however, presented a problem for the councillors and the council's notary as they were 'written in the Latin tongue.' As none of them understood Latin, Motolinia states that they were registered in the book of the

---

18 For his role as protector see Fidel de Chauvet, "Fray Juan de Zumárraga, Protector of the Indians," *The Americas* 5 (1948–49): 283–310. For a general bibliography, see Bautz, *Kirchenlexion*, vol. 14 (Herzberg, 1998), 605–607. For a general survey of the role of the bishop in the protection of Indians in this period see Dussel, *El episcopado latinoamericano*, 11–107.

19 The impact of the Franciscan mission in Mexico is studied in Brading, *First America*, Ch. 5.

20 "[N]o solamente entiende de las cosas tocantes à los descargos de conciencia, mas aun entremétense en usar de juridición civil é criminal e inyben por la corona de las justicias, que son cosas tocantes á la premiencia episcopal," Toribio de Benavente Motolinia, *Memoriales ó libros de las cosas de la Nueva España y de los naturales de ella*, ed. Edmundo O'Gorman (1541; México, 1971), 424–425.

21 "[N]o puede haber obispo por sus magestades y traer con su bula provisión del rey para ello." Ibid., 424.

cabildo simply as two bulls 'in leather parchment and sealed with two red seals.'[22] The presiding councillor then proceeded to place the *cédulas* and bulls above his head, thus declaring obedience to them 'as letters of their King and natural lord.' After this, however, Motolinia claims that the councillor recorded his doubts as to whether the bulls genuinely granted any use of jurisdiction and 'civil and criminal judicature' to the Franciscan mission in Mexico.[23]

If the text of the rescripts refers only to travel licenses, it is evident that Motolinia based his claim of jurisdictional faculties on the Papal bulls taken to the cabildo. These bulls were *Alius felicis* and *Exponi nobis fecisti*. The first was issued in 25 April 1521 by Leo x (*r.*1513–21) and authorised two Franciscan fathers to undertake a mission to Mexico, granting them full powers to carry out pastoral duties in the absence of normal diocesan structures. The second was *Exponi nobis fecisti*, issued in 10 May 1522 by Hadrian v (*r.*1522–23), to renew the authorisation of the mendicant order to evangelise the newly conquered region and to empower the friars with episcopal faculties until the bishop himself arrived in Mexico.

Therefore, the 'power granted by the Pope' which Motolinia refers to, was in fact contained in the bull *Exponi nobis fecisti*. A manuscript copy of this document found in the Mexican collection of the Lilly Library provides the key to the friars's claim to possess both episcopal faculties and secular jurisdiction. Its text thus established that,

> so that the said conversion of the infidels may better be achieved, and the salvation of all the souls living at the time in the said lands of the Indians may better be assured, we desire, and in the tenor of the present letter we grant from the fullness of power, that the said friars chosen as their leader and other to whom those of the friars shall entrust authority, in areas in which no bishoprics have yet been created, or if they have been, where neither they nor their officials can be found within the space of two days' travel, shall have our all-encompassing authority in both courts [utroque foro], both as far as their brothers and other of any order whatsoever, who shall have been deputed there for this task, and over the Indians converted to the faith of Christ, and also other Christians accompanying them for this work[24]

22 "[E]scritos en lengual latina en pergamino de cuero y sellados con dos sellos de cera colorada encajados en cajitas de palo pendientes en cintas verdes." Ibid., 425.

23 "[C]artas de su rey y señor natural…y judicatura civil y criminal." Ibid., 425.

24 "[U]t melius prefata conversio infidelium fieri valeat, et saluti animarum omnium in pre fatis terris Indorum pro tempore degentium provideatur, volumus, et tenore presentium

Whereas the friars' episcopal powers were clearly established ("in quibus nondum fuerint Episcopatus creati...ominmodam authoritate nostram"), its attributions "in utroque foro" were interpreted by Motolinia as civil and criminal jurisdictional powers over Indians and non-Indians. However, this was not the consensus among the authorities in Mexico. In fact, Motolinia himself would admit that university graduates Juan de Ortega and Alonso Pérez disagreed with his interpretation after being consulted by the *cabildo* of Mexico on the matter, and concluded that the authority granted to the friars was only limited to matters of conscience and ecclesiastical courts.[25] This situation would prompt Antonio de Mendoza (1493?–1552), viceroy of Mexico, to later regret how the King's officials and the friars had 'destroyed the poor Indians, and spent so much time and ink in making and unmaking...provisions, one contrary to other.'[26]

Contrary to the viceroy's belief, Jerónimo de Mendieta (1525–1604), Motolinia's chief disciple, claimed that for the Franciscans the 'office of the judicature' would become detrimental 'towards the conversion of the Indians' and that their leader agreed to 'relinquish the jurisdiction' regarding the Spanish population. Mendieta would also state that, although secular authorities continuously infringed the 'authority and jurisdiction' granted to the friars, these powers were used reluctantly and often 'compelled by necessity.'[27] Testimony would suggest that the scope of conflict between secular and spiritual authorities between 1524 to 1528, that is prior to the arrival of the bishop, was fairly limited; particularly as it could only comprise the jurisdiction of the

de plenitudine potestatis concedimus, utt prefati prelati fratrum. Et alii quibus ipsi de fratribus suis in predictis Indiis commorantibus duxerint committtendum, in partibus in quibus nondum fuerint Episcopatus creati, vel si fuerint tamen infra diarum dietarum spatium ipsi, vel officiales eorum inveniri minime possint, tam quoad fratres suos, et alios cuiuscumque ordinis, qui ibidem fuering ad hoc opus deputati, ac super Indos ad fidem Christi conversos, quam et alios Christicolas ad dictum opus eosdem comitantes, omnimodam auctoritatem nostram in utroque foro quantam ipsi." In "Adrianus Papa Sexto, bulla Pro conversione Indorum...," Lilly Latin American mss. Mexico, 1522, May 10, f. 2. Trans. by Geoffrey Symcox, ed. *Italian Reports on America, 1493–1522: Letters, Dispatches and Papal Bulls* (Turnhout, 2001), 134–136.

25 Motolinia, *Memoriales*, 30.

26 "Relación de don Antonio de Mendoza sobre las Indias" (1551), in Manuel Fernández Alvarez, ed. *Corpus documental de Carlos v*, vol. 3 (Salamanca: 1977), 256.

27 "[S]e desasosegaban con el cargo de la judicatura, y les era detrimento para la conversión de los indios y aprovechamiento de los españoles, acordó dejar y renunciar la jurisdicción en cuanto á lo que tocaba á los españoles." Gerónimo de Mendieta, *Historia eclesiástica indiana*, ed. Joaquín García Icazbalceta (1870; Mexico, 1971), 315.

cabildo of Mexico City by then under the authority of the audience of Santo Domingo.[28] Moreover, the fact that the episcopal prerogatives invoked by the friars were established by 1528, suggests that the influence of the contesting parties would often depend on extra-legal factors to exert their authority, with threats of excommunication being the friars's main instrument.[29] Thus, the conflict between secular and ecclesiastical authorities in Mexico would acquire its real magnitude only after the establishment of the audience and the arrival of Bishop Zumárraga in Mexico in 1528.

Zumárraga was appointed first bishop of Mexico City and protector of Indians in 1528 by virtue of a *real cedula* enacted in Burgos by Charles V and Queen Juana (1479–1555). The text that set out the obligations of Zumárraga as protector began by insisting that Indians should be treated as vassals and free subjects. The office would ensure not only their conversion to Christianity but also their conservation. The protector, therefore, would not consent to any wrongdoing towards Indians and would make sure that ordinances regarding their good treatment were being obeyed. The *cedula* also indicated that these ordinances should be kept even at the expense of the property and persons of those who infringed them, and empowered the protector to prosecute and execute—using both material and personal punishment—persons who infringed the ordinances. To ensure adequate protection for the Indians, the office's jurisdiction included all dependencies of government, and collaboration was requested from the president and *oidors* of the newly created audience of Mexico (1528). Failure to help the protectorship of Indians in any of its attributions had, as a result, a penalty of 10,000 maravedíes for the royal treasury.[30] In other words, the faculties given to Bishop Zumárraga as protector gave him effective jurisdictional powers in Indians matters.

The use of these assumed jurisdictional powers by Zumárraga would only exacerbate the tensions between the secular and ecclesiastical powers. In a letter to Charles V, Zumárraga informed the emperor that after his arrival in Mexico City it had been proclaimed that he had been sent by the king as protector and defender of Indians. After this he had personally informed the *principales* and lords of New Spain that they were the king's vassals, that they would be well treated, and that they could denounce any mistreatment to him or any

28 Francisco del Paso y Troncoso, ed., *Epistolario de la Nueva España, 1505–1818*, vol. 1 (1505–1529) (Mexico, 1939), 87.

29 Mendieta, *Historia*, 314.

30 "[E]xecuteys en sus personas y bienes, las penas en ellas contenidas, pa lo qual…vos damos poder cumplido con todos sus icidencias y dependencias." Vasco de Puga, *Provisiones cedulas instrucciones de su Magestad…*(Mexico, 1543), 64v.

of his appointed lieutenants. The Indians were not obliged to give the bishop anything in return nor pay for this right. Indians, the bishop wrote, were moved by this and thanked the king for such protection. Soon after, Zumárraga claimed he received complaints of 'many thefts and force, and bad treatment' and other crimes committed against the Indians, some of them so abominable and devilish that he did not dare repeat them. Shielded by his prerogatives, Zumárraga would prosecute the perpetrators and take them to court.[31]

Although Zumárraga does not give details of the action he took to correct the abuses, the advice of the Real Audiencia of Mexico to cease acting as a 'judge' of Indians makes it clear that the bishop was hearing and solving legal disputes.[32] The bishop states that the *oidors* objected such hearings in view that these were matters solely for the secular high court. In turn he explained that he held a provision from the king granting him these powers and that the *oidors* were aware of such a provision. As relations with the audience were becoming 'damaged, blind and passionate,' Zumárraga claims in his letter to the king that he sought a conciliatory position and conceded that his sentences be heard in appeal by the high court, if in return he retained his veto on the approval of appointees to the position of visitadores. The audience, presided over by Beltrán Nuño de Guzmán (†1544), replied by sending official notification ordering the bishop to cease in his office of protector and defensor of Indians. The *oidors*, stated Nuño de Guzmán, would be thereafter the only 'lords' in Indians matters.[33]

The relations between the bishop and the *oidors* of Mexico had reached its historic low-point by March 1529 when two caciques who had taken refuge in the Franciscan convent of Huexotzingo were abducted by the audience. The caciques had reported to Zumárraga that the audience had burdened Huexotzingo, a repartimiento under the jurisdiction of Cortés, with excessive tributes. In view of this the bishop wrote to the *oidors* but Guzmán replied that the audience could demand any tribute they wished, regardless of whether people died trying to comply with it. The audience then ordered the capture of the caciques in Huexotzingo. The alguacil and his agents who carried out the order were met by the friars, who not only declared the audience the work 'of

31 Zumárraga to Charles V, Mexico, 27 August 1529, Joaquín García Icazbalceta, *Don Fray Juan de Zumárraga: Primer obispo y arzobispo de México* (México, 1947), 2: 221–223.

32 The best description of the conflict between Zumárraga and the audience is Georges Baudot, "Le 'complot' franciscain contre la première audience de Mexico." *Caravelle: Cahiers du Monde Hispanique et Luso Brésilien* 2 (1964), 15–34.

33 "[N]o entendiese en este cargo de protector y defensor de indios…porque ellos eran señores dello." Ibid, 226, 224–225.

the devil and of Satan.' They also excommunicated the alguacil, admonishing him that the audience should not deal with matters concerning Indians, nor should it invoke any provisions regarding them.[34] The violation of ecclesiastical asylum which permitted the capture and subsequent torture and murder of the two caciques was sanctioned by Zumárraga by excommunicating the audience and declaring the cessation *a divinis*, that is, the closure of all churches and termination of all sacraments in the capital of New Spain.[35]

In the midst of the conflict, Zumárraga wrote to the Charles v stating that the 'Dioclesian cruelties' which Indians suffered at the hands of the Spanish and, in particular, from those who held offices, convinced him of the fact that only members of religious orders could provide 'the medicine to cure' these wrongs and requested the king to ratify his jurisdiction over the protection and care of Indians, and to grant him powers to amend and suspend ordinances.[36] As the clergy could not dedicate themselves solely to legal disputes, he proposed the appointment of Indian alcaldes by the protector to settle civil and criminal lawsuits in towns and villages. Lastly, he requested new ordinances providing for the good treatment of Indians so that they could function as guide for all the protectors and defenders. These would include general guidelines and regulations on scales and punishments for the mistreatment of Indians.[37]

The conflict between the bishop and the high court ended with the appointment a new audiencia in 1530 under the presidency of Sebastían Ramírez de Fuenleal, former bishop of Santo Domingo, and the question on the protector of Indians' prerogatives was solved by a *real cédula*. In 2 August 1530, the Queen, observing that the exercise of the office of protector of Indians had been the cause of 'differences' between the bishop and the president of the audience, resolved to enact certain provisions that would modify the prerogatives of the office.[38]

---

34 Audiencia of Mexico, "Información fecha por mandato del Presidente y Oidores, contra ciertos frailes Franciscos de Guaxocingo, pueblos enconmendado a Cortés, donde se empieza en 22 de abril de 1529," García Icazbalceta, *Zumárraga*, 2: 105–106.

35 Zumárraga to Charles V, Mexico, 27 August 1529, García Icazbalceta, *Zumárraga*, 2: 237, 248, 255–257. The cessation *a divinis* was the usual censure in such cases. It was declared, for example in 1625 in Toledo where the Archbishop excommunicated the corregidor of the city for the seizure of a 'famous thief' in a church and later hanging him. Fernando Díaz-Plaja, *Historia de España en sus documentos: Siglo XVII* (Madrid, 1987), 113.

36 "[M]uy cumplido poder ... jurisdiccion dela proteccion y amparo de los indios." Zumárraga to Charles v, Mexico, 27 August 1529, García Icazbalceta, *Zumárraga*, 2: 235–236.

37 Ibid, 239–240.

38 Puga, *Provisiones*, 64v.

The first provision was related to the power of the protectors to appoint inspectors, and stated that such inspectors needed to be ratified by the audience. Secondly, the rescript established that although the protector would continue to inform himself of any ill treatment towards Indians, he could not impose any punishment. In other words, the audience would have exclusive control in the prosecution of those who perpetrated wrongs against Indians. In principle the bishop-protector could only arrest offenders, take them before the secular court and submit to the judicial authorities a report on the case. Thirdly, the protector and his lieutenants were granted the faculty to investigate the conduct of any crown official regarding his treatment of Indians. The findings, however, would be submitted to the audience which would decide whether or not to start judicial proceedings. In sum, the provisions stated that the protectors did not have 'any priority over the said justices.'[39] The only jurisdictional powers that remained with the office of protector were the right to impose fines up to 50 golden pesos and order imprisonment of up to ten days in jail, with no right of appeal. Bishop-protectors, however, lost their entire previous jurisdiction over criminal cases where both defendant and plaintiff were Indians.[40]

Zumárraga did not contest the measures. In part, this was due to the fact that a bishop had replaced Nuño de Guzmán in the presidency of the audience of Mexico, thus improving the relationship between the secular and ecclesiastical orders. In fact, Zumárraga continued to undertake his duties as 'judge and protector and defensor, by his majesty, of Indians' within the new framework imposed by the provisions of August 1530. In January 1531, for example, he commissioned Pedro de Orantes, his secretary and notary, to investigate claims of ill treatment towards and excessive tributes imposed on Indians. Following the new provisions the case was not heard by the bishop himself but taken to secular authorities.[41] In 1532, however, he requested the president of the audience, Bishop Ramírez de Fuenleal, to relieve him of his functions as protector. Fuenleal informed the king that Zumárraga had stated that the protectorship had been the root of all past differences and proposed that the audiencia should assume its functions. Naturally, Fuenleal shared this opinion stating

39 "[N]o es nuestra intencion y voluntad, que los protectores tengan su prioridad alguna sobre los dichos justicias." Puga, *Provisiones*, 65.

40 Ibid, 65.

41 "Ynforma*cio*n. Manda resevir por el Yllmo. Obispo Zumarraga como Protector de los Indios…" Lilly, Latin American mss. Mexico, 1531, Jan. 2.

that the king's justices were the 'true protectors' of Indians and that a special protector of Indians was in fact 'not a fruitful office.'[42]

Zumárraga's petition to be exonerated from the protectorship of Indians was accepted by the crown in a rescript of 28 September 1534. He duly complied by returning the provisions which had caused so much conflict. Much of the bitterness caused by the events of 1528–30, however, remained. Not one of the members of the first audience wished to receive absolution. In fact, *oidor* Diego Delgadillo stated that he preferred to go to hell before receiving absolution from a Franciscan friar.[43]

The Protector-audience Conflict Explained

Attempting to explain the conflict between Zumárraga and the audience, Fuenleal observed two main causes. The first had been the bishop's 'zealousness.'[44] The second had been the jurisdictional attributions that both the Franciscans and the bishop assumed. In Fuenleal's view the problem had been the 'brief of Adrianus, given by petition of Your Majesty, by which the friars of both orders have pretended to be bishops and even at times pontiffs.'[45] Zumárraga himself, writing to Charles V during the events of Huexotzingo, justified his actions by virtue of his "*cum omnimoda potestate in utroque foro.*"[46] These attributions, however, do not appear in his appointment as protector, but in *Exponi nobis fecisti*, the Papal bull cited by Motolinia to the town councillors of Mexico in 1525.

At another point in the conflict, however, when the audience questioned Zumárraga's legitimacy as 'judge' for Indians, the bishop replied that he was in possession of the King's provision granting him that right. Where, then, did Zumárraga's source of jurisdiction over Indian legal disputes reside? Part of the answer lies in the argument presented by the audience and Gonzalo de Salazar, governor of Huexotzingo, to undermine the bishop's claims. Both referred to the fact that at the time of the 1528–30 conflict Zumárraga could not enforce his rights as protector of Indians because he was still a 'simple friar.' By this

---

42 "No es oficio de algún fructo." Fuenleal to Charles V, Mexico, 30 April 1532, *Colección de documentos inéditos relativos al descubrimiento, conquista y colonización de las posesiones españolas en América y Oceanía*, vol. 13 (Madrid, 1870), 219–220.

43 Fernando Gil, *Primeras Primeras"Doctrinas" del Nuevo Mundo: Estudio histórico-teológico de las obras de fray Juan de Zumárraga (†1548)*, (Buenos Aires, 1993), 101.

44 Salmerón et al. to the Empress, Mexico, 30 March 1531, Garcia Icazbalceta, *Zumárraga*, 2: 291.

45 "[U]n breve de Adriano, dado à peticiòn de vuestra Majestad con el qual los frailes de ambos hordenes an pretendido ser obispos y aun tener veces de pontífices." Fuenleal to Charles V, Mexico, 30 April 1532, *Colección de documentos inéditos relativos al descubrimiento, conquista y colonización de las posesiones españolas en América y Oceanía*, vol. 13 (Madrid, 1870), 211.

46 Zumárraga to Charles V, 6 March 1530, Garcia Icazbalceta, *Zumárraga*, 2: 247.

they meant that he was only 'presented' as bishop, but had not taken possession of his ecclesiastical dignity.[47] While the argument indicates an implicit acceptance of the bishop's legitimate provision as protector, it nevertheless expresses reserves as to Zumárraga's actual status as a bishop.

The history of the formation of the diocese of Mexico partly proves the point made by Salazar and the audience. The see and diocese of Mexico were created by decree in 1527 by virtue of the royal patronage enjoyed by the kings of Spain in respect of 'ancient custom.'[48] However, although the King had established the diocese and nominated the bishop and all the members of the cathedral chapter, none of these could formally occupy their posts until the proclamation in Mexico of the Papal bull founding the diocese. As the bull arrived and had public validity in Mexico on December 28, 1533, the bishop and chapter became a canonically recognised body only from this date.[49] The jurisdiction granted to Zumárraga as protector of Indians was, therefore, fully valid from a secular point of view. However, the fact that the protectorship was also attached to his episcopal dignity gave valid grounds for questioning the legitimacy of using the protector's prerogatives before being formally recognised as a bishop in the Church.

The fact that defence and protectorship of Indians combined secular and ecclesiastical offices was not an uncommon feature in the Spanish Church. Royal patronage by the Spanish monarchs, for example, made bishops not only prelates of the Church, but also officials of the King. This fact is clear in a provision of 1480 by the Catholic Kings which refer to the bishops as being part of the King's State Council.[50] A clerical presence in government affairs of the peninsula can be traced back to as early as 1295 when the cities of Castile and Leon demanded that bishops, masters of military orders and abbots should abandon the palace and court. Intertwining between secular and ecclesiastical powers was also observed in the historical link in the Middle Ages between the prelates of Santiago and Toledo and the office of State Chancellor.[51] In the case of the Indies, the appointment of bishops by the King and their involvement in secular affairs had a more recent antecedent in the Spanish *reconquista* of

47 Motolinia, *Memoriales*, 433.

48 P.5.18. and *Nueva Recopilación* 1.6.1. The ancient custom refers to the reign of Recaredo (589).

49 García Icazbalceta, *Zumárraga*, 1: 115–116; John Frederick Schwaller, "The Cathedral Chapter of Mexico in the Sixteenth Century," *Hispanic American Historical Review* 61 (4) (1981), 654–655.

50 Javier González Echenique, "Los obispos de Indias como funcionarios de la corona," *Revista Chilena de Historia del Derecho* 6 (1970), 147.

51 P.2.9.4.

lands formerly ruled by the Moors. The active participation of the bishops in this process, often as heads of frontier posts,[52] and the fact that the *reconquista* and the creation of new sees in the former caliphates of Spain were key elements in the justification of royal patronage.[53]

The Bishop Protectors in Peru, 1529–54

The prerogatives of Hernando de Luque (†1534), as first bishop and protector of Indians in Tumbes and its provinces, which is to say the territory of Peru known thus far, were very similar to those of Zumárraga in 1528. In the *real cedula* of July 1529, Charles V stated the need to 'send a person of conscience to be protector and defender of the said Indians and to oversee their good treatment and conservation and conversion and to not allow wrongs.' This person would be Luque by virtue of his condition as bishop and of his trusted 'loyalty and conscience.' As in the case of the first *cedula* issued to Zumárraga, Luque was given full powers of visitation to supervise the good treatment of Indians and their instruction in the Catholic Faith, and, more importantly, jurisdictional faculties to impose fines and decree punishments, both material and personal, to those who did not abide by the ordinances in favour of Indians.[54]

Luque, however, remained in Panama after his appointment. The delay in his arrival in his diocese prompted the King to issue a *cedula* appointing Reginaldo de Pedraza, a Dominican friar due to join Francisco Pizarro's expedition to Peru, as interim protector of Indians. Pedraza's instructions as protector of Indians, detailed in a *cedula* of 4 April 1531, however would include the limitations to the office issued to Zumárraga in 1530. By 1532, when Luque was reinstated in his office and requested the payment of his salary of protector of Indians as 'bishop of the provinces of Peru,' his original provisions were modified.[55]

52 See José Manuel Nieto Soria, *Iglesia y poder real en Castilla: El Episcopado, 1250–1350* (Madrid, 1988), 34, 62–72.

53 "E esta mayoria e honrra han los Reyes de España por tres razones: la primera porque ganaron la tierra de los moros e fizieron las mezquitas Eglesias.... La segunda, porque fundaron de nuevo en logares donde nunca las ovo. La tercera porque las dotaron, e demas les fizieron mucho bien." P.1.5.18.

54 Raul Porras Barrenechea, ed., *Cedulario del Perú (siglos XVI, XVII y XVIII)* (Lima, 1944–1948) 1: 32–34.

55 Luque to Charles V, 20 October 1532, *Cartas del Peru (1524–43)*, vol. 3 of *Colección de documentos inéditos para la historia del Perú*, ed. Raul Porras Barrenechea (Lima, 1959), 35, 33.

The change in the provisions for the protectors of Indians, and the fact that neither Luque nor Pedraza effectively arrived in Peru, prevented conflicts between secular and ecclesiastical powers of the magnitude of those experienced in Mexico in 1528–30. Some tension between the protector and the *cabildo*, however, would follow the appointment of Vicente de Valverde (†1541), a Dominican friar, as Bishop of Cusco.

Valverde, who arrived in Cusco in 1538, was convinced that it was 'most important for the service of God and His Majesty to defend these people [i.e. the Indians] from the mouths of so many wolves.'[56] He therefore intended to make effective use of his powers as protector of Indians to exact fines of up to 50 gold pesos and to use his right to imprison wrongdoers for up to ten days in jail granted by the *real cédula* of 14 July 1536, a rescript which contained the exact terms as that of 1530 to Zumárraga.[57] In 22 January 1539, for example, he condemned a Spaniard, Francisco González, for hitting Popocoya, an Indian woman, to ten days in jail and a fine of 50 pesos in gold. On 6 February of that year he imposed a fine of 30 pesos and five days' imprisonment to Juan Veginés for similar reasons. As a result, the justices of the newly founded *cabildo* of Cusco (1534) wrote to the King denouncing Valverde's interference with ordinary justice.[58]

Similar tensions between bishop protectors and royal authorities occurred in other parts of America. In 1537 Francisco de Marroquín (*c.*1478–1563), Bishop of Guatemala, wrote to the King informing him that those who governed his province did not want protectors, 'nor any other [persons] with the powers of Your Majesty,' and that disputes on Indian matters had already caused much passion.[59] In view of the constant complaints against him, Bishop Marroquín demanded clarification of his jurisdiction. In 1539 he wrote once more to the King inquiring if the protectors were in fact 'judges' or not. If protectors were judges, he argued, then powers should be granted to appoint bailiffs, clerks and visiting judges for distant areas of the diocese. Marroquín also explained to the King that the hearing of Indian legal disputes was a consequence of both their great need for justice and their constant appeals to the bishop. Although he

56 Valverde to Charles V, Cusco, 20 March 1539, *Colección de documentos inéditos relativos al descubrimiento, conquista y colonización de las posesiones españolas en América y Oceanía*, vol. 3, 105.

57 "Nombramiento e instrucciones a Fray Vicente de Valverde como protector de los indios. Valladolid, 14 de julio de 1536," in Ruigómez, *Protector de Indios*, 187–88. Puga, *Provisiones*, 65.

58 Ruigómez, *Protector de Indios*, 60.

59 Marroquín to Charles V, Mexico, 10 May 1537, Francisco de Marroquín, *Cartas y testamento* (Guatemala, 1963), 5.

admitted that he had solved many lawsuits, he also stated that 'in most cases' he preferred 'to find an agreement.' In some disputes, however, the bishop did not dare to 'put his hand' to avoid being accused of 'taking more than what is mine.'[60]

Like Marroquín, Valverde also requested an explanation of his powers in a letter of 1538, claiming that the justices of Peru pretended that 'no one stopped their hands.'[61] The reply, a year later, provided some clarification on the dispositions contained in the 1530 *cédula* which granted the use of jurisdictional faculties to bishop protectors. The rescript stated that the attributions of the protector were only to 'inform himself of the wrongs done against Indians' as the prosecution of these crimes should be left to the royal justices. The King admonished Valverde, saying that he should not make decisions over legal disputes in Indian matters as this was the competence of the 'governor and his lieutenants.' This position was ratified in a real cédula in Valladolid, 13 February 1544, by which Philip II ordered Las Casas to give notice to the royal authorities of any mistreatment of Indians.[62]

The limitations imposed on Valverde, however, were not transferred to Jerónimo de Loayza (1498?–1575), who, in 1542, was appointed bishop protector of Indians in the newly created diocese of Lima (1541). Loayza's title contained the same dispositions as those in the 1530 *cédula* and, therefore, reproduced exactly the instructions and prerogatives given to Valverde, including those of imposing fines of 50 pesos and incarceration of up to ten days.[63] Moreover, a rescript of 14 May 1542 by Philip II to Governor Cristóbal Vaca de Castro (*r.*1540–42) ordered that Valverde should be granted a notary whose salary would be drawn from the fines imposed by the bishop as protector of Indians. Although the disposition arrived in Peru after the death of Valverde, there seems to be an indication that the crown desired the maintenance of the jurisdictional faculties of the bishop protector of Indians. However, unlike the former bishop of Cusco, there no evidence of Loayza solving Indian disputes.

60 "[Q]ué cosa es ser protector y a qué se extiende, y si somos jueces…otro si entre los indios hay muchos pleitos, y todos son civiles, que con poco se contentan y descontentan por su pobreza y mala ventura, y acuden a quien los oye y do hallan más consolación, y las más de las vezes procuro de los concertar, y algunas veces quedean algunos agraviados, por no osar meter la mano, y déjolo porque no digan que tomo más de lo que es mío." Marroquín to the King, 15 August 1539, ibid., 18.

61 "[P]retenden los justicias de esta tierra que nadie les vaya a la mano," in Manuel Olmedo Jiménez, *Jerónimo de Loayza, o.p.: Pacificador de españoles y protector de indios* (Granada, 1990), 138.

62 Ibid., 134.

63 *Real cédula*, Valladolid 4 April 154. Ibid., 146.

His relationship with the *cabildo* of Lima, founded in 1535, was basically limited to administration of the city's hospitals and the collecting of tithes.[64] Although there are records of Loayza requesting sanctions against, for example, butchers who sold meat to the sick without an ecclesiastical licence,[65] there is no trace of complaints from the *cabildo* of Lima to the Council of Indies regarding interference in jurisdictional matters.[66] Neither did Loayza, created archbishop in 1546, enter into disputes over jurisdiction with the audience of Lima, established in 1543.

Loayza's apparent inactivity as protector of Indians is partly explained by the virtual standstill of all judicial activity due to the cycle of civil war and rebellion which ended in 1554.[67] However, secret instructions despatched to the Viceroy of Mexico Antonio de Mendoza (*v.*1535–50) in 1537, point towards making the audience, in general, and its fiscal, in particular, responsible for the preservation and good treatment of Indians. As the secret instructions stated, even if the crown was well aware of the fact that corregidors and religious institutions contributed towards providing remedies for Indians, the viceroy and *oidors* provided the ultimate 'tutorship and shelter.'[68] These secret instructions were influenced, no doubt, by views such as those of Bishop Fuenleal who, after the appointment of Marroquin to Guatemala, suggested Charles V to end the double appointment of bishop protector, as the prelate's pastoral example, doctrine and council would be more fruitful than 'having jurisdiction' as protector.[69] The tendency towards making the ecclesiastical protector subordinate to the secular authority on Indian judicial matters, however, was in fact the general policy of the Spanish monarchy in this period.

One aspect of this policy was the creation of new offices to protect different aspects of the Indians' legal well-being. In certain cities in New Spain, Indians who came to sell fruit were protected in their commercial transactions by an

64 Respectively, entries of 2 May 1552, 10 June 1552 and 3 November 1553, Bertram T. Lee, ed. *Libros de cabildos de Lima* (Lima, 1935), 3: 559, 572; 4: 102.

65 Entry of 7 March 1550. Ibid., 3: 531.

66 See *Cartas de cabildos hispanoamericanos: Audiencia de Lima*, vol. 1 eds. Javier Ortiz de la Tabla Ducasse, María Jesus Mejías Alvarez and Agueda Rivera Garrido (Sevilla, 1999).

67 On La Gasca see Teodoro Hampe Martínez, *Don Pedro de la Gasca, 1493–1567: Su obra política en España y América* (Lima, 1989).

68 Lewis Hanke, ed, *Los virreyes españoles en America durante el gobierno de la casa de Austria: México*, vol 1, BAE 273 (Madrid, 1976), 35–36.

69 "[P]ues el que fuere Obispo mas frutos sacara sin poder de Protector con su doctrina y ejemplo y consejo y con mandalle que haga relacion, que no con tener jurisdicción." Ramírez de Fuenleal to Charles V, México, 8 August 1533, Mariano Cuevas, *Historia general de la Iglesia en Mexico*, 6th ed., ed. José Gutiérrez Casillas, 5 vols. (Mexico, 1992), 1: 258.

alguacil amparador, a bailiff.[70] In Peru, Pedro de la Gasca, president of the audience (1546–50) and responsible for its 're-foundation' after the civil wars, created Indian alcaldes to settle legal disputes of minor importance in an attempt to improve the availability of justice for the Indians.[71] The jurisdiction of these alcaldes would co-exist with that of the cacique, the local authority. In their district these alcaldes could even arrest Spaniards to take them in front of the local judge. Similarly, Viceroy Andrés Hurtado de Mendoza, Marquis of Cañete (*v.*1556–60), created four Indian alcaldes in rural Cusco, whose roles changed over time, by appointing local dignitaries to the post.[72]

The consolidation of secular jurisdiction in Indian matters would eventually end with the judicial attributions of the bishop protectors in the decade of the 1550s. In 1550 the audience of Santa Fe had already obtained a royal charter which allowed it to appoint a layman as Protector of Indians instead of its appointed bishop, Juan de Barrios.[73] In 1554, and following the precedent of the Council of Indies, the *fiscales* of the audiences gained control over the legal protection of Indians in judicial matters.[74] In 1557 the council reiterated this view with a rescript to the audience of Quito ordering it to prosecute and decide in all Indian matters, even in mistreatment committed by bishops themselves.[75] Only in the Philippines would bishop protectors remain in office, only to be removed in 1590 at the request of the bishop himself, who argued that he was unable to attend the judicial diligences that required his personal presence.

---

70 Charles R. Cutter, *The protector de indios in colonial New Mexico, 1659–1821* (Albuquerque, 1986), 15.

71 An explanation of why the earliest records of litigation in Peru date from the decade of 1550 is the 're-foundation' of the audience by Pedro La Gasca in 1548–49 during the period of civil war. See, for example, the judicial section of the cabildo of Lima, AGN, CA JO 1, caja 33, whose first lawsuit (doc. 1, 183 fs.), the impugnation of the testament of Diego Hernández, dates from 1552. In the case of the audience, the earliest record, also a matter of inheritance, dates from 1543, " Autos seguidos en grado de apelación, nulidad y agravio, por Francisco de la Feria, estante en la ciudad de Los Reyes, contra los bienes y herederos de Francisco Dávalos (muerto en 1539)," AGN, Real Audiencia, Causas Civiles, leg. 1, c. 1, fs. 146.

72 The Viceroy Count of Nieva (*v.*1560–64), however, limited the capacity of these magistrates to civil lawsuits, and Viceroy Lope de Castro, provisional governor of Peru (1564–69) eventually suspended the appointment of alcaldes. See Guillermo Lohmann Villena, *El Corregidor de Indios en el Perú bajo los Austrias* (Madrid, 1957), 15–17.

73 Ruigómez, *Protector de indios*, 63.

74 *Recopilación de leyes de los reynos de Indias*, 4 vols. (1681; reprint, Madrid, 1943), 2.5.1.

75 Diego de Encinas Encinas, *Cedulario Indiano*, 4 vols, ed. Alfonso García Gallo (1596; reprint, Madrid, 1945), 2: 36.

Although the bishop protectors were eliminated de facto in 1554, prelates in the New World would continue to maintain the title of 'Protector of Indians.' In part this was a consequence of their traditional role as protectors of the unfortunate and poor, a category with which Indians were being associated. In Church teachings the poor and miserable (or unfortunate) represented the face of Christ on earth and fulfilled a eschatological mission by inducing charity into the hearts of people. It was not in vain, as Domingo de Soto (1494–1570) explained, that God was many times called 'lawyer and father of the poor;' and this was why, following this example, canon law had given the protection of the poor to the prelates of the Church.[76] Although the role of the Church in the welfare and relief of the poor and miserable is well documented and varied enormously,[77] in Castile, the Partidas sanctioned the house of the prelates to be like 'hospitals' where the poor would be sheltered and fed.[78] These functions of prelates, and in particular bishops, were already under way in Visigoth Spain, where their houses were called the 'house of poor' referring in turn to the tradition of the bishops organising institutions such as the *matricula*, itself deriving from the *annona* in Rome, which gave one-tenth of the harvest produced by the deaconry to the *matricularii*, who were the most indigent and destitute portion of the community. By the time the bishop protectors were

76 Domigo de Soto, *Al muy alto y muy poderoso señor el Príncipe de España...Deliberación en la causa de los pobres* (Salamanca, 1545), 22.

77 General works on the Iberian peninsula include *Pobreza e a assistancia aos pobres na Peninsula Iberica durante media*, Actas de las primeras jornadas Luso-Españolas de historia medieval (IX-1972), 2 vols (Lisboa, 1973); Carmen López Alonso, *La pobreza en la España Medieval: Estudio histórico social* (Madrid, 1986); Carmelo Viñas y Mey, *Notas sobre la asistencia social en España de los siglos XVI y XVII* (Madrid, 1971). For Castile see Linda Martz, *Poverty and Welfare in Habsburg Spain: The Example of Toledo* (Cambridge, 1983); Jon Arrizabalaga, "Poor Relief in Counter Reformation Castile: An Overview," in *Healthcare and Relief in Counter-Reformation Europe*, Peter Grell and Andrew Cunningham, eds. (London, 1999); Michel Cavillac, introduction to *Amparo de Pobres*, by Cristóbal Pérez de Herrera (Madrid, 1975); Jose Antonio Maravall, "De la misericordia a la justicia social en la economía del trabajo: La obra de Fray Juan de Robles," in *Utopía y reformismo en la España de los Austrias* (Madrid, 1982). For Catalonia see Manuel Riu, ed., *Pobreza y asistencia a los pobres en la Catalunya medieval, Anuario de Estudios Medievales* 9–11 (Barcelona, 1980–82). General works on poverty in Medieval and Modern Europe are Michel Mollat, *The Poor in the Middle Ages: An Essay in Social History* (New Haven, 1986); Jean Louis Goglin, *Les misérables dans l'Occident Médiéval* (Paris, 1976); Bronislaw Geremek, *Les fils de Caïn: L'image des pauvres et vagabonds dans la littérature européenne du XV au XVII siècle* (1980; Paris, 1991), *La potence et la pitié: L'Europa et les pauvres du Moyen Age a nos jours* (1978; Paris, 1987) and *Poverty: A History* (Oxford, 1994) all including bibliographies.

78 P.1.5.40.

being eliminated, Celse Hugue Descousu (*c.*1480–1540), wrote in his repertoire of Castilian Law that the Church should give succour to the poor, to the extent of selling its property for this purpose if necessary.[79]

More to the point, however, dispositions such as a 1582 rescript by Philip II ordered the bishops and archbishops of the New World to use all their 'intelligence and prudence' to avert oppression and disorder in the treatment of Indians.[80] In Peru, Bishop Loayza undertook this responsibility, mainly in three different ways: the enactment of protective dispositions in favour of Indians, the writing of informative memorials to the crown, and the promotion of Indian settlement in pueblos. Examples of the first are seen in the first Council of Lima (1551–52), where Loayza provided for the brevity of suits, granted the right of appeal to superior tribunals and ordered that no rights should be exacted when Indians litigated in ecclesiastical courts.[81]

In the case of informative memorials, Loayza played an instrumental role in the fight against the perpetuation of encomiendas, and petitioned for the appointment of Indian alcaldes in place of Spanish corregidors. Loayza also wrote a number of memorials denouncing abuse by certain encomenderos (1549) and general ill-treatment of Indians in Peru (1564).[82] The tradition of bishops writing informative memorials in favour of Indians would continue in the seventeenth century, and would have its epitome in Juan de Palafox y Mendoza (1600–59), Bishop of Puebla, who composed a treatise on the virtues and qualities of the Indians, demanding more favour and protection from the Spanish Crown.[83]

The necessity of Indian settlement or *asiento* in pueblos is primarily observed in the second Council of Lima (1567–68), presided over by Loayza, which established that in order to eliminate the 'pestilent vice of inebriation'—the root of all infidelity and countless other evils—it was necessary that Indians should live in peace and order.[84] Settlement in pueblos constituted not only the best way of Christianising and instructing Indians, but also the only manner of protecting them from wrongs committed towards them by Spaniards, which had

79 Hugo de Celso, *Repertorio universal de las leyes destos reynos de Castilla....*(1553; Madrid, 2000), 262v.

80 *Real Cédula*, Philip II, Lisbon, 17 May 1582. In Cuevas, *Historia de la Iglesia*, 1: 259.

81 Rubén Vargas Ugarte, *Concilios Limenses (1551–1772)*, vol. 1 (Lima, 1951).

82 Olmedo, *Loayza*, 245, 272–273.

83 Juan de Palafox y Mendoza, "Memorial al Rey por don Juan de Palafox y Mendoza, de la naturaleza y virtudes del indio," in *Memoriales civiles y espístolas-tratados*, vol. 2 of *Tratados mejicanos*, Francisco Sánchez Castañer, ed. BAE 218 (Madrid, 1968), 91ff.

84 Vargas Ugarte, *Concilios*, 255.

been numerous in the period of civil wars.[85] This preoccupation with Indian settlement was also exhibited by Vasco de Quiroga (*c.*1477–1565), Bishop protector of Michoacán.[86] Between 1531–65 Quiroga, whose previous experience included that of oidor in the audience of Mexico under the presidency of Fuenleal, founded a number of hospital-pueblos where Indians would be instructed in agriculture, and taught the benefits of charity, virtue and prudence. These were directed towards attaining good order, which was contrary to a 'rustic, barbarous, divided and scattered, uncultivated, savage' existence. As life in hospitals would steer Indians away from pride, greed and ambition, there would be no need to take disputes before a secular court—a place, Quiroga thought, where justice had a price and Indians ended in jail. Instead, all differences would be settled in a 'plain and amicable' manner or resolved by elected Indian justices or priests.[87] In sum, the hospital-pueblos were places where the unfortunate Indians were considered not merely people towards whom one should feel pity and compassion, but, more importantly, also candidates for moral improvement. This illustrates the change in perception that operated towards the poor and unfortunate in sixteenth century Spain, and its influence in the New World.[88] As Juan Luis Vives (1492–1540), a Valencian humanist, proclaimed miserability and poverty was not a matter of moral charity but a 'political' issue.[89]

In the case of the protector of Indians studied in this chapter it is precisely the 'political'—understood, as in Vives, as simply non-ecclesiastical—aspect that constitutes the problematic issue when examining the institution in the period 1516–54. In part, this difficulty arises from the fact that not all those who

85 Olmedo, *Loayza*, 230–231.

86 For a survey of Quiroga's life and work see Francisco Martín Hernández, *Don Vasco de Quiroga (Protector de Indios)* (Salamanca, 1993).

87 Vasco de Quiroga, "Reglas y ordenanzas para el gobierno de los hospitales de Santa Fe de Mexico y Michoacán" in *Don Vasco de Quiroga: Documentos*, ed. Rafael Aguayo Spencer (Mexico, 1939), 249–263.

88 This shift is illustrated even in theological works such as those of Gabriel de Toro, *Tesoro de la misericordia divina y humana* (Salamanca, 1536) or Alejo Venegas, *Agonía del tránsito a la muerte* (Toledo, 1537) which stated that sloth not only had a spiritual dimension but was also a matter of social ethics and condemned the false beggars as thieves. See also Martz, *Poverty and Welfare*, 11–12; Michel Cavillac, Introduction, LXXXI, XCV–VI. For the influence of Thomas More's *Utopia* in the hospital pueblos of Quiroga the classic work remains Silvio Zavala, "La 'Utopía' de Tomás Moro en la Nueva España" in *La utopía mexicana del siglo XVI: Lo bello, lo verdadero y lo bueno*, ed. Octavio Paz (1930; reprint Mexico, 1992).

89 Juan Luis Vives, *De subventione pauperum*, in vol. 6 of his *Opera Omnia* (1532; Valentiæ, 1782), 475–476.

used the title of 'protector' of Indians were, in fact, officials responsible for exercising either effective jurisdiction, or the legal defence of Indians before judicial authorities. In the early years of the Spanish settlement in Chile, for example, Domingo de Santo Tomás (†1570), the Dominican provincial of Peru, sent three friars as 'protectors' to the Araucanian Indians in the Kingdom of Chile. None of these, however, had a royal appointment.[90] As I have observed in section II, this was neither the case of the protectorship of Bartolomé de las Casas. Despite his title of 'Universal Procurator and Protector of Indians' the actual appointment does not refer to jurisdictional prerogatives, the right to file lawsuits on behalf of Indians, nor the possibility of assuming their defence before royal justices. In the *real cedula* of 17 September 1516, Las Casas is ordered to travel to Hispaniola, Cuba, San Juan, Jamaica and the mainland thus far discovered, to collect information on the spiritual and corporal 'health' of Indians, and to propose measures towards their well being.

The limitations of the appointment were noticed by Antonio de León Pinelo (†1660), the chief compiler of the Laws of the Indies, who observed that Las Casas 'took as office' the defence of Indians. This point is made by León Pinelo to indicate that Las Casas was not given a royal office proper regarding the defence of Indians.[91] In sum, setting aside the significance of Las Casas' endeavours in favour of the natives of the New World, his appointment as universal protector was devoid of any judicial powers, and, therefore, did not have any relevance within the legal systems of Spain or the New World, either in the form of effective jurisdiction or simple judicial defence.

Protectors of Indians would assume effective civil and criminal jurisdiction and legal defence in Indian matters as from 1527–28 when the first bishop protectors were appointed by the Spanish crown. Until the de facto elimination of the institution in 1554, I have identified two distinct periods in this office. The first, between 1527–30, is characterised by the right to hear cases brought by Indian plaintiffs, both in civil and criminal matters, and also to prosecute and try Spaniards for mistreatment or abuse of Indians. Although the bishops of Nicaragua and Santa Marta were granted these powers,[92] it is Bishop Juan de Zumárraga in Mexico who constitutes the emblematic case study. In great measure, this is due to the fact that Mexico was both the seat of the diocese and the royal audience. Infighting between them ensued as soon as Zumárraga

90 *Real cedula*, Philip II, 4 September 1571. Ramón Ramírez, *Fr. Gil Gonzalez de S. Nicolas, Dominico: el primer defensor del los indios en Chile* (Santiago, 1986), 3.

91 Antonio de León Pinelo, *Tratado de confirmaciones reales* (Madrid, 1630), 6v.

92 Respectively Diego Alvarez de Osorio by *real cedula* of 2 May 1527; and Fr. Tomás Ortiz by *reales cedulas* of 15 February and 17 August 1528.

made effective use of his rights, thereby disputing the monopoly over secular justice which the audience claimed. The conflict ended in 1530 with the ousting of the members of the audience and a drastic reduction in the attributions of the bishop protector.

The trimming down of the bishop protector's prerogatives in 1530 reduced his jurisdiction to imprisonment of up to ten days, and fines limited to 50 pesos, but the possibility of hearing Indian cases was completely eliminated. Appointments under these prerogatives constitute the second phase of the institution of the bishop protector of Indians in 1530–54. In Peru, three bishops and one interim protector were appointed in this period. Of these, Hernando de Luque, bishop protector of Tumbes (1529–34), and Reginaldo de Pedraza, interim protector (1531), never took possession of their office. Only Vicente de Valverde, bishop protector of Cusco (1538) and Francisco de Loayza, bishop protector of Lima (1546–54), presented to the local authorities their title and took possession of their office. Evidence suggests, however, that only Valverde effectively exercised the jurisdiction attached to his office in the city of Cusco. Loayza's inactivity in this respect is partly explained in the virtual halt of all judicial activity until the decade of the 1550s due to civil wars. But in the end, more important were the efforts of the Spanish Monarchy to increase secular involvement in Indian legal disputes through the creation of special magistracies. These efforts would be consolidated in 1554 when the fiscal of the audience assumed judicial responsibility for Indian matters and protection. Although Loayza's title was not revoked, this measure would effectively bring the institution of the bishop protectors of Indians to an end.

If anything, the circumstances around the elimination of the bishop protector only confirm the fact that, ultimately, it was a secular office. Gaspar de Villarroel (1587–1665), a prelate and jurist in Spanish America, recognised in his treatise on royal patronage that bishops could have jurisdiction over lawsuits by miserable persons in certain particular circumstances;[93] a statement both supported by the *ius commune*, in two imperial constitutions, of the years 318 and 333,[94] and by Holy Scripture where it was legitimised by St Paul.[95]

93 Gaspar de Villarroel, *Gobierno Eclesiastico-pacifico, y union de los dos Cuchillos Pontificio, y Regio*...(1656 7; Madrid, 1738), 2.14.3.43.

94 The constitutions permitted the parties of a lawsuit to take their dispute to the bishop, whose jurisdiction and sentence would be fully recognised by secular justices. It was even possible for the bishop to decide on procedures already initiated in civil courts. C.Th. 1.27.1.

95 Audet aliquis vestrum habens negotium adversus alterum, iudicari apud iniquos, et non santos?...Ad verecundiam vestram dico. Sic non est inter vos sapiens quisquam, qui possit iudicare inter fratrem suum? Sed fratrer cum fratre iudicio contendit: et hoc apud infideles? 1 Cor. 6.1; 5–6.

This historical claim would explain why, in 1527, the Council of Indies noted that the Bishop of Cuba should be protector of the Indians therein, as it was originally 'granted to all prelates.'[96] On the other hand, evidence suggests that the bishop protectors themselves were conscious of this fact: Valverde, for example, would always claim he was 'sent by His Majesty' to defend and shelter the Indians of Peru.

The idea that the bishop protector of the Spanish Monarchy was ultimately a royal office is furthered by the legal characteristics of the appointments themselves. In his treatise on the the office of *fiscal* Francisco Alfaro (*c.*1551–*fl.*1628), an *oidor* in Lima and Charcas, established that royal offices needed three elements to be valid: title, acceptance and exercise.[97] A simple review of all the *reales cedulas* granted to the protectors, as well as their claims to secure office, prove the first and second requisites. In the case of the actual exercise, Alfaro points out that the 'reception' of the title by the local magistrates should precede this. Proof of this in the case of Mexico is Motolinia's vivid account of how the members of the *cabildo* placed the cedulas above their heads, even if they disagreed—or did not fully understand—their contents. In the case of Peru, there is an account by Fernando de Montesinos (†1644) of the 'reception' of Valverde in 19 May 1538 in Cusco also by the *cabildo* of the city.[98] The importance of the royal appointment, however, can be seen more clearly in the case of Mexico where Zumárraga exercised his legal authority even if his confirmation as bishop by the Holy See had not arrived in the diocese. In fact, legal doctrine in the Indies considered the consecration of a bishop without the executor of the Council, as had occurred with Cipriano de Medina y Vega (1594–1664) the Bishop-elect of Huamanga, the chief impediment to the valid exercise of the bishopric as it was dismissive of royal authority.[99]

On the whole, the protectors of Indians between 1516 and 1554 are an example of the vital role played by the Church in the first decades of Spanish settlement, in accordance with the Pontifical title deeds to the New World. In practice, the incorporation of two bishops in the re-composition of the audience of Mexico after its confrontation with Zumárraga illustrates the degree to which prelates were involved in obtaining an enduring political order.

96 *Colección de documentos inéditos de ultramar*, vol. 22, 11, quoted in Bayle, *Protector*, 34.

97 See Francisco de Alfaro, *Tractatus de officio fiscalis* (Valladolid, 1606), glos. 27.4.

98 Fernando de Montesinos, *Anales del Perú, 1498–1642* (Madrid, 1906), 106.

99 Manuel José de Ayala, *Notas a la recopilación de Indias: Origen e historia ilustrada de las leyes de Indias*, ed. Juan Manzano Manzano, 2 vols (Madrid, 1945–46), 1: 122–123. Royal patronage of the Catholic Kings was ratified by a cédula of 1574, see Encinas, *Cedulario*, 1: 83. For Castilian Law see P.1.5.8.

But more significantly, the history of protectorship in this period represents the continuous adaptation of institutions to the new realities of Colonial life, and the efforts of the Crown to give adequate protection to Indians in a legal context. This adaptation was marked, as seen in this chapter, with a great amount of confrontation between ecclesiastical and secular powers. In Peru this confrontation would be permanently solved with the death of Bishop Loaysa in 1575 and the creation of the Defensor of Indians by viceroy Francisco de Toledo the same year.

CHAPTER 2

Protectors of Indians in the Audience of Lima

Although historians have increasingly recognised the impact of the re-settlement of the Indian population and the revival of the mining industry during the government of Viceroy Francisco de Toledo, they have paid little attention to his reforms in the administration of justice.[1] In an extensive report from Cusco, the former Inca capital, Viceroy Francisco de Toledo wrote to King Philip II that in Peru the absence of justice was, above all, the 'root and principle…of the ruin of this land.'[2] The present chapter will study the history and structure of one of the most significant institutions in the context of the legal reforms undertaken by Toledo: the Defensorship of Indians. The institution was created to monitor dealings with the indigenous population and to bring legal action on their behalf before the courts of justice. It thus helped to establish a system of legal protection for Indians before the judiciary in secular hands; and, at the same time, provided a form of continuity to the institution of the bishop-protectors. The chapter begins with an analysis of the Toledan ordinances for the Defensors of Indians in 1575, and then moves on to trace its transformation throughout the seventeenth century until its effective disappearance in 1741 and formal abolition in 1821. Emphasis is placed on the officials that worked within the high court in Lima. Unless referring to the officials' specific titles (Defensor General of Indians, Advocate of Indians, etc.) defensorship is used to refer to the institution and protector and defensor for the head of the institution.

The Defensor General of Indians (1575–1640)

The Ordinances of 1575

On 10 September 1575 Viceroy Francisco de Toledo (1515–82) issued a set of ordinances which created an institution of crown appointed officials charged with

1 For a guide to Toledo's writings and bibliography see León Gómez Rivas, "Don Francisco de Toledo, comendador de Alcántara, virrey del Peru: Guía de Fuentes," parts 1 and 2, *Anuario de Estudios Americanos* 49, supplement 1 (1992): 123–171; supplement 2 (1992): 95–152.

2 "[R]raiz y principio y medios del daño desta tierra." Toledo to Philip II, Cusco, 1 March 1572. Roberto Levillier, ed., *Gobernantes del Perú: Cartas y Papeles, siglo XVI*, 14 vols. (Madrid, 1921–26), 4: 139.

 | DOI 10.1163/9789004305175_004

the protection of Indians before the colonial administration. At the seat of the royal audience of Lima, the institution was comprised of the Defensor General of Indians, who acted as an adjutant to the viceroy in Indian matters, as well as the Advocate and Procurator of Indians, who would represent indigenous lawsuits at the high court; at a local level, the most important *corregimientos* would have a protector to aid Indians in their petitions and to guarantee fair treatment before first instance magistrates. The ordinances expected that these men would ensure that Indians were 'defended, sheltered and set free of any grievances that they had received, as H.M. wishes and orders.'[3]

The head of this institution was the Defensor General of Indians. This official would replace the *fiscal* of the audience of Lima, the magistrates originally charged with the defence of Indians in all 'things and matters in which they should be defended and protected' by virtue of a royal cedula of 1554.[4] Unlike the *fiscal*, Toledo established that the Defensor General would neither be a member of the high court, nor a university trained official. Setting aside those prerogatives dealing with administrative minutiae, such as the designation of interpreters (§VIII, XIII) and the provision of paper and ink (§XIV), the ordinances were mainly concerned with providing better protection for Indians before the government and courts of justice.

Toledo framed his ordinances in such a way that the Defensor General was granted special access to the viceroy regarding Indian matters (§II, XIII). As such, he was the only officer entitled to receive and record petitions on behalf of Indians, and also the only person authorised to forward such demands to the viceroy (§VI). Consequently, the ordinances established that only important matters ('grave businesses') should be taken before his consideration (§XI), and that these were to be taken before the viceroy every week on Tuesdays and Wednesdays (§VII). In the case of issues that could cause damage to Indians due to undue delays, the ordinances granted the Defensor General access to the viceroy's household and private chambers at any time (§XV).

The ordinances also established that the Secretary of Government would keep the Defensor General informed of all the provisions concerning Indian

3 "[T]odo lo que conviniere al bien de los dichos indios contra todas y cualesquiera personas de cualquier estado y condición que sean que les hubieren agraviado...y en todas e cualesquier demandas y cosas y negocios que se les ofrecieren y sean de su bien y utilidad para que en todo sean defendidos y amparados y desagraviados de cualesquier agravios que hubieren recibido." Francisco de Toledo, *Disposiciones gubernativas para el virreinato del Perú*, ed. Maria Justina Sarabia Viejo (Sevilla, 1986–89) 2: 102.

4 "Cosas y casos que deben ser defendidos y amparados, así en general como en particular," Diego de Encinas, *Cedulario Indiano* (1596; reprint Madrid, 1945), 2: 268–269.

matters enacted by the king, viceroy, or audiences; in particular those concerning personal services, payment of salaries, unlawful taking of property by Spanish or caciques, or tributes exceeding those established in the *tasa* (§XXI). In addition, it was prescribed that the Defensor General should be provided with ink and paper (§XIV) and an interpreter (§VIII). Both would be instrumental in ensuring that the defensor kept his own account of Indian demands. This fact is recurrent in the ordinances, which strongly discouraged the practice of accepting Indian petitions directly (§VI, XIV).[5]

The ultimate purpose of the ordinances was to provide the indigenous population with a framework that would protect their interests when entering legal demands or lawsuits—a matter in which the Viceroy had taken a great interest since the first years of his government. In this respect, the Defensor General of Indians was charged with the responsibility of undertaking the legal defence of Indians in the audience of Lima by means of both the newly created offices of Advocate of Indians and the Procurator General of Indians (§V). The defensor had the duty to ensure that royal provisions dispatched by the audience to provincial corregimientos ordering judicial diligences reached their destinations in due course (§XVIII), as well as informing the lesser courts of the audience's rulings (§V). The Defensor General, the advocate and the procurator of Indians could not exact fees from Indians for any action taken on their behalf. To avoid graft or corruption resulting from inadequate compensation, it was thus established that defensors should have a 'competent' salary (§IX).[6]

In this respect the Defensor General of Indians was to ensure that appeals of Indian cases to the Council of the Indies be dispatched in the first fleet leaving for Spain (§III). In the case of appeals from either local courts or *corregimientos*, the Defensor would determine whether these should be dispatched to the audience (§IV). This would be done with the help of the Advocate of Indians and the *fiscal* of the audience (§XVI).

The 1575 ordinances concluded with the appointment of Baltazar de la Cruz y Aspetia (*fl.*1594) as first Defensor General of Indians, with an instruction to procure the swift dispatch to the audience of Lima of pending appeals remaining in the corregimientos visited by the viceroy. He would also inform himself of Indian non-legal petitions. To aid him in this task Toledo assigned Gonzalo de Holguín, the viceroy's personal interpreter, plus 200 pesos for ink and paper to record such demands.[7]

5 Toledo, *Disposiciones*, 2: 103, 111–112.

6 Ibid., 2: 105–106, 110.

7 Ibid., 2: 107, 105.

In addition to the Defensor General and Advocate and Procurator of Indians resident at the seat of the audience, the 1575 ordinances decreed that protectors should be appointed for 'each city of Spaniards of this Kingdom,' that is, in each of the Spanish corregimientos. The memorial written by Nicolás Matías del Campo (1630–*fl.*1682) records at least 21 corregimientos where protectors were appointed by Viceroy Toledo.[8] These officials would not only ensure the general well-being and good treatment of Indians, but were also entitled to receive their petitions and complaints and to submit memorials to the authorities at the royal audiences. Within the administration of justice, the duties of *corregimiento* protectors included countersigning Indians' pleadings before the corregidor, providing that appeals against resolutions from local authorities reached the corregidors, and submitting appeals to rulings by the latter to the high courts.[9]

These provincial appointments also took into account the particular situation of Indians in different areas or regions. The *corregimiento* protectors appointed to Potosí and Huancavelica in 1577, for example, stipulated that one of the chief purposes of these officials was to ensure that the work-load for Indians did not exceed the legal limits, that payment was sufficient and punctual and that working conditions were adequate. More specifically, their instructions pointed towards involvement in the security measures of mines, control of work in dangerous shafts and the prohibition of direct contact with mercury in the refineries. The instructions also stipulated that Indians should not stay in mining towns longer that the length of their *mita*, as this caused them enormous damage.[10]

Defensors General of Indians were also established in audiences such Santiago de Chile and Manila following the Toledo ordinances. In other jurisdictions the emplacement was discarded. In 1577, for example, the Council of the Indies reported that the magistrates of the high court of Quito had argued

8 The *corregimientos* were: Ica, Jauja, Huancavelica, Castrovirreyna, Cusco, Carabaya, Vilcabamba, Arequipa, Arica, Trujillo, Cajamarca and Huánuco, in the audience of Lima; Potosí, Cochabamba, La Paz and Chucuito, in the audience of Charcas; and Quito, Chimbo Riobamba Tacunga, Cuenca, Loja, and Jaén de Bracamoros, in the audience of Quito. See Nicolás Matías del Campo y la Rynaga, *Memorial historico y ivridico que refiere el origen del Oficio de Protector general de los Indios del Perú…*(Madrid, 1671), 22–22v. The appointments of the protectors of Potosí and Huancavelica are available in Toledo, *Disposiciones*, 2: 289–301. For the case of Huamanga, where the Protector of Indians was granted a salary of 600 pesos, see AGN, Derecho Indígena, leg. 3, c.25 (1578), f.1.

9 Toledo, *Disposiciones*, 2: 105.

10 Ibid., 2: 289–301.

against the institution of protectors 'due to the inconveniences of this office.'[11] The oidors of the audience of Guadalajara, New Spain, reported in turn that its *fiscal* had pleaded Indian lawsuits following the disposition of 1554 and thus a Defensor of Indians following the ordinances of Toledo had never been established within its territory.[12]

Abrogation and Restoration

It would be, however, one of these adverse reactions against the Defensors of Indians that eventually led to its first overturn. Following a petition from the oidors of the audience of Mexico which stated that *corregimiento* defensors had caused 'notorious damage and detriment to the said Indians, for many causes and reasons of consideration,' the protectorship of Indians established in 1575 by Viceroy Toledo was abrogated by the Council of the Indies on 27 May 1582.[13] It is not surprising, therefore, that although it is most likely Cruz remained in his post until the end of Toledo's government in May 1581, the defensorship took part in scarcely any activity during its first years.[14]

The lack of protectors, however, generated a void in many of the high courts. Gabriel de Ribera, the procurator of the Philippines in Spain, for example, was ordered by the Governor of the islands to consult on who should be responsible for Indian lawsuits in lieu of the protectors.[15] Similarly in Peru, Viceroy Fernando de Torres y Portugal, Count of Villar dom Pardo (*v.*1585–90) wrote to the King in 1585 expressing his concern about the situation of Indians in the

11 "A nos se ha hecho relación que essa ciudad de San Francisco de Quito está proueido vn promotor de los Indios naturales de ese distrito; y porque no conuiene que aya este oficio, por los inconvenientes que representan que con él pueda aver, vos mando que os informéis y sepáis si está proueido el dicho oficio" in Constantino Bayle, *El protector de indios* (Sevilla, 1945), 90.

12 See Woodrow Borah, *Justice by Insurance: The General Indian Court of Colonial Mexico and the Legal Aides of the Half Real* (Berkeley and Los Angeles, 1983), 371.

13 Encinas, *Cedulario*, 4: 333.

14 The surviving documentation of his government in the National Archive in Lima (AGN) regarding judicial aspects comprises a few documents in the Superior Gobierno—Contencioso section: a provision in favour of Captain Cáceres (1570, leg. 1, c. 5, fs. 2) now stolen; a provision appointing a corregidor (1580, leg. 3, c. 8, fs. 3); and a provision on encomiendas (1585[?], leg. 1, c. 9, fs. 1). Other than this, there are no relevant documents in the Superior Gobierno—Político Administrativo section (GO.BI 1, caja 22, c. 1–15, 1558–1644) nor in the Superior Gobierno—Hacienda section (GO-BI 2, caja 63, c.1–36, 1596–1699).

15 Heredia, *Consultas*, 1: 411.

great silver mine of Potosí, as they were continually subject to abuse and violence. There were not enough magistrates in that city, he wrote, to deal with these cases and so, without a *fiscal* to procure Indian lawsuits, he petitioned for the reinstatement of the protector.[16] A year later, the viceroy would report to Madrid that the *oidores* of Lima were requesting a second *fiscal* with exclusive responsibility over Indian lawsuits.[17]

The Council of the Indies replied to these demands in 1589 by issuing a rescript that restored the 1575 ordinances on the grounds that the elimination of the protectors had caused more trouble than good.[18] It was Viceroy García Hurtado de Mendoza (*v.*1590–95) and his successors who restored the protectorship designed by Toledo and, before the end of the sixteenth century, three defensors, one advocate and three procurators of Indians successfully obtained their letters patent and commission.[19] An addition was made to the institution in the early seventeenth century, when the Marquis of Montesclaros created a second advocate of Indians in 1608 to plead cases when both parties were indigenous.[20] In decades that followed, therefore, the institution of protectorship was composed of the Defensor General, the first and second advocates and two procurators of Indians.

Following the precedent set in the 1575 ordinances where Toledo refers to Baltazar de la Cruz as someone 'close to my person,' appointments of Defensors General of Indians until the first decades of the seventeenth century were

16 Carmen Ruigómez Gómez, *Una política indigenista de los Habsburgo: el Protector de Indios en el Perú* (Madrid, 1988), 71.

17 Count of Villar dom Pardo to Philip II, Callao, 25 May 1586, Levillier, *Gobernantes*, 10: 105. The petition was loosely based on the *Leyes Nuevas* (1542–1543), which established that the audiences should keep themselves informed of 'the excessive and bad treatments' towards the Indians, and should 'punish those found guilty with all rigour, in conformity with justice' (§ 20), in José Sánchez-Arcilla Bernal, ed., *Las ordenanzas de las audiencias de Indias (1511–1821)* (Madrid, 1992).

18 See the *real cedula* of 10 January 1589, Encinas, *Cedulario*, 4: 334–335. Further evidence of the reception of this decision in Lima is found in a letter from García Hurtado de Mendoza, fourth Marquis of Cañete (*v.*1590–95) to Philip II written in Lima on 17 May 1590, in Levillier, *Gobernantes*, 12: 164.

19 See Campo, *Memorial*, 4v. For the appointment of Antonio Heredia (1590), Antonio Torres de la Fresneda (1597), and Doctor Antonio de Ibarra (1599) as Defensor General of Indians see Levillier, *Gobernantes*, 14: 63, 164, 234 as well as the respective entries in appendix 1. In the case of Procurators of Indians Diego Gil de Avís and Antonio de Neyra, see AGN, Derecho Indígena, leg. 39, c. 793 (1596) and "Juan Narváez, indio, como marido de Dña. Barbola Charachumbi, contra Juan González Cornejo y Cristóbal de Palacios, sobre las tierras de que fueren despojadas y rematadas en los susodichos," (1599) BNP ms. A 353, f.33.

20 Campo, *Memorial*, 4.

usually drawn from the viceregal entourage.[21] Antonio Heredia (DGI 1590), for example, was the personal secretary to Viceroy García Hurtado de Mendoza (*v.*1589–1596), prior to his appointment as protector.[22] Domingo de Luna (DGI 1630–33) not only was advisor to the Count of Monterrey, but also a witness in his testament of 1608.[23] Similarly, advocates Alberto de Acuña (AI 1590–97), Antonio de Ibarra (AI 1599), Leandro de la Rynaga (AI 1601–*c.*24) and Juan del Campo (AI 1626–47) were all appointed advisors (*asesor letrado*) to various viceroys (see Table 2).

Evidence is somewhat sketchy, but it appears that the Defensors General were predominantly actively involved in promoting measures concerning the well-being of Indians and in protecting their interests in legal transactions. The ordinances for Baltazar de la Cruz, for example, established express orders to counter litigiousness.[24] In turn, Pedro Balguer de Salcedo (DGI *c.*1599–1604) successfully argued for the establishment of a special court to expedite justice to Indians living within the *corregimiento* of Lima.[25] On the other hand, there are numerous references to the defensors' intervention in Indian contracts concerning the sale of real estate and in countersigning judicial writs and petitions.[26]

The burden of the work in the audience of Lima, however, rested upon the procurators and advocates of Indians. Of the procurators there is little to be

---

21 "Y si el tal negocio, o negocios fueren de calidad que pare perjuicio notable la dilación, en cualquier hora, y dia podreis venir con el dicho Interprete a su Excelencia, que por la presente mando al Mayordomo de mi casa, y a los de mi Camara, y aqualquiera dellos que os de para ello la puerta." "[C]erca de mi persona." Toledo, *Disposiciones*, 1: 102.

22 Levillier, *Gobernantes*, 14: 63, 164, 234.

23 Luis Antonio Eguiguren, *Diccionario histórico cronológico de la Real y Ponitifica Universidad Mayor de San Marcos y sus colegios: Crónica e Investigación,* 3 vols. (Lima, 1940–1951), 1: 389. Networks of loyalties are also visible through appointments as visitation judges and *corregimientos* bestowed on defensors. Until the government of Viceroy Melchor de Navarra y Rocafull, Duke of La Palata (*v.*1681–89) the posts in El Cercado, Andahuaylas, Canta and Chincha were all distributed directly by the viceroy, and not by the Council of the Indies in Madrid. See Lohmann, *El Corregidor de Indios* 2002, 160.

24 Toledo, *Disposiciones*, 2: 107.

25 See Woodrow Borah, "Juzgado general de indios del Perú o juzgado particular de indios del cercado de Lima," *Revista chilena de Historia del Derecho* 6 (1970), 134. There is an incomplete transcription of the provision enacted upon Balaguer's proposal on 11 July 1603 by Viceroy Luis de Velasco in Bernabé Cobo, "Fundación de Lima, escripta por el P. Bernabé Cobo de la Compañía de Jesus. Año de 1639," in *Obras del P. Bernabé Cobo*, BAE 91–92 (Madrid, 1956) 2: 349–350.

26 Juan de Solórzano, *Política Indiana*, eds. Francisco Tomás y Valiente and Ana María Barrero (Madrid, 1996), 2.28.42, 44–46.

said: appointed by the viceroy, and accountable to the advocate, they oversaw legal proceedings. On the other hand, the Indians' advocates played a significant role in the protectorship by undertaking the defence of indigenous plaintiffs at the high court of justice. In the context of a general increase in litigation throughout the sixteenth and seventeenth centuries, advocates pleaded many of the Indian cases heard at the royal audience of Lima.[27] Advocates also had a determinant role in shaping the legal doctrine that equalled Indians to the *miserables*—an institution developed by the *ius commune* (see Chapter 7). The appointment of prestigious university professors and practitioners as both first and second Indian advocates between 1590 and 1626, and their role in representing Indian lawsuits further contributed to consolidate the structure of an institution that remained unchanged until the 1640s.

Defensors and *Fiscales* (1640–1680)

Proposals for Change

At the time the first memorials discussing the institution of the protectorship of Indians began to appear in the early seventeenth century, however, a number of key elements of the 1575 ordinances were brought into question, especially the idea that the institution was headed by gentlemen drawn from the viceregal entourage who possessed no professional legal training. This, and a dose of Creole Patriotism, resulted in calls for change towards a protectorship connected to the university-trained viceregal learned elite.

On 20 August 1614, Doctor Cristóbal Cacho de Santillana (†1640), the *fiscal* of the audience of Lima, wrote to Philip III (*r.*1598–1621) explaining the shortcomings of the office of Defensor General of Indians. For the magistrate, not only did the defensors fail to undertake their obligations, but also their only aspiration was to 'draw their salaries, and receive everything they could from Indians.' Although the King promptly issued a rescript on 17 October of that same year admonishing the Prince of Squilace to ensure that the office was performed with 'Christianity, *limpieza* and punctuality,' he did not reply to Cacho de Santillana's proposals to improve the institution.[28]

27 See for example, Steve J. Stern, *Peru's Indian Peoples and the Challenge of Spanish Conquest: Huamanga to 1640*, 2nd ed. (Madison, 1993), 114–137. An interesting testimony is found in "Memorial para el buen asiento y gobierno del Perú" c.1550, *Colección de documentos inéditos para la historia de España*, vol. 94, ed. Marqués de la Fuentesanta del Valle (Madrid, 1889), 180.

28 Solórzano, *Política Indiana*, 2.28.48.

This would occur in August 1620 when Philip III requested the viceroy's opinion on whether granting university trained Defensors a seat at the audience and the right to the *garnacha* (magistrate's toga), would yield a more 'authoritative' defence of Indian interests.[29] The proposals included in Cacho de Santillana's letter inspired two memorials published in the 1620s. The first is an anonymous memorial published in Madrid in 1622.[30] The second, also published in Madrid in 1626, was written by Juan de la Rynaga Salazar, a procurator for the city of Lima in Spain who was *regidor* of the city (1611–21), first professor of decretum at San Marcos (1618), later *oidor* in Panama (1628–35) and member of a prominent family linked to the protectorship institution as advocates for Indians.[31]

Both memorials are divided into four articles. The first article gives a brief description of the institution and its history. The second describes its problems or 'inconveniences.' The third provides a set of solutions based on the proposals in Cacho de Santillana's letter drafted in 1614. The fourth point is a working plan to achieve the proposed reforms and argues for their expeditious solution.[32]

The memorials proposed the removal of the protection of Indian interests from the defensorship system established by Viceroy Francisco de Toledo, and to entrust it to the *fiscales* of the Council of the Indies and the royal audiences. Their argument was based on the 'inconveniences' of the system headed by the Defensor General of Indians created in 1575.

In the first place, the memorials criticised the fact that the Defensor of Indians, as a 'layman of *capa y espada*,' could not undertake the legal defence of Indians without the help of the *abogado de indios*. For Rynaga the Defensor General's only role was to take Indians to the house of the advocate of Indians, for it was he who made petitions, wrote memorials, headed businesses and defended Indian lawsuits. The fact that the Defensor General required a second

29 Solórzano, *Política Indiana*, 2.28.47, 48. On the concept of limpieza de sangre see Chapter 3, Section 2.

30 *Memorial al Rey N.S. Don Felipe IIII. A favor de los indios del Piru Sobre el oficio de Protector General en la ciudad de Lima, corte y cabeza del Piru* (Madrid, 1622), arts. II, III.

31 Juan de la Rynaga Salazar, *Memorial discursivo sobre el oficio de Protector General de los Indios del Piru* ([Madrid], [1626]). He was the eldest son of Leandro de la Rynaga, advocate of Indians from 1601 to 1624. His family connections and links to the protectorship see Chapter 3.

32 The similarities in content of both memorials has prompted historians to attribute the anonymous 1622 memorial either to Cacho de Santillana himself or to Rynaga. See Francisco Cuena Boy, "Utilización pragmática del derecho romano en dos memoriales indianos del siglo XVII sobre el protector de indios," *Revista de Estudios Histórico Jurídicos* 20 (Valparaíso) (1988), 119.

'protector' to fulfil his duties was a waste of Indian tribute. This would explain why the city of Cuzco, for example, requested their Protector of Indians to possess a university degree.[33] Similarly, Procurators of Indians were appointed without the appropriate examination required by Castillian law.[34] The memorial of 1622 also found that viceroys were not rigorous with the appointment of procurators and that some procurators could even 'barely write.'[35]

Another negative factor was the viceroy's influence in the appointment and removal of defensors. For the 1622 memorial defensors were not only appointed by, but also 'accommodated' in all matters to, the viceroy.[36] As a consequence of this, Rynaga stated that defensors undertook their offices without contradicting the viceroy, even if at the cost of the 'miserable Indians.'[37] On the other hand, the memorials observed that absolute powers to remove the Defensor General often resulted in officials lacking the necessary experience in Indian matters. Although this anomaly was modified by a royal *cédula* of 1621 requiring that defensors could be removed only with a legitimate cause, the memorials recognised that such a cause was always at hand.[38]

The memorials also questioned the extent to which a poor Defensor General of Indians could confront 'the well positioned gentleman and encomendero, and the merchant and the wealthy miner.'[39] This problem, however, not only affected the Defensor General but also the advocates and procurators of Indians. Insufficient salaries, for instance, prevented advocates dedicating themselves completely to their office. Instead, they were required to lecture at university and set up private practices. In fact, Rynaga estimated that in some 25,000 pesos were owed to advocates and other officials working in the defensorship of Indians.[40] The memorials also found that the Defensor General had no influence

---

33 Rynaga, *Memorial*, 5v–6;

34 *Recopilación de leyes de estos reynos...* [i.e. Nueva Recopilación 1567] (1640; facsimile edition, Valladolid, 1982), 2.24.1.

35 "[R]especto de los procuradores, es, que los virreyes los nombran sin preceder examen…a veces tan incapaces, que ha habido Procurador, que apenas sabia firmar." *Memorial* (1622), 7v.

36 "El segundo inconveniente es, ser nombrado por el virrey, y de ordinario pretensor con él de otras cosas, obligado por lo primero, deseoso de obligar por lo segundo; por lo cual contemporiza en todo con el virrey, y en nada le replica, haciendo su negocio a costa de los miserables indios." *Memorial* (1622), 5v.

37 "[P]por lo qual con capa de agradecimiento, contemporiza en todo con el Virrey, haziendo su negocio a costa de los miserables Indios." Ibid., 6; and Rynaga, *Memorial*, 7–7v.

38 Rynaga, *Memorial*, 7–7v.

39 "[Y] hacer rostro al cavallero y encomendero bien quisto, y al mercader y caudaloso minero."Rynaga, *Memorial*, 6v–7.

40 Ibid. 9.

or authority within government and judicial spheres. This lack of influence was the cause of prolonged lawsuits, considerable expenses, frequent illnesses or even the death of Indians who travelled to Lima. This was particularly dramatic in the case of Andean Indians, whose vulnerability to the coastal climate was noted by diverse authorities such as José de Acosta, Bartolomé de las Casas and Gregorio López.[41] In many cases, Rynaga stated, Indians found that going to Lima had the same effect as going to the slaughterhouse.[42]

The memorials concluded that the remedy to this situation was to institute a Protector of Indians with the same salary, prerogatives and honours as a *fiscal*. The protector-*fiscal* would replace the Defensor General and Advocate of Indians established in 1575. The fact that Indian protectors would be able to sit in the *estrados* of the audience, enter the *real acuerdo* and have the 'hand and authority' of the *fiscal* would give Indian plaintiffs enormous benefits. In sum, the memorials maintained that a protector-*fiscal*, with an attached procurator to help with the legal proceedings, ensured a more professional defence in court, a considerable amount of influence and speed in the dispatch of lawsuits.[43]

The fact that the memorials proposed that protectors-*fiscales* and their procurators would earn, respectively, 3,000 and 600 pesos per annum, would not alter the finances of the protectorship of Indians as it stood in the seventeenth century. In 1615, the defensorship system considered 1,000 pesos for the Defensor General, 1,000 and 600 pesos for the first and second advocates of Indians and 500 pesos for each of the two procurators. The sum of these salaries resulted in the 3,600 pesos necessary to pay the *fiscal* and his procurator. In addition to this, the protector would be appointed by the king and not the viceroy, which, in turn, would make his office more independent.[44]

Although having a protector-*fiscal* appointed by the king would solve the inconveniences cited earlier, the memorials stressed the importance of the candidate's 'experience in the matters of the Indies.' This implied knowledge of the government, customs, condition and laws pertaining to Indians. Particular stress was placed on the need to know the Indian tongue. To justify this point, Rynaga would cite examples from antiquity to demonstrate that judges of the Kingdom of Israel knew 70 languages, and King Mithridates alone could speak many of these. The importance of magistrates that could speak the native tongues was contrasted with the great damages that interpreters could cause, and cited the

41 *Memorial* (1622), 6v–7; Rynaga, *Memorial*, 7v–8.

42 Rynaga, *Memorial*, 8v.

43 *Memorial* (1622), 7v–8; Rynaga, *Memorial*, 10–11.

44 *Memorial* (1622), 8, 14; Rynaga, *Memorial*, 10, 30v,19–20v.

case of Felipillo, the interpreter of Francisco Pizarro held responsible for the death of Atahualpa. More to the point, however, the memorials pointed out that only those born in Peru were legitimately called to be protectors-*fiscales*. Although knowledge of the land and previous experience with Indians were important factors, these were not greater than love of the *patria*.[45]

The memorials employed three arguments to defend creole participation as protector-*fiscales*. For Rynaga, the norms in Castilian and Roman Law indicating that magistrates should hold their offices in jurisdictions different to their places of origin, did not constitute an absolute prohibition.[46] He claimed that, despite the fact that the Partidas considered the employment of magistrates in their place of birth as 'sacrilegious,' ratification by the sovereign in this post removed all illegitimacy. In Peru, Rynaga cited the case of Alonso Bravo de Sarabia y Sotomayor (1571?–1620), the son of a Spanish *oidor*, who was appointed *alcalde del crimen* in Lima in 1602.[47]

The second argument stated that the prohibitions in Roman and Castilian law did not include 'municipal' magistrates. The term was not employed in the sense of local authorities, but as used by seventeenth century juristic doctrine to describe the legal status of the Indies.[48] On this point, the memorials relied on authorities such as Camilo Borrell, *De Magistratibus* and Jerónimo Castillo de Bovadilla, who stated that town councillors (*regidores*) should be born in, or be neighbours (*vecinos*) of the city; and Emperors Marcian and Valentinian whose rescripts regarding the praetors of Rome and Constantinople considered a similar principle.[49]

Thirdly, the memorials justified the appointment of creoles to the post of protector-*fiscal* by stating that the office combined the functions of the

45 *Memorial* (1622), 9v–10v; Rynaga, *Memorial*, 11v–13.

46 Rynaga, *Memorial*, 15v. References are made to C.1.41.1 (Ut nulli patriae suae administratio sine speciali permissu principis permittatur), P1.18.11 and the 1567 Recopilación of Castile, 3.2.10.

47 Rynaga, *Memorial*, 16–16v. Reference is made to P.1.18.11.

48 It referred to the idea that the Indies were, as Solórzano suggested, similar to Roman *municipia*, *Política Indiana*, passim. The use of this term was maintained until the end of the eighteenth century as evidenced, for example, by a 1794 report of Joaquín Pérez de Uriondo, protector-*fiscal* of Chile, to Governor Ambrosio O'Higgins, Santiago, referring to the Laws of the Indies as 'municipal.' ANCH, Real Audiencia, vol. 1589, pz. 3, fs 229v–230. On the use of Roman comparisons by Solórzano see Francisco Cuena Boy, "El ejemplo de los romanos," *Revista Chilena de Historia del Derecho* 22 (2010), 103–124. See also David A. Lupher, *Romans in a New World: Classical Models in Sixteenth-Century Spanish America* (Ann Abor, 2003).

49 *Memorial* (1622), 15. See Jerónimo Castillo de Bovadilla, *Política para corregidores y señores de vasallos*...(1597; Barcelona, 1624), 3.8.5.

Advocate General and Defensor General of Indians. As advocate, the protector was responsible for Indian lawsuits being appealed before, or originating in, the audience of Lima. In his position of Defensor General, the protector had the duty to care for all Indians of 'the Kingdom and provinces of Peru, the mainland and Chile, and those of Mexico, China, and Japan, who went to Peru.' Whereas there was no legal impediment for Peruvians, and even *limeños*, to hold the advocacy of Indians, Rynaga argued that the Defensor General's jurisdiction was so vast that it was impossible to apply any parameters of exclusion from office.[50] In other words, the idea of *patria*, restricted to the 'city, villa, place or province' of origin, could not be applied to the larger political units—kingdoms, *capitanías*, audiences—that were part of the Spanish Monarchy in the Indies. Anything different would alter the principle set in the laws of the Indies which prohibited magistrates from exercising their offices in their place of birth. Should a broader principle be applied, a person born in Quito was limited to magistracies in the audiences of Mexico, Guadalajara, Panama, Guatemala or Santo Domingo, that is, those beyond the limits of the viceroyalty of Peru.[51]

In ultimate terms, the memorials argued that merging the Defensor General, advocates and procurators of Indians into a protector-*fiscal* and a procurator did not constitute a significant innovation. Not only were the audiences responsible for the well-being of Indians, but also *fiscales* had been appointed as protectors of Indians in the past. In certain audiences like Chacras, moreover, this practice still prevailed. To merge the offices, therefore, would be like 'putting back the nuts into the pitcher, and to resurrect that which was old and forgotten.'[52] As for increasing the number of fiscales to three, Rynaga stated that the Romans had increased the number of praetors in accordance to the needs of the Empire. In a similar fashion, he argued that the audience of Lima (1542) was originally founded with four *oidores*, but currently had eight *oidores*, four *alcaldes del crimen*, and two fiscales each. If the Spanish monarch employed twelve *fiscales* for the defence of the crown's interests, would it not be worthy and pious to give Indians one protector paid with their own tribute?[53]

Both memorials ended lamenting by the fact that no formal resolution had been taken since Cacho de Santillana's letter of 1614.[54] At one level, Rynaga was of the opinion that the Council of the Indies should decide on the matter despite the fact that the viceroy's reply to a 1615 rescript on this matter was

---

50 "[T]odo Indio de todos los Reynos y Prouincias del Pirù, Tierrafirme, y Chile, y de los de Mexico, de la China, y del Iapon, q[ue] fueren al Pirù." Rynaga, *Memorial*, 17v.

51 *Memorial* (1622), 12; Rynaga, *Memorial*, 17–18.

52 "[B]olver nueçes al cantaro, y resucitar lo antiguo y ya olvidado." Rynaga, *Memorial*, 27.27v.

53 Rynaga, *Memorial*, 28v–29.

54 *Memorial* (1622), 15; Rynaga, *Memorial*, 21v.

FIGURE 1
Diego de León Pinelo. 17th century. Painting by unknown artist in Universidad Nacional Mayor de San Marcos. Despite the fact that he was professor of prime and vespers in canon law, he is holding the book of the Digestum Vetus (also in the library shelves), denoting the prestige of Roman Law. The elevation of the protectorship to the rank of fiscal *of the audience entitled him to wear the* garnacha *(gown of office).*
PHOTOGRAPH WILFREDO LOAYZA

still pending (21v). The fact that two former *oidores* of Lima, Juan de Villela (1562–1639) and Alonso Maldonado de Torres (†1628), as well as *limeño* Diego Ramírez de Cepeda, former Bishop of Cartagena, were councillors of the Indies, provided this institution with considerable experience in Peruvian matters (22v–23). At another level, there was no economic reason preventing the institution's reform, particularly as the protector's salaries were not paid with the resources of the royal treasury but with Indian tribute (25v). Rynaga concluded by stating that if the Indians provided the monarchy with 'the necessary food of gold and silver,' their king was obliged to provide these vassals with the necessary 'consolement, shelter, and protection' (30). In turn, the 1622 memorial called Peru the Atlas upon which rested the old world.[55]

The memorials proposed the elimination of the troika established in 1575 and its replacement by a *fiscal* of the audience devoted to Indian lawsuits aided by a procurator. By elevating the rank of the Defensor General to that of *fiscal* they effectively acknowledged the importance of the legal defence of Indians within the protectorship institution. The centrality of their role at the courts of justice, as opposed to that of furthering policy measures in favour of Indians, is evidenced by the high consideration the memorials had for advocates (depicted as accomplished jurisprudents) which contrasts with the existence of little or

55 "La provincia del Pirú, Atlanta, que sobre sus hombros sustenta al mundo viejo, y sus gastos y prodigialidades de millones." Memorial (1622), 18v.

no reference in the texts to the men appointed as defensors general. On the other hand, the project of having a second *fiscal* position that would almost exclusively be staffed by Spanish Americans reveals the general discourse of Creole Patriotism of the seventeenth century.[56] Despite the fact that both memorials were published in Madrid, there is no evidence to assess their influence at the Council of the Indies. About a decade and a half after their publication, however, part of their demands were answered when a protector of Indians with the prerogatives of an audience *fiscal* was appointed for the jurisdiction of Lima.

The Protector-fiscal

On 31 October 1640, a *real cédula* issued by the Council of the Indies appointed Doctor Francisco de Valenzuela (†1655) protector-*fiscal* of Peru as reward for a payment of 9,000 pesos, his 'letters' and 'great services, inherited and proper' to the Spanish Crown.[57] The purpose of this office, which was created for the audiences dependent of the vice-royalty of Peru (Lima, Quito and Charcas) was to act as Crown attorney in cases concerning Indian plaintiffs. The appointment of Valenzuela not only created a new position within the colonial bureaucracy, but also implied changes in the structure of the audiences where it was established, thereafter composed of *oidores* and *alcaldes del crimen*, as well as three *fiscales*: Civil, Criminal and Protector of Indians. As its civil and criminal counterparts, the protector-*fiscal*, would be entitled to the use of *garnacha*, seats in the royal *acuerdo*, and all the other honorific prerogatives enjoyed by a minister of the audience.[58] The appointment was sufficiently significant to be mentioned by Juan de Solórzano Pereyra when he stated that at the time in which the *Política*

56 David Brading, *First America: The Spanish Monarchy, Creole Patriots, and the liberal state, 1492–1867* (Cambridge, 1993), 224–225, 232–233, 317, 321, 329–330 and Chapter 14.

57 See Ruigómez, *Protector de indios*, 81 and Ernesto de la Torre Villar, *Los pareceres de Juan de Padilla y Diego de León Pinelo acerca de la enseñanza y buen tratamiento de los indios* (Mexico, 1979), 82. In the same rescript Valenzuela was also appointed *fiscal* of the Tribunal de la Santa Cruzada, an office which was traditionally exercised by a *fiscal* of the royal audiences in the Indies. The Tribunal de la Santa Cruzada was a specialised tribunal which determined the rights of those exercising the ecclesiastical privileges attached to the *Bula de la Santa Cruzada*, a form of Church indulgence.

58 The garnacha was the robe which distinguished *oidores* and Crown Prosecutors of the Audiences. It was an black ankle-length gown with sleeves. From the early seventeenth century it was used with the *golilla*, a simple, starched pointed white collar. Since the mid-seventeenth century the *golilla* replaced the ruff as sign of honour and was promoted by the Count-Duke of Olivares as one of the measures of austerity in the Spanish court (see Plates 1–4). John Elliot, *The Count-Duke of Olivares: Statesman in an Age of Decline* (New Haven, 1986), 147.

Indiana was being written (1639–46) the vice-royalty of Peru had been granted protectors with 'titles of *fiscales*, and other honours and privileges.'[59]

The fact that the defence of Indians would be undertaken by a protector-*fiscal*, that is, a *letrado* with the rank and privileges of an audience official, appears to have initially produced no visible changes in the structure of the protectorship. The fact that Juan del Campo remained in his post as Advocate of Indians (a position which would have overlapped with the functions of protector-fiscal) suggests that the institution took some time to settle. In 1648, however, a royal *cedula* issued by the Council of the Indies to Viceroy Count of Salvatierra (*v.*1648–55) stated that the protectors-*fiscales* were not performing their obligations in an adequate manner and ordered that protectors appointed for the audiences Lima, Quito and Charcas should return to their 'old institute.' To compensate those who had bought the office, the rescript ordered immediate reimbursement.[60]

The viceroy could not undertake these instructions because funds to reimburse the office holders could not be drawn from the royal treasury, but had to come from local resources. In two reports of 1650 and 1652, Salvatierra informed King Philip IV (1621–65) that the amount needed to reimburse those who had purchased office was 'considerable,' and there were no means other than the royal treasury for compliance. As a result, Valenzuela remained in office until his death in 1655 and, that same year, Salvatierra's successor, Viceroy Count of Alva de Aliste (*v.*1655–61), appointed Alvaro de Ibarra (1621–75) as second protector-*fiscal* of the audience of Lima under the terms of the 1640 rescript (see Plate 2, below).[61] Ibarra was commissioned to Chile to investigate the deposition of the governor of Concepción shortly after he entered office, which allowed the appointment of Diego de León Pinelo (1608–71) as interim protector-*fiscal* of Indians of Lima in June 1655 (see Plate 1, above).[62]

59 "En efecto yá hoy quando esto se escribe se han puesto Protectores Letrados, y con Garnacha, títulos de Fiscales, y otros honores y privilegios en todas las Audiencias del Perú: quiera Dios que cumplan bien su oficio." Solórzano, *Política Indiana*, 2.28.49.

60 Real Cédula 28 August 1648, Madrid, in Ruigómez, *Protector de indios*, 216.

61 For a general account of his life see Guillermo Lohmann Villena, *El Conde de Lemos: Virrey del Perú* (Madrid, 1946), 133–149, and *Los ministros*, 172–173. An account of later appointments is found in Lilly, Latin American mss. Peru, 1673, Sep.18.

62 Nicolás Matías del Campo states that Ibarra, 'maintained' his appointment as protector-*fiscal* of Lima for a period during his time in Chile and that this absence permitted the interim appointment of 'other lawyers' to the protectorship of Indians. See Campo, *Memorial*, 12–13. The bibliography on the Leon bothers is legion. A guide to the various writings on this family is found in Juan E. Morón Orellana, *Antonio de León Pinelo* (Lima, 1993), 18–20.

FIGURE 2
*Alvaro de Ibarra. 17th century. Painting by unknown artist in Universidad Nacional Mayor de San Marcos. The Protector-*fiscal *is depicted with the books of the Code and Infortiatum, representing the chairs held by him at San Marcos. The mitre of bishop, alludes to his posthomous appointment as bishop of Trujillo.*
PHOTOGRAPH WILFREDO LOAYZA

However, less than two years after these appointments took place the office of protector-*fiscal* of Indians came to an end by means of a real *cedula* enacted on 1 February 1657. The *cedula* ordered the abrogation of the protectors-*fiscales* appointed to the royal audiences of Lima, Charcas and Quito, and the reinstatement to its 'ancient state'—that is the 1575 ordinances of the defensorship of Indians. In view of past difficulties, the *cedula* authorised the use of royal treasury funds to reimburse those who had paid for their office. Unlike previous attempts to eliminate the protectorship, on this occasion the financial circumstances were less pressing: the titular protector-*fiscal* in Lima (Ibarra) was absent, that of Quito had died, and there was only the protector of Charcas to reimburse.[63]

Based on the fact that, in September 1660, Diego de León Pinelo claimed to have been Protector of Indians for 'five years and three months,' it is safe to conclude that there was functional continuity of the protectorship institution.[64] In other words, after the enactment of the 1657 *cedula*, the office of León Pinelo changed from interim protector-*fiscal* to Defensor General of Indians and he exercised his office under the terms of the 1575 ordinances. For viceregal authorities only the office of protector-*fiscal*, not the office of

63 Real Cédula 1 February 1657, Madrid, in Ruigómez, *Protector de indios*, 217.
64 León Pinelo, *Mandó que se imprimiesse este escrito*...([Lima?], 1660), [1].

Protector of Indians as instituted by Viceroy Toledo, had been abrogated by the 1657 rescript. On 2 October 1664, however, the Council of the Indies agreed under a special consideration to appoint León Pinelo as protector-*fiscal* of Indians with the 'same honours and prerogatives' as Francisco de Valenzuela.[65] As protector-*fiscal*, León Pinelo remained a full member of the royal audience of Lima until his death in 1671.

The apparent conflict between León Pinelo's 1664 appointment and the 1657 rescript abrogating the protectors-*fiscales*, was solved by a *real cedula* of 28 December 1671. Enacted after his death that same year, the rescript explained that 'as Protector General of Indians in the district of the royal audience' of Lima, León Pinelo was appointed fiscal in view of his 'letters, parts and merits.' This provision, however, was a consequence of his 'particular considerations' and could not, by any mean, be an 'exemplar' to further appointments. By virtue of this rescript the Council of the Indies restated that the 'provision and grade' of the office of protector or defensor general had been 'reduced' to its 'ancient form' in the terms established by the *cedula* of 1657. In other words, future appointments to the office of protector general of Indians would be granted within the framework of the 1575 ordinances.[66]

Restoration, Honorific *Fiscales* and Decline (1680–1821)

Restoration: The Defensor General and the 1680 Recopilación

The publication of the *Recopilación de las Leyes de Indias,* or Laws of the Indies, in 1681 confirmed the provisions set in the 1657 *real cedula* and brought back the 1575 ordinances for the protectorship of Indians. It thus validated the structure of Defensor General, advocates, procurators and provincial defensors of Indians (Recop. 6.6.3,4). The Defensors General were charged with writing briefs for the viceroy, audience and Council of the Indies on issues such as indigenous demography, the treatment of Indians by officials and the undertaking of Christian instruction; as well as drafting proposals concerning the improvement of 'teaching, relief, and conservation' of Indians (Recop. 6.6.12).

65 Francisco and José Mugaburu, *Chronicle of Colonial Lima: The Diary of Josephe and Francisco Mugaburu, 1640–1697*, ed. Robert Ryal Miller (Norman, Okla., 1975), 88; Torre Villar, *Pareceres*, 83; and Campo, *Memorial*, 20. Based on the fact that he enjoyed the same prerogatives as Valenzuela, León Pinelo petitioned the Council of the Indies for his appointment as *fiscal* of the Tribunal de la Santa Cruzada without success; the office was also requested by Juan Bautista Moreto *fiscal* for civil and criminal. The discussion is found in the transcripts made by Torre Villar, *Pareceres*, 81–88.

66 Real Cedula de 28 de diciembre de 1671, Madrid, in Ruigómez, *Protector de indios*, 219.

In turn, the defence of indigenous plaintiffs in court would be undertaken by the advocate and procurators ordering the *fiscal* of the audiences to resume the obligation of defending one party, if both plaintiffs were Indians (Recop. 6.6.3,4; 2.15.37; 6.6.13). Despite attempts at reforms by the memorials of 1622 and 1626, the compilers of 1680 determined that appointments of protectorship officials would remain a prerogative of the viceroy (Recop.6.6.5).

The Laws of the Indies of 1680, however, introduced some innovations to the 1575 ordinances. It placed special emphasis, for example, on the fact that mestizos were prohibited to be defensors—reinstating a 1578 rescript reporting that mestizo defensors of Indians had caused 'much damage to Indians' (Recop. 6.6.6,7).[67] Another innovation was the obligation of caciques to contribute to the salary of their *corregimiento* defensor (Recop. 6.6.11). Finally, the *Recopilación* instituted a Defensor General in the audience of the Philippines, where the defence of Indians had previously been in the hands of the bishop, and a special defensor was also appointed for the vagabond Indians of the Magdalena river in New Granada (Recop. 6.6.9).

Despite the formal abolition of the office of protector-*fiscal* in 1657, protectors continued to be referred as *fiscales*. The successor to León Pinelo, Alonso Hurtado de Mendoza (†1695), for example, would refer to himself in judicial dealings as protector-*fiscal*; yet the fact that he was a *regidor* of the city of Lima between 1661 and 1695—a post which was not compatible with an audience position—indicates that the use of the title of *fiscal* was merely honorific.[68] The practice of granting the title of *fiscal* to Defensors or Protectors (the term more commonly used after 1680) General of Indians was a common feature in the seventeenth and eighteenth centuries.[69] In view of the restrictions set in the Laws of the Indies and the pressure to appoint local-born officials, viceroys developed a practice by which they appointed short-term, *interim* protectors

67 Richard Konetzke, ed., *Colección de documentos para la historia de la formación social de Hispanoamérica, 1493–1810*, 4 vols (Madrid, 1953–58), 1: 512.

68 See "Autos que sigue Juan de Campos Villacataparaco sobre el cacicazgo…" 1680, Apr. 20—1695, Apr. 14, Lilly, Latin American mss, fol. 29v. For his role as advisor to the *cabildo*, see AGN, GO-BI 5, leg. 139, c.100, f. 3. A short biography is found in Guillermo Lohmann Villena, *Los regidores perpetuos del cabildo de Lima (1535–1821): Crónica y estudio de un grupo de gestión*, 2 vols. (Sevilla, 1983), 2: 154–155.

69 Pedro de Santiago Concha,for example, referred to himself in his last will as "Fiscal protector General de los naturales de la R.A. [Real Audiencia]," in Francisco Cayetano y Arredondo, AGN protocolos notariales s. XVIII, protocolo notarial 64, 1734, f. 544. In the case of universities, see transcripts of the *colegiales* catalogues of the royal colleges of San Martín and San Felipe y San Marcos (Archivo Histórico de Madrid códice 164 and signature 239b), in Eguiguren, *Diccionario*, vol. 2: 133–255 and vol. 1: 523–540.

also with the rank of *fiscal* as a starting point in their careers (see chapter 5). Even some eighteenth century Peninsular-born *letrados* accepted these honorific appointments when transferred to the Indies as protectors-*fiscales*.[70] Honorific or not, perhaps the most significant consequence of the title of *fiscal* was the fact that, from 1640 onwards, all Defensors General were university *letrados* or university graduates. That the head of the institution was now a *letrado* would change the protectorship structure, making the office of Advocate of Indians redundant: After the death of Juan del Campo Godoy in the mid sixteenth century no further appointments were made.

Honorific Fiscales

The legal nature of the title of *fiscal* held by protectors was the cause of debate within the Council of the Indies. Between 1758 and 1763, for example, Fernando Bustillos and Antonio de Porlier (1722–1813), respectively protectors-*fiscales* in Santa Fe and Charcas, requested an increase in their salaries to the level of audience ministers on the grounds that their appointments were granted by Real Confirmación.[71] However, in a report of 28 April 1763, the Council's *fiscal* replied to the request stating that, although protectors of Indians had the right to wear the magistrate's gown, they did not possess the rank of *fiscal*, and therefore could not be considered as ministers of the audience (f.105v).[72]

The point made by the Council in 1763 had been established a few years earlier following a petition entirely different in nature. Following his engagement to a local bride (and his niece), Tomás de Azúa e Iturgoyen (1700–69),

70 This is case of Brun and Mier (who rejected the appointment as protector and agreed to travel after securing an Alcalde del Crimen position). See Mark A. Burkholder and D.S. Chandler, *From Impotence to Authority: The Spanish Crown and the American Audiencias, 1687–1808* (Columbia, 1977), 72.

71 Manuel Josef de Ayala, "Consultas y pareceres, dado a S.M. en asuntos del gobierno de Indias recopiladas a materias del A.B.C.D…," vol. 5 (1768), AHN, códices 756-B, f.104v, 105. Porlier was later oidor in Chacras (1765–66), *fiscal* of crimen in Lima (1769–75), *fiscal* in the Council of the Indies for New Spain (1773) and Governor of the Council in 1792 until the Napoleonic invasion. In 1791 he was created Marquis of Bajamar. See Mark A. Burkholder and D.S. Chandler, *Biographical Dictionary of Audiencia Ministers in the Americas, 1687–1821* (Westport and London, 1982), 266–267, and Lohmann Villena, *Los ministros de la Audiencia de Lima en el reinado de los borbones (1700–1821)* (Sevilla, 1974), 103–104.

72 Ayala, "Consultas y Pareceres," vol. 5 (1768), AHN, códices 756-B, fs. 104v–106v. The councillors were Abaria, Arco, Valdelirios, Manuel Pablo de Salcedo, Joseph Banfi, Marcos Ximeno, Domingo Trespalacios y Escandón, Pedro Calderón de la Barca, and the Marquis of Aranda. The increase would have been from 1,000 pesos to 2,940 pesos per annum.

protector-*fiscal* of Indians in the audience of Chile, wrote to the Council in 1749 to obtain confirmation that the dispositions prohibiting ministers of the audience marrying into families under their jurisdiction stated in the Laws of the Indies (2.16.82) were not applicable to protectors of Indians as this office did not constitute a '*fiscal* of the audience proper.' As the protector-*fiscal*'s main obligation was to plead Indian lawsuits, he argued that the office had 'no link whatsoever with...the administration of justice.' Therefore, Azúa concluded that the protectorship was not bound by the hindrances caused by the 'alliances and friendships which follow marriages.'[73]

The Council agreed with Azúa that the protector-*fiscal*'s 'principal and only assignment' was the defence of Indians in all their lawsuits. It also made clear that such responsibility did not imply being part of the judiciary; even if many audiences had often 'elevated' the protector of Indians to the 'honorific class of togate' this fact did not alter the office's 'true nature.'[74] In view of this, the Council of the Indies agreed to grant Azúa dispensation to marry his niece on 27 June 1749.[75] The councillors confirmed the status of protectors of Indians as officials below the rank of audience magistrates and, therefore, the precedent established in the 1681 Laws of the Indies prevailed.[76]

---

73 "[P]rotector de los Indios en su distrito cuyo único cargo es defender en sus causas, y pleytos, sin enlace alguno con los intereses de V.M. ni con la administracion de Justicia, por lo que no puede el Protector incurrir en los embarasos que para admnistrarla con enteresa, sin dar ocasión à quejas, y recusaciones, suelen causar las alianzas, y amistades que se siguen a los casamientos." "[E]l principal, o único encargo de los Protectores de Indios es... abrazar por ellos, y defenderlos en todas sus causas y negocios sin la menor intervencion della administracion de justicia."Ayala, "Consultas y pareceres," vol. 4, AHN, códices 755-B, fs. 177–177v. The local bride was his niece Clara María Marín de Poveda y Azúa. On the prohibition of marriage between magistrates and local women see Daisy Rípodas Ardanaz, "El 'Tratado analítico sobre la cédula real de 10 de febrero del año 1575. Y otras semejantes, que estrechísimamente prohiben el matrimonio de los oidores y otros ministros en las provincias de las Indias,' de Bernardino de Figueroa y de la Cerda," *Revista de Historia del Derecho* 1 (Instituto de Investigaciones de Historia del Derecho, Buenos Aires) (1973), 391–96.

74 "[S]u elevacion en Chile, y en otras Audiencias a la clase honorifica de toga, en nada hà alterado su verdadera naturaleza." Ibid, f.177v.

75 The councillors were Romay, Agüero, Cornejo, Abaría, Geraldino, Osorio, Fernández Molinillo, Matallana, Arco and José de Laysequilla y Palacios (*c.*1677–1755), former *oidor* of Santo Domingo (1704), Quito (1709–12), Bogotá (1719–22), and fiscal of the council in the secretariat of Peru (1723). See Burkholder and Chandler, *Biographical Dictionary*, 179–180. The marriage was celebrated in Santiago on 22 December 1750.

76 As for the rules concerning marriage dispensations for ministers of the audience in 1767, the council would state that licences to marry local women in American audiences were

A similar view was adopted by the Council of the Indies in the case of Ignacio Negreiros, a merchant who purchased the *fiscal*-protectorship of Indians in Chacras. In 1755 Negreiros requested the audience that he assume the responsibilities of the civil and criminal *fiscales* in their absence. Unable to decide on this matter, the *oidores* in Charcas consulted on the matter with the Viceroy, Count of Superunda (*v.*1745–61), who, in turn, wrote to the Council of the Indies. In the *consulta* sent to the council Superunda pointed out that, according to the *oidores* in Charcas, Negreiros not only possessed a 'turbulent' personality but did not profess 'jurisprudence;' that is, he lacked a university degree. The Viceroy pointed out that, although Negreiros had previously served as corregidor of Urubamba and Cusco, he was only a merchant and not a *letrado*, and thus, in the opinion of the *oidores* of Charcas, his pretensions to exercise the functions of *fiscal* would cause 'grave inconveniences' in the dispensation of justice.[77]

As expected, the *fiscal* of the Council of the Indies considered Negreiros' lack of university education an insurmountable obstacle for exercising an audience rank office. In his report, he stated that even if the royal decree which appointed Negreiros as *fiscal*-protector had binding force comparable to an 'onerous contract,' this contract could nonetheless be annulled when some 'notable and substantial' error was discovered. In this case, the error had been found after he entered the contract and this was the fact that Negreiros was an 'idiot, not proficient [in law], and versed only in matters of commerce.' Had his condition of non-*letrado* been known to the king, the *fiscal* explained, such an appointment would not have occurred. Even if the king had acted in good faith, the 'contract' was void due to the absence of proper consent, a vital element for the sustaining of any contract.[78] As a consequence of this, the *fiscal* recommended that

---

normally granted by virtue of 'custom,' an argument cited in 1767 when Joseph Perfecto de Salas (1714–78), the advisor to Viceroy Amat and fiscal in the *audience* of Chile, requested a pension for his children. The council cited dispensations of 1755 and 1766 as antecedents. See Ayala, "Consultas y pareceres," vol. 4, AHN, códices 755-B, f.332. Marriage dispensations would cease in the nineteenth century. See Burkholder and Chandler, *Impotence to Authority*, 110–112.

77 Ayala, Consultas y pareceres (1768), vol. 5, AHN, códices 756-B, fs. 274 275. "[G]raves inconvenientes que pueden seguirse, de que tan importante ministerio se exerza por una perona absolutamente ajena de la mencionada facultad."

78 Ayala, Consultas y pareceres, 1768, vol. 5, AHN Códices 756-B. "[S]ugeto al riesgo de nulidad, ò currescision, quando aparesca posteriormente, ò que intervino algun notable, y sustancial error, que impidiese al principio el consentimiento, ò que el succesivo [f.275r] implemento de la gracia manifiesta despues el perjuicio, que con su subsistencia se irroga a la República, cuya utilidad como tan especial, y privilegiada siempre, se entiende libre,

Negreiros be removed from office with 'gibe to his person, blush to his companions, rebuff to the toga, and discredit...to the tribunal' (fs. 276–77).[79]

The case of Negreiros reveals the complexities of the legal status of the protector of Indians by the mid-eighteenth century. That a merchant, without a university education, was allowed to perform the duties of Protector General of Indians only confirms the legal standing of the 1575 Ordinances of Viceroy Toledo, which established that non-*letrados* could be appointed to this office. In other words, if Negreiros had not requested to replace the civil and criminal *fiscales*, both the councillors of the Indies and the magistrates of Charcas would have continued to accept his appointment as protector and allowed him to remain in office. The case also reveals that, by the mid-eighteenth century, it was preferable for Protectors General to hold a university degree in order to exercise the office. The fact that in audiences such as Lima all protectors-*fiscales* appointed between 1680 and 1781 were *letrados*, partly explains why the Council of the Indies considered that Negreiros's protectorship had been obtained 'surreptitiously' from the Crown.[80]

Decline and Abrogation

Despite the fact that protectors considered their office to be one of the 'most serious and heavy ministries' it appears that the office of protector-*fiscal* came to a halt in the second part of the eighteenth century.[81] This is partially explained by the drastic reduction in the number of Creoles in the audience of Lima after the arrival of its first regent, Melchor Jacot Ortiz Rojano (†1794), in 1776.[82] As Burkholder and Chandler have shown in their study of the American

---

y exempta de las comunes reglas de todo contrato" [f.275v]. "Que era idiota, imperito, y versado solo en materias de comercio" [f.275v]. "[P]or faltar el consentimiento, que es tan preciso, para que subsista el contrato" [f.276].

79 Ibid. "[S]in escarnio de su persona, sonrojo de sus compañeros, desayre de la toga, y menoscabo del respeto tan debido al tribunal donde hablaba," f.276.

80 Ayala, Consultas y pareceres (1768), vol. 5, AHN, códices 756-B, fs. 276–76v.

81 "[C]uyo ministerio es de los mas graves, y pesados." "Relacion de los grados y servicios del Licenciado Don Francisco Ruiz y Berecedo, Protector Fiscal de el distrito de la Audiencia del Reyno de Chile" (1716), BNCH, Medina mss. vol. 23, pieza 23, n/f.

82 Burkholder and Chandler, *Impotence to Authority*. For the effect of reform on these tribunals, see Leon G. Campbell, "A Colonial Establishment: Creole Domination of the Audienica of Lima during the Late Eighteenth Century," *Hispanic American Historical Review* 52 (1972): 1–25; and Mark A. Burkholder, "From Creole to Peninsular: The Transformation of the Audiencia of Lima," *Hispanic American Historical Review* 52 (1972): 395–415. Equally useful for this period is John Fisher, *El Perú borbónico, 1750–1824* (Lima, 2000), Chapter 2.

Audiences, unlike Creoles who were willing to accept lesser *letrado* positions such as the protector of Indians, Peninsulars were averse to accepting any American post below a rank of civil and criminal *fiscal*, *oidor* or *alcalde del crimen*. In fact, the perception was that none of the other *letrado* positions—*asesor general* (legal advisor to the viceroy), *teniente asesor* (legal advisor to intendant) and war auditor—provided either a decent salary or a reasonable prospect for promotion, and did not justify the transatlantic journey from Spain. Thus is the case of Spanish-born Cosme de Mier, who refused his appointment as protector-*fiscal* in Lima, and travelled to America only after he was offered the position of *alcalde del crimen*.[83]

However, the chief reason for the lack of protector-*fiscal* appointments in Lima after 1741 was the decision to diminish or abrogate the office by political authorities both in the Indies and in Spain. The first indications of this phenomenon would appear in 1730 when the Marquis of Casafuerte, Viceroy of New Spain (1722–34), ordered the abrogation of the office in Mexico. The order, issued on 20 March 1730, stated that the protector had attempted to encroach the functions of the *fiscal*. In his report to the Council of the Indies, Casafuerte explained that protector Felipe Tineo (†1753), who had exercised his office since his arrival in Mexico in September 1728, had appointed visitors and agents to supervise Indian tax collection, traditionally a prerogative of the *fiscal* for civil cases.[84] For the viceroy the fact that Tineo was usurping functions proved that the protectorship in itself had none, and was, therefore, a useless institution.[85]

Tineo, a former corregidor of Illescas in Spain (1711–15), opposed the measure, arguing that, without the protectorship, Indians would risk losing all their property and would find it impossible to redress their wrongs in the courts of justice due to their 'common misery, and limited capability'(f.233v–234). In addition to this he stated that the civil and criminal *fiscales* were already 'overwhelmed' by work and could not divert their attention to Indian lawsuits

83 Between 1687 and 1750 a total of 311 men were appointed to letrado positions. Of these 138 were Creoles; 157 Spanish; and 16 of unknown origin, Burkholder and Chandler, *From Impotence to Authority*, appendix 1.

84 His appointment was by *real cedula* of 1 April 1727, AGI, Contratación, 5476,N.27, f.3v; available at http://pares.mcu.es/. Tineo was a licentiate in 1729 when he requested the position of Alcalde del Crimen in Mexico.

85 "[P]retendió nombrar apoderados, o agentes para la formacion de los cuentas, y visita de los tributos de aquel Reyno, y que el Fiscal lo havia executado hasta entonces no lo hiciere, pues no le tocaba, exponiendo que el citado empleo de Protector era inutil, porque convendría le extinguiese." Ayala, "Consultas y pareceres," vol. 9 (1771), AHN Códices 759-B, fs. 233v–234, 235.

(f.234). The Council of the Indies, however, ratified Casafuerte's decision on 19 January 1732, ordering that Indian lawsuits should be pleaded by the civil *fiscal* who would, in turn, be assisted by four advocates and a procurator. After relocating Tineo as *alcalde del crimen* (1734–35) and *oidor* (1735–53), on 22 December 1736 Casafuerte issued a *real cedula* officially suppressing the protector-*fiscal* of Indians in the audience of Mexico (235).[86] Although the Archbishop of Mexico sought to annul the *cedula* by appealing to the council, there is no record that the viceroy's decision was effectively reversed.[87]

Similarly, in 1761 Manuel Amat y Juniet (1702–82), Governor General of Chile, abolished the protector-*fiscal* of Indians within the district of the audience. Unlike Casafuerte's order, Amat's decision was not motivated by any particular case. In a letter of 21 August 1761 to the Council of the Indies he briefly stated that protectors were essentially 'useless…and extremely burdensome due to their large salaries.' As as consequence of this they could easily be replaced by the *fiscal* of the audience.[88] As in the case of Mexico, the decision was supported by the Council of the Indies.

However, on 3 October 1762, Félix de Berroeta, interim president of the audience of Chile (1761–62), wrote to the Council conveying the difficulties in undertaking the governor's order. Firstly he stated that there was no financial backing to reimburse the current protector, particularly as he had just acquired the office. More importantly, Berroeta was of the opinion that replacing the protector by a *fiscal* could lead to incompatibilities in the magistracy. As the *fiscal* usually acted as prosecutor in crimes committed by Indians, he explained that the same officer that 'demands a punishment, could not litigate on behalf of the defendant.' He therefore requested the council to reverse its resolution.[89]

The opinion of the *fiscal* of the Council of the Indies on this situation was drafted in a report of 10 August 1763. On one hand, he stated that the concerns about the incompatibilities of merging the two offices were essentially correct. On the other, he accepted the idea that having a protector with the prerogatives of an audience minister was useless and costly to the royal treasury. He thus proposed that an 'advocate of satisfaction' should be appointed to act as Protector of Indians in the district of audience of Chile. In what seems a

86 "[P]or su comun miseria, y limitadad capacidad a defenser por si sus causas, y deducir en juicio sus derechos, estàn oy expuestos (no haviendo quien de oficio, y con graduada representacion tome la voz por ellos) à perder (233v) enteramente lo poco que tienen, y no resarcir nunca lo que por no poder, y no saber defender se les usurpase." Ibid.

87 Ayala, "Consultas y pareceres," vol. 2 (1765), AHN Códices 753-B, fs. 2, 2v.

88 Ayala, "Consultas y pareceres," vol. 6 (1768), AHN Códices 757-B, f.263v.

89 "[P]or no poder el mismo empleo que demanda la pena, defender al reo." Ibid., 264v.

reference to the case of Mexico, the Council's *fiscal* stated that this scheme was already practised in other audiences (f.268). The members of the Council, however, resolved on 12 September 1763 to abrogate the office of Protector of Indians in Chile. The resolution also ordered that the protector's functions would be undertaken by the audience's *fiscal*; only in lawsuits where this magistrate faced a clear incompatibility would a second advocate be appointed by the audience. The Council stressed that this advocate would be a 'temporary post' paid for by the audience, and under no circumstances by the Indians (f.268v–269).[90]

Although the appointments of Ruiz Cano in 1778 and Baquíjano in 1783 suggest that the office was not completely abrogated in the audience of Lima, the sentences issued at the Council of the Indies, and the lack of appointments after Lasso de la Vega in 1741, at least demonstrate a loss of interest in this institution, if not its effective abrogation at least for three decades. This would be the prelude for the complete abrogation of the protector of Indians on 11 January 1821.[91]

The position of Defensor General of Indians, the *corregimiento* protectors, as well as the Advocate and Procurator General of Indians were created by Viceroy Toledo to assume the protection and defence of Indians in Peru. The measure was part of an effort towards the establishment of an effective and coherent system of solving Indian legal disputes. Their formal institution in 1575 coincided with the territorial consolidation of the audience of Lima and the inception of a three-tier structure of judicial administration. When the protectorship became fully operative in the decade of 1590, it became apparent that its core duty, that is, the defence of Indian lawsuits in court, was undertaken by the Advocate of Indians—a university trained professional lawyer. The importance of *letrados* would be assessed in two memorials drafted in Lima in the decade of 1620 proposing that the Defensor General of Indians should have the same rank, pre-eminences and salary as that enjoyed by a Crown Procurator or *fiscal* at the audience. The enactment in 1640 of a *real cedula* appointing a protector-*fiscal* of Indians in the audience of Lima materialized some of the ideas put forward by the memorials and effectively changed the structure of the audience of Lima by increasing the number of *fiscales* from

90 Ibid., 268v–269. The resolution was signed by councillors the Marquis of San Juan de Piedras Albas, Esteban J. de Abaria, Fernández Molinillo, Gerónimo de Sala, Vásquez de Agüero, the Marquis of Valdelirios, Felipe de Arco, Joseph Moreno and Pedro de León.

91 Facsimile of the *real cédula* providing for the termination of the office of Protector of Indians. In Charles Cutter, *The Protector of Indians in Colonial New Mexico, 1659–1821* (Albuquerque, 1986), fig. 2.

two (civil and criminal) to three (protector of Indians). It was also exceptional in its outlook and would soon be revoked.

The enactment of the Laws of the Indies in 1680 confirmed the return of the 1575 Ordinances. However, the influence of the memorials, the 1640 rescript and the pressure of creoles for *letrado* appointments, resulted in two features that would be predominant from 1680 onwards. In the first place, political authorities, both in Lima and Madrid, conferred the honorific title of *fiscal* on Defensors General of Indians and gave them the privilege of wearing the magistrate's gown. Secondly, would-be protectorship officials were predominantly recruited within the *letrado* class.[92] Between 1680 and 1781 all appointments of protectors in the audience of Lima possessed both features. The fact Defensors General were now university trained lawyers with the rank of *fiscal*, provided, no doubt, considerable leverage for Indian plaintiffs, but also sparked debate. By the mid-eighteenth century, the Council of the Indies reviewed several cases concerning the legal nature of the office of protector-*fiscal* and its position as togate magistrate, and ruled that protectors could not be considered ministers of the royal audiences. Similar debates led to the abrogation of the institution in certain jurisdictions such as Chile and Mexico; in Lima, appointments came to a virtual standstill. The abrogation of the Defensor General of Indians in 1821 only confirmed the trend that had started more than half a century previously.

---

92 On the influence of letrados, see Jean Marc Pelorson, *Les letrados: Juristes castillians sous Philippe III* (Poitiers, 1980) and Richard Kagan, *Students and Society in Early Modern Spain* (Baltimore, 1974).

CHAPTER 3

Social Characteristics

The scarce references made in Peruvian literature to protectors of Indians, or their kinsmen, allude to their social standing. A satirical verse published during the government of Viceroy Marquis of Castelfuerte (*v.*1724–36), for example, mocked the accursed and humble origins of a recently titled protectorship family.[1] In contrast, one of the traditions of Ricardo Palma (1833–1919) stressed the 'first water' nobility of an eighteenth century protector's maternal family, on the grounds that their arms proudly displayed quarterings with the shields of Navarre and Aragon.[2] In the same vein, Nicolás Matías del Campo declared that creoles of noble birth were bound to the protection of Indians due to 'the obligation of their blood, and the secret love for their *patria*.' Following the example of the Inca rulers, who entrusted the protectorship of Indians only to those of royal blood, Campo considered that vice-regal officers should be noblemen of pure actions, gifts and virtues. Perhaps taking into account that both his father and grandfather were advocates of Indians, and that his 'great uncles' were bishops protectors Vicente de Valverde and Jerónimo de Loaisa, Campo reflected that, throughout the institution's history, kinship networks had been bound by service to the indigenous cause.[3] The same considerations had been put forth, half a century earlier, by Campo's uncle, Juan de la Rynaga who emphasized that the protectorship had always been entrusted to people of 'importance.'[4] This chapter thus focuses on the social status and characteristics of protectorship officials. It is, therefore, the result of coupling genealogical information with contemporary *relaciones de méritos y servicios* (memoirs attesting to personal qualities and accomplishment presented in support for a

1 "¿No te acuerdas de Benito,/vuestro abuelo, aquel maldito,/que del polvo de la tierra/se apellidaba Salvatierra?" quoted in Luis Alberto Sánchez, *La literatura peruana: Derrotero para una historia cultural del Perú* (Lima: P.L. Villanueva Editor, 1973), 2: 632. Reference is made to the family of Luisa Mayor Méndez de Salvatierra y Cabello (*fl.*1653–1700), Pedro de Santiago Concha's maternal grandmother.

2 "La excomunión de los alcaldes de Lima (1717)" in Ricardo Palma, *Tradiciones Peruanas*, ed. Edith Palma, 6th ed. (Madrid, 1968), 534. Reference is made to the Híjar y Mendoza family.

3 Nicolás Matías del Campo y de la Rynaga, *Memorial historico y ivridico, que refiere: El origen del Oficio de Protector general de los Indios del Perú* (Madrid, 1671), 16–16v, 15v.

4 Juan de la Rynaga Salazar, *Memorial discursivo sobre el oficio de Protector General de los Indios del Piru* ([Madrid], [1626]) 2v.

 | DOI 10.1163/9789004305175_005

position), notarial records, judicial dossiers and a number of edited collections of documents, diaries, and travellers accounts. As many other attempts of collective biography, it follows the steps of a number of important, often path-breaking, studies.[5] After discussing the sources of, and persons appointed to, the posts of Defensor General, Advocate, and Protector-Fiscal of Indians, the chapter continues with an analysis of the origin, parentage, marriages, and networks of these men. The purpose of this group portrait, therefore, is to cast further light on the men who occupied significant positions in the non-*letrado* and *letrado* bureaucracies of the Spanish Empire.

Sources and Appointments

Available documentation suggests that the institution of the Defensorship of Indians in Lima was not fully implemented following the ordinances issued in Arequipa in September 1575. Thus, between 1575 and 1582, Baltazar de la Cruz y de Aspeitia (*fl.*1575–94) was the sole official in Lima, combining his functions of defensor with those of provincial protectors. Accordingly, he was ordered to dispatch all pending appeals that remained in the *corregimientos* he visited to the royal audience in Lima.[6] Although this situation should have lasted until

5 In the case of Latin American historiography, I have greatly benefited from Guillermo Lohmann Villena, *Los americanos en las orden nobiliarias (1529–1900)*, vol. 1 (Sevilla, 1947), IX–LXXXII (preliminary study); David Brading, *Miners and Merchants in Bourbon Mexico, 1763–1810* (Cambridge, 1971); Susan Migden Socolow, *The Merchants of Buenos Aires, 1778–1810: Family and Commerce* (Cambridge, 1978); Fred Bronner, "Elite Formation in Seventeenth Century Peru," *Boletín de Estudios Latinoamericanos y del Caribe* 24 (1978), 24; Magnus Mörner, "Factors and Stratification in Colonial Spanish America with Special Regard to Elites," *The Hispanic American Historical Review* 63 (2) (1983), 335–69; John Kicza, *Colonial Entrepreneurs: Families and Business in Colonial Mexico City* (Albuquerque, 1983); Paul Rizo-Patrón, *Linaje, Dote y Poder: La nobleza de Lima de 1700 a 1850* (Lima, 2001); and Tamar Herzog, *Upholding Justice: Society, State, and the Penal System in Quito* (1650–1750), chap. 3. Equally useful have been Lawrence Stone, *The Crisis of the Aristocracy, 1558–1641* (Oxford: Clarendon Press, 1965) and *The Family, Sex and Marriage in England, 1500–1800* (1977; London, 1990); Guy Chaussinand-Nogaret, *The French Nobility in the Eighteenth Century: From Feudalism to Enlightenment* (Cambridge: Cambridge University Press, 1985); Wilfrid Prest, *The Rise of the Barristers: A Social History of the English Bar, 1590–1640* (Oxford: Clarendon Press, 1986); Jonathan Dewald, *The European Nobility, 1400–1800* (Cambridge, 1996); and Ellis Watson, *Aristocracy and the Modern World* (London: Palgrave, 2005).

6 To aid him in the task of dispatching Indian demands, Toledo assigned to Cruz, Gonzalo de Holguín, his personal interpreter, plus 200 pesos for ink and paper to record such demands. Toledo, *Disposiciones*, 2: 107, 105.

the return of the Viceroy and the visitation committee to Lima in November 1575, it was extended until 28 August 1577, when provincial protectors were appointed for the mining cities of Potosí and Huancavelica.[7] A report by Viceroy García Hurtado de Mendoza (*v.*1590–96) to Philip II confirms that Baltazar de la Cruz remained as defensor throughout the government of Francisco de Toledo (1575–82), and until the abrogation of the institution by royal cedula of 27 May 1582.[8]

Nominations were resumed by viceroy García Hurtado de Mendoza, soon after he received the order of the restoration of the institution by cedula of 10 January 1589.[9] During this period viceroys reported the elections of Antonio Heredia (1590), Antonio Torres de la Fresneda (1597), and Doctor Antonio de Ibarra (1599) to the office of Defensor General of Indians.[10] Coinciding with the lists of advocates of Indians provided by the memorials of Rynaga (1626) and Campo (1671), there are records of Alberto de Acuña (1565–1630) pleading before the audience as General Advocate of Indians in 1593.[11] Also from the decade of 1590 are the designations of Diego Gil de Avís (1596) and Antonio de Neyra as Procurators General (1599).[12] Although the evidence is somewhat sketchy, it appears that the viceroys of Peru appointed at least three more Defensors General of Indians between 1603 and 1643: Pedro Balaguer de Salcedo (DGI 1603), Domingo de Luna (DGI 1630), and Francisco Carrasco del Saz (PGI 1635).[13]

In addition to the office holders registered in vice-regal reports, judicial dossiers often record a number of 'defensors general' pleading in legal disputes. Between 1576 and 1580, for example, one Alonso de Lucio signed his writs as

7 Francisco de Toledo, *Disposiciones gubernativas para el virreinato del Perú*, ed. Maria Justina Sarabia Viejo (Sevilla, 1986–89), 2: 289–301.

8 Diego de Encinas, *Cedulario Indiano* (1596; reprint Madrid, 1945), 4: 333.

9 Encinas, *Cedulario*, 4: 334–35.

10 Roberto Levillier, ed., *Gobernantes del Perú: Cartas y Papeles, siglo XVI*, 14 vols. (Madrid, 1921–26), 14: 63, 164, 234.

11 "Testimonio de una Real Provisión de Don García Hurtado de Mendoza despachada en la casa que se seguía por ante la Real Audiencia entre Doña Florencia de Mora y Escobar, vecina de la ciudad de Trujillo y encomendera de Huamachuco, y los caciques y principales del dicho repartimiento..." AGN, Derecho Indígena, leg. 3, c. 37 (1594), fs. 1, 6.

12 See, respectively, AGN, Derecho Indígena, leg. 39, c. 793 (1596) and "Juan Narváez, indio, como marido de Dña. Barbola Charachumbi, contra Juan González Cornejo y Cristóbal de Palacios, sobre las tierras de que fueren despojadas y rematadas en los susodichos," (1599), BNP ms. A 353, f.33.

13 AGN GO-BI 5, leg. 139, c.100, f. 11v; Buenaventura de Salinas Córdova, *Memorial de las historias del nvevo mvndo Pirv*. eds. Luis E. Valcárcel and Warren L. Cook, Colección de Clásicos Peruanos 1, (1635; Lima, 1957), 293–94, 300.

'defensor general of the Indians of this kingdom' when representing various indigenous clients: the Indians of the encomienda of Rodrigo Niño de Guzmán (1510–75) in a dispute with Guzmán's heirs over the validity of his testament;[14] the Indians of the valley of Trujillo against the Spanish citizens or *vecinos* of the city for the revision of the tributary *tasas* due to the 'great rains and water tides' that had occurred the previous year;[15] and the Indians and caciques of Ilo, Arica and Tarapaca in their dispute with Gonzalo de Valencia, administrator of the encomienda to which they were subject.[16]

However, there is evidence to conclude that the title of 'defensor general' used by Lucio in these dossiers did not imply his appointment as Defensor General of Indians. First, Baltazar de la Cruz was the sole defensor in Lima between 1575 and 1582. Other than the nominations of provincial defensors for Potosí and Huancavelica in 1577, there is no proof of other appointments to the defensorship system in this period.[17] Secondly, there is sufficient evidence to suggest that, within the legal profession, Lucio was not a university trained advocate but that he belonged to the branch of *procuradores* or procurators. As such he was elected 'procurator minor' by the *regidores* of the city of Lima between 1565 and 1571,[18] and acted as private procurator in a number of cases involving Spanish, Creole and Indian clients.[19]

---

14 The suit was heard by Captain Juan de la Rynaga (*c.*1505–1600) *alcalde ordinario* of Lima, who ordered that 3,600 pesos from the estate of Niño de Guzmán should be paid to the Indians as this had been stipulated in the will. AGN, Cabildo Justicia Ordinaria, CA-JO 1, caja 33, doc. 9, f.13.

15 See the account of Francisco Alarcón in Lorenzo Huertas Vallejos, ed., *Ecología e historia: Probanzas de indios y españoles referentes a las catastróficas lluvias de 1578 en los corregimientos de Trujillo y Saña* (Chiclayo, 1987), 33–36.

16 The encomienda was the property of Lucas Martínez Vegazo, a supporter of Gonzalo Pizarro. AGN, Derecho Indígena, leg.2, c.15 (1572), fs.487ff.

17 Toledo, *Disposiciones*, 2: 289–301.

18 In 1565–66, the city of Lima was employing him as a 'procurator minor,' a position he retained throughout 1571 to 1581. See *Libros de Cabildos de Lima*, ed. Bertram T. Lee (Lima, 1935–67), 6: 315, 413; 7: 173; 9: 20, 301–2, 318–19.

19 In 1571, for example, Lucio represented Luisa Merino, the peninsular widow of licentiate Salido de Ortega of Trujillo in the matter of a debt of 2,000 pesos, plus interest, against Diego de Mora and his Indians. That same year he defended Beatriz de Isásaga, a prominent landowner in Trujillo, against the demand of her former procurator in Lima, Luis Rodríguez, for payment of fees. More important, however, is the fact that Lucio also had considerable experience of Indian lawsuits. In 1568, for example, he represented the claim presented by the visitador Diego Hernández de Mendoza on behalf of the Chicha Indians in his suit against Francisco Maduciño and María Mendoza, encomenderos in Arequipa, for excessive and illegal exaction of tributes. In 1574 he defended Pablo Curas, a

Usage of the title of 'defensor general' of Indians in legal proceedings, therefore, did not necessarily refer of the office holder of the Defensorship General of Indians. As in the case of Alonso de Lucio, it is unclear if Sancho Verdugo (1609), Alonso Padilla (1638) and Gerónimo de Samanez (1622), who employed this title to countersign various writs, were in fact appointed to the office of Defensor General.[20] In the absence of conclusive evidence, it would appear that the title it was employed by the Procurator General of Indians. If anything, this is supported by the fact that not all procurators pleading Indian cases employed in their proceedings the title 'defensor of Indians.' A good example of this is Francisco Falcón (1521–87), a prominent procurator in the audience of Lima, and advisor to Archbishop Jerónimo de Loaisa (1498–1575) on indigenous matters. In the proceedings of the case involving the 'poor' Indians of Laraos and Mangos against the heirs of *encomendero* Fernando Martel (1585–87) Falcón did not use the title of 'procurator' or 'defensor' of Indians.[21] Similarly, an analysis of the lawsuits defended by Leandro de la Rynaga Salazar as advocate of Indians (1596–1624) reveals that he used a number of procurators: Juan de Santelices (1596), Jacome Carlos (1599–1600), Francisco de Avendaño (1604–5), and Lúcas Jiménez (1611). Of these, however, only Carlos and Avendaño appear in the proceedings as 'Procurators General of Indians' (see Appendix 1). In sum, leaving aside those appearing as 'defensors' of Indians in judicial

'principal' Indian, in his dispute for the cacicazgo of the *huaranga* of Ichochonta. See "Expediente sobre la causa seguida entre Alonso Moreno, en nombre de Diego de Mora encomendero del valle de Trujillo y sus indios, contra el Lic. Salido de Ortega, por censos," (1571), BNP ms. A 453, 73fs; "Autos seguidos por Alonso de Luzio, en nombre de Beatriz de Isásaga, vecina de la ciudad de Trujillo … contra Luis Rodríguez quien reclamaba sus salarios por los servicios prestados a doña Beatriz," AGN, Real Audiencia, causas civiles, leg.11, c.59 (1571); AGN, Derecho Indígena, leg.2, c.10 (1568); y AGN, Derecho Indígena, leg.3, c.19 (1574).

20 For Lucio, Verdugo and Padilla see Carmen Ruigómez Gómez, *Una política indigenista de los Habsburgo: el Protector de Indios en el Perú* (Madrid, 1988), 224, 106, 107. In the case of Samanez see "Causa de don Geronimo Polan, indio, con Francisco Chancoy sobre el cacicazgo del pueblo de Begueta del distrito de la villa de Chancay," Lilly Latin American mss. Peru 1621, Oct. 26—1625, May 16, f.20; BNP ms B19.

21 Falcón obtained a resolution which allowed the release of 200 pesos from the estate of Fernando Martel, their former encomendero, who had left these funds in his will. See "Carta de pago de los doscientos pesos que se dieron a los indios Mangos y Laraos para el repartimiento de los pobres," Los Reyes 18 January 1587, BNP ms. A 261. Falcón was involved in the indigenous cause through Archbishop Loayza and in 1567 wrote a memorial on the coercive work to which Indians were forcibly subject, Guillermo Lohmann Villena, "El licenciado Francisco Falcón (1521–1587): Vida, escritos y actuación en el Perú de un procurador de indios," *Anuario de Estudios Americanos* 27 (1970).

dossiers and considering those included in vice-regal reports, there is evidence of at least five appointments to the office of Defensor General of Indians between 1575 and 1643: Baltazar de la Cruz, Antonio Heredia, Antonio Torres de la Fresneda, Pedro Balaguer de Saledo, Francisco Carrasco del Saz (see Table 1).

In the case of the Advocate of Indians, the memorial by Nicolás Matías del Campo y de la Rynaga, published in 1671, provides a comprehensive list of office holders appointed in the audience of Lima between 1575 and 1643. Campo lists a total of eight law graduates appointed to the office of *abogados de indios*. Five were appointed to the post of *first* advocate of Indians between 1593 and 1643 (Alberto de Acuña, Alvaro de Ibarra, Leandro de la Rynaga, Juan del Campo and Antonio Maldonado de Silva) and three to that of *second* advocate of Indians (Diego Hurtado de Avendaño, Francisco de Sosa and Cipriano de Medina). Although the office of second advocate of Indians remained in place until 1643, there were no appointments after the death of Medina in 1635.

Further findings, however, suggest that, with the exception of Antonio Maldonado de Silva (†*c*.1651), all *letrados* listed by Campo worked as Advocates of Indians in the jurisdiction of the audience of Lima. As Maldonado de Silva himself indicates in his last will and testament, after a brief spell as corregidor of the Juzgado General de Indios in Lima he was appointed *abogado general de indios* of the audience of Charcas, a post he held between 1608 and 1610. Upon his return, he was professor of Decretum at San Marcos, and devoted most of his life to private practice in law.[22] Therefore, with Maldonado de Silva discarded from the list of occupants of the advocacy of Indians in Lima, it is possible to conclude that a total of seven law graduates were appointed to the post of Advocate General of Indians (see Table 2).

On the other hand, the task of establishing a comprehensive list of Protector-*Fiscales* between 1643 and 1781 has benefited from the seminal work of Guillermo

22 Not to be confused with Francisco Maldonado de Silva (1592–1639), a doctor of medicine condemned for Jewish practices by the Inquisition. See Nathan Wachtel, "El cielo cara a cara: Francisco Maldonado de Silva y la Inquisición," in *El hombre y los Andes: Homenaje a Franklin Pease G.Y.*, vol. 2, eds. Javier Flores Espinoza and Rafael Varón Gerbi (Lima, 2002), 929–37. Antonio Maldonado de Silva (†*c*.1651) was born in Lima to Juan Pérez Maldonado and María de Silva; he was a terciary member of the Order of St. Francis and doctor in Laws. See AGN, Protocolos Notariales siglo XVII, protocolo 1092, Francisco de Medina 1651–53, fs 207v-9; Luis Antonio Eguiguren, *Catálogo Histórico del Claustro de la Universidad de San Marcos, 1576–1800* (Lima, 1912), 33. It is interesting to note that Maldonado de Silva possessed a 500 volume library which was, unfortunately, not inventoried.

Lohmann Villena on the audience of Lima (1700–1821),[23] the studies of Mark Burkholder and D.S. Chandler on the American audiences (1687–1808),[24] and a number of monographs on magistrates who were appointed protectors-*fiscales* as part of their bureaucratic careers.[25] In many cases, however, notice of office holders has been found in diverse sources such as notarial records, judicial dossiers, vice-regal letters, *relaciones de méritos y servicios* (memoirs attesting to personal qualities and accomplishment presented in support for a position) and even contemporary paintings. In all, a total of nineteen protector-*fiscales* were appointed between 1643 and 1781. This list includes Cosme Antonio de Mier y Trespalacios (†1805) who declined the nomination made by the Council of the Indies in 1776,[26] as well as the interim appointments made after this date of Francisco Ruiz Cano y Saenz Galeano and José Baquíjano Carrillo, respectively in 1778 and 1781 (see Tables 3 and 4).[27]

It would appear that the title of protector of Indians was widely used in the courts of justice of Lima in the last quarter of the sixteenth century. Not all those who employed it, however, were royal appointed officials enrolled in the protectorship institution founded by Viceroy Toledo in 1575. The continuous appointment of advocates of Indians as from the decade of 1590 and the elevation of the

---

23 Guillermo Lohmann Villena, *Los ministros de la Audiencia de Lima en el reinado de los borbones (1700–1821)* (Sevilla, 1974).

24 Mark Burkholder and D.S. Chandler, *From Impotence to Authority: The Spanish Crown and the American Audiences, 1687–1808* (Columbia, 1977), and *Biographical Dictionary of Audiencia Ministers in the Americas, 1687–1821* (Westport and London, 1982).

25 This is the case of Diego de León Pinelo (1608–71) and José de Baquíjano Carrillo (1751–1817). See Juan E. Morón Orellana, *Antonio de León Pinelo* (Lima, 1993), 18–20. In the case of Baquíjano see José de la Riva Agüero, "Don José Baquíjano y Carrillo," in *Estudios de Historia Peruana: La emancipación y la república*, vol. 7 of *Obras Completas* (Lima, 1971), 21–109; Mark Burkholder, *Politics of a Colonial Career: José Baquíjano and the Audience of Lima* (Albuquerque, 1980); and José de la Puente Brunke, José *Baquíjano y Carrillo*, Colección Forjadores del Perú 12 (Lima, 1995).

26 Mier was latter offered the post of *alcalde del crimen* in Lima (1776), which was declined in favour of the same position in the audience of Mexico (1776–85), where he became regent (1804). See Lohmann, *Los ministros*, 70–71.

27 See AGN, protocolos notariales s.XVIII, protocolo 1143, Marcos de Uceda 1739, f.232 (Barrientos); "Libramiento de 711ps. 6ro. en comisos al Dr. Dn. Pedro Bravo de Castilla, Fiscal Protector Interino…," Lima, 14 December 1736, BNP ms. C92 (1736), fs. [3v]–[4] (Bravo de Lagunas); Alfredo Moreno Cebrián, *El virreinato del Marqués de Castelfuerte, 1724–1736* (Madrid, 2000), 261 (Santiago Concha); and AGN, protocolos notariales s. XVIII, protocolo 873, Agustín Gerónimo de Potalanza 1770–77, fs. 731–31v (Lasso de la Vega). Reference to these appointments is also found in Lohmann, *Los ministros*, 10, 17–18, 34–35, 59–61.

institution to an audience magistracy in 1643, contributed to differentiate the protectors of Indians from other legal professionals. By the time appointments to this office ceased in the second half of the eighteenth century, references to this institution filled many *relaciones de servicios*, memorials and even stately portraits. Present evidence suggest that, throughout its existence, the secular institution of the Protectorship of Indians, counted at least six Defensors of Indians whose royal appointments date between 1575 and 1635; seven advocates of Indians between 1590 and 1624; and nineteen protectors with the rank of fiscal of the audience appointed between 1643 and 1781.

Geographical Origin and Parentage

Geographical Origin

The Protectorship of Indians was largely recruited from men born in the urban centres of Spanish America. The exception to this general observation were the Defensors General of Indians, who appear to have been mostly born in Spain. As notarial records indicate, this was the case of Antonio Torres de la Fresneda (DGI 1597), Pedro Balaguer de Salcedo (DGI 1603) and Francisco Carrasco del Saz (PGI 1635).[28] The origins of Baltazar de la Cruz y de Aspeitia (DGI 1575–89), Antonio Heredia (DGI 1590) and Domingo de Luna (DGI 1630), however, cannot be ascertained. Nonetheless, considering the period of Cruz's tenure, it is highly probable that he was also of Peninsular origin. It is possible, therefore, that the only Spanish American of the defensors might have been Luna, one of the retainers of Viceroy Count of Monterrey both in Mexico and Lima, chiefly on the grounds that he completed his studies in Mexico City.[29] However, this is speculative.

In contrast to the fragmentary information available for the Defensors General, the origins of the advocates and protectors-*fiscales* are more discernible due to the availability of sources. The majority of advocates of Indians listed by Nicolás Matías del Campo in 1671 were Creoles or Spanish Americans. Of this group, Francisco de Sosa and Antonio Maldonado de Silva were born in

28 See AGN, protocolos notariales s.XVII, protocolo 819, Francisco Hernández 1606–1608, f. 312 (Torres de la Fresneda); and protocolo 788, Pedro Gonzáles Contreras 1605 (1606), f. 20371 (Balaguer). Biographical details on Defensor of Indians Carrasco del Saz are found in the work about his distinguished relative and namesake, Guillermo Lohmann, "Francisco Carrasco del Saz, jurisconsulto y tratadista," *Revista Histórica* 39 (1996–98), 168.

29 Luis Antonio Eguiguren, *Diccionario histórico cronológico de la Real y Pontificia Universidad de San Marcos y sus colegios: Crónica e investigación*, 3 vols. (Lima, 1940–51), 1: 389.

Lima; Leandro de la Rynaga and Juan del Campo in Osorno, Chile; and Antonio de Ibarra a *vecino* of Mexico City. Similarly, men of Creole extraction dominated appointments to the office of protector-*fiscal*. Of the eighteen magistrates that effectively served in this post, fourteen were born within the territories of South American royal audiences: ten in Lima, two in Santiago de Chile (Ruiz de Berecedo and Felipe Barrientos), and one in Córboda, Charcas (Diego de León Pinelo). The list of protector-*fiscales* also included three Peninsulars (Alonso Hurtado de Mendoza, Tomás de Brun and Pedro de León y Escandón). Judging from the documentation regarding licenses-of-passage to Lima, it would also appear that Francisco de Valenzuela (1641) and José Martínez de España (1728) were also of Spanish extraction.[30]

In terms of geographical origin, most advocates of Indians and protectors-*fiscales* were born within the vice-royalty of Peru, and a high proportion of these in Lima itself. This tendency supports the orthodox view that, until 1776, the royal audience of Lima was dominated not only by Spanish Americans, but by *limeños* themselves.[31] In fact, available information suggests that other vice-regal institutions staffed by members of the upper branch of the legal profession were equally dominated by Spanish Americans. A glimpse of the lists of professors of Canon Law appointed at the University of San Marcos, for example, evidences that sixteen of the eighteen academics appointed by the crown between 1576 and 1792 were born in the vice-royalty of Peru, twelve of whom were natives of Lima.[32] Even if there are virtually no systematic studies of the numerous jurisdictions that existed in addition to ordinary civil and ecclesiastical courts, this was also the trend amongst the officers of other specialized tribunals.[33] Judging from the list of attorneys (*fiscales*) who served in the

30 See, respectively, AGI, Contratación, 5424,N.1,R.7 and 5476, N.61, available at http://pares.mcu.es.

31 See Mark A. Burkholder, "From Creole to Peninsular: The Transformation of the Audiencia of Lima," *Hispanic American Historical Review* 52 (1972): 395–415; Leon G. Campbell, "A Colonial Establishment: Creole Domination of the Audienica of Lima during the Late Eighteenth Century," *Hispanic American Historical Review* 52 (1972): 1–25; Lohmann, *Los ministrios*, XXV–XXXV; Mark A. Burkholder and D.S. Chandler, *From Impotence to Authority*; and John Fisher, *El Perú borbónico, 1750–1824* (Lima: IEP, 2000), Ch. 2.

32 Eguiguren, *Catálogo Claustro*, 23–25.

33 With the exception of the Tribunal de Minería and the Tribunal de Cuentas, there is virtually no information on the tribunals of Protomedicato (Medics), Mesta (cattle), Santa Hermandad (1631) and Acordada (1722) (violent crime and prohibited liquors) or the Juzgados de Cofradías, Testamentos y Obras Pías (lay groups, wills and) and Correos (1776), among others. For a general glimpse of these jurisdictions see M.C. Mirow, *Latin American Law: A History of Private Law and Institutions in Spanish America* (Austin, 2004),

Tribunal of the Bull of Crusade in Lima from 1603 to 1641, it would appear that whenever these institutions were not dominated by creoles, this group represented at least half of the appointments.[34] The advocates and protectors of Indians were, therefore, not an exception to this general phenomenon.

These figures, however, do not take into account the extent to which Spanish-born officials who served in the protectorship could have been considered Spanish American citizens at the time of their appointments. As a recent study of citizenship in the Spanish Monarchy points out, prolonged settlement or residence enabled Peninsulars to become citizens of American cities and, as such, acquire political rights in these communities. The fact that advocate Antonio de Ibarra claimed to be a *vecino* of Mexico City, for example, indicates in the political language of the late sixteenth century that he considered himself a citizen of this jurisdiction regardless of his place of birth. On the other hand, the fact that Hurtado de Mendoza was a *regidor pepetuo* of Lima since 1661, evidences that vice-regal authorities considered him no longer a citizen of Zaragoza upon his nomination as protector-*fiscal* in 1680. Similarly, upon his nomination as Defensor General of Indians, Pedro Balaguer de Salcedo had been a resident of Lima for more than ten years; a period which juristic doctrine considered to be sufficient proof of his intention to abandon his native Madrid, and reside permanently in the New World.[35]

Even if they did not fulfil these conditions at the time of their appointments, an important group of non-*limeño* protectorship officials were certainly citizens of Lima in the making. Take, for example, Seville born advocates of Indians Cipriano de Medina and Alberto de Acuña. The first had been a resident of the City of Kings for nine years (during seven of which he was married to a native of the city) at the time of his appointment in 1593. In turn, Acuña married his second *limeña* wife (herself the daughter of a city councillor and an *encomendera*) during his tenure as advocate between *c.*1590 and 1597. Natives of Osorno, Chile, Leandro de la Rynaga and Juan del Campo, settled in

---

28–33; Miguel Molina Martínez, *El Real Tribunal de Minería de Lima, 1785–1821* (Sevilla: Diputación Provincial de Sevilla, 1986); and Ronald Escobedo Mansilla, *Control fiscal en el virreinato peruano: El Tribunal de Cuentas* (Madrid, 1986).

34 José Antonio Benito Rodríguez, *La Bula de Cruzada en Indias* (Madrid, 2002), 139.

35 Tamar Herzog, *Defining Nations: Immigrants and Citizens in Early Modern Spain and Spanish America* (New Haven and London, 2003), 51–56; for the concept of *desavecinamiento* or the undoing of citizenship see 31–35. The discussion of citizenship in the New World also extended to the prohibition of the marriage of magistrates in their jurisdiction. See Juan de Solórzano, *Política Indiana*, eds. Francisco Tomás y Valiente and Ana María Barrero (Madrid, 1996), 5.9.56–71.

Lima after obtaining their law degrees at San Marcos. In a similar vein, the authorities of San Marcos considered that Diego de León Pinelo's true "patria" was Lima, even if he was a native of Córdoba (one of the leading cities of the audience of Charcas), the son of a Portuguese, and a graduate from Salamanca.[36]

For these, and other, officials such as Tomás de Brun and Felipe Barrientos, the city of Lima was the place of birth of their wives and the *patria* of their children; as well as the community where they established their legal practices, served as local magistrates and lectured as university professors. As Tamar Herzog points out, in the seventeenth and eighteenth centuries citizenship ceased to be tied to administrative procedure, but became a matter of social recognition and reputation.[37] In this context, present evidence indicates that Francisco Ruiz de Berecedo and Pedro de León y Escandón were the only two officials who, by returning to their places of origin and not acquiring significant family or professional ties with Lima, could duly have been considered as non-citizens of the capital of the vice-royalty of Peru.

Status

Either by virtue of their passing to the Indies, their bureaucratic posts or university studies, the officers of the protectorship of Indians were presumed to be men of unblemished stock, and even noblemen. In principle, a number of rescripts issued between 1518 and 1602 established that neither Jews, Moors, Gypsies, heretics nor recent converts, could be allowed passage to the Indies.[38] These dispositions, enacted along the lines of the *Inter Coetera* bull of 1493, implied that only 'Old Christians' that is, men who could assert an untainted bloodline (*limpieza de sangre*) were to settle in the New World; the idea being that only such men could serve as examples to new converts, and undertake the defence of Catholic orthodoxy. As an institution of Castilian nobiliary law, the *limpieza de sangre* was also a requisite for those who pursued royal and ecclesiastical posts.[39]

By the end of the seventeenth century, the Recopilación de Indias reinstated the requirement that protectorship offices should be held by men of

---

36 Eguiguren, *Catálogo*, 23. On the concept of *patria* and creole patriotism see D.A. Brading, *The First America: The Spanish Monarchy, Creole Patriots and the Liberal State (1492–1867)* (Cambridge, 1991) 97; 293–313.

37 Herzog, *Nations*, 56–59.

38 Recop. 9.26.15, 16, 20; 7.4.5; 7.5.29; 9.27.9. See Luis Lira Montt, "El estatuto de limpieza de sangre en Indias," *Boletín de la Academia Chilena de la Historia* 108–9 (2000), 91.

39 Siete Partidas, 7.24.3. On this subject see Luis Lira Montt, "El estatuto de limpieza de sangre en Indias," *Boletín de la Academia Chilena de la Historia* 108–9 (2000), 85–112.

competent age, Christianity and *limpieza*.[40] Similar considerations were required for admission at the royal colleges of the University of San Marcos in Lima, as well as for the university itself. At least until 1816 the statutes of this institution not only excluded from its studies Jews, Moors and non-Indian converts, but also those of mixed blood such as 'mestizos, zambos, mulattoes and quarter-bloods.'[41] As a result, authors such as Melchor Cabrera Nuñez de Guzmán (*fl.*1670), a bureaucrat of the later Habsburgs, believed that members of the legal profession could not have 'impure' ancestry, nor forbears who had been condemned by the Holy Office or who exercised vile and mechanical offices.[42]

In addition to these requirements of *limpieza de sangre*, tradition prescribed that service to the King was also a path towards attaining ennoblement. For Nicolás Matías del Campo, Defensors of Indians had been men of "capa y espada."[43] Although this condition normally referred to men without a university education, Joaquín Bastús y Carrera (1799–1873), a Valencian priest, considered that "capa y espada" offices were granted to men of 'high birth' or distinguished military service.[44] In the same manner, the Council of the Indies ordered that the "beneméritos," that is, the first discoverers, conquistadors, or

40 Recop. 6.6.1.

41 Constitución XIV, título 7, "de los estudiantes y oyentes," 1735, in *Constituciones de la Universidad Mayor de San Marcos de Lima: Epoca del coloniaje* (Lima: Universidad Mayor de San Marcos, 1938). This disposition is also mentioned in the proposed reform plan of the university of 1816 "Plan de reforma de la Real Universidad de San Marcos enviado por el virrey de la Pezuela al rector de la universidad para su aprobación," Lima, 18 de diciembre de 1816, mss BNP, D 521, f. 4v. On this subject see the useful study, inventory and bibliography of Luis Lira Montt, "Las colegiaturas en los colegios mayores y seminarios reales de América como actos positivos de hidalguía," *Boletín de la Academia Chilena de la Historia* 112 (2003), 97–120. The struggles to establish these nobiliary requirements in Spain are studied in Baltazar Cuart Monet, *Colegiales mayores y limpieza de sangre durante la Edad Moderna* (Salamanca, 1991).

42 Melchor Cabrera Núñez de Guzmán, *Idea de un abogado perfecto, deducido de reglas, y disposiciones del Dercho, comprobada con la autoridad de sus interpretes* (Madrid, 1693), 63–64.

43 Campo, *Memorial*, 6.

44 Joaquín Bastús, *Suplemento al diccionario histórico enciclopédico* (Barcelona: Imprenta de Roca, 1833), 589. An example of the role of these men in government positions in the Kingdom of Aragon is found in Margarita Ortega López, "El Consejo Supremo de Aragón y la supervisión de la justicia del reino aragonés durante el siglo XVII," *Manuscrits* 8 (1990), 139–62; and Enrique Gimenez López, "Caballeros y Letrados. La aportación civilista a la administración corregimental valenciana durante los reinados de Carlos III y Carlos IV," *Anales de la Universidad de Alicante* 8–9 (1988–90), 167–82.

founders of cities, should have preference when it came to royal offices and appointments; thus establishing the foundations of a noble estate in the New World.[45] Whereas the ennoblement of the conquistadors followed the established European view of nobility as a conquering race, the sixteenth century also foresaw the increased importance of *letrados* in the councils and courts of Spain, and indeed other European nations.[46] Although juristic doctrine noted that 'noble, grave and prudent men' were best suited for appointments to public office in the Indies, eventually office-holding itself became an outward sign of nobility.[47] The rise of this administrative nobility also influenced the professions. It was not surprising to find authors such as Francisco Bermúdez de Pedraza (1585–1655), stating that university trained lawyers should be reputed as honourable, egregious, and noble.[48] Even if Bermúdez de Pedraza, a rector of the University of Granada, based his assertions on Biblical, Classical and Roman Law sources, these nonetheless reflect the manner in which the Spanish crown perceived its civil servants as honourable and distinguished men.[49]

Formal control over immigration, university education, and service to the crown could, therefore, lead to certain assumptions regarding social standing in the Spanish Monarchy. These assumptions, however, should be placed against many caveats. Although the Casa de Contratación exercised control over emigration, it appears that this could be easily circumvented either due to the impossibility of this institution being able to investigate effectively the backgrounds of all sea-bound travellers, notwithstanding illegal immigration itself.[50] Furthermore, the union of the crowns of Spain and Portugal between

45 See, for example, Solórzano, *Política Indiana*, 3.3.1, and Recop. 1.6.27; 1.28.3; 2.1.19; 2.2.27; 2.37.1, 3; 2.33.2–7. A discussion of this issue is found in Luis Lira Montt, "Los beneméritos de Indias y la gestación de la nobleza en América," *Hidalguía* 268–69 (1998), 504.

46 See Jonathan Dewald, *The European Nobility, 1400–1800* (Cambridge, 1996), 36–40; Richard Kagan, *Students and Society in Early Modern Spain* (Baltimore, 1974).

47 Solórzano, *Política Indiana*, 5.1.10. Lohmann, *Los americanos*, 1: XV–XVIII.

48 See Francisco Bermúdez de Pedraza, *Arte Legal para estudiar la Ivurisprudencia* (Salamanca, 1612), 24–26. Melchor Cabrera Núñez de Guzmán, considered lawyers to be members of the 'first nobility.' See *Idea de un abogado perfecto*, 63–64. For a general outlook on the *Speculum jurisconsultorum* genre see Helmut Coing, ed. *Handbuch der Quellen und Literatur der neueren europäischen Privatrechtsgeschichte*, 2 vols. in 3, Max-Planck-Institut für Europäische Rechtsgeschichte (München: C.H. Beck'sche Verlagsbuchhandlung, 1973–77), 2: 724–54. A discussion on these texts is found in Donald R. Kelley, "Jurisconsultus Perfectus: The Lawyer as Renaissance Man," *Journal of the Warburg and Courtauld Institutes* 51 (1988), 84–104.

49 See Dewald, *European Nobility*, 16.

50 There is evidence that during the sixteenth century, not only English merchants, but also a Turkish Emir, obtained licences to travel and trade in the Indies. Similarly, it

1580 and 1640 facilitated movement across borders in the Peninsula and the New World; thus large numbers of Portuguese Jewish *conversos*, for example, were able to find their way to the vice-royalties of Mexico and Peru with relative ease.[51] On the other hand, sources point out that by the eighteenth century the requirements of *limpieza* for entry into the royal colleges and university were loosened or simply not applied: A Royal Rescript of 1738, for example, referred to the 'pernicious consequences' brought by the 'multitude of lawyers of obscure birth and bad customs' which graduated from the University of San Marcos.[52] In a much broader sense, the degree to which public office ennobled its holder was repeatedly placed in question in the light of the various tides of sales of jurisdictional and non-jurisdictional bureaucratic positions carried out by the Spanish Crown between 1591 and 1750.[53]

---

would appear that approximately one percent of the total number of Italian immigrants to the vice-royalty of Peru filed formal petitions for entry. See, respectively, José Luis Martínez, *Pasajeros de Indias* (Madrid, 1983), 32–36, and Sandro Patrucco, *Presencia italiana en la Lima borbónica: 1701–1800* (New York, 2006), Chapter 2. The story of the Turkish Emir is found in Nicolás Martínez de Arzans y Vela, *Historia de la Villa Imperial de Potosí* (1705). On the Casa de Contratación see Antonio Acosta Rodríguez, et. al. Eds. *La Casa de Contratación y la navegación entre España y las Indias* (Sevilla, 2003). Besides the monumental work of Peter Boyd-Bowman, Ida Altman provides an important case study of Spanish emigration to America and reviews the main issues around this area of study in *Emigrants and Society: Extremadura and America in the Sixteenth Century* (Berkeley, 1989).

51 See for example, Henry H. Keith, "New World Interlopers: The Portuguese in the Spanish West Indies, from the Discovery to 1640," *The Americas* 25 (4) (1969), 361–62. On Portugese *conversos* in Peru see Irene Silverblatt, "New Christians and New World Fears in Seventeenth Century-Peru," *Comparative Studies in Society and History* 42 (3) (2000), 524–46.

52 "[P]erniciosas consecuencias... multitud de abogados de obscuro nacimiento y mala costumbre." Cited in Paul Rizo-Patrón, *Linaje, dote y poder: La nobleza de Lima de 1700 a 1850* (Lima, 2001), 96–97.

53 See John H. Parry, *The Sale of Public Offices in the Spanish Indies under the Habsburgs* (Berkeley: University of California Press, 1963); Leon G. Campbell, "A Colonial Establishment: Creole Domination of the Audienica of Lima during the Late Eighteenth Century," *Hispanic American Historical Review* 52 (1972): 1–25; Alfredo Moreno Cebrián, "Venta y beneficios de los corregimientos peruanos," *Revista de Indias* 36 (143–44) (1976), 213–46; Fernando Muro, "El 'beneficio' de oficios públicos en Indias," *Anuario de Estudios Americanos* 35 (1978), 1–67; Kenneth J. Andrien, "The Sale of Fiscal Offices and the Decline of Royal Authority in the Viceroyalty of Peru," *The Hispanic American Historical Review* 62 (1) (1982), 49–71; Burkholder and Chandler, *From Impotence to Authority*.

In more than one aspect, entry to one of the four military Spanish orders of knighthood (Santiago, Montesa, Calatrava and Alcántara) illustrates the degree in which noble status was often an issue of juridical formality. Instead of providing documentary proof of their nobility, most Creole applicants, for example, presented a number of testimonials commenting on their qualities and genealogies. However, even if these testimonials represented only 'procedural truths,' the Council of the Orders had no constraints in placing them at the same level as the traditional instruments of evidence in nobiliary law such as letters patent, pedigrees, or registration in the nobility rolls (*padrones de hidalgos*).[54] In this respect, virtually all Spanish Americans potentially belonged to the *hidalgo* class. Moreover, the absence of taxpayers (*pecheros*) of Peninsular descent in the New World, further contributed to blurring the distinctions between noble and commoner within this segment of society in Peru.[55] Nonetheless, although protectorship officials were presumed to possess personal nobility by virtue of their office, this juridical unity should not make us lose sight of the differences that put one official in a different class from another in the noble category. An enquiry on their status among the noble and distinguished persons that formed the court of the City of Kings is, therefore, a complex task, due to the highly mobile, and at the same time hierarchical and stratified, nature of Peruvian society throughout the vice-regal period.[56]

Parentage

Evidence of origins, class and the family entourage of Defensors of Indians, is limited to Pedro Balaguer de Salcedo. As a "familiar" of the Holy Office of Lima he would have submitted proof of purity of blood (*limpieza de sangre*) upon entry to this institution.[57] In addition, his hidalgo background would have

---

54 Miguel Luque Talaván, *Bibliografía Española de Genealogía, Heráldica, Nobiliaria y Derecho Nobiliario en Iberoamérica y Filipinas (1900–1997)* (Madrid, 1999), 65–67; Lohmann, *Los americanos*, 1: LV–LXII. On testimonials in Castilian Law see Marta Madero, "Façons de croire: Les témoins et le juge dans l'œuvre juridique d'Alphonse X le Sage, roi de Castille," *Annales HSS* 1 (janvier-février) (1999): 197–218.

55 Richard Konetzke, "La formación de la nobleza en Indias," *Anuario de Estudios Americanos* 3 (10) (1951), 356.

56 See Fred Bronner, "Elite Formation in Seventeenth Century Peru," *Boletín de Estudios Latinoamericanos y del Caribe* 24 (1978), 24; Magnus Mörner, "Factors and Stratification in Colonial Spanish America with Special Regard to Elites," *The Hispanic American Historical Review* 63 (2) (1983), 335–369.

57 P, 7.24.3. On this subject see Luis Lira Montt, "El estatuto de limpieza de sangre en Indias," *Boletín de la Academia Chilena de la Historia* 108–109 (2000), 85–112.

been theoretically scrutinized by the Council of Orders in Spain upon the admittance of his grandson Pedro de la Cueva y Balaguer (1598) to the Order of Santiago in 1628.[58] In all other cases evidence of the parentage of Defensors of Indians is either non-existent or too fragmentary to establish any conclusions. The testament of Alonso Torres de la Fresneda, for example, only reveals that he was married to Spanish-born Mariana de Zuñiga, and came to Peru after the birth of their son Juan de Torres y Fresneda.[59]

In contrast, advocates and protectors of Indians were a heterogeneous group, summarised in Appendix 1, which included titled aristocrats, *encomenderos*, sons of merchants, members of *letrado* dynasties, lesser nobles and even descendants of Jewish converts. Until the grants of titles of nobility by King Charles II (*r.*1665–1700) in the second half of the seventeenth century, the most prestigious members of Peruvian society were the descendants of conquistador or *encomendero* families.[60] Most of the advocates born in the New World belonged to the group which represented, until the end of the colonial period, the foundational military aristocracy of the vice-royalty.[61] The father of Francisco de Sosa, for example, was captain Diego de Sosa, a native of Toledo who was famous as conquistador of Peru and encomendero of Yanahuaras Malmayas (*c.*1572) in Cuzco, Yuminas and Canchis in Arequipa.[62]

58 Lohmann, *Los americanos*, 1: 119. It is worth noting that one Gregorio Balaguer de Salcedo, was protonotary, *camarero* of popes Paul III and Julius II and curate of the parish of Fuencarral, who died and was buried in this parish in 1556.

59 See the testament and last will of Juan Torres y Fresneda, AGN, protocolos notariales s.XVII, protocolo 819, Francisco Hernández 1606–1608, fs. 312–13. Note that in 1546 one of the notaries (*escribano*) of Alcalá de Henares was one Francisco Torres de la Fresneda, and that in 1625 one Gaspar Torres de la Fresneda was councillor of this city. See, respectively, Juan de la Barrera y Acedo-Rico, *Viejas Familias de Alcalá de Henares* (Madrid: Editorial Complutense, 2003), 27, and Evangelina Muñoz Santos, "Alcalá de Henares por la Inmaculada Concepción: Votos de la Magistral, Universidad y Consejo (s.XVII) fiesta y arte" (n/p, n/d).

60 See José de la Puente Brunke, *Encomienda y encomenderos en el Perú: Estudio social y político de una institución colonial* (Sevilla, 1992), 233. For Juan de Solórzano *encomiendas* granted 'much honour, estimation and authority.'

61 See José Durand, *La transformación social del conquistador*, 2 vols. (Mexico, Porrúa y Obregón, 1953), 2: 29–30.

62 See "Razon de la ascendencia del Sr. Dr. Dn Francisco de Sosa y Rengifo…" (c.1625). BNP mss. B 841; "Información de legitimidad y nobleza de Francisco de Sosa, vecino y regidor de Toledo, y del cap. Diego de Sosa, su hermano, conquistador el Perú, hijos legítimos de Francisco de Sosa y de María del Corral, su mujer." BNP, Archivo Astete Concha, mss. Z270; Salinas, *Memorial*, 168; and Puente, *Encomienda*, 380, 425. The encomienda of Yanahuaras Malmayas was still in the possession of Francisco de Sosa in 1634.

Leandro de la Rynaga Salazar, was the son of captain Juan de la Rynaga Salazar (1505/11-1600), an *infanzón*, or member of the lower nobility in the Basque country, who arrived in America in 1534 to participate in the conquests of Peru and Chile. Rynaga gained recognition by supporting the royalist cause in the uprising of Gonzalo Pizarro (†1548); he was thus awarded two encomiendas in Huánuco, and appointed corregidor of Osorno (1563–64) and Chachapoyas (1571–74), alcalde ordinario of Lima (1570, 1576), and alcalde of Huánuco (1597).[63] Both the parents of Juan del Campo Godoy (1591–*fl.*1653) were encomenderos. Isabel Rosa de Godoy, inherited from her father, captain Juan de Godoy (†1598), the encomiendas of Lomas and Copallán in Chile. His father, Francisco del Campo y Gómez Ahumada (†*c.*1601), an army officer with a record of service in the wars of Sicily, Flanders and Italy, was bestowed with the encomienda of Sicasica, south of La Paz in Charcas. In addition to this, Governor Alonso de Sotomayor (1555–1610) appointed him to the office of corregidor of Arica and the honorific title of *maestre de campo* (see Chart 1, below).[64] Also of encomendero and conquistador stock was Antonio de Ibarra, a nephew of Francisco de Ibarra (1539–75), the explorer and conqueror of New Biscay in Mexico.[65]

Even if their parentage was diverse, there were a few protectors who possessed titles of nobility and, as such, were placed at the very top of the social hierarchy in eighteenth century Peru. The first of these was García José Lasso de la Vega e Híjar (1705–75), fourth count of Villanueva del Soto, after the death of his maternal uncle García José de Híjar y Roldán in 1729. His father was a city councillor and his mother a member of a grand but impoverished family: Viceroy Prince of Santo Buono (*v.*1716–20) observed that Lasso de la Vega's grandfather, García de Híjar y Mendoza (†1718), second count of Villanueva del

63 The first of which had 320 tributaries and an annual income of 1,000 pesos.

64 See Pedro López de Echaburu, *Relación de los servicios del doctor Don Nicolás Matías del Campo y de la Rinaga, abogado que ha sido de la Audiencia de Lima* (Madrid? 1666?) and Joseph de Aguilar, *Bachiller don Joseph de Aguilar, Bilicia y Godoy, Cura de San Christoval de los Guachos en el obispado de Guamanga…* (Madrid, [1664]). The various testaments of Isabel Rosa de Godoy are found in AGN, protocolos notariales, Pedro Gonzáles Contreras 1612, ff. 195–203v.

65 For Javier Barrientos Grandon, Antonio de Ibarra was the son of Juan de Ibarra, who was appointed governor of New Biscay in 1576, but died before embarking for Mexico; see "La creación de la audiencia de Santiago y sus ministros fundadores," *Revista de Estudios Histórico Jurídicos* 25 (2003), 233–338. On the other hand, Guillermo Porras Muñoz, claims that he was the son of Francisco's elder brother Martín Ibáñez de Ibarra, "Diego de Ibarra y la Nueva España," *Estudios de Historia Novohispana* 2 (1968), 48–78.

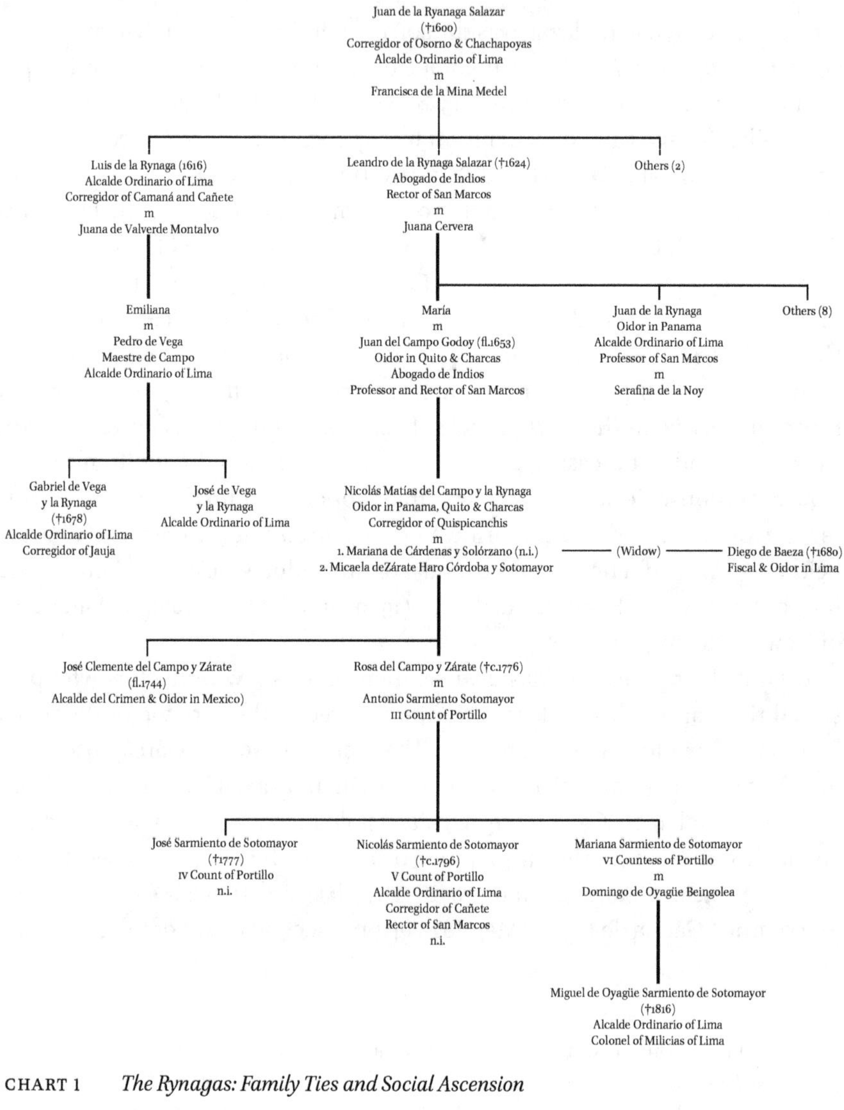

CHART 1 *The Rynagas: Family Ties and Social Ascension*

Soto, 'had no funds.'[66] The father of Francisco Ruiz Cano y Sáenz Galeano (1732–92), fourth marquis of Sotoflorido, was a Castilian from Ocaña of

66 See Bertrando del Balzo, "Familias nobles y destacadas del Perú en los informes secretos de un virrey napolitano (1715–1725)," *Revista del Instituto Peruano de Investigaciones Genealógicas* 14 (1965), 109. Nonetheless, his mother was given a dowry agreed on 17 March 1704, see BNP, ms. Z 235. She was the daughter of Diego Miguel de la Presa Carrillo de Albornoz (1695–1750), fourth count of Montemar, and Mariana Bravo de Lagunas y Villela (1705–1749), lady of the Castle of Mirabel. See Rizo-Patrón, *Linaje*, 76–78. Lasso de la Vega and his cousin, however, litigated against each other as evident in BNP, ms. Z 253.

unknown origin, who in 1749 obtained appointment as governor of Chucuito, a strategic jurisdiction that controlled the *mitayo* manpower of Puno to the silver mines of Potosí.[67] The title of marquis was inherited by Francisco's mother, who was the niece of the first and second marquises, both non-*letrado* officials appointed as general paymasters of the Armada of the Southern Seas in the port of Callao.[68]

In turn, José de Baquíjano y Carrillo (1751–1817), third Count of Vistaflorida in 1807, was the son of a successful Basque merchant who was bestowed with a nobility title in 1753 after a generous contribution to the crown for the reconstruction of Lima following the 1746 earthquake (see Plate 3). Although his father was a newcomer, his mother's family, the Carrillo de Córdovas, possessed an impeccable lineage that could be traced to conquistadors and indigenous caciques.[69] Pedro de Santiago Concha y Roldán-Dávila, heir presumptive to the Marquisate of Casa Concha until his untimely death in 1735, possessed a background similar to that of Baquíjano; whereas the ascendancy of his father, a prosperous merchant turned high court magistrate, was placed in doubt by contemporaries,[70] the Roldán Dávilas enjoyed high social standing as landowning *encomenderos*, and descendants of the first governor of Trujillo.[71]

Prestigious social position was also asserted by means of possessing a distinguished family ancestry. Despite his relatively modest upbringing, for example, Pedro José Bravo de Lagunas belonged to one of the most notable families of

---

67 See Enrique Tandeter, *Coacción y mercado: La minería de la plata en el Potosí colonial, 1626–1826* (Madrid: Siglo Veinituno de España Editores,), 261.

68 Respectively Tomás (1659–1707) and José González Galeano (1662–1735). For Ruiz Cano see Guillermo Lohmann, ed., *Un tríptico del Perú virreinal: El virrey Amat, el marqués de Soto Florido y la Perricholi. El drama de dos palanganas y su circunstancia* (Chapel Hill: University of North Carolina Department of Romance Languages, 1976), 22–51.

69 María Ignacia Carrillo de Córdoba y Garcés de Mansilla, was the daughter of Carrillo de Córdoba y Agüero, and Rosa Garcés de Mansilla e Irrarázaval. She was descended from Diego de Agüero, Nicolás de Ribera el Mozo, and the cacica of Talagante in Chile. Details on her ascendency are found in José de Amézaga, "El conquistador don Diego de Agüero y los mayorazgos de su casa," *Revista del Instituto Peruano de Investigaciones Genealógicas* 15 (1970), 165–176; Jorge Zevallos Quiñones, "Los Lisperguer en el Perú," *Revista del Instituto Peruano de Investigaciones Genealógicas* 7 (1954), 98–118; Juan Luis Espejo, *Nobiliario de la Capitanía General de Chil*e (Santiago, 1967), 526–531.

70 See Luis Alberto Sánchez, *La literatura*, 2: 632–633.

71 The Roldán Dávila family was founded by conquistador Juan Roldán Dávila (†*c.* 1538). References of their background and economic position are found in Susan Ramírez, *Provincial Patriarchs: Land tenure and the economics of power in colonial Peru* (Albuquerque: University of New Mexico Press, 1986), 46, 55, 81, and figure 5; Lohmann, *Los americanos*, 1: 363–366.

FIGURE 3
José de Baquíjano y Carrillo. 20th century. Copy of painting by unknown artist in Instituto Riva Agüero. The protector is depicted wearing his gown of office and the Order of Charles III pinned to his chest. The coronet of Count of Vistaflorida surmounting his personal arms can date the portrait after 1807. The library holds, among other the books, the Constitutions of the University of San Marcos an institution where Baquijano was professor of Institute and vespers of laws.
IMAGE COURTESY OF INSTITUTO RIVA-AGÜERO, PONTIFICIA UNIVERSIDAD CATÓLICA DEL PERÚ.

Peru (Plate 4).[72] Their recognition began with Sancho Bravo de Lagunas, a knight of Alcántara and *gentilhombre* of Emperor Charles V, whose grandson Fernando (1589–1650) moved to Peru where he was appointed corregidor of Piura and Chiclayo, as well as contador of the Tribunal Mayor de Cuentas. Through his paternal line of Bedoya, Pedro José was also a direct descendant of Pedrarias Dávila (*c.*1440–1531), founder of Panamá, and linked with three fifteenth century mayorazgo families in Spain, including one founded by a member of the Council of the Catholic Kings.[73] The social prestige of the family was

72 In 1721 viceroy Santo Buono commented that Bravo de Laguna's father 'had children and was poor.' See Balzo, "Familias," 119.

73 The first was founded in Guadalajara by Rodrigo Campusano, comendador of the Order of Santiago (1465); the second also founded in Guadalajara by Alonso de Bedoya (1490),

further heightened by the lengthy pedigree of Bravo de Lagunas's mother, whose genealogy included direct parentage with bishops Jerónimo de Loaisa (†1575), St. Toribio of Mogrovejo (1538–1606), and similarly important bureaucrats, audience judges, and city councillors.[74]

A similar case is that of Peninsular Alonso Hurtado de Mendoza, a member of the Zaragoza branch of the illustrious house of Mendoza founded by Diego Hurtado de Mendoza and Leonor Lasso de la Vega in the fourteenth century.[75] His noble origins are confirmed by the fact that his father was deputy of the hidalgo class in the Cortes of Tarazona (1592). On the other hand, his mother was part of the extended Beaumont Navarre clan founded by Luis de Beaumont Navarre (†1432), great-grandson of Philip III of France, first Count of Lerín, and hereditary Condestable of Navarre.[76]

---

included the right to be interred in the parish of San Andrés dating from 1338; and the third was founded in Buitrago by Gonzalo del Castillo, a member of the council of the Catholic Kings, and his wife Inés de Contreras (1475). All of these were inherited by Pedro José's uncle Fernando Bravo de Lagunas y Bedoya in 1704. See Guillermo Swayne y Mendoza, *Mis antepasados* (*Genealogía de las familias Swayne, Mariátegui, Mendoza y Barreda*) (Lima, 1951), 504–510.

74 Through the Castilla Altamirano line, Mariana de Castilla y Loaisa, descended from Fernando de Castilla Altamirano (1613–*fl.*1643), knight of Santiago and alcalde of Lima, whose uncle was the Count of Santiago Calimaya in Mexico, and from captain Ruy Barba Cabeza de Vaca, who was part of the expedition of Pedro de Alvarado. The line of Loaisa included as ascendants *oidor* Juan de Loaisa Calderón (†1632), and captain Rodrigo de Esquivel y Cueva (1519–*fl.*1581), 'conquistador' of Peru and corregidor of Arequipa with La Gasca. The Mogrovejo line included Franciso de Quiñones (1540), corregidor of Lima (1583), captain general of Chile (1599), and alcalde of Lima (1603). Quiñones married Grimanesa de Mogrovejo, sister of St. Turibius. A number of circumstances eventually made Pedro José both head and mayorazgo of the house of Mogrovejo. References to the different lines of Pedro Bravo de Lagunas are found in Lohmann, *Los americanos*, 1: 94–95, 149; Swayne y Mendoza, *Mis antepasados*, 503–519; Espejo, *Nobiliario*, 670–671; and Paul Rizo-Patrón, *Linaje*, 204.

75 See, for example, Helen Nader, *The Mendoza Family in the Spanish Renaissance, 1350–1550* (New Brunswick, 1979), Ch. 4. The text is now available at http://libro.uca.edu/mendoza/mendoza.htm.

76 A short biography is found in Guillermo Lohmann Villena, *Los regidores perpetuos del cabildo de Lima (1535–1821): Crónica y estudio de un grupo de gestión*, 2 vols. (Sevilla, 1983), 2: 154–155; Juan Luis Espejo, *Nobiliario*, 471–472. Leonor de Cosgaya Antillón Beaumont y Navarra was the daughter of Alonso de Cosgaya (*fl.*1609–1639), a captain of the guards in Pamplona who died in the Wars of Flanders, and Ana de Antillón. It would appear, however, that Cosgaya was accused of bigamy as he had been married in San Sebastián before marrying Ana de Antillón. The military actions in which Cosgaya participated in Flanders are seen in *Varias Relaciones de los Estados de Flandes, 1631 á 1656* vol. 14 of *Colección de Libros Españoles. Raros ó Curiosos* (Madrid, 1880), 239, 243. References to the Hurtado de

Below the members of aristocratic and great families, was the group formed by the sons of military officers, government officials, and knights. The largest group was composed by the sons of militia regiment officers (Ibarra, Peralta Sanabria, Márquez de Mansilla, Ruiz de Berecedo). In most cases these were purely decorative, or at best, part-time royal commissions designed to raise and command militia units within the vice-royalty of Peru. The army's aristocratic tradition, however, gave lustre to less prestigious occupations: Ibarra's father, captain Gregorio de Ibarra y Ruiz de Loyoza, for example, earned his living in trade.[77] As sons of knights of Santiago, León Escandón and López de Eceiza were automatically part of the nobility class. Similarly, as the son and grandson of royal officials, as well as a magistrate in his own right, Francisco de Rojas Acevedo would have earned the right of hereditary transmissible nobility.[78] Many of these families reproduced the archetypical marriage unions of government officials and distinguished creoles. Márquez de Mansilla's mother was a Vásquez de Acuña, and thus a member of the extended family of the counts of Vega del Ren (1686).[79] At a more provincial level, Ruiz de Berecedo's mother belonged to the prestigious Del Pozo clan established in Concepción in Chile.[80]

Not all advocates and protectors-*fiscales* were members of elite families by birth. Other than the fact that Alberto de Acuña's father held a licentiateship degree, the parentage of advocates Cipriano de Medina and Diego Hurtado de Avendaño is not readily discoverable. Similarly, there is no precise information on the parentage of protectors Barrientos, Brun, Martínez de España, or Francisco de Valenzuela. In a society obsessed with lineage, the testaments of some of these men provide no hint to suggest other than common birth. This could even include, as in the case of Diego de León Pinelo (1608–71), Jewish descent. León Pinelo was born in Córdoba, in the audience of Charcas, to

---

Mendoza-Cosgaya marriage in 1607 are found in José Yanguas y Miranda, *Adiciones al diccionario de antiguedades de Navarra* (Pamplona, 1845), 205.

77 Kenneth J. Andrien, *Crisis and Decline: the viceroyalty of Peru in the seventeenth century.* (Albuquerque, 1985), 120.

78 Gregorio de Rojas Acevedo (1622–80), was a law professor at San Marcos and *fiscal* at the audience of Charcas (1678), and Pedro de Rojas Acevedo (1594–1642), was governor of Buenos Aires (1640).

79 See Rizo-Patrón, *Linaje*, 17, 74, 256.

80 This included Juana's great-grandfather Alonso del Pozo Silva (Seville), who moved to Santiago where he was depositario general (1605), Treasurer of Santa Cruzada (1606) and chancellor of the Real Audiencia (1609–45), and corregidor of Maule (1628); and great-uncle Fernando del Pozo y Lemos (1624–56), captain of the wars in Arauco, alcalde of Concepción and encomendero of Hualqui. See Espejo, *Nobiliario*, 157–158, 660–661.

Portuguese emigres who moved to the Vice-royalty of Peru in 1601. Both his paternal grandfather, and other relatives, were burnt at the stake as Judaisers by the Holy Office in Lisbon. Although his father entered into the priesthood in 1621 and became the trusted chaplain of Hernando Arias de Ugarte, archbishop of Lima (1630) and former *oidor* in the audiences of Panama (1595), Charcas (1597) and Lima (1603), the family was accused in 1637 before the Inquisition of Judaisers of practices against the Catholic Faith.[81]

By virtue of their studies and royal office, defensors, advocates and protectors were unified in the single social category of the Spanish Monarchy's *noblesse de robe*. From a social perspective this apparent unity was merely theoretical. In reality, protectorship officials belonged to diverse social circles. Some were part of the top echelon of prestige and distinction, comprised of families of *encomenderos* and, as from 1680, titled nobles. The power of this background often blurred a tarnished origin. Direct descent from the conquistador of New Biscay no doubt prompted Antonio de Ibarra to style himself 'gentleman hijodalgo' even if there were doubts about his own legitimacy.[82] Diego de León Pinelo, grandson of a Jewish convert, claimed the status encomendero for his family in his *relación de méritos*.[83] The title of marquis gave Pedro de Santiago Concha's family the lustre and prestige that their meritocratic origins lacked. The bulk of the institution, however, was composed of sons of untitled nobles, members of the military, magistrates, and minor bureaucrats. In many cases these were related to noble families. The social origin of the Peninsular officials is, on the other hand, largely unknown. Most of them acquired permanent citizenship in Lima, where their office provided them with a fitting social rank. However, as the following section proves, it was their marriage alliances which consolidated, and often heightened, their social position in the vice-regal capital.

81 The bibliography on the Leon bothers is legion. A guide to the various writings on this family is found in Juan E. Morón Orellana, *Antonio de León Pinelo* (Lima, 1993), 18–20. The transcripts of the accusations of 1637, which compiled testimonials undertaken in Buenos Aires, Charcas, Santiago del Estero, and Lima, are found in Ernesto de la Torre Villar, *Los pareceres de Juan de Padilla y Diego de León Pinelo acerca de la enseñanza y buen tratamiento de los indios* (Mexico, 1979), 55–65.

82 "[C]aballero hijodalgo de solar conocido, limpio de generación." See Porras Muñoz, "Diego de Ibarra," 48–78.

83 Torre Villar, *Pareceres*, 66.

Marriage and Networks

Marriage Alliances

There is evidence that at least two defensors, five advocates and ten protectors-*fiscales* of Indians married. This represents approximately fifty percent of protectors-*fiscales*, and seventy percent of advocates of Indians. Advocates were married between the ages of 23 and 29 years. Considering that the average age for entry to the royal colleges was 15, these unions either occurred soon after graduation, or early in their legal careers; thus virtually all were married before obtaining their royal appointments. In contrast, the ages of marriage of protectors-*fiscales* varied considerably. León Pinelo, Santiago Concha and Barrientos, for example, married in their mid-twenties; others, such as as Hurtado de Mendoza, Rojas and Lasso de la Vega, did so in their thirties. The marriage of Brun at 44 was not entirely unusual in the context of Bourbon's policy of discouraging marriages between royal bureaucrats and local women.[84] Considering the low life expectancy in eighteenth century Peru, the second marriages of Lasso de la Vega at 61 years of age, and Ruiz de Berecedo at 72 were perhaps exceptional.

The vast majority of the wives of these officials were born within the viceroyalty of Peru. With the exception of Alonso Torres de la Fresneda, who married a Spanish-born bride, all wives of defensors, advocates or protectors-*fiscales* were of creole birth. As seen in appendix 1 and Charts 1 and 2, the pattern of marriage that united Creole women to Spanish men was also repeated by many of the protectors' parents, daughters or nieces. In this respect, the family arrangements of advocates and protectors of Indians were no different to those of Peninsular-born audience magistrates or merchants who settled in Spanish America.[85]

Even if the sanctity of individual free will was zealously backed by the Catholic Church, the marriages of protectorship families were often carefully crafted alliances.[86] It would appear, for example that the main objective of the wealthy, albeit newly established, Santiago-Concha and Baquíjano clans was to

---

84 Manuel de Arredondo y Pelegrín (*c.*1738–1822), for example, married for the first time in 1797 at 59 years of age. After the death of his first wife, he became betrothed once again in 1804 at 64 years of age, but his bride died before a license was obtained from the Council of the Indies.

85 SeeBrading, Miners and Merchants, 348, Appendices 1–4; Socolow, The Merchants of Buenos Aires, 37–38; Kicza, Colonial entrepreneurs, 38–39.

86 The issue of free choice of vocation and spouse among individuals in seventeenth and eighteenth century Lima is discussed in Bianca Premo, *Children of the Father King: Youth, Authority and Legal Minority in Colonial Lima* (Chapel Hill, 2005), 60–68.

expand their patronage networks and power within the upper officialdom of vice-regal courts. Thus the direct family entourage of José de Baquíjano Carrillo included at least four ministers of the audiences of Lima and Charcas.[87] The 1734 marriage of protector-*fiscal* Pedro de Santiago-Concha made him the brother-in-law of an *oidor* in Santiago for more than three decades.[88] In turn, Melchor de Santiago Concha y Errazquín (1716–95), Pedro's half-brother, was an *oidor* in Santiago and Lima who married the daughter of the Marquis of Rocafuerte, president of the audience of Charcas. Both the Santiago-Concha Errazquín sisters married magistrates of the high court of Lima.[89] In turn, the marriage of advocate Cipriano de Medina's younger son to the daughter of a rich *mayorazgo*, alcalde of Lima, and descendant of one of Francisco Pizarro's companions, certainly matched the need of the rising Medina Vega clan to establish an alliance with an ancient lineage that would match their recent success in the academic, political and ecclesiastical spheres. The fact that the bride was a first cousin of the portentous archbishop Felicano de Vega y Padilla—who was the chief driving force behind the clan—also hints to the fact that this was a kin, rather than an individual, decision.[90]

In the case of older houses, family planning usually combined social prestige, power and wealth, depending on collective needs and wants. As members of an eminent but impoverished family, both of Pedro José Bravo de Lagunas's

87 Baquíjano was a nephew of José Casimiro Gómez García (†1761), *fiscal* of Charcas (1724–51) and *oidor* in Lima (1751–61). His sister Mariana married Jerónimo Manuel de Ruedas y Morales (†1779), *fiscal* (1769–75) and *oidor* (1776) in Lima and regent of Charcas (1776–79). His younger sister María Josefa was the daughter-in-law of the *oidor* and regent of Charcas (1807–13), Gaspar Antonio Remírez de Laredo (c.1748–1831), third count of San Javier and Casa Laredo. Her niece Rosa Ramírez de Arellano y Baquíjano married Gaspar Antonio de Osma (1775–1848), *alcalde del crimen* (1806–15) and *oidor* (1816–21) in Lima. See Lohmann, *Los ministros*, 49–50, 91–92, 115–116.

88 José Clemente Trasalviña y Oyagüe (1714–90) was *oidor* in Chile (1740–76). See Ibid., 34–35.

89 Juana Rosa de Santiago-Concha y Errazquín married José Antonio de Villalta y Núñez (1699–1775), *oidor* in Charcas (1729–38) and supernumerary *oidor* of Lima (1738). In turn, Josefa married Antonio Hermenegildo de Querejazu y Molinedo (1711–92), *oidor* in Lima from 1744 to 1791.

90 María Magdalena de Agüero was the daughter of José de Agüero y Bravo de Lagunas (1563–*fl.*1608), familiar of the Holy Office (1587), corregidor of Huaylas (1592), and alcalde of Lima (1600); granddaughter of Diego de Agüero Garay (*c.*1544–1618), alguacil del Holy Office (1571); and great-granddaughter of Diego de Agüero y Sandoval (1511–44). The mayorazgo of Agüero lasted until 1824. See Rizo-Patrón, *Linaje*, 50.

siblings married noble and rich partners.[91] This was also the case of the titled branches of the Híjar y Mendoza family (see Chart 2).[92] The Count of Villanueva del Soto's first wife was the daughter of a merchant, sister of the president of the audience Charcas, as well as aunt to an *oidor* in the audience of Lima.[93] By virtue of his three marriages, the count's first cousin, the seventh Marquis of San Miguel de Híjar, entered into useful political alliances, noble lineages, and substantial amounts of property and cash.[94] For Spanish-born officials marriage alliances were often the central plank to heightening their social standing. The most consummate expression in this respect was the spectacular marriage of Tomás de Brun, an Aragonese bureaucrat of unknown origins, to the great—and also, it would appear, generous—Catalina Isidora de Vargas Carvajal y

---

91 Grimanesa Bravo de Lagunas married Antonio de Bejarano Fernández de Córdova, second count of Villaseñor. The first Count of Villaseñor was described by Viceroy Caraciolo as someone 'with money and a hacienda,' see Balzo, "Familias nobles," 109. José Bravo de Lagunas married Ana de Zavala y Vásquez de Velasco. A detailed account of the Zavala Vásquez de Velasco estate is found in AGN, protocolos notariales s.XVIII, protocolo 647, Francisco Luque, 1784, fs.853ff. On the Vásquez de Velascos see Ferdinand de Trazegnies, "Los Vásquez de Velasco: Historia genealógica de una noble e ilustre familia española del Perú," *Histórica* 16 (1945), 7–41.

92 At the time of her death in 1744, the widow of the sixth Marquis of San Miguel de Híjar and third Count of Villanueva del Soto declared that her only goods were the oil paintings hanging in her house and three slaves. See AGN, Protocolo Notariales, PN 1148, Marcos de Uceda 1744, fs. 298v.–299v. The titles were inherited by his nephews protector-*fiscal* García José Lasso de la Vega and Fernando de la Fuente Rojas e Híjar. Details of this arrangement are found in BNP, ms. Z 253. Nonetheless, his mother was given a dowry agreed on 17 March 1704, see BNP, ms. Z 235.

93 María Francisca de Jáuregui Aguirre was sister to Domingo de Jáuregui Aguirre (1707–91), president of the audience Charcas, as well as aunt of Pablo de Olavide Jáuregui (1725–1803), *oidor* in the audience of Lima, writer and academic.

94 The three wives of Fernando de la Fuente Rojas e Híjar (fl.1743–76) were: María Antonia Cavero y Espinoza (married in 1743) daughter of Alvaro Cabero de Céspedes (1682–1739), *oidor* of Lima and Governor of Huancavelica, and his cousin Catalina de Espinoza y Medoza; Grimanesa Bejarano Bravo de Castilla (married, 1748), daughter of Antonio Bejarano Fernández de Córdova, second count of Villaseñor, and Teresa Bravo de Castilla, sister of Pedro José Bravo de Lagunas y Castilla; and Isabel Carrillo de Albornoz (1747–1817) (married in 1757), daughter of Diego Miguel de la Presa Carrillo de Albornoz (1695–1750), fourth count of Montemar, and Mariana Bravo de Lagunas y Villela (1705–1749), lady of the Castle of Mirabel. The Carrillo de Albornoz were one of the wealthiest noble families of Peru in the second half of the eighteenth century. See Bertrando del Balzo, "Familias nobles y destacadas del Perú en los informes secretos de un virrey napolitano (1715–1725)," *Revista del Instituto Peruano de Investigaciones Genealógicas* 14 (1965), 109. See Rizo-Patrón, *Linaje*, 76–78.

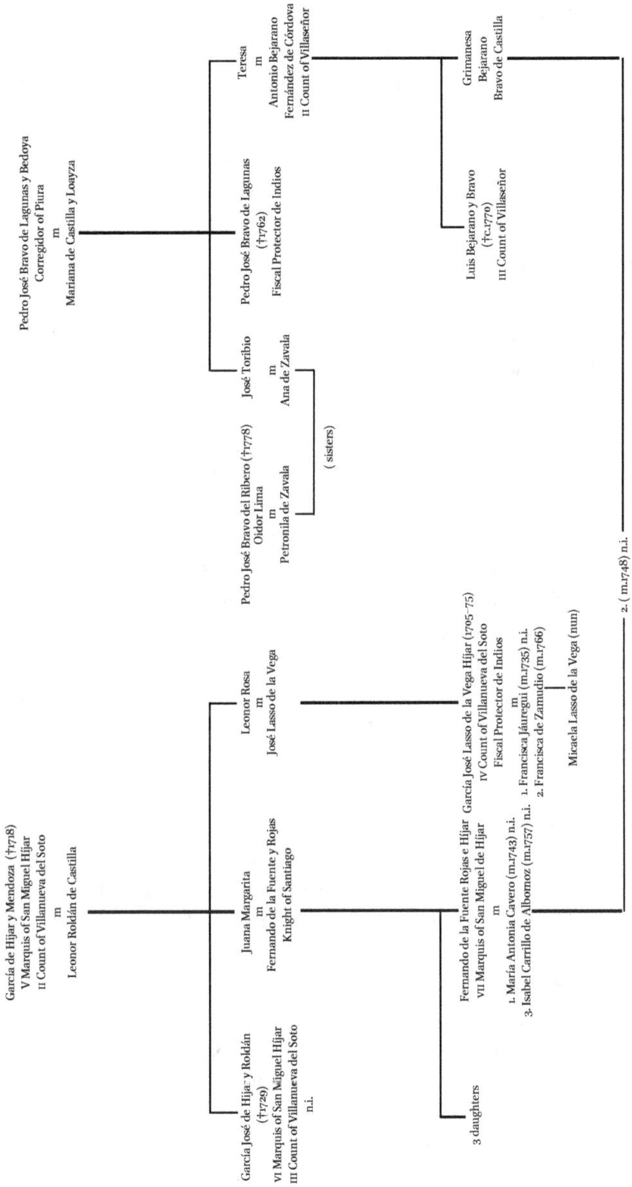

CHART 2 *Lasso de la Vega and Bravo de Lagunas: Ties between two Fiscal Protectors*

Hurtado de Quesada (1688–*c.*1759).[95] Besides the prestige this union brought to Brun, it would secure the titles of countess of El Puerto and Castillejo, their respective estate and entails, and the hereditary office of chief master of postal services of the Indies (*Correo Mayor de Indias*) for his only daughter, a dignity obtained by the Carvajal family in 1514.[96] Perhaps less aristocratic, but equally prestigious were the marriages of Alberto de Acuña into *encomendero* families of Lima, both of which possessed close ties with the city government. Through his first wife Acuña also became briefly related to two vice-regal secretaries of government.[97] On a humbler plane, the testament of Alonso Torres de la Fresneda, a Defensor General of Indians with no university education, reveals that his Spanish-born son married the daughter of licentiate Lerma, a citizen of Tucumán in Charcas.[98]

While marriage to the daughter of a high court magistrate may not have been an infallible road to success for protector-fiscal Francisco de Rojas

---

95 See AGN, protocolos notariales s. XVIII, protocolo 597, Francisco Luque, 1759, fs.1118v–1120. Catalina Isidora was the daughter of *Maestre de Campo* Diego Estaquio de Carvajal Vargas Marroquí (1651-c.1689) and his first cousin Magdalena Hurtado de Quesada (b.1664). Catalina Isidora's brothers were Diego Gregorio Joaquín Carvajal Vargas (1686-*c.*1731) (knight of Santiago, and Correo Mayor de Indias and Count of Castillejo) married to Constanza de la Cueva y Urdanegui, countess of Santa Lucía de Conchán and encomendera of Checras (Chancay); Josefa, married to García de Híjar, count of Villanueva del Soto and Marquis of San Miguel de Híjar. As Diego Gregorio died without issue, Catalina Isidora inherited the titles of Castillejo and the office of Correo Mayor. See Lohmann, *Los americanos* 1: 83; Alberto Rosas-Siles, "La nobleza Titulada del Virreinato del Perú," *Revista del Instituto Peruano de Investigaciones Genealógicas* 21 (1995), 367–372. Upon her death after a 'long and neat illness' ("larga y prolija enfermedad") on 24 March 1760, Catalina was described as someone in whom 'charity always shinned, in the many alms which which she socoured the poor' ("en quien resplandeció siempre la charidad en las muchas limosnas con que socorria a los pobres, y en concurrir a toda obra, que conducía a la piedad"). See *Gaceta de Lima de 1756–1762: De Superunda a Amat*, José Durand, ed. (Lima, 1982), 239–240.

96 Joaquina María Brun de Carvajal y Vargas married a close relative, Fermín Francisco de Carvajal y Vargas (1722–90) who would become the first duke of San Carlos. See Lohmann, *Los americanos* 1: 88; and Rosas-Siles, La nobleza, 47–56.

97 Lohmann, *Los ministros*, 151–152; Moreyra Paz Soldán, 134–135. His second wife was related to Sebastián Sánchez de Merlo, secretary to Governor Cristóbal Vaca de Castro (and also a *regidor* and encomendero), and to Alvaro Ruiz de Navamuel y de los Ríos (†1613), secretary of the government of Peru (*secretario mayor de gobernación*) for four decades.

98 Licenciate Lerma was married to Mariana de Quesada, and should not be confused with Hernando de Lerman, the founder of Salta. See the testament and last will of Juan Torres y Fresneda, AGN, Protocolos Notariales siglo XVII, protocolo 819, Francisco Hernández 1606–1608, fs. 312–313.

Acevedo, it was far from a hindrance. His network within the magistracy would have been consolidated through his sister's marriage to *oidor* Miguel Nuñez de Sanabria (1645–1729), who served forty years as *alcalde del crimen* and *oidor* of the audience of Lima (1686–1729) and regent of the vice-royalty (1710). Juan del Campo Godoy succeeded his father-in-law in the office of advocate of Indians. By virtue of his brother's marriage, Bravo de Lagunas became indirectly related to the powerful Pedro José Bravo del Ribero (1701–86), *oidor* in Lima for four decades (1735–78) (see Chart 2).[99] In turn, Esteban Marquez de Mansilla's father-in-law was the secretary to Viceroy Count of Lemos and inspector (*veedor*) of the Spanish Armada in the South Seas.[100]

Marriage was not always about social advancement. Diarist José de Mugaburu, for example, reports that the 1675 union between eighteen-year old José de Ortega y Oviedo and the daughter of protector-*fiscal* Alonso Hurtado de Mendoza, had been due to the couple's 'own desires' and because the bride was 'most beautiful.'[101] Lasso de la Vega's second marriage at 61 years of age to the daughter of the Marquises of Villar del Tajo gives the impression of being purely based on affectionate considerations, as does the union of Ruiz de Berecedo at 71 years of age. The fact that aristocratic women usually had more freedom to chose who they espoused in their second marriages could also suggest that the nuptials of Catalina Isidora de Vargas Carvajal—at the time the childless, but financially independent, widow of an aristocratic army general—with Brun had a more personal motivation.[102] On the other hand, there were many well balanced matches in wealth, hierarchy and honour amongst advocates and protectors. Santiago-Concha married into the equally aristocratic Traslaviña Oyagüe clan; the son of an audience magistrate, Rojas saw fit to wed the daughter of an *oidor*; it would also appear that the commoner but

99 In a 1780 dispatch during a visitation, José Antonio de Areche stated that Bravo del Ribero was one of the four creoles who effectively administered the vice-royalty of Perú. See Lohmann, *Los ministros*, XLIII. His vast estate is found in AGN, protocolos notariales s.XVIII, protocolo 649, Francisco Luque, 1786, fs. 405–480.

100 Lucía Francisca de Colmenares y Vega was sister of Sebastían Francisco de Colmenares y Vega, and was the first count of Polentinos (1716). The position of the Colmenares in vice-regal society was qualified by Santo Buono as being "principal" and was maintained until Independence. See Balzo, "Familias," 110; and Rizo-Patrón, *Linaje*, 235. For the economic position of the Rynagas see Chapter 5.

101 "[P]or su gusto, y por ser la desposada hermosísima." See José de Mugaburu and Francisco de Mugaburu, *Diario de Lima (1640–1694)*, vol. 2, ed. Carlos A. Romero (Lima, 1935), 188.

102 See, for example, Ellis Watson, *Aristocracy and the Modern World* (London, 2006), 62.

meritocratic Barrientos married a social equal in Petronila de Ardiles. The belief that marriage was an insoluble bond determined that couples stayed together throughout their lives, even if against their will. Bravo de la Laguna's mother, for example, complained that her husband 'violently forced' her into certain financial decisions.[103] The fact that a distant relative of Lasso de la Vega murdered his wife does not suggest a harmonious union.[104] In all cases, there are no hints to suggest if these were happy marriages or not.

Networks

Whether marriages were motivated by personal or collective interests, the resulting networks were tightly-knit units. Bravo de Lagunas, for example, named his niece's husband, the Marquis of San Miguel de Híjar, as executor of his will.[105] Similarly, Rojas appointed his brother-in-law, *oidor* Miguel Núñez de Sanabria, as executor.[106] In turn, he himself was appointed perpetual patron to the endowment established in 1703 in memory of Diego de León Pinelo, possibly by virtue of his marriage to his niece, María Andrea Correa de León Pinelo.[107] Thus, in the second half of the seventeenth century, the families of Rojas, León Pinelo and Peralta, became intertwined in a complex structure of kinship, patronage and alliances. The close ties forged between aristocratic families is exemplified in the 1756 report of the funeral of Manuel de Zavala Vásquez de Velasco held in the Church of La Merced, whereby the brother-in-law of the deceased, doctor Pedro José Bravo del Ribero (1701–86), is plainly referred to by *La Gaceta de Lima* as his 'brother.'[108]

The duration of these networks was often ephemeral. The vast majority of protectors-*fiscales* had no issue, and only a few marriages had children who survived into adulthood. Brun lost his male heir in childhood; Lasso de la Vega his four male sons. It is significant in this respect that none of the titled protectors were able to pass on their nobiliary dignities to their sons or daughters.

103 "[D]eclaro que las dichas obligaciones no las hice voluntariamente sino contra mi dictamen y forzada y violentada por el dicho mi marido y por no faltar a su respeto." AGN, protocolos notariales, pn 1165, Lázaro Fransico Moscoso 1681, f. 571.

104 In December 1659 Cristóbal de Híjar y Mendoza murdered his wife María Hurtado de Mendoza (not related to the protector-fiscal). See Mugaburu, *Diario de Lima*, 35.

105 AGN, protocolos notariales s.XVIII, protocolo 77, Orencio de Ascarrunz, 1751–52, fs.272v–73v.

106 AGN, protocolos notariales s. XVIII, protocolo 1116, Gregorio de Urtazo 1719, f. 592.

107 This was established by his wife María Ana Gutiérrez. The first beneficiary was Diego de León Pinelo Gutiérrez, *racionero* of the cathedral and uncle of Rojas. AGN, protocolos notariales s. XVIII, protocolo 1116, Gregorio de Urtazo 1719, f. 588.

108 *Gaceta de Lima de 1756–1762*, 21.

In fact, the titles of Lasso de la Vega and Ruiz Cano became extinct after their death.[109] Of the nineteen protectors-*fiscales*, the families of León Pinelo, Hurtado de Mendoza, Brun and Barrientos, surmounted the high mortality rates and had grandchildren. Among this group, however, only the Hurtado de Mendoza clan was able to fill the upper ranks of the university and city government for two successive generations; the most prominent of these being Diego Hurtado de Mendoza e Iturrizaga (1694–1742), a distinguished lawyer and academic.

There were also a significant number of officials who remained lifelong bachelors. In some cases, these were the younger sons of the nobility for whom no marriage alliances had been made. This could have been the case of Pedro José Bravo de Lagunas, whose older brother José Toribio married Ana de Zavala y Vásquez de Velasco. Other protectors entered the clergy, as did Alvaro de Ibarra; or were intended by their families to do so, as in the case of Baquíjano.[110] Bravo de Lagunas also took holy orders after retirement in 1759, when 55 years of age. It was not uncommon for unmarried magistrates to form liaisons with young women which led to the birth of illegitimate children. Alonso Maldonado de Silva, advocate of Indians in Charcas, for example, had one daughter of fourteen at the time of his death in 1651.[111] Similarly, Hurtado de Mendoza fathered a daughter, Josefa, before he married.[112]

In contrast, to the situation of protectors-*fiscales*, advocates of Indians produced families of competitive individuals who entered the upper ranks of the civil service and Church institutions. One of Medina's sons became a fiscal in the audience of Lima, and the other a professor of San Marcos and bishop of Huamanga. The son of Acuña was an *alcalde ordinario* and corregidor. Few Lima families, however, have produced more university trained administrators, judges, and ecclesiastics than the clan founded by Leandro de la Rynaga Salazar and Juana Cervera de Rivadeneira (see Chart 1).[113] Although Juan de la

109 For the title of Villanueva del Soto, see the opinion of Joseph de Rezabal y Ugarte, *Tratado del real derecho de las medias anatas seculares y del servicio de lanzas á que estan obligados los Títulos de Castilla. Origen de este juzgado en el Reino del Perú* (Madrid, 1792), 175.

110 Burkholder, *Baquíjano*, 20–21.

111 AGN, Protocolos Notariales, 1092, Francisco Medina 1651–53, f.208v–209. This was also the case of another audience magistrate, Manuel de Gorena y Beiria (†1774), oidor of the audience of Lima. See AGN, protocolos notariales, siglo XVIII, protocolo 169, Tomás Ignacio Camargo 1771–76fs. 571v.

112 AGN, PN 496, Diego Fernández Montaño 1692fs. 915.

113 The best account for the history of this family until the mid seventeenth century is Nicolás Matías del Campo y de la Rinaga, *Memorial y discurso informativo…Representa los*

Rynaga Salazar is often reputed to have been the most distinguished of Leandro's sons, his brothers were all scholars at the royal college of San Martín, who either entered the Augustinian order—where one became *calificador* of the Holy Office—or obtained vice-regal appointments as corregidors in important cities such as Huánuco or Moquegua. The Rynagas would gain further advancement with the marriage of Leandro's seventh daughter, María (†1672), to Juan del Campo Godoy, who succeeded his father-in-law in the advocacy of Indians. Both their son Nicolás Matías, author of the 1671 memorial on the protectorship of Indians, and their grandson José Clemente del Campo were ministers of American audiences. The family achieved its social pinnacle when a daughter of Nicolás Matías married the third count of Portillo in 1715. Although no descendants of Leandro would occupy audience posts after 1741, in the next half century the line of the Counts of Portillo produced a professor and rector of the University of San Marcos. The last descendant of Leandro de la Rynaga to occupy the rectorship of San Marcos left the position in 1808 (see Chart 1).[114]

Advocates and protectors of Indians were part of family networks of diverse nature. Those consisting of aristocratic families tended to be more diversified, and included a combination of wealth, power and prestige. In other cases, alliances were formed within the legal profession. Their collective interests often explain marriage patterns. External causes, such as high mortality rates, affected the continuation of these networks over more than one generation. However, whenever families surmounted the threshold of infant mortality, they either emerged in the next generation occupying the same positions as their forbears, or gained further advancement in rank and honour.

The vast majority of Advocates and Protectors of Indians were born in the Vice-royalty of Peru. Among the officials of Peninsular origin, available evidence suggests that all but one became permanent residents of the city of Lima. With a few exceptions, geographical movement was almost entirely one way. Advocates and Protectors were all respectable members of society. Their

estudios, y ocupaciones propias en servicio de su Magestad; y las del Doctor Iuan Bautista del Campo y de la Rinaga, su hermano, cura rector de la Villa de Huancabelica...Informa la nobleza, y servicio de sus padres (Madrid, 1668). For a genealogical study of the Rynaga Salazar family in the 16th and 17th centuries see Guillermo Lohmann Villena, *Amarilis Indiana: Identificación y semblanza* (Lima, 1993), § 5, 329–342.

114 Nicolás Cayetano Sarmiento de Sotomayor y Haro (†*c.*1796), fifth count of Portillo and sergeant major of the noble regiment of cavalry in Lima, was rector of San Marcos between 1787 and 1790. His nephew, Francisco de Oyagüe y Sarmiento de Sotomayor (†1818), was professor of Prime of Canon Law, as well as rector of the university (1805–08). The testament of Nicolás Cayetano is found in AGN, Protocolos Notariales s.XVIII, protocolo 90, escribano Ignacio Ayllón Salazar, 1796, 2 January 1796, f.330–31v.

respectability, however, emanated from a variety of sources. Most of these officials claimed some connection to conquistador or *encomendero* families; others were members of the upper tiers of vice-regal officialdom; a few were part of the titled nobility. In addition to this, social status was also acquired through royal office, and could be increased by the possession of a law degree or a convenient marriage alliance.

By possessing one or more of these characteristics, advocates and protectors of Indians were members of a distinct urban elite which, for the most part, was composed of a fusion of *encomenderos*, magistrates, merchants, landowners and old aristocrats. Among the protectorship officers themselves, this ongoing class dialectic explains the considerable social mobility that existed among those of European descent in the cities of the vice-royalty of Peru. Therefore, the appointment of the grandson of a Jewish convert as a university professor and audience minister, or the marriage of a commoner Aragonese magistrate to one of the most aristocratic clans in Peru, were not entirely exceptional. Yet the personal standing attained by academic or governmental honours alone cannot blur the social differences that existed between the son of a mayorazgo and a newly appointed *fiscal* of the audience.

The general tendency amongst the officials was to marry local brides. Peninsular born advocates or protectors thus followed a trend which counts a myriad of examples among Spanish-born bureaucrats. Married or not, the position of these men also placed them in, or indeed exercising control over, elaborate networks of patronage and power. These were often the result of deliberate strategies, as in the case of most aristocratic families, or of education, as in the case of *letrado* dynasties. There was also the unforeseen. It is difficult to believe that an aspiring young lawyer such as Medina would have predicted the spectacular rise of his portentous brother-in-law, who was only six years old at the time of his marriage. Even if these networks seldom survived more than one generation, they could wield a considerable de facto authority within many spheres of vice-regal society. Status may not have been the reason for the successful careers of many protectors, but the access to powerful officials, merchants or academics that came with it would have been far from a hindrance.

CHAPTER 4

Advancement and Careers

In his *relación de méritos* of 1715 Francisco Ruiz de Berecedo stated that the 'ministry' of the protectorship of Indians 'was one the gravest, and more burdensome.'[1] This chapter examines the careers of the Defensors General, Advocates and Fiscales of Indians. Although Tables 1, 2 and 3 summarize the findings of this chapter, its chief purpose is to provide an overview of the involvement of protectorship officials in viceregal administration, government and jurisdictional courts. After discussing bureaucratic parcours of the non-*letrado* Defensors General appointed until 1640, it moves on to analyse the career paths of the legal professionals appointed as advocates and protectors-*fiscales*. It aims to demonstrate how these professionals used their position as protectors as a step towards further influence and how they built true family-bureaucratic networks. In all cases, details of the careers and social networks of these audience magistrates were provided by notarial records, *relaciones de servicio*, and official documentation.[2]

Defensors General (1575–1640)

The careers of Defensors General of Indians did not follow a discernible pattern. Evidence suggests that they occupied positions in judicial, taxation and military institutions. Existing documentation in Peru provides no evidence that Defensors General of Indians were matriculated as students of the royal colleges, nor graduated from the University of San Marcos; dossiers, on the other hand, bear no reference to usage of academic degrees in lawsuits, despite

1 "[L]e nombró el Presidente Don Francisco Ibañez de Peralta, por Protector General de Indios de aquel Reyno; cuyo ministerio es de los mas graves, y pesados, assi en la defensa de los indios en todos los Tribunales Eclesiasticos, y Seculares, como en el Juzgado de Censos de Indios." "Relacion de los grados y servicios del Licenciado Don Francisco Ruiz y Berecedo, Protector Fiscal de el distrito de la Audiencia del Reyno de Chile," Biblioteca Nacional de Chile, Manuscrito Medina, vol. 23, pieza 23.

2 Biographies added together include both too much and too little. On the origins, limitations and achievements of this mode of enquiry see Lawrence Stone, "Prosopography," *Daedalus, Journal of the American Academy of Arts and Sciences* 100 (1) (1970), 46–79.

 | DOI 10.1163/9789004305175_006

this being the usual practice in the Spanish Monarchy.[3] As stated earlier, the 1575 provisions by Viceroy Toledo established that Defensors General should be men of *capa y espada*, that is, gentlemen.[4] With the exception of the magistrates of the high courts of justice or audiences, a university degree was not a requirement to hold jurisdictional magistracies in the Spanish Monarchy until the second half of the eighteenth century.[5] Thus, despite the fact that viceroys of Peru and New Spain presided over the audience and held important jurisdictional powers they were not required to be *letrados*.[6] This was neither an impediment for corregidors, who constituted the highest jurisdictional authorities in provinces. In fact, *corregimientos*, as explained below, constituted the usual appointments for members of the vice-regal entourage which, until the eighteenth century, was largely composed of men of *capa y espada*, and not of letters.[7] The lack of a university degree, therefore, circumscribed the careers of defensors to non-*letrado* positions.

Not all defensors pursued a bureaucratic career. It would appear, for example, that Antonio Heredia (DGI 1590), secretary to Viceroy García Hurtado de Mendoza (*v.*1589–1596), held no other official post after the defensorship of Indians.[8] Similarly, Carrasco del Saz (DGI 1635), who arrived in the Indies

3 See "Catálogo de los Colegiales que hubo en el Real Colegio de San Martín desde el día 10 de agosto de 1582, en que se fundó siendo virrey don Martín Henríquez, hasta que 12 de enero 1771, y que se transfirio por el virrey don Manuel Amat al noviciado de los regulares de la compañía con el título de convictorio carolino," in Luis Antonio Eguiguren, *Diccionario histórico cronológico de la Real y Pontificia Universidad de San Marcos y sus colegios: Crónica e investigación*, 3 vols. (Lima, 1940–51), 2, 135–255; "Cuaderno de Grado de Bachiller, 1571–1664," Universidad Nacional Mayor de San Marcos, Archivo Histórico Domingo Angulo and "Actas de Grados," Universidad Nacional Mayor de San Marcos, Secretaría General, caja 17 (705).

4 Francisco de Toledo, *Disposiciones gubernativas para el virreinato del Perú*, ed. Maria Justina Sarabia Viejo (Sevilla, 1986–89) 2: 103ff.

5 Whereas high court appointments required a university degree, until the early eighteenth century it was not a necessary condition to be a graduate in Laws. See Tamar Herzog, "¿Letrado o teólogo? Sobre el oficio de la Justicia a principios del siglo XVIII," in *Fallstudien zur spanischen und portugiesischen Jutiz 15.bis 20. Jahrhundert*, ed. Johannes Michael Scholz, Rechtsprechung Materielen und Studien Veröffentlichungen des Max Planck Instituts für Europäische Rechtsgeschichte Frankfurt am Main 8 (Frankfurt am Main, 1994).

6 Juan de Solórzano explained the advantages of having a university trained viceroy. *Política Indiana*, eds. Francisco Tomás y Valiente and Ana María Barrero (Madrid, 1996), 5.12.12.

7 Studies on this matter are scarce, but a list of the 113 people who composed the entourage of Viceroy Count of Lemos is found in Guillermo Lohmann Villena, *El Conde de Lemos: Virrey del Perú* (Madrid, 1946), 28–31. Most of them consisted of military personnel.

8 Roberto Levillier, ed., *Gobernantes del Perú: Cartas y Papeles, siglo XVI*, 14 vols. (Madrid, 1921–26), 14: 63, 164, 234.

(1606) as part of the entourage of Juan de Loayza Calderón, oidor of Charcas and Lima, held the post after a stint as Defensor General in Charcas.[9]

For others the defensorship constituted an initial step in their careers in the vice-regal bureaucracy, eventually leading to *corregimiento* positions. After his tenure as defensor, Baltazar de la Cruz y Aspetia (*fl.*1594) was appointed corregidor of Canta by the Count of Villar dom Pardo in 1589, and corregidor of Tarma and Chincha by Hurtado de Mendoza—Villar's successor—in 1594. In this period Cruz was also considered as a candidate for the post of defensor by Hurtado de Mendoza when the office was reinstated in 1590; but it is unclear if he was elected or declined the offer.[10] Similarly, two years after serving as Defensor, Antonio Torres de la Fresneda (DGI 1597) was appointed corregidor of Andahuaylas in 1599 by Viceroy Luis de Velasco (*v.*1596–1604). From this position, he secured a post in the government of the city of Lima, where he was elected by councillors of the *cabildo* as supletory administrator of *alcabalas*, a sales tax for real estate, in 1603.[11] Torres de la Fresneda, however, maintained personal connections with royal officials such as Perafán de Ribera, corregidor of Huamalíes, to whom he was bondsman.[12]

Some Defensors General of Indians were already experienced officials in the vice-regal administration at the time of their appointments. The credentials of Pedro Balaguer de Salcedo (1545–*c.*1605), for example, can be traced to before his arrival in Peru. During this period he was Secretary of the University of Alcalá, and secretary and accountant for Francisco Zapata de Cisneros y Ossorio (*fl.*1550–85), first Count of Barajas, corregidor of Córdova, majordomo to Queen Ana of Austria (1579), president of the Royal Council of Castile (1585) and member of the Councils of State and War (1585).[13] Once in Peru he was named to organise the system of *chasquis*, the postal service (1590), and eventually rented the office of

9 See Lohmann, "Francisco Carrasco del Saz, jurisconsulto y tratadista," 168. Oidor Loayza Calderón was married to Mariana de Quiñones y Mogrovejo, niece of St. Turibius de Mogrovejo (1538–1606), Archbishop of Lima.

10 See Carmen Ruigómez Gómez, *Una política indigenista de los Habsburgo: el Protector de Indios en el Perú* (Madrid, 1988), 70. The appointments of Cruz as corregidor are found in *Libros de Cabildos de Lima*, ed. Juan Bromley (Lima, 1935–67) 11: 95–100; 12: 89–99.

11 The other candidate was the current administrator, Diego Núñez de Figueroa. *Libros de Cabildos de Lima*, 13: 227; 14: 484, 489–490.

12 *Libros de Cabildos*, 14: 490.

13 See Guillermo Lohmann, *Los americanos en la órdenes nobiliarias*, 2nd ed. (Madrid, 1993), 1: 119. A biography of Zapata de Cisneros is found in Luis Vilar y Pascual, *Diccionario histórico, genealógico y heráldico de las familias ilustres de la monarquía española* vol. 2 (Madrid, 1859), 451–52. His son was Antonio Zapata de Cisneros (1550–1635), bishop of

Correo Mayor de Indias (1595) to the widow of Diego de Vargas Carvajal (†1593).[14] On the direct instructions of Viceroy García Hurtado de Mendoza, fourth marquis of Cañete (*v.*1590–95), Balaguer also participated in military action against the incursions of Richard Hawkings in Lima and Valparaíso (1594). He was further appointed corregidor of El Cercado, official of the Royal Treasury (Cajas Reales) of Lima, and familiar of the Holy Office (1597–1601).[15] Evidence of his dealings as procurator for the Villa Rica de Oropesa in Huancavelica, and a request to the audience of Lima to travel to Spain to pursue trade (1588) suggest that Balaguer de Salcedo was also active in business.[16]

Perhaps slightly extraordinary, but exemplary nonetheless, was the career of Domingo de Luna (*fl.*1595–33). After serving as advisor to the Count of Monterrey in his governments in Mexico (1595–1603) and Peru (1604–6),[17] he successfully held the positions of corregidor of Indians in El Cercado, Lima (1606); visitation judge (*juez visitador*) in sixteen *corregimientos* in Cusco, Arequipa and Arica; and visitor of Indian *reducciones* (1608). In 1621 he was appointed judge of land (*composición de tierras*) in the valley of Carabayllo in Lima and administrator of Censos of Indians.[18] His appointment as Defensor General of Indians in 1633 was, therefore, the last position he held in colonial administration.

It thus becomes apparent that one of the main characteristics of the career paths of Defensors General between 1575 and 1640 was the exercise of *corregimiento* positions. Corregidors were invested with administrative, military and judicial authority within the territorial subdivisions of the royal audience in the vice-royalty of Peru. In this respect, they presided over a retinue of civil lieutenants (*tenientes*), Indian alcades, notaries (*escribanos*), sheriffs (*alguaciles*),

---

Cádiz, Pamplona and Burgos, Cardinal in the Catholic Church, councillor of State for Philip III, viceroy of Naples and Inquisitor General.

14 See Julio César Ponce Lozada, *Las comunicaciones en el Virreynato del Perú: siglos XVI, XVII y XVIII* (n.p., 2004), 46–47.

15 Paulino Castañeda Delgado and Pilar Hernández Aparicio, *La Inquisición de Lima: 1570–1635*, vol. 1 (Madrid, Deimos), 27.

16 See, respectively, García Hurtado de Mendoza to Philip II, Callao, 1 May 1590, Levillier, *Gobernantes*, 12: 1590; provision of 21 November 1590 by the viceroy Marquis of Cañete. Lilly Latin American mss. Peru, 1590, Nov. 21, f. 1; García Hurtado de Mendoza to secretary Juan de Ibarra, Lima 19 August 1594, Levillier, *Gobernantes*, 13: 188–93; and Archivo General de Indias, Indiferente, 2097, N.183, f.1. Available at http://pares.mcu.es.

17 Eguiguren, *Diccionario*, 1: 389.

18 See, respectively, Real Cédula of 4 February 1606 by Count of Monterrey in *Libros de Cabildos de Lima*, 15: 29–33; Luis Miguel Glave, *De rosa y espinas: Economía, sociedad y mentalidades andinas, siglo XVII* (Lima, 1998), 37–41; and Eguiguren, *Diccionario*, 2: 960.

TABLE 1 *Protectors general of indians 1529–1635.*

Year	Name	Origin	University	Audiencia posts	Other posts	Entourage
1529–34	Hernando de Luque (†1534)	P	?	—	Bishop of Tumbes (1529–34)	Francisco Pizarro
1530	Gabriel de Rojas	P	No	—	—	Francisco Pizarro
1538–41	Vicente de Valverde (†1541)	P	Salamanca	—	Bishop of Cuzco (1538–41)	Francisco Pizarro
1546–54	Jerónimo de Loayza (†1575)	P	Sevilla, Valladolid	—	Archbishop of Lima (1543–75)	—
1554–75	Fiscal of Real Audiencia					
1575–89	Baltazar de la Cruz y de Aspeitia	P	—	—	Advisor to Viceroy Corregidor Canta (1589) Corregidor Chincha (1594)	Toledo Villar dom Pardo G. Hurtado de Mendoza
1590	Antonio Heredia	P?	?	—	Secretary to Viceroy	G. Hurtado de Mendoza
1597–1605	Antonio Torres de la Fresneda (†1619)	P	?	—	Corregidor Andahuaylas (1599)	Velasco
1603	Pedro Balaguer de Salcedo (†c.1605)	?	?	—	Corregidor Cercado Oficial Real Military Familiar Santo Oficio	G. Hurtado de Mendoza Velasco
1630–33	Domingo de Luna	P?	?	—	Tesorero (1604) Corregidor JGI Cercado (1606) Juez Visitador (1608)	Monterrey
1635	Francisco Carrasco del Saz (†1639)	P	?	—	PGI Potosí	Oid. Juan Loayza Calderón (Charcas)

P: Peninsular; C: Creole; JGI: Juzgado General de Indios; PGI: Protector General de Indios.

SOURCES: AGN, BNP, LEVILLIER 1921–26, LIBRO DE CABILDOS DE LIMA, LILLY, LOHMANN 1974, LOHMANN 1983, LOHMANN 19992000, SALINAS 1957.

interpreters, tax collectors and other minor officials.[19] The accumulation of power, as well as extended ill practices such as the forced sale of goods to Indians, resulted in permanent criticism of corregidors throughout the vice-regal period.[20] Among the countless testimonies of abuses by corregidors, Guamán Poma de Ayala, for example, considered that these officials should be blamed for 'great damages to these Kingdoms of Peru.'[21] In the eighteenth century these critics also included members of the protectorship of Indians, such as the anonymous Procurator General of Indians of Peru, who considered corregidors 'absolute lords' who inflicted countless damage, including forced sales, abusive administration of justice, and coercive work on Indians and Caciques.[22]

The importance of *corregimientos*, however, depended on territorial extension, population and economic performance. Balaguer de Salcedo and Luna, for example, were appointed corregidors of Indians of El Cercado in Lima. This was a jurisdictional district within Lima created in 1590, with autonomy from the authority of the city's *alcaldes ordinarios*. This judicial district consisted of thirteen *repartimientos* within a radius of 20 kilometres from the city of Lima which, in 1602, had a total population of approximately 1,780 people, including 490 tributaries.[23] As corregidors of El Cercado, these officials also presided over the General Indian Court (Juzgado General de Indios), an Indian tribunal with extended jurisdiction in civil and criminal matters established in 1603 by

---

19 Guillermo Lohmann Villena, *El Corregidor de indios en el Perú bajo los Austrias* (Madrid, 1957), 437–454.

20 The standby texts on this institution in Peru remain Lohmann, Corregidor, and Alfredo Moreno Cebrián, *El Corregidor de Indios y la economía peruana en el siglo XVIII* (Madrid, 1977). In a recent study, however, Jeremy Baskes argues that the repartimiento was designed to facilitate contract enforcement and economize on transaction costs in cross-cultural trade and, as result, served in its expansion. Jeremy Baskes, *Indians, merchants, and markets: a reinterpretation of the Repartimiento and Spanish-Indian economic relations in colonial Oaxaca, 1750–1821* (Stanford, 2000).

21 "A resultado muy grandes daños en estos rreynos del Pirú. Y al cabo salen del corregimiento con hazienda de mas de cinqüenta mil pesos a la costa y daños de los pobres yndios de todo este rreyno." Felipe Gumán Poma de Ayala, *El primer nueva corónica y buen gobierno de Felipe Guaman Poma de Ayala*, eds. John V. Murra and Rolena Adorno (1616; México, 1980), §489 vol. 2: 454, §484, p. 453. See also Solórzano, *Política Indiana*, 5.2.24–28.

22 Procurador y Diputado General…de Indios, *Manifiesto de los agravios, bexaciones y molestias, que padecen los Indios del Reyno del Peru* (N.p., n.e. [1731]), *passim*.

23 The repartimientos were Guancayo, Comas-Carabaillo, Surco, Puruchuco, Lati, Chuquitanta, Maringa-Guatca, Magdalena, Lurigancho, Pachacamac, Guanchoguaylas, and Cacahuasi. See Noble David Cook, "Population Data for Indian Peru: Sixteenth and Seventeenth Centuries, " *Hispanic American Historical Review* 62 (1) (1982), 83–84.

Viceroy Luis de Velasco (*v.*1596–1604) by recommendation of Balaguer de Salcedo.[24] For the Jesuit chronicler Bernabé Cobo (1580–1657), the court's ultimate aim was to expedite justice in all cases of Indians living in the Cercado of Lima, the City of Lima and its province, and to the numerous non-resident Indians who flocked to Lima from all parts of Peru.[25]

A different case is that of Torres de la Fresneda who, as Corregidor, was responsible for the six repartimientos in Andahuaylas, an outpost in the Southern highlands. In 1573 his jurisdiction comprised a population of approximately 36,275 people, including 6,836 tributaries.[26] However, under-capitalised sugar estates, subsistence agriculture and isolation made Andahuaylas one of the poorest provinces in Peru—an observation still valid today.[27] A report issued during the government of the Prince of Squilace, for instance, noted how the tax levied could not even cover the salary of 1,000 pesos per annum assigned to the corregidor.[28] On the other hand, it would appear that the economies of the *corregimientos* of Canta and Chincha granted to Baltazar de la Cruz were more integrated to Lima and, therefore, more prosperous. Canta, for example, had a population estimated in 1589–91 at 10,053 people, including 2,511 tributaries, but was the main supplier of snow to Lima.[29] Similarly, even if Chincha contained only one repartimiento of Indians, it had a strategic position as a

24 See "Testimonio de los autos seguidos por Don Antonio Berzosa, corregidor del cercado de Lima, contra el Alcalde Ordinario, sobre la jurisdicción en el conocimiento de las causas de los indios…," AGN GO-BI 5, leg. 139, c.100, fs. 9v–12v. On the General Indian Court see Woodrow Borah, "Juzgado general de indios del Perú o juzgado particular de indios del cercado de Lima," *Revista chilena de Historia del Derecho* 6 (1970), 129–142.

25 Bernabé Cobo, "Fundación de Lima, escripta por el P. Bernabé Cobo de la Compañía de Jesus. Año de 1639," in *Obras del P. Bernabé Cobo*, BAE 91–92 (Madrid, 1956), 2: 349–350. The court was still functioning in the decade of 1790 near the royal hospital of Santa Ana and, if the 1793 complaints of the court's notary are true, it dealt with a significant number of legal disputes. See BNP ms. C 3396, fs. 1–2, 4v.

26 Cook, *Population*, 100–101.

27 In Concolorcorvo or Alfonso Carrió de la Vandera (1715–83) would state that even the landowners in Andahuaylas were people of 'little economy, or that the haciendas, in reality did not cover their costs' ("Parece que los dueños de estas haciendas son personas de poca economía, o que las haciendas, en la realidad, no se costean, porque a los cañaverales llaman engañaverales y a los trapiches trampiches"). See Concolorcorvo, *El lazarillo de ciegos caminantes desde Buenos Aires hasta Lima, 1773* (Buenos Aires, 1942), 345.

28 Lohmann, *Corregidor*, 161.

29 Cook, *Population*, 83; Rubén Vargas Ugarte, S.J., *Historia General del Perú*, vol. 3 *Virreinato (1596–1689)* (Lima, 1966), 261.

storage location for mercury before it was delivered to the mines of the southern Andes.[30]

By holding *corregimiento* positions defensors acquired some knowledge of finances, considering they were liable for the collection of Indian and sales taxes, and administered the Indians' community funds (Cajas de Comunidad); both duties subject to strict control norms.[31] It would also appear that many were well-versed in fiscal matters and accountancy skills. Balaguer, for example, not only was the accountant for a grandee in Spain, but also a prominent businessman and official of the Royal Treasury. Luna was treasurer to the Indian court of El Cercado prior to his appointment as corregidor.[32] These skills come of use when Defensors General of Indians exercised a degree of control in the administration of Indian community funds. Francisco Carrasco del Saz, for example, was appointed by the Count of Monterrey to review the accounts of Diego Gil de Avís, who was Depositario General of Censos of Indians in Lima until 1606.[33]

The careers of Defensors General of Indians suggest that, although some held significant posts within the vice-regal government, there is no evidence that they obtained *ascenso* or promotion through a hierarchy of bureaucratic offices. Instead, it would appear that their careers remained in the sphere of local government. Corregidors and defensors were highly compatible positions, due to their responsibilities in Indian affairs.[34] This would explain why the officials studied in this section moved from one position to the other with apparent ease. The appointments that shaped the defensors' careers were also dependent on personal and political alliances with the viceroy. Even if these alliances provided many defensors with considerable experience in the intricacies of Colonial administration, ambition to occupy the upper echelons of vice-regal power was curtailed by their lack of an academic degree. In this respect, these officials would soon be outweighed in influence by those who

30 Vargas Ugarte, *Historia*, 228; Lohmann, *Corregidor*, 239.

31 Lohmann, *El Corregidor*, 330–331.

32 *Libro de Cabildos*, 15: 30.

33 See "Petición presentada por el oydor Carrasco del Saz, para que cite a Francisco de Avendaño, Procurador General de los Naturales del Perú a que presencia la toma de cuentas de los hijos de Diego Gil Davis, Los Reyes 29 de julio 1606," BNP, mss. B19, fs.1–3AGN, Derecho Indígena, leg. 31, c.619 (1589), fs. 1–3; and Derecho Indígena, leg.3, c.31; leg. 39, c.793 (1596).

34 Ordinances §XVII and XIX established that they had a well defined role in supervising the treatment local authorities gave to Indians. See Francisco de Toledo, *Disposiciones gubernativas para el virreinato del Perú*, ed. Maria Justina Sarabia Viejo (Sevilla, 1986–89), vol. 2.

held *letrado* positions within the defensorship: the advocates and protectors-*fiscales* of Indians.

The *Letrados*: Advocates and Protectors-*Fiscales* of Indians (1593–1781)

University Studies

The *letrados* or university graduates were a key element in the functioning of the protectorship of Indians. Since it began fully operating in the decade of 1590, the institution had a university-trained official to represent Indian plaintiffs in accordance with the Ordinances of 1575 and the royal decree of 1563 establishing that only those in possession of a university degree could be admitted in the audiences to exercise advocacy.[35] This role was initially undertaken by the Advocate of Indians who performed these duties between 1593 and 1640. From 1640 onwards, however, the representation of Indian lawsuits would be assumed by the Defensor General as a consequence of the office gaining the full or honorary position of *fiscal*.

Between 1593 and 1781, a total of 26 *letrados* held protectorship offices at the Royal Audience of Lima either as advocates (8) or protectors-*fiscales* (18) (see Tables 2, 3 and 4). With the exception of Antonio de Ibarra, who had a bachelor degree in canon law from the University of Mexico, all advocates of Indians possessed at least one of their degrees from the University of San Marcos.[36] Similarly, the proportion of protectors-*fiscales* in office between 1643 and 1781 with degrees obtained in universities other than San Marcos is minimal. Although Diego de León Pinelo and Alonso Hurtado de Mendoza obtained their bachelor degrees from Salamanca, they would both undertake doctoral studies at San Marcos. Similarly, Francisco Ruiz de Berecedo, a master of Arts and doctor of Theology from the Jesuit college of Santiago, obtained his licentiate in Laws in Lima. Thus, of the eighteen protector-*fiscales* in office during this period, only Tomás de Brun, a doctor in Laws by the University of Huesca, did not undertake any studies in San Marcos. An overview of the law graduates

35 Antonio de León Pinelo, *Recopilación de las Indias*, ed. Ismael Sánchez Bella (Mexico, 1992), 5.8.66 (2: 1470). In general the dispositions of Indian Law for advocates were few and referred mostly to ethical principles, as found also in León Pinelo, 5.9.1–11.

36 For the case of Ibarra see AGI, Mexico, 220, N.20, fs.1–20; available at http//.aer.mcu.es, cod. ES.41091.AGI/16403.13.22/ Mexico, 220, N.20; and "Causas sobre el cacicazgo del Pueblo de Quinti. Huaman Chata, Miguel et. al." Lilly Latin American mss. Peru, 1596, Aug.23—1626, Mar.13, fs. 43–43v.

from San Marcos, therefore, provide an excellent framework to establish career paths for protectorship officials.

Legal studies in Lima began in 1571–76 when Viceroy Francisco de Toledo established and endowed five chairs for the teaching of law at the University of San Marcos: Prime and Vespers of Laws, Prime and Vespers of Canon Law and Institute. The first appointee to the professorships of Institute, and Prime and Vespers of Laws was Jerónimo López Guarnido (1525–96) in 1571, followed by Fernán Vásquez de Fajardo (1534–97) for the professorship of Prime of Canon Law in 1575.[37] The chair of Institute was envisaged as an introduction to Roman Civil Law, as this text covered the essential parts of the law of persons, things, inheritances, obligations and actions. Professors of Laws read the *Infortiatum* (books 24 to 38 of the Digest) and the *Digestum Novum* (books 39 to 50 of the Digest). In turn, the teaching of Canon Law included the *Decretales*, *Sextum* and the *Clementinas*, thus covering the core of ecclesiastical dispositions issued until the fourteenth century.[38]

Evidence is somewhat fragmentary, but it appears that Canon Law was the preferred subject of study among law students in Lima during the seventeenth and eighteenth centuries. A 1694 account of the royal college of San Martín reveals, for example, that 47 percent of the students were matriculated in canon law, and only 6 percent did so in Civil Law.[39] Following this trend, dossiers of lawyers admitted to the Real Audiencia of Lima between 1648 and 1770 evidence that only Manuel de la Bodega Cuadra y Mollinedo (1752–*fl.*1789), a *colegial* of San Martín and future *oidor* in Guatemala, declared not to have studied canon law.[40]

The preference for Canon Law is also reflected in the course of study selected by both advocates and protector-*fiscales* of Indians. In the first case, Medina, Sosa, Hurtado de Avendaño, and Maldonado de Silva were all doctors in canon law; Rynaga was professor of prime and dean of the faculty of canon law; and Acuña, Medina and Del Campo were all lecturers in this subject. In the case of protector-*fiscales*, León Pinelo, Peralta, Ruiz de Berecedo, Bravo de Legunas and León Escandón had degrees in canon law; and León Pinelo, Ruiz de Berecedo, Barrientos and Bravo de Lagunas were professors in this subject.

37 Luis Antonio Eguiguren, *La universidad en el siglo XVI*, 1 vol. in 2 books of *Historia de la Universidad* [San Marcos] (Lima, 1951), 1: 494, 475.

38 Luis Antonio Eguiguren, *Catálogo Histórico del Claustro de la Universidad de San Marcos, 1576–1800* (Lima, 1912), 23–43; Francisco Javier Alejo Montes, *La universidad de Salamanca bajo Felipe II: 1575–1598* ([Burgos], 1998), 117–120, 243.

39 Real Colegio de San Martín, *Parnaso*, passim.

40 AGN, Grados de Abogados, leg. 1, exp. 51, fs.1–1v.

TABLE 2 *Abogados de indios in the* Memorial Histórico *of Nicolás Del Campo, 1671.*

Year	Name	University	Academic career	Audiencia posts	Other posts	Entourage
1590–1597	Alberto de Acuña (Jaen (Spain), 1565-Lima, 1630)	B. Laws, Salamanca Licenciate, Seville Dr. Laws, SM	Prof. Vespers of Canon Law (1589)	Oidor Panama (1598–1602) Oidor Quito (1602–3) A. Crimen Lima (1604–7) Oidor Lima (1607–25, 1628–30) Pres. Guadalajara (1625) (elect)	Viceregal Advisor (Villar dom Pardo) Advisor Tribunal Santa Cruzada Probate Judge Land Judge (1595)	Villar dom Pardo Velasco
1593–*fl.*1626	Cipriano de Medina (Seville, *c.* 1559–Lima, 1635)	Licenciate (Seville?) Dr. Canon Law, SM	Lecturer Institute, Canons & Laws Vice-rector SM (1592) Rector SF & SM (1604) Rector SM (1605, 1617)	—	Lawyer of the Poor (1591–c.1597)	Feliciano de Vega (Rector SM, Bishop of La Paz & Popayán)
1599–1600	Antonio de Ibarra (Durango, (Spain)	B. Canon Law, Mexico Dr. Canon Law	—	Fiscal Lima (1600–1) Fiscal Charcas (1607)	Corregidor Cajamarca (1602) Corregidor Jauja (1604) Fiscal Santa Cruzada (1604)	Velasco

1601–*c.* 1624	Leandro de la Rynaga (Osorno (Chile), *c.*1562 Lima, 1624)	Dr. Laws, SM Col. SF & SM?	Prof. Institute (1589) Prof. Prime of Canons (1596) Rector SF & SM Dean Faculty of Canon Law Rector SM (1599, 1603, 1609, 1619, 1619, 1621)	—	Viceregal Advisor Asesor Santa Cruzada (1601) Regidor Cabildo Lima (1611–21) A. Ordinario Lima (1622)	Monterrey Montesclaros Esquilache Guadalcázar
1608	Diego Hurtado de Avendaño (Madrid, b.*c.*1582)	Col. SM (m.1596) Col. SF & SM (m.1599) Dr. Canon Law, SM (1622)	?	?	?	?
*c.*1608–10 (Charcas)	Antonio Maldonado de Silva (Lima-†*c.*1651)	Col. SF & SM (m.1598) Dr. Canon Law, SM	Prof. Decretals	—	Corregidor JGI Advisor Salvatierra	Montesclaros Salvatierra
c. 1616	Francisco de Sosa (Lima, 1577–Charcas, 1653)	Col. SF & SM (m.1592) Dr. Canon Law, SM	Lecturer Institute (1600) Prof. Prime of Canon Law (1607) Rector SM (1611)	Oidor New Granada (1621–1633) Oidor Chacras (1634–51)	A. Ordinario Lima (1613) Visitor Royal Navy	?

TABLE 2 *Abogados de indios in the Memorial Histórico of Nicolás Del Campo, 1671* (cont.)

Year	Name	University	Academic career	Audiencia posts	Other posts	Entourage
*c.*1624–1647	Juan del Campo Godoy (1591–*fl.*1653)	Dr. Laws, SM	Lecturer Vespers of Laws Prof. Institute (1620) Prof. Prime of Canon Law (1632) Prof. Vespers of Canon Law (1636) Rector SM (1630)	Oidor Quito (1647–52) Oidor Chacras (1653)	Viceregal advisor (Mancera and Chinchón)	Guadalcázar Chinchón Mancera

A: Alcalde; AGI: Abogado General de Indios; B: Bachelor; C: Creole; Col: College; JGI: Juzgado General de Indios, Cercado; P: Peninsular; SF & SM: Real Colegio de San Felipe y San Marcos; SM: University of San Marcos.

SOURCES: AGI, AGN, BNP, ARCHIVO DOMINGO ANGULO, LILLY, LA RYNAGA SALAZAR 1626, CAMPO Y LA RYANAGA, 1671, LEVILLIER 1921–26, EGUIGUREN 1951.

TABLE 3 *Protectors*-Fiscales *of Indians, 1643–1701.*

Year	Name	University	Academic career	Audiencia posts	Posts/Honours	Entourage
1640–55	Francisco de Valenzuela (†1655)	Dr. SM	?	—	Fiscal Tribunal Santa Cruzada (1638)	?
1655	Alvaro de Ibarra (Lima, 1621–75)	Col. San Martin (m.1633) Dr. Laws, SM Dr. Canon Law, SM	Prof. Code (1647) Prof. Prime Laws (1650)	Oidor Santiago (1655) Oidor Quito (1664–68) Pres. Lima (1669–74)	Canon Lima (1648) Inquisitor (1658) Bishop of Trujillo (elect)	Alva de Aliste Lemos
1655–71	Diego de León Pinelo (Córdoba de Tucumá, 1608 Lima, 1671)	BCL, Salamanca Licentiate, SM Dr. Canon Law, SM	Prof. Code (1633) (substitute) Prof. Vespers Canon Law (1636) Prof. Prime Canon Law (1647) Rector SM (1656)	Fiscal Crimen Lima (1671) (elect)	—	F.Arias de Ugarte (Archbishop of Lima)
1680	Alonso Hurtado de Mendoza (Zaragoza-Lima,1692)	Licentiate Salamanca	—	Relator Santiago (1629) PGI Chile Fiscal Crimen Lima	Regidor Cabildo Lima (1661–95) Advisor Viceroy	Santisteban Lemos Castellar Monclova
1689	Esteban Márquez de Mansilla (1645–*c.*1700)	Col. SF & SM	Rector SF & SM	Oidor Panama		Lemos

TABLE 3 *Protectors-Fiscales of Indians, 1643–1701* (cont.)

Year	Name	University	Academic career	Audiencia posts	Posts/Honours	Entourage
1692	Juan de Peralta Sanabria (Lima, †1706)	Col. San Martín (m.1664) Dr. Canon Law, SM	Prof. Code (*c.*1690) Prof. Institute (1688)	Sup. Oidor Lima (1704)	—	—
1693–1701	Francisco de Rojas Acevedo (Lima, 1652–1716)	Col. San Martín (m.1667) Dr. Laws, SM	Prof. Code (subs.) Prof. Prime Canon Law (subs.) Prof. Vespers of Laws (subs.)	A. Crimen Lima (1701–2, 1710) Oidor Santiago (1703–9)	Advisor Viceroy (Monclova)	Monclova

A: Alcalde; BCL: Bachelor in Canon Law; C: Creole; Col: College; Lic: Licenciate; P: Peninsular; PGI: Protector General of Indians; SF & SM: Real Colegio de San Felipe y San Marcos; SM: University of San Marcos.

SOURCES: AGN, BNP, LILLY, BURKHOLDER AND CHANDLER 1982, LOHMANN 1974.

TABLE 4 *Protectors*-Fiscales *of Indians, 1708–1781*

Year	Name	University	Academic career	Audiencia posts	Posts/Honours	Entourage
1708–20	Isidro López de Eceiza (†1739)	Col. San Martín (m1697)	—	Fiscal Protector Quito Fiscal Guatemala (1721)	—	—
1720–23	Tomás de Brun Normante (1680–1728)	Col. Real de San Vicente Mártir (Huesca) Dr. Laws, Huesca	Rector Col. San Vicente (Huesca) Prof. Digestum Vetus	A. Crimen Lima (1723)	Advisor Viceroy Contador of Juntas Count of Castillejo and El Puerto (consort)	Castelfuerte
1723–28	Francisco Ruiz de Berecedo (†1752)	San Felipe Chile Master of Arts Dr. Theology Col. San Martín (m.1692)		PGI Santa Fe (1720) Oidor Santiago (1730)		
1728–30	José Martínez de España		—	—		
1730	Felipe Barrientos Díaz (*c*.1678–1739)	San Martín (m.1695) Doctor	Prof. Institute (1720) Prof. Vispers in Law (1722) Prof. Prime of Canon Law (1731)	A. Crimen Lima	Advisor Cabildo Advisor Viceroy	Villagarcía

TABLE 4 *Protectors*-Fiscales *of Indians, 1708–1781* (cont.)

Year	Name	University	Academic career	Audiencia posts	Posts/Honours	Entourage
1730–35	Pedro de Santiago Concha (1706–35)	Col. San Martín (m.1718) Dr. Laws, SM	—	Councillor Indies (1737) (honorary & posthumous)		J.de Santiago Concha (Oidor Lima)
1735–36	Pedro Bravo de Lagunas (1704–62)	Col. San Martín (m.1717) Col.SF & SM (m.1727) Dr. Laws, SM Dr. Canon Law, SM	Lecturer Visperos of Canon Law Prof. Digestum Vetus (1729) Prof. Code (1735) Prof. Prime of Laws (1742) Rector SM (1728)	Oidor Lima (1746) Councillor Indies (1751) (honorary)	Ecclesiastical judge Señor of House of Mogrovejo	Villagarcía
1736–39?	Pedro de León Escandón (c.1708–70)	Col. San Martín (m.1724) Col. SF & SM (m. 1736) BCL, SM Dr. Canon Law, SM	—	Oidor Valladolid Councillor Indies (1752) Councillor Castile (1766)		Castelfuerte F. A. de Escandón (Archbishop of Lima)
1741	García José Lasso de Vega (1705–75)	Col. San Martín (m.1721) Col. SF & SM (m. 1724) Dr. Laws, SM	—	—	IV Count of Villanueva del Soto	

1776 (*)	Cosme de Mier Trespalacios (†1805)			A. Crimen (1776), Oidor (1785), Regent (1804) Mexico	—
1778	Francisco Ruiz Cano (1732–)	Col. San Martín (m.1743) Col. SF & SM (m.1759) Doctor	Prof. Arts (1750–54) Prof. Code (1763–81) Prof. Vespers of Canon law (1779) Prof. Prime Canon Law (1783) Rector SF & SM (1761–62)	Interim Fiscal Crime	III Marquis of Sotoflorido Advisor Guiror Procurator SM (1781–83) Consultor Inquisition
1778–81	José de Baquíjano Carrillo (1751–1817)	Col. Santo Toribio (1762) BCL, SM Dr. Laws, SM	Prof. Institute (1778) Prof. Vispers of Laws (1780) Prof. Prime of Canon Law (1792) Dir. Studies San Carlos (1806)	A. Crimen Lima (1797) Oidor Lima (1807) Councillor of State (1812)	Judge Consulado Judge Minería II Count of Vistaflorida

A: Alcalde; BCL: Bachelor in Canon Law; C: Creole; Col: College; Lic: Licenciate; P: Peninsular; PGI: Protector General of Indians; SF & SM: Real Colegio de San Felipe y San Marcos; SM: University of San Marcos.

SOURCES: AGN, BNP, LILLY, BURKHOLDER AND CHANDLER 1982, MORENO CEBRIAN 2000, LOHMANN 1974. (*) DID NOT ASSUME OFFICE.

This tendency ratifies the view of Alonso de Solórzano y Velasco (*fl.*1628–64), a former rector and minister in four American audiences, who admitted that although the professorship of Digest constituted the base for all the other chairs, it was the professorship of canon law which held the 'primacy' among the teaching of Law.[41]

Studies were initially pursued independently at San Marcos, as in the case of advocate of Indians Leandro de la Rynaga and practitioner Diego de Salinas (1558–95), reputed to be the university's first graduates in Law around 1578.[42] The establishment of the royal colleges from the decade of 1580 both consolidated the teaching of Law and provided a place of study for members of the Creole and Indigenous elite.[43] In this respect, the college of San Felipe y San Marcos, founded in 1581 for the descendants of conquistadors, held some prerogatives regarding the teaching of the *corpus iuris civilis* until 1623 when the college of San Martín, a Jesuit institution founded in 1582 for the study of liberal arts and theology, obtained a royal authorization for the establishment of legal studies.[44] Most advocates of Indians and protector-*fiscales* in office until the 1680s were therefore members of San Felipe y San Marcos either as law students or fellows. Francisco de Sosa, for example, was among the first seventeen boys who received a scholarship to the college in 1592.[45] Similarly, Antonio Maldonado de Silva (1598) and Diego Hurtado de Avendaño (1599) obtained their doctorates in this institution. In turn, Cipriano de Medina and Esteban Márquez de Mansilla were elected rectors of the college in the seventeenth century. At least four future eighteenth century protectors matriculated in this college to pursue higher degrees: García José Lasso de la Vega (1724), Pedro

---

41 Alonso de Solórzano y Velasco, "Panegírico sobre los sujetos, prendas y talentos de los doctores y maestros de la real é insigne universidad de San Marcos" (1651) BNP, ms. B208, fs.3v–4v.

42 See Oswaldo Holguín Callo, "El doctor Diego de Salinas (1558–1595): Primero lances de un limeño ambicioso," *Boletín del Instituto Riva Agüero* 14, 1986–87, 28; and Eguiguren, *Diccionario*, 1: 324.

43 In 1621 viceroy Prince of Squilace founded the college of El Príncipe for the sons of caciques and noble Indians. See Eguiguren, *La universidad*, 1: 154–155.

44 Christoval Suárez de Figueroa, *Hechos de don García Hurtado de Mendoza, Quarto Marqués de Cañete* (Madrid, 1613), 184–85; Eguiguren, *La universidad*, 1: 140–52. For the prerogatives of the college of San Felipe y San Marcos in the teaching of the Digest see Solórzano y Velasco, "Panegírico," fs. 4–4v. The text of the royal rescript was given by Philip III in Madrid, 17 August, 1623. Its text is found in León, *Recopilación*, Pinelo, 1.23.14.

45 Eguiguren, *Diccionario*, 1: 275.

Bravo de Lagunas (1727), Pedro de León Escandón (1736), and Francisco Ruiz Cano (1758).[46]

The position of the San Felipe y San Marcos in educating future lawyers would be altered after the royal college of San Martín began producing law graduates by the end of the 1620s. The surviving dossiers of admission of lawyers to the royal audience reveal, for example, that in the first half of the eighteenth century, most newly incorporated lawyers were previously affiliated with the college of San Martín (46 percent), followed by students of San Felipe y San Marcos (21 percent), *manteístas* or without college affiliation (21 percent), and Santo Toribio (13 percent), a theological college.[47] During the Bourbon era (1700–1821) about one third of the ministers of the audience of Lima were graduates of San Martín—a figure that increases to 62 percent when counting only Creoles.[48] With the exception of those who studied outside Lima, virtually all protector-*fiscales* appointed after 1690 matriculated in San Martín. This is also the case of newly arrived Peninsulars who sought legal education, such as Pedro de León Escandón who received his bachelor's degree in canon law as *colegial* of San Martín. The royal colleges of San Martín and San Felipe y San Marcos became central to the education of the lettered elite of the vice-royalty and, as the matriculation registers show, provided a starting point for prominence in the governmental, ecclesiastic and academic fields.[49]

46 "Catálogo de los Colegiales que tuvo el Real y Maior de Sn. Felipe y Sn. Marcos desde su primitiva fundación que hizo el Virrey D. Francisco de Toledo, y principalmente desde 28 de Junio de 1592, en que empezó a poblarse…hasta el 12 de Enero de 1771 en que fue extinguido por el Virrey D. Manuel de Amat…," in Eguiguren, *Diccionario*, 1: 524, 530, 535, 539. Hurtado de Avendaño's membership of the college is also noted in Universidad Nacional Mayor de San Marcos, Archivo Histórico Domingo Angulo, Cuaderno de Grado de Bachiller, 1571–1664, fs. 105.

47 See AGN, Grados de Abogados, leg.1, exps.1–25 (1648–1760).

48 This is obtained crossing the information available in Guillermo Lohmann Villena, *Los ministros de la Audiencia de Lima en el reinado de los borbones (1700–1821)* (Sevilla, 1974), with the list of colegiales of San Martín avaiable in Eguiguren, *Diccionario*, 2: 135–255.

49 The list of members from prominent families linked to the protectorship and judiciary, such as Hurtado de Mendoza, Híjar y Mendoza, Jiménez de Lobatón, Puente, Santiago Concha and Tagle Bracho linked to San Felipe y San Marcos is a good starting point. See Eguiguren, *Diccionario*, 1: 533–34, 2: 186, 190, 199, 202, 227, 229, 233–34, 236, 239. Sons of Alonso Hurtado de Mendoza, Diego (matriculated 1709), José (matriculated 1717) and Francisco (matriculated 1717) Hurtado de Mendoza Iturrizarra were all members of the college.

Letrados *and Careers*

An overview of a catalogue of the *colegiales* (college members) of San Felipe y San Marcos, however, provides some information on the career paths followed by university graduates during the vice-royalty.[50] Table 5 summarizes the available data of those who matriculated between 1592 and 1760, the year of entry of protector-*fiscal* Francisco Ruiz Cano. It classifies *colegiales* in fourteen cohorts, largely composed of professionals and public officials (I–XII); but also takes into account graduates solely as possessors of nobiliary or chivalric dignities (category XIII), as well as the 112 men whose careers were not recorded by college authorities. Although it may have been possible to discover more about the occupations of this cohort of San Felipe y San Marcos graduates through the time-consuming scrutiny of primary and non-primary sources, it was beyond the scope and resources of this study. As a result, college members such as the brothers Diego (matriculated 1610) and Luis de Agüero (matriculated 1615), respectively a presbyter in the church, and a mayorazgo, landowner and encomendero, have been classified in category XIV as a consequence of their being listed by name alone in the catalogue.[51] Therefore, *colegiales* have been placed in their respecting headings taking into account only the descriptions found in the admission register.

A substantial one third of all the graduates of San Felipe y San Marcos who matriculated up to 1760 entered the church. This includes not only those who solely remained in holy orders, either as secular priests, religious, dignitaries or prelates (category I), but also the clerics who combined their ministry with legal practice or university appointments (categories II and VII). Since the occupational cohorts of table 5 only provide, as manner of avoiding overlapping categories, for single or double occupations, the *colegiales* with three or more career shifts, have been ranked in one of the two-fold combined categories (II, IV, VI–VIII, X) following the order placed in the admissions list. For instance, Andrés de Valverde y Contreras (m.1690), Fernando Inclán de Valdez y Guzmán (m.1690) and Juan de Moncada Hurtado de Chávez y Escobar (m.1696), were all registered advocates of the audience of Lima and rectors of

50 "Catálogo de los Colegiales que tuvo el Real y Maior de Sn. Felipe y Sn. Marcos," in Eguiguren, *Diccionario*, 1: 523–540. The register lists a total of 475 college members of which there is information on their careers.

51 Diego and Luis de Agüero were the sons of Marcela de Padilla y Celis, and José de Agüero y Bravo de Lagunas (1563–*fl.*1608), familiar of the Holy Office (1587), corregidor of Huaylas (1592), *alcalde* of Lima (1600), and first holder of the second mayorazgo established by Diego de Agüero Garay (*c.*1544–1618) in 1581. José de Amézaga, "El conquistador don Diego de Agüero y los mayorazgos de su casa," *Revista del Instituto Peruano de Investigaciones Genealógicas* 15 (1970), 173.

TABLE 5 *Colegiales of San Felipe y San Marcos: Careers, 1591–1771*

		Number	Percent
I	Ecclesiastics	109	23
II	Ecclesiastics/University	27	6
III	Audience Ministers	25	5
IV	Audience Ministers/University	27	6
V	Practitioners	22	5
VI	Practitioners/University	37	8
VII	Practitioners/Ecclesiastics	20	4
VIII	Practitioners/Office (inc. Audience)	23	5
IX	University	16	3
X	University/Office	11	2
XI	Corregidors	11	2
XII	Military and other offices	28	6
XIII	Other (knights, encomenderos)	7	1
XIV	Unstated or unknown	112	24
	Total	475	100

SOURCE: "CATÁLOGO DE LOS COLEGIALES DEL REAL Y MAIOR DE SN. FELIPE Y SN. MARCOS" IN EGUIGUREN, *DICCIONARIO*, 1: 523–40.

university colleges before entering the priesthood; they are thus ranked, according to our rules, as practitioners who held university positions (category VI). It is readily apparent, therefore, that totals presented for ecclesiastics (I, II and VII) must be regarded as lower-limit figures.

College members also held public offices, university positions or practised law at some point of their professional lives. One quarter (26 per cent) of *colegiales*, for instance, were bestowed with crown appointments. About half of this group entered *letrado* positions in one of the royal audiences (III, IV, and VIII); the rest would become city councillors, corregidors, viceregal advisors or honorary army officers and commissioners (categories VIII, X–XII). A similar group of graduates (25 percent) obtained university positions, either as professors, substitute lecturers, rectors, faculty deans or minor administrative authorities (categories II, IV, VI, IX–X). Entering the legal profession was, in turn, the choice of approximately one fifth (22 percent) of the student body.

Whereas ecclesiastics constitute the largest of all single cohorts (23 percent), university professors and authorities were slightly better represented if double cohorts are included (25 percent). In fact, legal practitioners who were also nominated as university professors and rectors amount to a significant eight percent of all graduates. It should be noted, however, that the San Martín and San Marcos college register provides no information of the faculty in which the college members matriculated. Therefore, categories such as ecclesiastics (I, II, VII) would have included graduates in Canon and Civil Law, Theology or Arts. This might have not been the case of audience ministers or lawyers (categories III–VI), where a majority of law graduates is expected. However, the cases of Pablo de Olavide (1725–1803) or Gaspar Antonio de Ceballos (†1820) evidence that it was not unheard of to find an *oidor* with a degree in Theology.[52]

In this respect, smaller samples of *colegiales* enable us to compare the career trends of law graduates within the general trend of university students. Perhaps the most valuable of these is the *Parnaso del Colegio de San Martín* (1694) a collection of poetry works by 85 members of the royal college of San Martín, matriculated between 1686 and 1691.[53] It is interesting to note that half of the most literary accomplished college members during the end of the seventeenth century pursued legal studies. Among those for whom there is some information available, either through the manuscript annotations to the text itself or other sources, it would appear that six followed ecclesiastic careers, six became audience magistrates, three established private legal practices as attorneys, and the other three entered the royal service in non-*letrado* positions. Some of these men also obtained prominent university appointments: Juan de Vergara, accountant at the Tribunal Mayor de Cuentas, was rector of San Marcos; José Belaochaga Aranzimendi, *regidor perpetuo* of Lima, was professor of Institute; Andrés de Munive, canon and provisor of the Archbishopric of Lima, was professor of decretals; and Miguel Núnez de Sanabria, *oidor* in Lima, was professor of vespers of law.[54]

---

52 See AGN, grados de abogados, (1793). This has been studied by Tamar Herzog, "'Letrado o teólogo?' Sobre el oficio de la Justicia a principios del siglo XVIII." In *Fallstudien zur spanischen und portugiesischen Jutiz 15.bis 20. Jahrhundert*, ed. Johannes Michael Scholz. Rechtsprechung Materielen und Studien Veröffentlichungen des Max Planck Instituts für Europäische Rechtsgeschichte Frankfurt am Main 8 (Frankfurt am Main, 1994).

53 Real Colegio de San Martín, *El parnaso del real colegio de San Martín* (Lima, 1694), 122, 143, 157. The information about the graduates' careers was annotated posthumously by an unknown writer. The edition is kept at the Biblioteca Nacional del Perú.

54 Ecclesiastics: Andrés de Munibe (canon and provisor Lima); Juan José Canal (canon Lima); Fernando Román de Aulestia (*fiscal* of the Holy Office, canon Lima and Synod examiner); Pedro Romaní Carrillo (procurator of the University of Huamanga and curate of Huancavelica); Diego Frías (chaplain of the Hospital of San Bartolomé); and Luis de Sotomayor (doctoral canon Trujillo). Audience magistrates: Pedro Vásquez de Velasco (*fiscal* Lima and *oidor* Charcas), Tomás Fernández Pérez (*oidor* Santo Domingo, Captain General of Caracas, Cuba and Puerto Rico, and later dean of the cathedral of Cuzco);

It becomes readily apparent that the career paths available to recent law—and indeed university—graduates were centred in the church, university and state service. More significantly, dossiers of admission to the Real Audiencia of Lima available until the year of the appointment of Baquíjano (1781) reveal that graduates in civil and canon law could take these options at various stages of their lives.[55] It was not uncommon, for example, to find a number of aspiring lawyers in holy orders prior to their admission to the royal audience; once this was secured, many went on to occupy positions as curates, bureaucrats and dignitaries in provincial dioceses. The aristocratic Buenaventura de Tagle Bracho e Isásaga (1746–*fl.*1801), was in possession of the minor holy orders (porter, exorcist, acolyte) at the age of seventeen, that is, two years before obtaining his bachelor's degree; it was after his admission as advocate of the audience, however, that he served as rector of San Marcos and curate of Chilca and Huancayo, and later as canon and archdeacon of the metropolitan chapter of Lima.[56] Domingo de Larrión y Cortés (†1812), a clergyman, practised law for ten years before his election as professor of Digestum Vetus (1759), followed by a nomination to the cathedral chapter of Lima (1777) and subsequent promotion to the chair of Prime of Laws (1788).[57] Manuel de Salas Corvalán (1754–1841) was an army captain in nobility regiments of Chile and Peru prior to his admission to the audience of Lima in 1773; upon his return to his hometown Santiago, he was elected alcalde and member of the Tribunal del Consulado, and later director of the national library and minister of the new

---

Francisco Ruiz de Berecedo (protector-*fiscal* of Indians); José de Mena (oidor); Miguel Núñez de Sanabria y Rojas (1645–1729) (*oidor* in Lima 1694–1729); and Ignacio del Castillo (oidor in Chile and Charcas) Nicolás Manrique de Lara (1677–1753), councillor of the Indies. The attorneys were Juan de Sobarco; Isidro de Olmedo, rector of San Marcos 1707–9; and Juan Eusebio Merino de Heredia. In turn, José Belaochaga Aranzamendi purchased the position of regidor perpetuo of Lima (1715–20) and was appointed professor of Institute at San Marcos; Juan de Vergara was appointed contador mayor del Juzgado de Bienes de Difuntos, rector of San Marcos and knight of Calatrava; Cipriano Seminario Calderón was captain of the cavalry regiment and royal official in Piura. Real Colegio de San Martín, *Parnaso*, passim.

55 The sample I will refer to consists of 47 dossiers for the years 1732 to 1781. Although the section of Grados de Abogados starts in 1648, there is only one dossier for the seventeenth century; dossiers thus start with regularity in 1750. Ella Dunbar Temple, ed., *La universidad. Libros de posesiones de cátedras y actos académicos 1789–1826. Grados de bachilleres en cánones y leyes. Grados de Abogados*, tomo 19, vols. 1–3, de *Colección Documental de la Independencia del Perú* (Lima: Comisión Nacional del Sesquicentenario de la Independencia del Perú, 1972–74); AGN, Grados de Abogados, leg. 1, exp. 51, fs.1–1v.

56 Archivo Arzobispal de Lima, Expedientes de Ordenaciones de Curas, leg. 70, exp. 5; AGN Grados de Abogados, leg. 1, 54.

57 AGN, Grados de Abogados, leg. 1, exp. 4.

republic of Chile.[58] Nicolás Manrique de Lara (1677–1753), future marquis of Lara (1739) and, at the apogee of his career, member of the Royal Councils of War, Castile and Indies, left his legal practice in Lima and Charcas, to attend his to mayorazgos and lordships in Spain.[59]

Evidence tends to suggest that only a few *letrados* pursued activities outside the professions or state service. Miguel Cornejo and José de Agüero, both students of San Felipe y San Marcos in the early seventeenth century, seem to have devoted their efforts to their encomiendas and properties.[60] This was also the case of advocates admitted to practice in the royal audiences. Juan Fulgencio de Apesteguía y Torre (†*c.*1793), second marquis of Torre Hermosa, returned to manage his haciendas in Cañete and Ica after his admission to the audience in 1750.[61] In turn, Agustín de Quijano Velarde y Tagle (1752–*c.*1838), a doctor in canon law admitted to practice in 1778, entered the burgeoning world of transatlantic trade as part of the business emporium founded by his grandfather in the early eighteenth century.[62] Although there is little doubt that a law degree would have provided these men with an immense range of practical applications in their business activities, it was far from their main activity.

---

58 AGN, Grados de Abogados, leg. 1, exp. 60.

59 Eguiguren, *Diccionario*, 1: 532; Alberto Rosas-Siles, "La nobleza Titulada del Virreinato del Perú," *Revista del Instituto Peruano de Investigaciones Genealógicas* 21 (1995), 151–157.

60 See José de la Puente Brunke, *Encomienda*, 277; and José de Amézaga, "El conquistador don Diego de Agüero y los mayorazgos de su casa," *Revista del Instituto Peruano de Investigaciones Genealógicas* 15 (1970), 173.

61 The properties were eventually inherited by *oidor* Manuel de Arredondo y Pellegrín (*c.*1738–1822), who married Apesteguía's widow, Juana Josefa de Herce y Dulce, in 1797. See AGN, Protocolos Notariales s. XVIII, protocolo 728, Justo Mendoza y Toledo, 1798–1799, fs. 373v, 374v, 375–375v and Protocolos Notariales s. XIX, protocolo 406, Justo Mendoza y Toledo, 1802–1804, fs. 808–809. One of these properties, the hacienda Montalván in Cañete, inspired a tradición of the same name by Ricardo Palma, in which Apesteguía is described as a 'bobalicón.' See "Montalván (1779)" by Ricardo Palma, *Tradiciones* 676–677.

62 AGN, Grados de Abogados, leg. 1, exp. 67. The founder of the family business was his maternal grandfather, José Bernardo de Tagle Bracho y Pérez de la Riva (1648–1740), first marquis of Torre-Tagle who settled in Lima in 1705. Agustín was the son of Gaspar de Quijano Velarde y Zevallos (*n.*1713), born in Puilma, Santander, a merchant who obtained the rank of honorary colonel in the infantry regiment of the merchants of Lima (Comercio de Lima), as well as the title of count of Torre Velarde (1745), and was elected mayor of Lima (1747). On the diverse family interests and history see Carlos Escudero Ortiz de Zevallos, "La familia Tagle Bracho en el Perú: Apuntes genealógicos," *Revista del Instituto Peruano de Investigaciones Genealógicas* 20 (1994), 79–93; y Susy Sánchez, "Familia, comercio y poder: Los Tagle y su vinculación con los Torre Velarde (1730–1825)," en *Los comerciantes limeños a fines del siglo XVIII: Capacidad y cohesión de una elite, 1750–1825*, ed. Cristina Mazzeo de Vivó (Lima, 1999).

In this context, the careers of the twenty-six advocates and protectors-*fiscales* of Indians appointed between 1593 and 1781 were divided into those who attained audience appointments and those who were engaged in private practice, university lecturing and non-audience positions. In terms of the career paths reviewed in this section, the vast majority of *letrados* (20 of 26) can be placed within the cohort of graduates which held audience appointments (III and IV), and only a small proportion (3 of 26) within the practitioners and university lecturers (V and VI). As explained in the next section, both career paths were representative of a relatively small (around 10 percent), but significant proportion of university graduates.

Career Paths Explained: Magistrates and Practitioners

Audience Appointments

In many ways, the professional development of Alberto de Acuña (1565–1630), first appointee to the post of advocate of Indians, anticipated the career pattern followed by many other officials in the protectorship of Indians. A graduate from the universities of Salamanca and Seville, Acuña arrived in Peru in 1584 as part of the entourage of Viceroy Count of Villar dom Pardo (*v.*1585–90).[63] He was nominated for two influential positions: *asesor letrado* to the viceroy and advisor of the Tribunal of Santa Cruzada. Acuña would gain further prestige with his 1589 election to the chair of Vespers in Canon Law at the University of San Marcos. Prior to the departure of Villar dom Pardo in 1590, he was appointed General Advocate of Indians.[64] From this position he was promoted seven years later to that of *oidor* in the audiences of Panama (1597–1602) and Quito

63 For a general account of the life and career of Acuña see Manuel Moreyra Paz-Soldán, *Oidores y Virreyes*, vol. 2 of *Estudios Históricos*, ed. Grover Antonio Espinosa Ruiz (1957; Lima, 1994), 137–146, and Lohmann Villena, *Los ministros*, 151.

64 The appointment had an annual salary of 2,000 pesos. See Buenaventura de Salinas Cordoba, *Memorial de las historias del nvevo mvndo Pirv*, ed. Luis E. Valcárcel and Warren L. Cook. Colección de Clásicos Peruano 1. (1630; Lima, 1957), 139. For his appointment at the university see Eguiguren, *La universidad*, 451. For his early activities as advocate of Indians see "Auto político que el Dr. Alberto de Acuña eleva ante las autoridades correspondientes con recomendaciones para una buena administración de estos dominios del Perú," BNP ms F261, 43fs. The memorial would state that Indians were "miserables" and poor (f.30), that tribute paid for the defensors of Indians (f.30v) and advises that chasquis should be paid by corregidores from the funds of the *caja de comunidad*, administered by the protector of the *corregimiento* (f.40–40v). Only parts of the manuscript are legible as it was affected by one of the fires in the National Library of Peru. A transcription is found in Eguiguren, *Diccionario*, 2: 499–506.

(1602–03).[65] In 1603 he returned to Lima as *alcalde del crimen*, a high court judge with criminal jurisdiction, and served in this post until 1607. That same year he was elected *oidor* of the audience of Lima, a position he held until his retirement in 1628. In 1625, however, he declined an offer to preside at the audience of Guadalajara in Mexico.

There was a total of twelve protectorship officials who, like Acuña, obtained appointments as appellate judges (*oidor* or *alcalde del crimen*) in the audience of Lima; of these, nine started their professional careers in academic positions. For Nicolás Matías del Campo, the most accomplished example of a protector-*fiscal* ascending from a university chair to the ranks of the upper bureaucracy and government in Peru was Alvaro de Ibarra. Appointed professor of Codex at 28 years of age (1647), and promoted as protector-*fiscal* and *oidor* in Santiago de Chile eight years later (1655), Ibarra was considered by the 1671 memorial as a man of 'superior talent' who flourished in his century for 'the emulation of those of the past, and envy of those of the future.'[66] Equally conspicuous was the case of Francisco de Sosa, professor of prime of Canon Law (1607) and rector of San Marcos (1611) prior to his appointments as advocate of Indians and *oidor*, who was hailed by Buenaventura de Salinas y Córdoba (1592–1653) as someone 'most eminent in jurisprudence.'[67] Another example is that of advocate Juan del Campo Godoy (1591–*fl.*1647), whose scholarly merits as professor and university rector—as well as his participation in the military defence of the port of Callao—would prompt poet Rodrigo de Carbajal y Robles (*fl.*1632) to write at the time,

> Era digno Rector de esta academia
> De Minerba, el Doctor acreditado
> Don Juan del Campo, hijo y heredero
> Del Coronel, que a Julián Romero,
> Pudiera enseñar leyes de Soldado[68]

---

65 For his appointment to Panama see Velasco to Philip II, Callao, April 1557, Levillier, *Gobernantes*, 14: 63; and Juan de la Rynaga Salazar, *Memorial discursivo sobre el oficio de protector General de los Indios del Piru* ([Madrid], [1626]), 2v.

66 Nicolás Matías del Campo y la Rynaga, *Memorial historico y ivridico que refiere el origen del Oficio de Protector general de los Indios del Perú*...(Madrid, 1671), 12v.

67 See "Razon de la ascendencia del Sr. Dr. Dn Francisco de Sosa y Rengifo..." (c.1625). BNP mss. B 841; "Información de legitimidad y nobleza de Francisco de Sosa, vecino y regidor de Toledo, y del cap. Diego de Sosa, su hermano, conquistador el Perú, hijos legítimos de Francisco de Sosa y de María del Corral, su mujer." BNP, Archivo Astete Concha, ms. Z270; Salinas, *Memorial*, 168.

68 "Was worthy rector of this academy/of Minerva, the accredited doctor/Don Juan del Campo, son and heir/of the colonel, who to Julián Romero/could teach the laws of soldiery. Julián Romero was a Spanish commander in the battle of St. Quintin (1557). Rodrigo

FIGURE 4
*Pedro José Bravo de Lagunas y Castilla. Lima, 1752. Oil on canvas by Cristóbal Lozano. Bravo de Lagunas represents the height of creole power in the royal audience of Lima. The appointment as protector-*fiscal, *noted in the inscription, constituted an important part of the colonial* cursus honorum. *Besides the attributes of minister of the audience* (garnacha *and* golilla), *his desk displays the crowned* beca *of the college of San Felipe y San Marcos (light blue). Unfortunately no probate inventory survives of the magnificent library used as background.*
CASA ALIAGA COLLECTION (LIMA)

The careers of Juan de Peralta Sanabria (1648–1706), Felipe Santiago de Barrientos y Díaz (*c.*1678–1739), and Pedro José Bravo de Lagunas (1704–62) possessed similar milestones to those encountered in sixteenth and seventeenth century officials such as Acuña, Sosa, Ibarra and Campo (see Table 4). Even Peninsular-born Tomás de Brun Normante (1680–1728), was rector of the royal college of San Vicente at the University of Huesca, prior to his transferral to America as protector of Indians (1720–23) and later *alcalde del crimen* (1723–28) of the audience of Lima.[69] By the time the institution was formally abrogated by the Council of the Indies in 1821, advancement as audience judge through a university position and the protectorship of Indians, was a well trodden path among officials.

---

de Carvajal y Robles, *Fiestas que celebró la ciudad de los Reyes del Perú, al nacimiento del Serenísimo Príncipe don Baltazar Carlos de Austria* (1632; Sevilla, 1950). The verses were reproduced in Nicolás Matías del Campo y La Rynaga, *Memorial y discurso informativo… Representa los estudios, y ocupaciones propias en servicio de su Magestad; y las del Doctor Iuan Bautista del Campo y de la Rinaga, su hermano, cura rector de la Villa de Huancabelica… Informa la nobleza, y servicio de sus padres* (Madrid, 1668), 28v.

69 Lohmann, *Los ministros*, 21–22.

There were some exceptions to this trend. Perhaps the most notable is that of León Escandón, a protector-*fiscal* with no academic experience, who pursued a fruitful career in the upper echelons of power in the Royal Court in Spain moving from *oidor* in the chancery of Valladolid (*c.*1740) to member of various royal councils such as Indies, Castile, War and Holy Inquisition (*c.*1752–66).[70] Similarly, Rojas Acevedo and Ruiz de Berecedo attained high court judgeships without previously becoming law professors.[71] However, the relationship between university posts and advancement towards the upper echelons of the royal audiences is perhaps more evident among among the nine officials (eight protectors-*fiscales* and one advocate of Indians) who did not gain advancement beyond the position of *fiscal*. With the exception of León Pinelo and Ruiz Cano, both appointed to university chairs and the rectorship of San Marcos, there were no academics among the protectors-*fiscales* who failed to obtain promotion to *oidor* or *alcalde del crimen* positions.

Table 6 evidences that promotion from a protectorship position to one of judge in the high court would take sixteen years on average. This statistic is perhaps slightly distorted by the fact that advocates Sosa and Campo were promoted more than twenty years after assuming their academic chairs. However, unlike audience ministers (i.e. *oidor*, *alcalde del crimen*, and *fiscal*), advocates of Indians were able to retain their university posts during their time in office. At the other end of the spectrum was Brun, promoted after three years as protector-*fiscal*, followed by Ibarra, Ruiz de Berecedo and Rojas Acevedo who gained *ascenso* after seven or eight years in this magistracy. Even well connected members of vice-regal society such as Bravo de Lagunas and Baquíjano waited around eighteen years before entering the audience as appellate judges.

---

70 Details of his life are found in Joseph Antonio Alvarez y Baena, *Hijos de Madrid, ilustres en santidad, dignidades, armas, ciencias y artes de Madrid*...vol. 4 (Madrid, 1791), 258–59; and AGN, protocolos notariales s.XVIII, protocolo 506, Gregorio González de Mendoza, 1749–1752, fs.140–141.

71 Francisco de Rojas Acevedo (1652–1716), for example, moved from protector-*fiscal* (1693) and advisor in Indian matters to Viceroy Count of La Monclova (1697) to *alcalde del crimen* in the audiences of Lima (1701, 1710) and Chile (1703) without having any academic post. Similarly, Francisco Ruiz de Berecedo (*c.*1674–1752), was a well experienced protector-*fiscal* with postings in the audiences of Santiago (1707–13), Bogotá (1720–23), and Lima (1723–28) prior to his nomination as *oidor* in his home-town Santiago (1730). See "Relacion de los grados y servicios del Licenciado Don Francisco Ruiz y Berecedo, Protector Fiscal de el distrito de la Audiencia del Reyno de Chile" (1716), BNCH, Medina mss. vol. 23, pieza 23, n/f; and Lohmann, *Los ministros*, 123.

TABLE 6 *University and audience appointments: Time frame*

Name	I. Professor/Rector		II. Advocate/Protector-fiscal		III. Oidor/A. Crimen	
	Date	*Years (I to II)*	*Date*	*Years (II to III)*	*Date*	*Years (I to III)*
Acuña	1589	1	1590	8	1598	9
Sosa	1600		n/a		1621	21
Campo Godoy	1620	4	*c.*1624	23	1647	27
Alvaro de Ibarra	1647	8	1655	0	1655	8
Peralta Sanabria	1688	4	1692	12	1704	16
Rojas Acevedo	—	—	1693	8	1701	
Brun	n/a		1720	3	1723	
Ruiz de Berecedo	—	—	1723	7	1730	
Barrientos	1720	10	1730		n/a	10+
Bravo de Lagunas	1728	7	1735	11	1746	18
León Escandón	—	—	1736	14	*c.*1750	
Baquíjano Carrillo	1778	3	1781	16	1797	19
Average years		6		10		16

n/a: Date not available; * Interim appointment.
SOURCES: LOHMANN 1974, EGUIGUREN 1940–51

By contrast, it took six years on average for law professors to be nominated as either advocates or protectors-*fiscales*. The case of Acuña, who had been in possession of the chair of Vespers in Canon Law (1589) for a few months at the time of his appointment as General Advocate of Indians (1590), was thus somewhat exceptional;[72] as is the case of Barrientos, a native of Santiago de Chile, who remained in various university positions for ten years before obtaining an appointment as interim protector of Indians in 1730.[73]

The extended periods of time that passed between positions offered, nonetheless, important opportunities for these men. Prior to his appointment as advocate of Indians, for example, Francisco de Sosa served as *alcalde ordinario* of the city of Lima (1613). Upon his retirement as protector-*fiscal*, Pedro José Bravo de Lagunas was appointed *asesor general* (general advisor) to viceroys Marquis of Castelfuerte (*v*.1724–36) and Marquis of Villagarcía (*v*.1737–45). At the same time, Bravo de Lagunas resumed his academic career and was elected to the professorships of Vespers of Canon Law (1740) and Prime of Laws (1742)—both positions held until 15 June 1747, when he was elected as *oidor* of the audience of Lima, after buying a supernumerary position the previous year (25 June 1746).[74] In 1736 the city of Cusco hired Felipe Santiago Barrientos as an

72 The appointment had an annual salary of 2,000 pesos. Salinas, *Memorial*, 139. For his appointment at the university see Eguiguren, *La universidad*, 451. For his early activities as advocate of Indians see "Auto político que el Dr. Alberto de Acuña eleva ante las autoridades correspondientes con recomendaciones para una buena administración de estos dominios del Perú," BNP ms F261, 43ff. The memorial would state that Indians were "miserables" and poor (f.30), that tribute paid for the defensors of Indians (f.30v) and advises that chasquis should be paid by corregidors from the funds of the *caja de comunidad*, administered by the protector of the *corregimiento* (f.40–40v). Only parts of the manuscript are legible as it was affected by one of the fires in the National Library of Peru. A transcription is found in Eguiguren, *Diccionario*, 2: 499–506.

73 AGN, protocolos notariales s.XVIII, protocolo 1143, Marcos de Uceda 1739, f.232. Details of his judicial career are found in Lohmann, *Los ministros*, 10.

74 It is also worth noticing that Bravo de Lagunas' professional career continued after retiring as *oidor* in 1757, he was appointed appellate judge of the Tribunal del Consulado. See *Gaceta de Lima 1756–1762*, 58. Despite his importance in vice-regal society, the only bibliography on Bravo de Lagunas remains José Antonio de Lavalle, "Pedro José Bravo de Lagunas y Castilla (Apuntes sobre su vida y obras)," in *Estudios Históricos* (Lima, 1935). Evidence of his judicial career is found in BNP ms. C3698. His testament of 27 August 1751 is found in AGN, protocolos notariales s.XVIII, protocolo 83, Orencio de Azcarrunz, 1764–68, fs.476–78v. For his academic career see BNP ms. C92; Eguiguren, *Catálogo Claustro*, 27–28, 30, 36, 42; and "Catálogo Colegio de San Martín," in Eguiguren, *Diccionario*, 2: 227.

attorney to represent certain petitions before the viceroy.[75] After his interim appointment as protector-*fiscal* José de Baquíjano was elected professor of Prime of Canon Law (1792), and appointed magistrate of the tribunals of Minería (Mines) and Consulado (Merchant Guild).

The existence of this pattern should not lead us to conclude that this was an easy path. Campo, for example, waited almost four decades before occupying a position in the high court. Despite intensified lobbying by Nicolás Polanco de Santillana (1603–64), procurator of the university of San Marcos, and the cabildo of Lima in the decade of 1630, Campo received the eagerly sought for audience position as late as 1646, as *alcalde de corte* of Quito.[76] He served as magistrate in this city from 1649 until 1652. Following the death of Francisco de Sosa as senior magistrate of Charcas, Campo was promoted as *oidor* to this audience in 1651 but entered the post in 1653. He died a few years later.[77]

The same is true for university appointments. Evidence suggests that he applied eleven times to professorships in law; of these, three were obtained. Thus, he was professor of Institute (1620), Prime of Canon Law (1632)—where he replaced the eminent Feliciano de Vega—and Vespers of Canon Law (1636). Campo was also elected rector of San Marcos in 1630 and, in this capacity, presided over the celebrations of the birth of prince Baltazar Carlos (1629–46).[78]

75 "[P]ara que en nombre de esta ciudad besase las manos y diese la embajada a su excelencia." See Diego de Esquivel y Navia, *Noticias cronológicas de la gran ciudad del Cuzco*, ed. Felix Denegri Luna vol. 2, (Lima, 1980), 258.

76 See the petitions of 1633, 1637 and 1639 by the cabildo of Lima in *Cartas de Cabildos Hispanoamericanos: Audiencia de Lima*, vol. 1 eds. Javier Ortíz de la Tabla Ducasse et al. (Sevilla: Consejo de Superior de Investigaciones Científicas, Instituto Riva Agüero et al., 1998), 101, 118, 125. and In this same period *oidor* Nicolás Polanco de Santillana (1603–64) is quoted to have claimed that despite 'his studies, good conscience, integrity and zealousnes,[Campo] had white hair, and no prize.' See Campo, *Memorial y discurso informativo*, 5.

77 Details of his career as magistrate are found in *Autos Acordados de la Real Audiencia de Quito, 1578–1722*, Anuario Histórico Jurídico Ecuatoriano 2 (Guayaquil, 1971), 53–60, 63; Joseph de Aguilar, *Bachiller don Joseph de Aguilar, Bilicia y Godoy, Cura de San Christoval de los Guachos en el obispado de Guamanga…*(Madrid, [1664]), [1v–2]; Campo, *Memorial y discurso informativo*, 5; Salinas, *Memorial*, 293. In his memorial Aguilar, an ecclesiastical judge in Huamanga and first cousin of Campo, describes the ceremonial and procedure of Campo's resignation as president of the audience of Quito.

78 Accounts of the academic career of Juan del Campo are found in the *relación de servicios* of his son Nicolás Matías, *Memorial y discurso informativo*, 27v–28, and Pedro López de Echaburu, *Relación de los servicios del doctor Don Nicolás Matías del Campo y de la Rinaga, abogado que ha sido de la Audiencia de Lima* (Madrid?, 1666?), [2v].

To a number of advocates and protectors the rise to the honorary office of *fiscal* did not constitute a turning point towards further advancement in the upper echelons of the royal audiences. Even if their position as honorary 'advocates of His Majesty' placed them below *oidores*, *alcaldes del crimen* and full *fiscales*, obtaining an honorary togate magistracy was nonetheless a coveted reward for many individuals.[79] Alonso Hurtado de Mendoz, for example, was made protector-*fiscal* by petition of the city of Lima after 17 years of service as councillor and vice-regal advisor.[80] In turn, the aristocratic García José Lasso de la Vega e Híjar (1705–75), III count of Villanueva del Soto, held no other post during his lifetime.[81]

It would thus appear that letrados who remained as *fiscales* obtained this position at the end of their careers or obtained lateral promotion. Take for instance Antonio de Ibarra, one of the advisors of Viceroy Luis de Velasco (*v*.1596–1604), who in 1601 obtained a rapid promotion from advocate of Indians to *fiscal* of the audience of Lima.[82] After remaining in this post for nine months, he served five years as corregidor of various provinces before returning to one of the royal audiences as *fiscal* of Charcas.[83] Diego de León Pinelo (1608–71), on the other hand, obtained this office 33 years after his appointment as substitute professor of Code at San Marcos and a prolific career as a lawyer.[84] Similarly, Isidoro Lopez de Eceiza served as fiscal in Guatemala after his period as protector in Lima.[85] In turn, Francisco de Valenzuela (†1655) would seek permission from the crown to combine his office of protector with that of attorney (*fiscal*) of the Tribunal de la Santa Cruzada, an office he

79 See Manuel Fernández de Ayala, *Práctica y formulario de la Chancillería de Valladolid* (Valladolid, 1667), 25.

80 *Cartas de Cabildos*, §382, §398 (195, 203).

81 AGN, protocolos notariales s. XVIII, protocolo 873, Agustín Gerónimo de Potalanza 1770–1777, fs. 731–31v (Lasso de la Vega). Reference to these appointments is also found in Lohmann, *Los ministros*, 10, 17–18, 34–35, 59–61.

82 Ibarra served as *fiscal* in Lima until December 1601 when he was replaced by Pérez Merchán. He was then appointed corregidor of Parinacochas, Cajamarca (1602–4) and Jauja (1604–7). Levillier, *Gobernantes*, 14: 202, 249; Lilly Latin American mss. Peru,1600, Nov. 18–1602, Jan. 22. f48.

83 *Libros de Cabildos*, 14: 804, 746–749.

84 "Méritos y cargos del Dr. Diego de León Pinelo y de su hijo Diego de León Gutiérrez" (1648), in Ernesto de la Torre Villar, *Los pareceres de Juan de Padilla y Diego de León Pinelo, acerca de la enseñanza y buen tratamiento de los indios* (Mexico,1979), 65–79.

85 Burkholder and Chandler, *From Impotence to Authority*, 39.

purchased in 1638 for 24,000 pesos.[86] This allowed Valenzuela to be part of an institution of considerable economic importance; as Diego Salazar, the sub-delegate commissar of Lima, reported in 1687, the income derived from the Bull of the Crusade alone could levy around half a million pesos per annum.[87]

Practitioners and Academics

As stated earlier, the careers of the advocates of Indians were not solely oriented towards the judiciary. In many ways, however, this was exceptional both in terms of the broader trends of vice-regal *letrados*, and in terms of protectorship official themselves. Neither Diego Hurtado de Avendaño, Cipriano de Medina, nor Leandro de la Rynaga Salazar obtained a position within the judiciary. Hurtado de Avendaño, for example, served as advocate of Indians between 1608 and 1616, shortly after graduating as licentiate and doctor of Canon Law at San Marcos (1607). Evidence suggests, however, he did not hold any other position, in either government or academic spheres.[88] On the other hand, Medina discarded any possibility of pursuing a career in one of the high courts of justice when in 1609 when the Council of the Indies denied him a 'togate' magistracy in the audience of Quito after being presented by Cristóbal Pérez de Urísar. In the case of Rynaga the possibility of an *audiencia* position was denied earlier, in 1599, despite the fact that Viceroy Velasco himself had proposed him as someone 'proficient in advocacy.' A further petition in 1612 by Viceroy Montesclaros was equally unsuccessful.[89]

86 Torre Villar, *Pareceres*, 82. Valenzuela requested permission to travel to Peru on 31 May 1641, AGI, ES.41091.AGI/1.16419//PASAJEROS,L.12,E.333, at http://pares.mcu.es. For the office of *fiscal* of Santa Cruzada see the *real cédula* of 26 October 1626 which established that this office should be undertaken by the most senior *fiscal* in the audiences of Lima and Mexico. Recop.1.20.4.

87 José Antonio Benito Rodríguez, *La Bula de Cruzada en Indias* (Madrid: Fundación Universitaria Española, 2002), 101, 139 40, 81. The office of fiscal of the Tribunal of Santa Cruzada was traditionally exercised by a *fiscal* of the audience. "[E]ntre los remoas de que se compone el Tesoro de V.M. es el más pingüe y seguro el de la limosna de la Santa Bula," 322.

88 The only reference to the life of Hurtado de Avendaño is a request to Feliciano de Vega, dean of the faculty of Canon Law at San Marcos, to extend a copy of his degrees. Universidad Nacional Mayor de San Marcos, Archivo Histórico Domingo Angulo, Cuaderno de Grado de Bachiller, 1571–1664, fs. 105–109.

89 Levillier, *Gobernantes*, 14: 63.

In principle dispositions of 1589, 1603 and 1629, the University of San Marcos prohibited audience ministers to obtain nominations from rectors or professors.[90] The logic behind the prohibition was to protect the university council from the influence of 'powerful persons.'[91] Holding magistracies below audience rank, however, opened possibilities of advancement in other spheres. The first of these was the university of San Marcos, where Cipriano de Medina and Leandro de la Rynaga had distinguished careers. Medina, for example, was incorporated to San Marcos in 1598, one year after receiving his doctorate. Although he does not appear as professor in any of the chairs of laws in San Marcos, there is evidence of him as lecturer. Not only is there a volume of his 'lectures' in his library,[92] but also the fact that he appears as substitute professor of Institute, under Francisco de León Garavito (1541–1612), prime of laws, under Jerónimo López Guarnido (1525–96), and vespers of canons under Fernán Vásquez de Fajardo (1534–97). Medina was elected vice-rector (1592) and rector (1604) of the Real Colegio Mayor de San Felipe y San Marcos. The apex of his academic career would be his election as rector of the university of San Marcos in 1605 and 1617. He would remain part of the university at least until 1619.[93] In turn, Rynaga was incorporated as a teaching member of the university shortly after his graduation as bachelor in Canon Law (1586). He was appointed professor of Institute (1589) and prime of Canon Law (1596). The consolidation of his academic career came with his election as rector of the college of San Felipe y San Marcos and of the university of San Marcos (1599), where he was re-elected on four occasions (1603, 1609, 1619 and 1620).

Perhaps the most significant characteristic of those advocates of Indians who did not enter the judiciary was their independent practice of the law. Evidence of Medina's rise as a successful independent lawyer go back to 1593, when he was already considered one the *letrados* of more fortune and businesses in Lima.[94] As it is seen in Chapter 5, the inventory of his property made after his death in 1635 proves that Medina still maintained a comfortable economic position late in life.[95] Similarly, there is considerable evidence that

90 Reales Cédulas of Philip II, Aranjuez, 19 de April 1589; Philip III, Ventosilla, 29 January 1603; and Philip IV, Madrid 21 June 1629. Antonio de Léon Pinelo, *Recopilacón de las Indias*, ed. Ismael Sánchez Bella, (México, 1992), 1: 302.

91 Eguiguren, *Diccionario*, 1: 547; Lourdes Díaz-Trechuelo López-Spínola, *La vida universitaria en Indias. Siglos XVI y XVI* (Córdoba, 1982), 16.

92 "Ittem un quaderno de las lecturas antiguas que izo el Sr. Doctor." See Appendix 2, §476.

93 Eguiguren, *Catálogo Claustro*, 21–43; Eguiguren, *Diccionario*, 1: 385–386, 328, 442.

94 Eguiguren, *Diccionario*, 1: 386–387.

95 Cipriano Medina y Gómez, Inventario de bienes. 4-I-1635, AGN Protocolos Notariales s.XVII, protocolo notarial 818, escribano Diego Gutierrez, 1635, fs. 494–96v.

Rynaga possessed an extensive clientèle for his professional services in Lima.[96] Among these were important members of the local elite, such as Juan de Lumbreras, who in 1617 founded his *mayorazgo* under the advice of Rynaga.[97] Evidence suggests that former advocates of Indians in other jurisdictions, were successful legal professionals, as is the case of Maldonado de Silva.[98]

There were also lateral advancements for Advocate of Indians who did not hold high court magistracies, and that was the exercise of public positions compatible with their office. In the same period he served in the Defensorship of Indians, Medina was also named advocate for the poor of the audience of Lima (1591–*fl.*1597). Likewise, during his tenure as advocate of Indians, Leandro de la Rynaga was named advisor to five viceroys, advisor to the Tribunal of Santa Cruzada (1601), as well as *regidor perpetuo* (1611–21) and *alcalde ordinario* (1622) of the city of Lima.[99] The position in the Tribunal of Santa Cruzada, a jurisdictional body that determined the controversies arising from the administration of the alms of the bull of Crusade, would enable Rynaga to forge links with one of the most powerful economic institutions in the Spanish Monarchy.[100] On the other hand, the *cabildo* of Lima, a caucus of the city's leading families, represented the highest level of urban power in the viceroyalty of Peru. As *regidor* or councillor of this institution Rynaga would oversee a number of issues. An overview of the minutes of 1616, for example, reveals that councillors elected at least sixteen offices, and regulated matters such as the distribution of water, administration of sales taxes, or licensing of banks, shops and clothiers; and at the same time performed ceremonial and

96 An example of Rynaga's range of businesses and legal transactions is found in the records of notary Cristóbal Aguilar de Mendieta, AGN Protocolos Notariales s.XVII, Protocolo Notarial 45, 1602–1603, fs. 248v, 289, 610, 725, 747, 770v, 974v, 984, 1679v, 1681v, 1732, 1733; and Protocolo Notarial 46, 1603–1604, fs. 326, 475v. See also Chapter 5.

97 "Razon de los instrumentos del vínculo de mayorazgo, que mandó fundar Juan Lumbreras en el poder que dio para testar al Dr. Dn. Leandro de la Rinaga Salazar, regidor de esta ciudad de los Reyes y abogado de la Real Audiencia de élla, etc." (1617), BNP MS Z 291.

98 AGN, protocolos notariales s.XVII, protocolo 1092, Francisco Medina 1651–53, fs.207v–208.

99 Levillier, *Gobernantes*, 14: 63; Rynaga Salazar, *Memorial Protector General*, 4v; Eguiguren, *Diccionario*, 1: 385–86; Lohmann, *Amarilis*, 336; AGN, Cabildo Justicia Ordinaria, causas civiles, CA JO 1, caja 36, doc. 40 (1622), f.5v.

100 In addition to his the asesor of the Tribunal earned a salary of 250 pesos per annum. The members of the tribunal also had minor honorary privileges. See José Antonio Benito Rodríguez, *La Bula de Cruzada en Indias* (Madrid, 2002), 30–31, 72–73, 109–111.

lobbying functions.[101] As *alcalde ordinario*, Rynaga was the chief magistrate of the city with a jurisdiction of five leagues (5.5 km) around Lima.[102]

Protectorship officials occupied the highest and most prestigious positions that men could aspire to in the Indies. Evidence is scant, but that available suggests that there were at least three factors to promotion to audience positions. The first was purchase. With the exception of Valenzuela, who purchased the newly created office of *fiscal*-protector for 9,000 pesos, protectors Peralta, Rojas and Bravo de Lagunas purchased future or supernumerary audience magistracies of *oidor* or *Alcalde del crimen*. A second group of officials, such as Peninsulars Brun and Mier, and creole Baquíjano obtained their appointments directly from the Council of the Indies.[103] The third factor for promotion derives from local circumstances. An overview of the petitions for the Santiago or Calatrava knighthoods, for example, reveals that creoles used local institutions such as the *cabildo* or the cathedral chapter, as well as networks in Peru and Spain, for support.[104] Although it is difficult to point out the reasons why men were promoted, it would appear that the protectorship, as a viceroy appointed post, provided a good starting point in their careers. It is at this instance that the relationship with the viceroy should be explored.

Viceroys and Protectors: Politics and Fidelity

The fact that the 1575 Ordinances established that protectorship officials were not only vice-regal appointments, but could also present themselves to the viceroy 'at any time or day' instructing the members of the household to allow them permanent entrance (ordinances XV), anticipated the links that existed between these two men throughout the institution's history. It is no coincidence, therefore, that Toledo referred to Baltazar de la Cruz as someone 'close

101 *Libros de Cabildos* (1616), 18: 5–130. The various services which were responsibility of the cabildo are discussed in María Antonio Durán Montero, *Lima en el siglo XVII: Arquitectura, urbanismo y vida cotidiana* (Sevilla, 1994), 77–109.

102 See Guillermo Lohmann, "El corregidor de Lima," *Anuario de Estudios Americanos* 9 (1952), 131,137. Unlike other cities in Peru, Lima had the privilege of having *alcaldes ordinarios*, and not *corregidors* to impart justice in the city. This situation led to a number of debates disputing the jurisdiction of these magistrates which were settled in 1590 by a decision of the Council of Indies confirming the jurisdiction of the *alcaldes ordinarios* but ordering that their election by the cabildo be supervised by the Viceroy.

103 Burkholder and Chandler, *From Impotence to Authority*, 202–205.

104 See Lohmann, *Los americanos*, passim.

to my person';[105] that Antonio Heredia (DGI 1590) was Viceroy García Hurtado de Mendoza's (*v.*1589–1596) personal secretary;[106] or that Luna was both advisor and a witness of the Count of Monterrey's 1608 testament.[107] Similarly, an important number of *letrado* protectors were also part of the viceroy's close circle. Advocates Acuña, Ibarra, Campo and Rynaga were all appointed advisors (*asesor letrado*) to various viceroys. Similarly, protectors-*fiscales* Ibarra, Rojas, Barrientos, Bravo de Lagunas and Ruiz Cano were all vice-regal advisors at some point in their careers.

Although there is no study on the role of vice-regal advisors, there is fragmentary evidence that reveals the influence of these men as power brokers during the vice-regal period. Alvaro de Ibarra, for example, became one of the trusted men of Viceroy Count of Lemos (*v.*1667–72) during his government. He was thus appointed visitor general of Peru and, in this capacity, conducted numerous investigations into royal officials in Lima, promoted the revival of the mining industry, and attempted to reform the *mita* system in Potosí.[108] This trust also had a manifestation in private life. As diarist José de Mugaburu points out, the viceroy and his family were frequent visitors to Ibarra's property in Villa where they stayed for several days.[109] Following the death of Lemos on 6 December 1672, Ibarra became regent and captain general of the vice-royalty of Peru—possibly the most powerful position attainable by a Creole. He held the post until September 1674 when Viceroy Count of Castellar (*v.*1674–78) made his entry into the city of Lima.[110] Even if he retained numerous influential enemies from his time as advisor of Lemos, he was nonetheless appointed bishop of Trujillo, but was unable to take up this office due to his death in January 1675.[111]

105 "Y si el tal negocio, o negocios fueren de calidad que pare perjuicio notable la dilación, en cualquier hora, y dia podreis venir con el dicho Interprete a su Excelencia, que por la presente mando al Mayordomo de mi casa, y a los de mi Camara, y aqualquiera dellos que os de para ello la puerta." "[C]erca de mi persona." Ordinances, x. Toledo, *Disposiciones*, vol. 2.

106 Levillier, *Gobernantes*, 14: 63, 164, 234.

107 Eguiguren, *Diccionario*, 1: 389.

108 Kenneth J. Andrien, *Crisis and Decline: The viceroyalty of Peru in the seventeenth century* (Albuquerque, 1985), 179–184.

109 See José de Mugaburu and Francisco de Mugaburu, *Diario de Lima (1640–1694)*, vol. 2, ed. Carlos A. Romero (Lima, 1935), 119–20, 123. Ibarra spent Christmas Day of 1669 with the viceregal family.

110 Lilly, Latin American mss. Peru, 1673, Sep.18.

111 Eguiguren, *Catálogo Claustro*, 27.

Pedro Bravo de Lagunas gained considerable influence in government affairs as advisor to viceroys Marquis of Castelfuerte, Marquis of Villagarcía (*v*.1737–45) and Count of Superunda (*v*.1745–61). Unlike Ibarra, who maintained an intense loyalty towards Lemos, Bravo de Lagunas had serial, short term, loyalties with viceroys he served. In this respect, for example, he was entrusted with the defence in the *residencia* judgement of Villagarcía. Similarly, Superunda sought his advice to deal with the rebellion of the Indians of El Cercado of Lima in 1750, and appointed him to the Junta summoned by instruction of the Council of the Indies to regulate the repartimientos of the corregidors in 1751.[112] Accordingly, Bravo de Lagunas had an active part in the viceroy's faction during the conflicts that occurred with Pedro Antonio de Barroeta, archbishop of Lima; even if these were maintained maintaining civility.[113] Bravo de Lagunas, and three other notables of Lima, gave the bond (*fianza*) on behalf of Superunda after his departure from Peru in 1761.[114] Similarly, Viceroy Manuel de Guiror entrusted his former advisor Ruiz Cano with his defence in his residencia judgement.

Not all protectors, however, were part of the vice-regal entourage. Recent studies in the governments of Casteldosruis and Castelfuerte reveal that protectors serving in these periods remained outside their vice-regal clientèle. López de Eceiza, for example, remained completely outside the extensive group that collaborated with Casteldosruis in his contraband trade of cacao.[115] Similarly, other than being commissioned in 1724 as *alcalde del crimen* to seize the shipment of Pedro Morcillo, nephew of Archbishop Morcillo Rubio de Auñon, Brun does not appear in the list of 114 people who directly or indirectly benefited from Castelfuerte.[116]

The closeness to a particular viceroy could also imply problems. Ibarra, for example, made numerous influential enemies.[117] His funeral in January 1675 was not attended by Viceroy Castellar, nor by the ecclesiastics who, in the

---

112 Moreno Cebrián, *Corregidor*, 314–315.

113 In 1758, for example, Superunda, for example, lent his carriage for the departure of the Archbishop to assume the diocese of Granada. See *Gaceta de Lima 1756–1762*, 155. Writen in reply to *Concordia de la discordia* (Lima, 1749) by Jesuit Antonio de la Cueva y Ponce de León, Bravo de Laguna's *Discordia de la Concordia; manifiesto jurídico apologético por la jurisdicción real…*(Lima, 1761) was a defense of King of Spain's prerogatives regarding ecclesiastical appointments in the viceroyalty of Peru.

114 Vargas Ugarte, *Historia*, 4: 226 (residencia of Villagarcia), (rebellion) 248, San Lázaro (306).

115 Alfredo Moreno Cebrián y Nuria Sala i Vila, *Premio virrey*, 158, 122 (Bravo de Lagunas).

116 Ibid., 252–263.

117 Kenneth J. Andrien, *Crisis and Decline: The viceroyalty of Peru in the seventeenth century* (Albuquerque, 1985), 179–184.

words of Mugaburu, sought vengeance due to 'certain differences' with the former regent of Peru.[118] Similarly, loyalty to Viceroy Güiror, placed Ruiz Cano and other Creoles as targets of the *visitador* Antonio de Areche (1731–98). In a letter commenting on the residencia given to the Viceroy Marquis de Guiror, the *visitador* explained to Antonio Porlier (1722–*fl.*1791), secretary of justice affairs in the Indies, the enormous difficulties in knowing the truth in judicial matters due to the 'power and respect achieved there [in Lima] by the Sierra Bellas, the Bozas, the Soto-Floridos [Ruiz Cano's title], the marquises of Celada.'[119]

It is difficult to establish the exact implications of closeness or distance from power. It is somehow indicative that Bravo de Lagunas y Castilla obtained his appointment as *oidor* (1747–57) during the government of Superunda, the viceroy he advised. However, institutions such as the city council of Lima also seem to have been somewhat effective in promoting would be audience magistrates. Although the city repeatedly requested (1675 and 1677) a post of *oidor* for Hurtado de Mendoza, the fact that he obtained an appointment as *fiscal* suggests some degree of influence.[120] On the other hand, the petitions made on behalf of Medina by an agent of Viceroy Marquis of Cañete (Cristóbal Pérez de Urísar), and on behalf of Rynaga by viceroys Velasco and Montesclaros themselves proved to be unsuccessful in obtaining togate magistracies for these men. In any case, the degree of influence exercised by the viceroy would have been subject to a number of circumstances, starting by his own standing in court. That viceroys had, comparatively, short mandates also provides a limit to the patronage exercised. Equally, relationships would have changed once promotion to one of the royal audiences was achieved. The new condition of magistrates of the high court immediately placed these officials in an institution which traditionally competed with the power of viceroys. All this does not diminish the influence of the viceroys particularly in the first stages of the protectors' careers.

---

118 "[N]i tampoco fue en el entierro el Cabildo eclesiástico por ciertas diferencias, que depués de muerto se vengaron del difunto. Y siendo hijo de la tierra y habiendo ocupado tantos puestos honoríficos que le dio S.M., nada le valió a la muerte, y así no hay sino que servir a N.S. Jesucristo, que todo lo demás es burla." Mugaburu, *Diario*, 180.

119 "[C]uando median unos respetos y poder como el que logran allí los Sierra-Bellas, los Bozas, los Soto-Floridos, los marqueses de Celada." Antonio de Areche to Antonio Porlier, Madrid 7 April 1789, in "Los Ideólogos," vol. 3, tom. 1 of CDIP, 369. Porlier was marquis of Bajamar and secretary of the newly created office of Grace and Justice for the Indies. Alongside Ruiz Cano, the letter refers to Felipe de Colmenares, V marquis of Zelada de la Fuente, and to Boza family, composed by Boza Garcés de Mancilla and the descendants of general Jerónimo de Boza y Solís, I marquis de Casa Boza (1736).

120 *Cartas de Cabildos*, §382, §398 (195, 203).

To summarise, university education divided the careers of protectorship officials into two distinct groups. The office holders of the Defensorship General of Indians usually remained within the sphere of *corregimientos*, city magistracies or the vice-regal household. Considering that the institution revolved around the legal defence of Indians in court, the paths followed by these men are somewhat exceptional. By contrast, the majority of *letrados* who represented Indian plaintiffs by becoming Advocates of Defensors General of Indians between 1593 and 1781, were university professors and magistrates at the high courts of justice. In a few cases, they followed a route that led to private legal practice, lecturing and local office. An analysis of the careers of *letrados* throughout the vice-royalty using the prosopographical data provided by the college of San Felipe y San Marcos, suggests that advocates and protectors-*fiscales* were among the top 10 percent of graduates who obtained audience magistracies and professorships. There is, therefore, little doubt that these offices provided advancement for promising lawyers. In this light, the opinion of Nicolás Matías del Campo that the protectorship was entrusted to those university graduates who possessed 'more jurisprudence, better conscience, and superior cleanliness [*limpieza*]' is not as tainted by his family's own achievements as it would seem.[121] That these men owed their initial nomination to the person of the viceroy, if they were not altogether part of his entourage, provides an insight to the—largely unknown—mechanisms of patronage and politics during this period. However, as the previous and next chapters evidence, their exceptional advancement can only be explained by a diversified series of power relations (family, networks, university) rather than merely the supremacy of the viceroy.

121 Campo, *Memorial*, 4v.

CHAPTER 5

Economic Position

Reporting in 1763 on the request to increase the salary of the Protector of Indians of Santa Fe, the *fiscal* of the Council of the Indies concluded that it was impossible for someone, particularly an audience minister, to live with a salary of 1,000 pesos per annum, not only in terms of decorum and decency, but also in terms of sustaining a family.[1] A century earlier, in 1671, Nicolás Matías del Campo, the son of a prominent advocate of Indians, noted that throughout the history of the institution advocates had compensated their low salaries with other occupations such as private legal practice, university professorships and 'other offices and positions of the Republic.'[2]

The following chapter attempts to address the consistency of these observations primarily in the light of testaments, probate inventories, dowry contracts, and notarial transactions. Its chief objective, therefore, is to analyse the economic situation of advocates and protectors of Indians. It will first survey their salaries, sources of income and, where applicable, other indicators of wealth. The discussion then turns to the material culture and nature of consumption of these officials. The concluding remarks attempt to assess the significance of these elements in their lives and careers.

Wealth and Economic Performance[3]

Salaries

The Protectorship of Indians was, from its origins, a salaried office. Bartolomé de las Casas was granted 100 golden pesos per annum to act as protector of

1 "Tomo quinto de consultas y pareceres dado a S.M. en asuntos del gobierno de Indias recopiladas a materias del A.B.C.D. por Don Manuel Josef de Ayala, natural de Panamá Archivero de la secretaria del Despacho Universal de ellas, dedicado al Exmo señor Baylio Fr. Dn. Julian de Arriaga su Geffe. Año de 1768," AHN Códices 756-B, f.106v.

2 "[S]us Abogados defienden muchos pleitos de particulares; suelen ser Catedráticos, y tener otros oficios y cargos de la Republica: porque no pueden viuir estando atendidos al salario de los Indios, que es muy poco para solo, y tan mal pagado." See Juan de la Rynaga Salazar, *Memorial discursivo sobre el oficio de Protector General de los Indios del Piru* ([Madrid], [1626]), 8v and Nicolás Matías del Campo y de la Rynaga, *Memorial historico y ivridico, que refiere: El origen del Oficio de Protector general de los Indios del Perú* (Madrid, 1671), 8.

3 There is no universal agreement on the worth of unit of money in the viceregal period. Unless otherwise stated all monetary figures are stated in pesos fuertes of eight reales, each

 | DOI 10.1163/9789004305175_007

Indians, as were the bishop-protectors of Peru granted 1000 ducats or 375,000 *maravedíes*.[4] In his ordinances of 1575, viceroy Toledo established an annual salary of 1,000 pesos for the Protector General in Lima (plus 200 pesos in ink and paper), 1,000 pesos for the Advocate of Indians, 500 pesos for each of the two Procurators of Indians, and similar amounts for the provincial protectors.[5] The latter were in the range of 600 pesos, as evidenced by the salaries of the protectors of Potosí, Chucuito, Villarica de Oropesa and Huancavelica.[6] By the end of the government of Toledo in 1581, the audience declared that the total cost of the system of protectors of Indians amounted to 18,000 pesos.[7]

The cost of the protectorship system in Lima increased in 1608 with the creation of the second advocate of Indians, which was granted an annual wage of 600 pesos; later increased to 800 pesos by the decade of 1620.[8] By 1629 Bernabé Cobo, the Jesuit chronicler, reported that the Protector of Indians resident in Lima earned 1,200 pesos; the first and second advocates of Indians respectively 1,000 and 800 pesos; and the two procurators 500 pesos each.[9]

The appointment of protectors with the prerogatives of *fiscales* after 1641, often resulted in higher wages for the holder of this office, but also reveals a degree of autonomy in establishing salaries within the different audiences. In Lima, Francisco de Valenzuela, was granted 1,800 pesos in 1641, plus 250 pesos as *fiscal* of the Tribunal de la Santa Cruzada;[10] the same income, excluding the

---

containing thirty-four *maravedís* (a peso of 272 *maravedís*). All other figures are expressed in their original monetary unit.

4 Similar amounts were granted in 1527–39 to the bishop protectors of Nicaragua (100,000 maravedíes), Tierra Firme (200,000 maravedíes), Honduras (300,000 maravedíes), Nueva Galicia (300,000 maravedíes) and Venezuela (250,000 maravedíes). See Constantino Bayle, *El protector de indios* (Sevilla, 1945), 99; and Carmen Ruigómez, *Una política indigenista de los Habsburgo: El protector de indios en el Perú* (Madrid, 1988), 150.

5 Francisco de Toledo, *Disposiciones gubernativas para el virreinato del Perú*, ed. Maria Justina Sarabia Viejo (Sevilla, 1986–89) 2: 103, 107.

6 See Toledo, *Disposiciones*, 2:295–296, and Ruigómez, *El protector*, 151.

7 Nicolas Matías del Campo cites an *auto acordado* of the audience of Lima establishing this amount on 8 February 1581. See Campo, *Memorial*, 3v. It is unclear, however, if this referred to the total cost of the institution per annum (i.e. the protectorship in Lima and in the provinces), or to the accumulated cost of the protectorship in Lima.

8 Rynaga, *Memorial*, 4v.

9 Bernabé Cobo, *Historia de la fundación de Lima*, ed. M. Gonzalez de la Rosa (1639; Lima: Imprenta Liberal, 1882), 115–116.

10 Juan Baptista Moreto to the Council of Indies, Lima, 8 November 1664, in Ernesto de la Torre Villar, *Los pareceres de Juan de Padilla y Diego de León Pinelo, acerca de la enseñanza y buen tratamiento de los indios* (México, 1979), 82.

250 pesos as *fiscal* of Santa Cruzada, was assigned to Diego de León Pinelo.[11] On the other hand, the appointment of José de la Concha Bernardo de Quiroz as interim protector-*fiscal* of the audience of Quito in 1646, reveals that the annual salary of this office was 2,000 pesos.[12] Carmen Ruigómez, points out that in 1688 the Protector of Indians of this same audience was being paid 1,890 pesos.[13] In the eighteenth century, however, the protectorship salaries seem to have returned to the levels established in 1575.[14] In 1736, for example, Pedro José Bravo de Lagunas was paid 711 pesos of 6 reales, for his service as interim *fiscal*-protector during eight months.[15] Likewise, in 1758 Fernando Bustillos, Protector of Indians in the audience of Santa Fe de Bogotá, declared an annual salary of 1,000 pesos.[16]

As established by Toledo in 1575, the protectorship wages continued to be financed with Indian tribute at least until the mid-eighteenth century.[17] The variable nature of this source of funding could imply that the payment of these was often delayed, or left outstanding. Whereas the anonymous memorial states that in 1619 the unpaid salaries of an Advocate of Indians amounted to

---

11 Diego de León Pinelo to King Philip IV, Lima, 12 November 1665, in Ernesto de la Torre Villar, *Pareceres*, 84–85.

12 Archivo Nacional de Ecuador, Gobierno, caja 3, exp. 15 (13.XII.1646), fs. 1–2.

13 Ruigómez, *El protector*, 151.

14 The causes for this may vary, but there is a consensus on the general stability of prices during the Viceregal period. The stand-by works in this subject are Pablo Macera, *Precios del Perú: XVI–XIX Fuentes*, 3 vols. (Lima, n.d.), and Guillermo Lohmann, "Apuntaciones sobre el curso de los precios de los artículos de primera necesidad en Lima durante el siglo XVI," *Histórica* 29, (Lima, 1966), 79–104. More specifically, however, a study of urban development in Lima, reveals that the prices of bricks and other construction material remained stable throughout the seventeenth century. María Antonia Durán Montero, *Lima en el siglo XVII: Arquitectura, Urbanismo y Vida Cotidiana* (Sevilla, 1994), 52. Prices for many consumables in the first half of the seventeenth century are also found in Bernabé Cobo, *Historia de la fundación de Lima*, ed. M. Gonzalez de la Rosa (1639; Lima, 1882), 68–73.

15 "Libramiento de 711 ps. 6rs. en comisiones al Dr.Dn Pedro Bravo de Castilla, Fiscal Protector Interino...," Lima, 14 December 1736, BNP mss, c92 (1736), fs.1–4.

16 "Tomo quinto de consultas y pareceres dado a S.M. en asuntos del gobierno de Indias recopiladas a materias del A.B.C.D. por Don Manuel Josef de Ayala, natural de Panamá Archivero de la secretaria del Despacho Universal de ellas, dedicado al Exmo señor Baylio Fr. Dn. Julian de Arriaga su Geffe. Año de 1768," AHN Códices 756-B, f.105v.

17 "Tomo segundo de consultas y pareceres dado a S.M. en asuntos del gobierno de Indias recopiladas a materias del A.B.C.D. por Don Manuel Josef de Ayala, natural de Panamá Archivero de la secretaria del Despacho Universal de ellas, dedicado al Exmo señor Baylio Fr. Dn. Julian de Arriaga su Geffe. Año de 1765," AHN Códices 753-B, 2v.

4,000 pesos, Juan de la Rynaga claimed that the accumulated debt to the officials involved in the protectorship of Indians was in the range of 25,000 pesos.[18] In 1706 José Mejía de Estela declared that he was owed 20,643 pesos in unpaid salaries as Procurator General of Indians.[19]

Although this situation applied to other crown officers—Maldonado de Silva, advocate of Indians in Charcas, for example, declared in his testament that he was owed 6,000 to 7,000 pesos for his salaries as corregidor of El Cercado in Lima[20]—there is a consensus in these tracts that the annual income of protectors and advocates implied a life of 'discomfort.'[21] The idea that the officers involved in the protectorship of Indians were ill paid is recurrent throughout the existence of this institution. When considering the appointment of Ignacio de Aybar Eslava (1649–1706) as protector-*fiscal* for Quito, viceroy Melchor de Navarra y Rocaful (*v.*1681–89), for example, remarked that the salary was 'too short.'[22] In similar fashion, the memorials on the Protector of Indians published between 1622 and 1671, all proposed that an adequate annual salary for the *fiscal*-protector should be 3,000 pesos. To further this point, Nicolás Matías del Campo compared the salary of a protector (between 1,000 and 1,800 pesos per annum), with the 7,000 or 8,000 pesos per annum he estimated that an advocate in private practise could earn in Lima.[23]

In sum, despite the stark differences between one and the other, the comparison drawn by Campo was perhaps exaggerated. Considering the earnings of other crown officers in Peru, the wages of advocates and protectors were close to that of a commissar general of cavalry (1,500 pesos), and below that of

---

18 Rynaga, *Memorial*, 8v-9.

19 AGN, protocolos notariales s.XVIII, protocolo 475, Nicolás de Figueroa 1705–1706, f. 241v.

20 AGN, protocolos notariales s.XVII, protocolo 1092, Francisco Medina 1651–53, fs.207v–208.

21 "[D]esacomodados," Rynaga, *Memorial*, 8v–9.

22 "Sobre ser muy cortos." See *Memorias de los virreyes que han gobernado el Perú durante el tiempo del coloniaje español* (Lima, 1859), vol. 2, 99. Ignacio de Aybar (or Martínez de Aybar), a graduate of the universities of Santo Tomás of Quito and San Marcos, had been *teniente de corregidor* (1676, 1678–81) general war auditor (1680), and interim protector of Indians in Quito (Aug.1679–Oct.1680). In 1683 he purchased the position of protector-*fiscal* of this audience for 13,000 pesos with a futurario position as *oidor*. He served as protector from 1686 until his death in 1706. See Tamar Herzog, *Los ministros de la audiencia de Quito (1650–1750)* (Quito, 1995), 50–53.

23 *Memorial al Rey N.S. Don Felipe IIII. A favor de los indios del Piru Sobre el oficio de Protector General en la ciudad de Lima, corte y cabeza del Piru* (Madrid, 1622), 7–8; Rynaga, *Memorial*, 20v; and Campo, *Memorial*, 13. Complaints of ill payment in the seventeenth century from other audiences are also found in Bayle, *Protector*, 100.

an *oidor* of the audience (3,000 pesos).[24] In this respect when in 1763 Antonio de Porlier (1722–1813), *fiscal* of the Council of the Indies, reviewed the proposal to increase the salary of protector of Santa Fe de Bogotá to 2,940 pesos, he considered it to be disproportionate and instead suggested 2,000 pesos.[25]

Income

The protectorship salaries were not the only source of income for advocates and protectors of Indians. As stated above, a marked characteristic of the seventeenth-century memorials on the protectorship of Indians in Peru, was their concern with the inadequacy of the wages paid to these officials. For the memorial of 1622, the need for extra income often implied that, in addition to their other occupations, advocates and protectors 'defended other many lawsuits, are professors, and have other offices and occupations.'[26] This was the case of Diego de León Pinelo who in 1665 informed King Philip IV (*r.* 1621–65) that during his ten years as protector he had the 'profits of lawyer and professor of Prime of Canon Law.' However, once he was elevated to the rank of protector-*fiscal* in 1665 these activities became incompatible with his new position of minister of the audience of Lima, and thus his salary of royal official alone would not allow him to sustain his wife and daughters.[27]

León Pinelo was among the many advocates and protectors that combined their office with legal practice and work at the university of San Marcos (see Chapter 4). Evidence is scattered but it appears that Cipriano de Medina, Leandro de la Rynaga, and Alonso Hurtado de Mendoza obtained additional income as private attorneys. Medina, for instance, was already considered as one the *letrados* of most fortune and businesses in Lima by the time of his appointment as advocate of Indians in 1593, and continued to practice the

24 See Cobo, *Historia*, 115 and Frèzier, *Relación*, 194. In this respect it is interesting to note that Hurtado de Mendoza, upon his retirement as *regidor perpetuo*, received 1,700 pesos from the Cabildo of Lima. See AGN, protocolos notariales s.XVIII, protocolo 835, Pedro Pérez Cabañas 1705, fs. 1559–62v.

25 "Tomo quinto de consultas y pareceres…," AHN Códices 756-B, f.104v. Porlier was later *oidor* in Chacras (1765–66), *fiscal* of crimen in Lima (1769–75), *fiscal* in the Council of Indies for New Spain (1773) and governor of the Council in 1792 until the Napoleonic invasion. In 1791 he was made Marquis of Bajamar. See Mark Burkholder and D.S. Chandler, *Biographical Dictionary of Audiencia Ministers in the Americas, 1687–1821* (Westport, 1982), 266–67; and Guillermo Lohmann Villena, *Los ministros de la Audiencia de Lima en el reinado de los borbones (1700–1821)* (Sevilla, 1974), 103–4.

26 *Memorial* (1622), 7.

27 "[L]ucro de abogado y catedrático de Prima de Cánones." Diego de León Pinelo to King Philip IV, Lima, 12 November 1665, in Torre Villar, *Pareceres*, 84.

law at least until he was seventy-two years old.[28] On the other hand, the power of attorney given to Rynaga by Diego de los Rios, evidences that legal services for a single client in the period of four years could amount to 550 pesos, that is 137.5 pesos per annum. To judge from the power of attorney given by Lope de Mendoza, corregidor of Quito, to collect an obligation of 1,050 pesos it would appear that Rynaga's practice extended beyond the audience of Lima.[29] In the case of Hurtado de Mendoza, his testament indicates that the mercury miners of Potosí paid him an annual fee of 500 pesos to take care of their legal affairs.[30] Legal practice was also undertaken by protectors in audiences other than Lima: Maldonado de Silva of Charcas, for example, declared that he earned '300 to 500 pesos' in legal fees to defend the Indians of Cocharcas.[31]

With the exception of Antonio de Ibarra, Diego Hurtado de Avendaño and Tomás de Brun (who was rector of the college of San Vicente in Huesca), all advocates and protectors of Indians held chairs or lectureships at the University of San Marcos (see Appendix 1 and Tables 2–4).[32] Although Alvaro de Ibarra, Diego de León Pinelo, and Juan de Peralta Sanabria did not hold their professorships at the same time as their office of protector-*fiscal*, Table 7 indicates that this appointment could provide a significant additional annual income. Acuña and Sosa, for example, earned three times as much as professors of prime of Canon Law (1500 pesos per annum) than as advocate of Indians (500 pesos per annum). With the exception of the professorship of Institute (400 pesos per annum), all legal chairs at the university paid higher salaries than those of the advocates of Indians. It is revealing, for instance, that the professorships of prime of Laws or Canon Law themselves provided an annual income similar to that of a protector-*fiscal* (1,500 pesos). Therefore, even within the lowest paid chairs, holding a university position could add between thirty

28 Eguiguren, *Diccionario*, 1: 386–387. An entry of 22 May 1631 in the diary of Juan Antonio Suardo, reveals that Medina's *solicitador* Juan de Guedexas, was badly injured shortly after leaving his house where they had "dispatched a certain lawsuit [pleyto]." See Juan Antonio Suardo, *Diario de Lima*, ed. Rubén Vargas Ugarte (Lima, 1935), 132.

29 AGN, Protocolos Notariales s. XVII, protocolo 45, Cristóbal de Mendieta 1603, fs. 747–48; fs. 984–990.

30 AGN, protocolos notariales s.XVII, protocolo 496, Diego Fernández Montaño 1692, f. 915.

31 AGN, protocolos notariales s.XVII, protocolo 1092, Francisco Medina 1651–53, fs.207v–208.

32 Prime of Law (Alvaro de Ibarra, Bravo de Legunas), Vespers of Law (Campo, Barrientos), Prime of Canon Law (Acuña, Rynaga, Sosa, Campo, León Pinelo, Barrientos, Baquíjano), Vespers of Canon Law (Campo, León Pinelo, Bravo de Lagunas), Decretals (Maldonado de Silva), Institute (Medina, Rynaga, Sosa, Campo, Peralta, Barrientos, Baquíjano), Code (Ibarra, León Pinelo, Peralta, Bravo de Lagunas), and *Digestum Vetus* (Bravo de Lagunas).

TABLE 7 *Professorships at San Marcos, annual salaries 1570–1788*

Chair	1570–c.1617	c.1617–1689	c.1689–1788
Prime of Canon Law (1570)	1500	1600	1000
Prime of Laws (1570)	1500	1000	1000
Vespers of Canon Law (1570)	1000	600	600
Vespers of Laws (1570)	1000	600	600
Decretals	1000	600	600
Institute (1570)	500	400	400
Code (1620 / 1668)		300	300
Digestum Vetus (1694)			400

SOURCE: VALCÁRCEL 2001

and one hundred-fifty percent to the annual income of a protector or advocate of Indians.[33]

Notarial records also document that, besides private practice or university professorships, advocates and protectors had additional earnings deriving from either business transactions, real estate ownership, or family estates. A good example of an advocate actively involved in business is Leandro de la Rynaga. As early as 1586 Rynaga, then twenty-three years of age, purchased the 'principal houses' of the Monastery of the Holy Trinity using the 7,000 pesos brought as dowry by his wife, and later sold them for double that price at 14,000 pesos.[34] In a similar fashion, a number of transactional minutes of 1603–1604 registered by notary Cristóbal Aguilar de Mendieta, indicate that he invested the produce of tithes of the valley of Pisco which amounted to 2,950 pesos with cleric Crisóbal Ruiz Trujillo; lent 6,000 pesos to Andrés Nino Pedratas to buy wine and other goods; and lent 1,950 pesos to licenciate Cristóbal Ruiz, a presbyter in Lima.[35] During this same period his debts amounted to 1,616 pesos in three separate bonds.[36] The transactions of 1603–04 amounted to 12,541 pesos. In addition to

33 The statutes of the College of Santo Tomás in Quito, founded in 1683 established the following salaries for university professorships: Prime of Canon Law, 500 pesos; Prime of Laws 500 pesos; Vespers of Canon Law, 400 pesos; Vespers of Laws 400 pesos; Institute, 300 pesos; and Code. See Archivo Nacional de Ecuador, caja 3, exp. 15 (13.XII.1646), fs.18–18v.

34 AGN, protocolos notariales, s.XVII, protocolo 480, Antonio Fernández de la Cruz 1653, f. 1885.

35 AGN, Protocolos Notariales s. XVII, protocolo 45, Cristóbal de Mendieta 1603, fs. 248v–52v; 289–90; and Protocolo 46, Cristóbal de Mendieta 1603–1604, fs.326–27v.

36 Ibid., fs. 974v; 1732, 1733v.

this, the economic activities of Rynaga included the production of grain crops in his agricultural properties in the valley of Cacahuasi, Ate, East of Lima.[37]

A good example of the size of the business transactions undertaken by Rynaga in the last years of his life, is the 40,000 pesos offered in the bid for the hacienda of Santa Beatriz, eventually sold to the Noviciate of the Company of Jesus.[38] Similarly, the amounts of surplus cash he managed are illustrated in the sums paid to support his children: Juan was given 2,842 pesos for his trip to Spain; Bartolomé 6,000 pesos; Bernardo 5,978 pesos for his personal support; Jacoba 1,000 pesos to buy a cell at the Monastery of Encarnación; and María a dowry of 20,000 pesos upon her marriage to Juan del Campo Godoy. In all, the magnitude of the business activities undertaken by Rynaga is encapsulated by the debt of 118,000 pesos his widow inherited at the time of his death in 1634, including the 3,622 pesos for his funeral pomp.[39]

In a similar fashion, the inventory of goods of Juan de Peralta Sanabria reveals that he was actively involved in the trade of cloth and clothing. Among the pending transactions left by Peralta Sanabria, for example, there is the purchase of a shirt, taffeta trousers, and towel to for 165 pesos. He also left Chinese imports consisting of 26 varas (42.4 mts) of cloth embroided with flowers (*primavera de China*), and 46 varas (76.98 mts) of satin. More significantly, however, the accounts include unspecified instruments for 9,489 pesos; a court order to execute the land and goods of Alonso de Ita for 1,000 pesos; and accumulated debts in his favour for a total of 42,996 pesos registered in his account books for the period between 1699 and 1706.[40]

Advocates and protectors also had earnings deriving from real estate. Diego de León Pinelo, for example, 'punctually' paid Juan del Campo Godoy 500 pesos per annum as rent for his house.[41] Pedro Balaguer de Salcedo possessed

---

37 AGN, Protocolos Notariales s. XVII, protocolo 1984, Cristóbal de Vargas 1611, fs.2542–45v. Cacahuasi, however, had encumbered a chaplaincy (*capellanía*) which yielded 331 pesos of 4 reales per annum.

38 The property of Santa Beatriz remained with the Jesuits until their expulsion in 1767. See Fernando Flores-Zúñiga, *Haciendas y pueblos de Lima: Historia del Valle del Rímac*, vol. 1, Valle de Huatica, La Victoria, Lince y San Isidro (Lima, 2008), 153–54.

39 AGN, protocolos notariales s.XVII, protocolo 480, Antonio Fernández de la Cruz 1653, f. 1885.

40 One vara equalled approximately 163 cm. The debtors were Juan de Vechis Roncal for 1,080 pesos, 1,566, María de Esquivel, Diego Sáenz and Francisco de Campos 2,160; María de Esquivel and García Alson Falcón 3,696 pesos and 3,240 pesos; Manuela de Mendoza 4,320 pesos; Nicolás de Aramburú 1,080 pesos.

41 "Testamento de Diego de León Pinelo," (21.IV.1652), in Torre Villar, *Pareceres*, 104. The fact that Maldonado de Silva paid 200 pesos for the annual rent of a house, testifies of the

a house with seven shops, and a *solar* (an urban plot of land) and a half in the riverside property next to the Convent of Saint Francis in Lima—a development initiated by viceroy Luis de Velasco—acquired in 1602 with the condition of building within a year of the acquisition.[42] In addition to his home with four shops, Alvaro de Ibarra was also the owner of three houses in front of the Church of Belén.[43] Cipriano de Medina and Alonso Hurtado de Mendoza both declared they were proprietors of additional houses to their private residences.[44] Evidence varies, but it would appear that in seventeenth century Lima, rent for a house on the riverside (Balaguer de Salcedo) could reach 50 pesos per annum, whereas rents in the area of the Church of Belén (Ibarra) could reach 120 pesos per annum for a small house, and 400 to 650 pesos per annum for a large one. Pedro Bravo de Lagunas Bedoya, father of protector-*fiscal* Pedro José Bravo de Lagunas, for example, received 108 pesos per annum for a 'small house in the street of the Monastery of St. Clare.'[45] Larger rents could have been obtained from the properties of Hurtado de Mendoza in the street of the Church of La Merced, due to their proximity to the main square.[46]

Another source of income was agricultural production. In this respect Rynaga had properties in valley of Cacahuasi in Ate;[47] Medina a *chacra* in Miraflores in the valley of Magdalena in Lima;[48] Hurtado de Mendoza the *estancia* of La Angostura in Chile;[49] and Lasso de la Vega the haciendas of Santa Rosa and Surquillo.[50] Although there is no record of the income these properties yielded for their owners, the inventory of the goods of Lasso de la

---

additional income that property could yield. See AGN, protocolos notariales s.XVII, protocolo 1092, Francisco Medina 1651–53, f. 208.

42 See Antonio San Cristóbal, *La casa virreinal limeña de 1570 a 1687*, 2 vols. (Lima, 2003), 1: 145–146; and Durán Montero, *Lima en el siglo XVII*, 61.

43 AGN, protocolos notariales s.XVII, protocolo 1461, Pedro Pérez Landero 1675, f. 304v.

44 Medina declared that the house in La Merced street, was acquired for five lives to the Augustinian Order, for which he paid an annual fee of 517 pesos; for the other house he paid 180 pesos per annum. See AGN, protocolos notariales s.XVII, protocolo 496, Diego Fernández Montaño 1692, f. 915.

45 AGN, protocolos notariales s.XVIII, protocolo 444, Francisco Fernández Pagan 1722, f. 42.

46 See Durán Montero, *Lima en el siglo XVII*, 168, 170.

47 AGN, protocolos notariales s. XVII, protocolo 1984, Cristóbal de Vargas 1611, fs.2542–45v. Cacahuasi, however, had encumbered a chaplaincy (*capellanía*) which yielded 331 pesos of 4 reales per annum.

48 AGN, protocolos notariales s.XVII, protocolo 818, Diego Gutiérrez 1635, f. 475v.

49 Guillermo Lohmann Villena, *Los regidores perpetuos del cabildo de Lima (1535–1821): Crónica y estudio de un grupo de gestión*, 2 vols. (Sevilla, 1983), 2: 154–55.

50 AGN, protocolos notariales s.XVIII, protocolo 873, Agustín Gerónimo de Potalanza 1770–77, f. 734v.

Vega, reveals that he kept an account of the payments of *alcabalas* (real estate sales tax), purchase of slaves, or credit agreements. His papers also reveal that the hacienda of Surquillo had water rights disputes with the Indians of Surco and Miraflores, and that the hacienda of Santa Rosa included a lime concession.[51]

In other cases, however, the origin of this additional income is difficult to ascertain. The executors of Pedro Balaguer de Salcedo, granted powers of attorney to collect his debts in Potosí of 2,275 pesos and of 493 pesos of 9 reales, but give no information on the origins of these.[52] At the time of his death in 1635, Cipriano de Medina had 2,555 pesos of debts in his favour plus 76 rescripts and legal instruments (*escrituras*) 'of salaries of different persons.' Considering that his estate was composed of two houses and various goods, this income could derive either from legal practice or business. The fact that among his papers he possessed powers of attorney from a Mateo de Castroverde of Seville, also suggest that these activities had a transatlantic scope.[53] Similarly, Hurtado de Mendoza declared unspecified credits for 7,700 pesos. The fact that his brother in law, Antonio de Jaraquemada had previously owed him 6,000 pesos suggests that these transactions also involved family members.[54]

Other Indicators

The economic capacity of advocates and protectors can also be measured through other indicators. Good examples of this are sums paid to purchase royal offices and audience positions. In 1611 Rynaga, for example, paid 8,250 pesos for the office of *regidor perpetuo* vacated by Francisco de Valenzuela Loayza (*fl.*1569–1606) in 1606.[55] In turn, Francisco de Valenzuela paid 9,000

51 Among the papers found was a 'small notebook where the Count noted all the expenses of the hacienda of Surquillo' ("Un cuadernito en que el señor conde apuntaba los gastos de la hacienda de Surquillo"). See AGN, protocolos notariales s.XVIII, protocolo 873, Agustín Gerónimo de Potalanza 1770–77, f. 734v.

52 AGN, protocolos notariales s.XVII, protocolo 788, Pedro Gonzáles de Contreras 1606, fs. 20371–75v.

53 AGN, protocolos notariales s.XVII, protocolo 818, Diego Gutiérrez 1635, f. 496v. In the case of the 2,555 pesos the debtors were Juan de Valencia (250 pesos), Diego García de Palacios (55 pesos), María de Hinojosa (250 pesos), Jerónimo de Cavaría (500 pesos), Manuel Férnandez and Ana Marique (1000 pesos), Ana Manrique (500) pesos.

54 AGN, protocolos notariales s.XVII, protocolo 496, Diego Fernández Montaño 1692, f. 915. Debtors were Antonio de Oquendo, from Cusco (3,000 pesos), Francisco de Saldívar (700), Estate of Juan de Ubaque (3,000), and Antonio de Jacaremada, his brother in law (1,000 pesos, of an original obligation of 6,000 pesos).

55 Lohmann, *Regidores*, 1: 79.

pesos for the office of *fiscal*-protector.[56] Similarly, Moreno Cebrián indicates that the 1730 appointment of Pedro de Santiago Concha as protector was preceded by a payment to the royal treasury of 20,000 pesos.[57] On the other hand, Chandler and Burkholder indicate that Francisco de Rojas Acevedo, Juan de Peralta Sanabria, and Pedro Bravo de Lagunas purchased *letrado* positions in the audience of Lima. Although there is no indication on the amount paid by Rojas Acevedo, Peralta Sanabria and Bravo de Lagunas paid, respectively, 8,000 and 20,000 pesos for a supernumerary post of *oidor*.[58]

Evidence provided in testaments demonstrate that these officials were also beneficiaries of annuities. As patron of the lay chaplaincy of Santa Juana de Mora, for example, Bravo de Lagunas received an annual income of 200 pesos.[59] In other cases the amounts of money were more significant. The parents of Rojas Acevedo, for example, transferred him the annuity of the 8,000 pesos mortgage they had on an agricultural property next to the convent of Saint Francis in Lima.[60] In a similar fashion, Melchor de Santiago Concha, transferred to his son Pedro and his sister, the income of the 10,000 mortgage charged against his main house in Lima.[61]

Equally indicative of the economic situation of advocates and protectors were dowries, which consisted of cash and property, and were paid on marriage to be managed by the husband for the benefit of the wife and children.[62] The earliest record of this transaction is that of Leandro de la Rynaga, who received 7,000 pesos when he married Juana Cervera de Rivadeneyra in 1586. In turn, Rynaga would endow his daughter María with 20,000 pesos of dowry upon her marriage to advocate of Indians Juan del Campo Godoy.[63] The dowry

56 Real Cédula, Lima, 8 November 1664, in Ernesto de la Torre Villar, 82.

57 Alfredo Moreno Cebrián, *El virreinato del Marqués de Castelfuerte, 1724–1736* (Madrid, 2000), 261.

58 See Mark Burkholder and D.S. Chandler, *From Impotence to Authority: The Spanish Crown and the American Audiences, 1687–1808* (Columbia, 1977), Appendix III, 147–149.

59 See BNP, mss c96 (1736).

60 AGN, protocolos notariales s.XVIII, protocolo 1095, Gregorio de Urtazo 1704, f. 418.

61 See the testament of Melchor de Santiago Concha y Errazquín of 1729, AGN, protocolos notariales s.XVIII, protocolo 302, Pedro de Espino Alvarado 1742, f. 92v 94.

62 See M.C. Mirow, *Latin American Law: A History of Private Law and Institutions in Spanish America* (Austin, 2004), 56; Paul Rizo-Patrón Boylan, *Linaje, dote, y poder: La nobleza de Lima de 1700 a 1859* (Lima, 2001), 128–146; and Asunción Lavrin and Edith Couturier, "Dowries and Wills: A View of Women's Socioeconomic Role in Colonial Guadalajara and Puebla, 1640–1790," *Hispanic American Historical Review* 59 (2) (1979), 280–304.

63 AGN, protocolos notariales s.XVII, protocolo 480, Antonio Fernández de la Cruz 1653, f. 1885. Lohmann, *Regidores*, 2: 154–155

given to Alonso Hurtado de Mendoza in 1643 was agreed in 30,000 pesos, although it was not all effectively paid due to the 'shortness of goods' of the parents of his wife Isabel Jaraquemada. Doctor Cipriano de Medina gave her daughter Sebastiana the lavish amount of 45,000 pesos.[64] In any case, the estimation of the dowries granted to these advocates and protectors fits within the upper tier of dowries registered by Juan Antonio Suardo for Lima in the years 1629 to 1634, and certainly well above the amount Hurtado de Mendoza endowed Josefa, his illegitimate daughter (1,000 pesos).[65] By the end of the seventeenth century, Francisco de Rojas Acevedo received 14,051 pesos when he married the daughter of doctor José del Corral Calvo de la Banda (*c.*1625–86) in 1691.[66]

Higher dowries, in both cash and goods, were received by protectors-*fiscales* in the eighteenth century. In 1734, for example, Pedro de Santiago Concha received 56,174 pesos from Juan de Traslaviña and Juana de Oyague Beingolea, parents of María Teresa de Traslaviña Oyague, his future wife.[67] Equally exceptional were the 77,000 pesos received in 1735 by García José Lasso de la Vega from Domingo de Jáuregui and María Josefa de Jáuregui y Alvear, parents of his first wife, María Francisca de Jáuregui.[68] Based on the eighteenth century dowries inventoried by Swayne and Rizo-Patrón, the amount granted to both protectors is located in the upper tier. Thus, the amounts received by Santiago Concha and Lasso de la Vega exceeded those granted to diverse women belonging to the nobility of Lima. In this respect, these are in the range of the dowries granted to Juana Josefa Cabero Manrique de Lara in 1725 (78,220 pesos); Catalina de Baquíjano y Carrillo in 1773 (72, 515 pesos); and Petronila Carrillo de Albornoz y Salazar in 1790 (61,359 pesos).[69]

---

64 AGN, protocolos notariales s.XVII, protocolo 818, Diego Gutiérrez 1635, f. 477v.

65 AGN, protocolos notariales s.XVIII, protocolo 835, Pedro Pérez Cabañas 1705, fs. 1559–62v. Suardo noted the dowries of daughers of *oidor* Gabriel Núñez de Sanabria (30,000 pesos) and Gregorio de Ibarra (30,000 pesos in cash, and 10,000 as trousseau or *ajuar*)—incidently the father of Alvaro de Ibarra (PGI 1655)—; as well as that of Mariana de Urdanivia, wife of treasurer Miguel Azpurua (40,000 pesos). See Suardo, *Diario*, 178, 154, 181.

66 AGN, protocolos notariales s.XVII, protocolo 1497, Pedro Pérez Landero 1691, f. 38–43.

67 AGN, protocolos notariales s. XVIII, protocolo 64, Francisco Cayetano Arredondo 1734, fs. 544–47v.

68 AGN, protocolos notariales s.XVIII, protocolo 883, Salvador Jerónimo de Portalanza 1734–1735, f. 269–271v.

69 See Guillermo Swayne y Mendoza, *Mis antepasados* (*Genealogía de las familias Swayne, Mariátegui, Mendoza y Barreda*) (Lima, 1951), *passim*, and Paul Rizo Patrón, *Linaje*, Table 11, 134. Other than those mentioned above, the dowries registered are those of Ursula Fernández Maldonado in 1701 (2,006 pesos), Rosa Miranda y Caballero de Tejada in

FIGURE 5
Joaquina María Brun de Carvajal Vargas. 18th century. Painting by unknown artist in Museo Nacional de Chile. In Paul Rizo-Patrón, Linaje, dote y poder: La nobleza de Lima de 1700–1850 *(Lima, 2001). The marriage of protector*-fiscal *Tomás de Brun, an Aragonese of the lesser hidalgo class, to creole Catalina Isidora de Vargas Carvajal y Hurtado de Quesada, is a good case of upward mobility within the* letrado *ranks. The sumptuous appearance of their daughter Joaquina María (depicted here) matches the prestigious social standing and lineage displayed in her arms (1. Vargas 2. Carvajal 3. Chavez [de Quesada] and 4. Sotomayor) and the atributes of Correo Mayor de la Indias, surmounted by the coronet of countess of Castillejo and Del Puerto.*

In a broader perspective, the financial situation of the protectors is also revealed by family entourage. Cipriano de Medina, for instance, was married to Sebastiana de Vega, half-sister of bishop Feliciano de Vega who, by 1631, had amassed a fortune estimated in 450,000 pesos.[70] Although Medina's legal practice and business surely benefited from the system of patronage created by Vega, it was his son and namesake, friar Cipriano de Medina y Vega, who gained the material benefits of this fortune as patron of the lavish *capellanías* and pious works endowed by Feliciano in his testament of 1639.[71]

In a similar fashion, the marriage of Tomás de Brun to Catalina Isidora de Vargas Carvajal y Hurtado de Quesada (1688–*c.*1759) provided him with access

1702 (37,442 pesos), Mariana Bravo de Lagunas y Villela in 1723 (15,635 pesos), Andrea de los Rios Berris Miranda y Caballero de Tejada in 1732 (25,732 pesos), María Ignacia Carrillo de Córdoba y Garcés de Mansilla in 1746 (17,818 pesos), Josefa Román de Aulestia y Aulestia Cabeza de Vaca in 1747 (35,774 pesos), María Josefa de Eslava y Cavero in 1749 (36,233 pesos), Clara Carrillo de Albornoz (1755), and Catalina Sánchez Boquete y Román de Aulestia in 1789 (35,321 pesos).

70 Suardo, *Diario*, 161.

71 See the testament of Cipriano de Medina y Vega, AGN, protocolos notariales s. XVII, protocolo 612, Marcelo Antonio de Figueroa 1652, fs. 2396–2404v. There were, however, notorious disputes on the administration of Vega's legacy. See Diego de León Pinelo, *Por el Licenc. don Diego de Córdova, canonigo desta santa iglesia cathedral de Lima, albacea, y administrador que ha sido de los bienes del señor arzobispo de México de buena memoria, doctor Feliciano de Vega. En el artículo con el P.M. Fr. Cipriano de Medina...*(Lima, n.d.).

to the well-established Vargas Carvajal clan. At the age of eight years, Brun's brother in law, Diego Gregorio de Vargas Carvajal (1686–1731), inherited from his great uncle and namesake Diego Anastasio de Vargas Carvajal (1634–94) the office of Correo Mayor de Indias, and the countship of Castillejo. In economic terms, holding the Correo Mayor de Indias, bestowed in perpetuity to Lorenzo Galíndez de Carvajal (1472–*c.*1525) in 1514, implied for the office holder the right to eight *mitayo* Indians, and an estimated income of 7,000 pesos per annum.[72] The permanent assets linked to the title of Castillejo, founded in 1683, were the encomienda of Ichoguari in Conchucos, and the hacienda of Castillejo-Mamacona in Lurín, some twenty miles from Lima. This property, estimated in fifty-three *fanegas* (84.27 acres), had seventeen slaves, eighteen mules and six cows, as well as the right to three *mitayo* Indians.[73] Although, both the office and the entail were tied to numerous obligations, its possession allowed Diego Gregorio to declare in his testament of 1731 a personal estate (i.e. non entailed goods) 'oscillating between 20 and 30 thousand pesos.'[74]

The Vargas Carvajal's were also holders of the countship of Del Puerto, created in 1632, and eventually inherited by Catalina Isidora.[75] This title had two entails attached: That founded in Trujillo, Spain, by Alonso García de Vargas Valfondo in 1413; and that founded in Lima by Diego de Vargas Carvajal in 1557, with the *señorío* (lordship) of the Villa del Puerto. The properties in Spain included the Vargas palace in the plaza mayor of Trujillo, rights to twenty-three pasture lands, and three hundred *fanegas* (477 acres) of land, rented to the

72 José María Vallejo García-Hevia, "La asesoría general del juzgado de la renta de correos (1755–1762): Campomanes, precursor de la moderna administración del servicio postal," *Revista de Administración Pública* 146 (1998), 80.

73 See AGN, protocolos notariales s. XVIII, protocolo 609, Francisco Luque 1765, fs. 1307–1309v. The right to the mitayo Indians was granted to the first Count of Castillejo by the viceroy-archbisho Melchor de Liñan y Cisneros on 20 July 1679.

74 AGN, protocolos notariales s. XVIII, protocolo 64, Francisco Cayetano Arredondo 1731, fs. 88v–90v. Whereas the in 1731 the office of Correo Mayor had 16,000 pesos in liens in favour of two *capellanías*, in 1765 the entail of Castillejo was tied to contributions amounting to 700 pesos per annum in favour of various religious causes (e.g. 200 persos for the most senior Inquisitor, 100 for Holy Thursdays, etc.). See AGN, protocolos notariales s. XVIII, protocolo 609, Francisco Luque 1765, fs. 1342–49v.

75 Authors differ on wether Catalina Isidora was the third, sixth or seventh holder of the title. However, this dignity appears in her testaments of 1751 and 1759. See Alberto Rosas-Siles, "La nobleza titulada del virreinato del Perú," *Revista del Instituto Peruano de Investigaciones Genealógicas* 21 (1995), 441; Rizo Patrón, *Linaje, dote y poder*, 126; and Lohmann, *Los ministros*, 21.

local council at least until 1765. In addition to this, there was an orchard, and a rural property comprised by a house, sixteen *fanegas* (25.44 acres) of wheat, and eight *fanegas* (12.72 acres) of rye.[76]

On the other hand, the testament of Magdalena Hurtado de Quesada (1664–*c.*1746), Brun's mother in law, suggests that her entire estate was worth well over 75,000 pesos.[77] Such an important colonial fortune offers a striking contrast with Brun's wife—Catalina Isidora—assets at the time of their marriage in 1724. In 1753, for example, her personal, i.e. non entailed property, amounted to 2,000 pesos, two slaves, a gold and diamond "aderezo," and twelve bronze plates.[78] However, it is worth pointing out the fact that being a member of such a wealthy, prestigious and well-connected trans-Atlantic lineage, gave Tomas de Brun access to the upper echelons of Peruvian colonial society and furthermore, access to credit, business opportunities and honourable treatment; solely based on the respectability and wealth of his in-laws. The symbolic capital that came through his marriage to Catalina Isidora, was probably decisive for his career and businesses.

In sum, it would appear that the economic capacity of advocates and protectors of Indians was not limited to their income as crown officials. The vast majority held university positions with regular salaries that could increase their annual gains in the range of thirty to one hundred-fifty percent. In addition to this, notarial evidence suggests that their patrimonies were further increased by other economic activities. With the exception of legal practice, which was restricted only to non audience magistrates, protectorship officials endeavoured in real estate investment, agriculture, and trade; all these resulting in considerable revenues. Dowries and family entourage also gave advocates and protectors a powerful instrument to enlarge their wealth and access credit.

---

76 AGN, protocolos notariales s. XVIII, protocolo 609, Francisco Luque 1765, fs. 1342–49v. The annual obligations of the entail of Del Puerto in Spain amounted to 11,526 reales and 15 maravedíes vellón.

77 AGN, protocolos notariales s. XVIII, protocolo 373, Francisco Estacio Meléndez 1746, fs. 98v–103. The estimation is based on the fact that she declared that 12,000 pesos should be taken from the fifth part of her estate, to institute a chaplaincy in the convent of St. Francis in Lima.

78 AGN, protocolos notariales s. XVIII, protocolo 597, Francisco Luque 1759, fs. 1118v.–1122. The jewels were left to her grand-daughter María Magdalena de Vargas Carvajal, and the plates to her grandson Mariano Joaquín de Carvajal y Vargas.

Material Culture

Following the dispositions of viceroy Toledo, the Protector General, Advocates and Procurators of Indians were required to reside in Lima during their office tenure. The city of Lima was not only the religious and political capital of the Viceroyalty of Peru, but, in the words of the French traveller Amedée-François Frèzier (1682–1773), the 'deposit [its]…treasures.'[79] Reconstructing the private domestic world of the material culture of this city, let alone that of the protectors' themselves, is, however, a task constrained by limited available sources.[80] Leaving aside the surviving houses and artefacts, the material culture of the viceregal period is documented through a small number of chronicles, travellers' diaries, notarial records, portraits and pictures depicting domestic life.[81] In this respect, most studies in this field are limited to architecture,[82] although some insights on the households and living conditions of Lima are found in a number of monographs.[83] All these have contributed to place in context the

79 Amadeo Frèzier, *Relación del viaje por el Mar del Sur*, trans. Miguel Guerin, (1716; Caracas, 1982), 191.

80 For material culture as the study of meaning in consumption see Neil McKendrick, John Brewer, and J.H. Plumb, *The Birth of Consumer Society: The Commercialization of Eighteenth-Century England* (Bloomington, 1982), and John Brewer and Roy Porter, eds *Consumption and the World of Goods* (London: Routlegde, 1993). For Latin America see the essays in the special issue on material culture of *The Americas* 60 (3) (2004).

81 Only brief descriptions of houses and domestic life in Lima are found in Cobo, *Historia*, 49–54; Frèzier, *Relación*, 223–24; Vasili Mikhailovitch Golovnin, "Lima y Callao en 1818," in Estuardo Núñez, ed. *Relaciones de viajeros*, book 1, vol. 27 of *Colección Documental de la Independencia del Perú* (Lima, 1971), 154–156, 164; William Bennet Stevenson, "Memorias sobre las campañas de San Martín y Cochrane en el Perú;" and Alexander Caldcleugh, "El Perú en vísperas de la Jura de la Independencia (1821)," both in ibidem, book 3, 120–122, 165–166, 181, 184–185.

82 For the history of domestic life and architecture of Lima see Emilio Harth-terré, *Cómo eran las casas en Lima del siglo XVI* (Lima, n.d); Emilio Harth-terré and Alberto Márquez Abanto, "Historia de la casa urbana virreinal en Lima," separata of *Revista del Archivo Nacional del Perú* 26 (1962), 15–21; Héctor Velarde, *Arquitectura Peruana*, 3rd ed. (Lima, 1978); María Antonia Durán Montero, *Lima en el siglo XVII: Arquitectura, Urbanismo y Vida Cotidiana* (Sevilla, 1994); Richard Malachowski et al., *Casa Peruana* (Lima, 2000); and Antonio San Cristóbal, *La casa virreinal limeña de 1570 a 1687*, 2 vols. (Lima, 2003). Although it is a literary work, some insights of viceregal domestic world are found in the *Tradiciones Peruanas* of Ricardo Palma (1833–1919), published between 1863 and 1909.

83 See José Gávez, "Lima colonial," in *Lima en el IV Centenario de su fundación: Monografía del Departamento de Lima* (Lima, 1935); Jean Descola, *La vida cotidiana en el Perú en tiempos de los españoles, 1710–1820* (Buenos Aires, 1962); Alberto Flores

urban houses and domestic furnishings of the advocates and protectors of Indians, as the material expression of their social and economic place in the city and viceroyalty.[84]

Houses and Domestic Furnishings

There are a significant number of protectors that appear as house owners. In some cases there is evidence of their specific locations. Hurtado de Mendoza, for example, was the proprietor of a house in La Merced street, and Santiago Concha the owner of the Traslaviña house in Afligidos or Traslaviña street. Both houses were conveniently located, respectively, two blocks away from the main square. In other cases, there are indicators of some characteristics of the house. In 1592, for example, Balaguer de Salcedo commissioned three doorways and an upper floor for his main house. Two of these doorways would be in stone with the same architectural devices found in the residence of Alvaro Ruiz de Navamuel (1552–*c.*1613), secretary of government of Viceroy Toledo; and the upper floor was possibly intended to add more comfort to the house either as a second drawing room or a *cuadra de estrado*.[85] Similarly, the inventory of goods of Alvaro de Ibarra performed in 1675, indicates that his home had four shops (*tiendas*) overlooking the street.[86] With the exception of the house of Gregorio de Rojas Acevedo, located in the street of the Jesuit College or Estudios de la Compañia, and valued in 17,413 pesos, there is no specific indication of the market price of these properties.[87]

The ownership of a great house or *casa solariega*, considered by Frèzier as beautiful and spacious—but also as dark, humid and badly decorated—, was the most forthright statement of social and economic position.[88] The *casa*

Galindo, *La ciudad sumergida: Aristocracia y plebe en Lima, 1760–1830*, 2nd ed. (Lima, 1991); Rizo Patrón, *Linaje, dote y poder*; Eduardo Arrarte, ed. *La casa solariega de Aliaga* (Lima, 2004); Sandro Patrucco, *Presencia italiana en la Lima borbónica: 1701–1800* (New York, 2006). For Latin America see comments on domestic furniture found in Joseph J. Rishel, comp. *Revelaciones: Las artes en América Latina, 1492–1820* (México, 2007), 253–54.

84 In this field of study I am particularly endebted to the studies of Richard L. Bushman, *The Refinement of America: Persons, Houses, Cities* (New York, 1993); Richard Goldthwaite, *Wealth and Demand for Art in Italy, 1300–1600* (Baltimore, 1993), and Simon Shama, *The Embarrasment of Riches: An Interpretation of Dutch Culture in the Golden Age* (New York, 1997).

85 San Cristóbal, *La casa virreinal*, 1: 145–46.

86 AGN, protocolos notariales s.XVII, protocolo 1461, Pedro Pérez Landero 1675, fs. 302–10v.

87 AGN, protocolos notariales s.XVII, protocolo 1116, Gregorio de Urtazo, 1719, f.590.

88 Frèzier, *Relación*, 224–225.

solariega was usually a two-storey construction: The first built in adobe and the second in *quincha* (a frame of wood and cane held together by leather, and covered in mud), all covered in painted plaster. Scale and arrangements vary from case to case, but the basic house plan of the *casa solariega* consisted of a large doorway, usually elaborately decorated with a stone façade opening to a passage or entry foyer (*zaguán*) flanked by rooms overlooking the street. The *zaguán* opened to a patio, around which there was the *sala* or sitting room (usually opposite the *zaguán*), as well as the bed chambers, the *cuadra de estrado* (a room used exclusively for family entertainment), and rooms dedicated for specific activities such as the study or oratory. The area of service was usually around the second patio, and included the kitchen, pantry, carriage room and stables. Whereas the carriages could be placed in one of the rooms next to the *zaguán*, the patios or in the back of the houses, the stables were invariably situated at the very end of the house. In addition to this, the service area of the house could also include an orchard, hen house or garden.[89]

This pattern is found in the houses of Cipriano de Medina and García José Lasso de la Vega. Medina's house was composed of a chamber or drawing room, bedchamber, study, oratory, and pantry. The fact that he kept a carriage with two black mules, as well as a third mule "to bring logs," suggests that his residence had carriage room and stables. The property also had an infirmary, possibly used for charitable works, but also as bedchambers for the slaves.[90] In turn, the inventory performed on the Lasso de la Vega house indicates that, although the house was built 'from its foundations' in a ruinous property bought to the Augustinian Order, it remained unfinished by 1775. The finished rooms included a chamber, bedchamber, study, *tras estudio* (a room behind the study which served as a deposit), and a room next to the carriage-room, possibly used as sleeping quarters for the coachman. On the other hand, the fact that it had 'costly embankment,' suggests that it was located alongside the Rímac River.[91] In general terms, however, the number and arrangement of rooms in both houses suggests that they followed the pattern of a drawing

89 See San Cristóbal, *La casa virreinal*, 2: 652, 653–664; Emilio Harth-terré and Alberto Márquez Abanto, "Historia de la casa urbana," 15–21; and Harth-terré, *Cómo eran las casas*, 7.

90 AGN, protocolos notariales s.XVII, protocolo 818, Diego Gutiérrez 1635, fs. 494v–96v.

91 "La casa de la morada de los señores condes de Villanueva, fabricada desde sus cimientos y un costoso terraplén por las señora condesa antes de su fallecimiento, hasta el cuarto de dormir y si acabar las demás piezas está en pampa y ocupado solo de desmonte de la casa antigua arruinada que se necesitan limpiar y allanar el sitio para seguir la fábrica de la casa hasta concluirla." AGN, protocolos notariales s. XVIII, protocolo 873, Agustín Gerónimo de Potalanza 1770–77, f. 734v.

room parallel to the street (*sala atravesada*), dividing the two patios, with the specialized rooms (study, oratory, infirmary) around them.[92]

In other cases, the protectors' probate lists of goods provide clues of house arrangements, even if the notaries did not produce a room by room inventory. The house of Alvaro de Ibarra, for example, would have had enough rooms to accommodate a collection of more than 190 paintings, 440 books, seventy-two chairs, fifteen writing desks, and carriage.[93] He therefore lived in a *casa solariega* with at least a bedchamber, chamber, study, and carriage house. On the other hand, the fact that the inventory of goods of Felipe Santiago Barrientos included a mid-sized set of furniture, ornaments for mass in a cupboard, a library and a considerable amount of clothes, reveals that he lived in rented apartments composed at least of a bedchamber, chamber and possibly a third for the study or oratory.[94]

The domestic world of the advocates and protectors can also be reconstructed through notarial inventories and probate lists of goods. One of the main features of these domestic surroundings was the separation of public and private rooms. The separation of intimate and public spaces was a characteristic of houses of the upper echelons of society, and an outgrowth of the Renaissance Humanistic stress on civility and polite external behaviour.[95] In general terms, private quarters were not ostentatious. The bedchamber of Medina, for example, contained personal clothes and domestic utensils (six sets of bed linen, cushions, one silver plate, and four candlesticks), and was furnished with a wardrobe, two gold plate boxes, two large prints, twelve small old paintings, a crucifix, and a retable. Similarly, that of Lasso de la Vega contained a wardrobe, cupboard with silver furnishings, writing desk and folding screen; the walls were covered with eight devotional paintings of the Virgin: four of advocations—owned by the Countess—, and four depicting scenes of Her life.[96]

On the other hand, the decoration of rooms used for public functions varied from case to case. Medina's *sala*, for instance, was quite sparse as befitted a waiting area: a wooden sculpture, a wooden sideboard, an old bench, a two

92 San Cristóbal, 2: 427; Durán Montero, *Lima en el siglo XVII*, 163.

93 AGN, protocolos notariales s.XVII, protocolo 1461, Pedro Pérez Landero 1675, fs. 302–10v.

94 AGN, protocolos notariales s. XVIII, protocolo 1143, Marcos de Useda 1739, fs. 232–239.

95 See Laurence Stone, *The Family, Sex and Marriage in England, 1500–1800* (London, 1990), 171; Marvin Becker, *Civility and society in western Europe, 1300–1600* (Bloomington, 1988), 81; and Jessica Kross, "Mansions, Men, Women and the Creation of Multiple Publics in Eighteenth-Century British North America," *Journal of Social History* 33 (2) (1999), 385–408.

96 AGN, protocolos notariales s.XVII, protocolo 818, Diego Gutiérrez 1635, f. 494v; and protocolos notariales s. XVIII, protocolo 873, Agustín Gerónimo de Potalanza 1770–77, f. 733v.

vara (163 cm) buffet, and twelve chairs upholstered in silk.[97] In contrast, notary Agustín Gerónimo de Portalanza describes the *sala* of Lasso de la Vega as a more handsomely decorated room. It contained twelve wood inlaid chairs, seven gilded chairs, two canapés and three full-length curtains. The walls were decorated with four paintings depicting the life of the Virgin, Saint Turibius of Mogrovejo, Saint Francis Xavier, and portraits of the Count's forbearers.[98]

The place of precious furniture and paintings as a manifestation of taste among protectors is perhaps best represented by the household collection of Alvaro de Ibarra. The inventory performed in 1675 by notary Pedro Pérez lists twenty-four upholstered chairs embroidered with the cross of the Order of Alcántara, fifteen inlaid and fine wood writing desks, seven ebony mirrors, another sixteen embroidered chairs, an ivory crucifix, three brocade and six velvet upholstered chairs, one cocobolo wood and three inlaid buffets, and two inlaid chests.[99]

More significant, however, was the art collection composed of more than 190 unattributable paintings. Although these covered a broad spectrum of subjects, there appears to be a predominant taste for still-life and religious painting. The inventory lists at least fifty-five pictures depicting fruits, and another forty-three depicting flowers or plants. The fact that this genre painting was usually of Flemish or Italian origin reveals, in it itself, a pattern of sophisticated collection found in Spanish art patrons as from the 1590s.[100] As for religious themes, which constituted the focal point of viceregal art, there were at least forty-two pictures depicting a diverse range of subjects including Marian and Christological imagery, Biblical scenes, and depictions of the holy figures who shaped Christian history and doctrine.[101] His interest in Classical Antiquity

97 AGN, protocolos notariales s.XVII, protocolo 818, Diego Gutiérrez 1635, f. 494.

98 AGN, protocolos notariales s. XVIII, protocolo 873, Agustín Gerónimo de Potalanza 1770–77, f. 733v.

99 AGN, protocolos notariales s.XVII, protocolo 1461, Pedro Pérez Landero 1675, fs. 302–10v.

100 Jonathan Brown and Richard Kagan, "The Duke of Alcala: His Collection and Its Evolution," *The Art Bulletin* 69 (2) (1987), 238. There is, however, evidence of still-life painting being produced in Peru, particularly during the eighteenth century, due to the imports of Flemish paintings and engravings. In Cusco, for exmple, fruteros were not only painted by Cusco artists such as Quispe Tito, but also appear as part of eighteenth century collections. See José de Mesa and Teresa Gisbert, *Historia de la pintura cuzqueña*, 2nd ed. (Lima, 1982), 290; and Rishel, *Revelaciones*, 331.

101 This included two Immacualte Conceptions, Saint Catherine, Peter, Rita, Ana, two Geronimo, Francis, Michael, Teresa, Magdalena, Francisco Masias, Rose of Lima, John the Evangelist, Ignatius, flight from Egypt, and a 'Roman Pieta.'

was also extensive to judge from the twenty-eight paintings of Greco-Roman deities, and historical scenes such as the Rape of Lucretia.[102] Ibarra also displayed on the walls of his house representations of the glories of the Spanish Monarchy: four canvasses depicting the conquest, a large portrait of King Philip IV, and a number of battles, including a scene of the Battle of Pavia (1525), and landscapes of the cities of Seville and Huancavelica.[103]

The status of paintings as highly esteemed decorative objects is also visible in the 1706 inventory of Juan de Peralta Sanabria. This notarial document evidences that Peralta owned an ensemble of seventy-two pictures composed of twelve angels, twelve 'strong women,' twelve portraits of members of the Spanish Royal Family, twelve still life *fruteros*, eleven devotional paintings, and three small canvases framed in Huamanga stone. Whereas the devotional paintings had been produced in Cusco, the angels, women and still lives were Spanish imports.[104]

The central importance of prayer and piety within the viceregal household is evidenced by the handsome furnishings of the oratory or private chapel of Cipriano de Medina. This room held the complete liturgical utensils for mass: a gold plated cross; silver chalice, candlesticks; glass cruets and host box; altar linens and silk taffeta frontals. It would appear that the altarpiece was constituted by a sculpture of the Virgin and Child, crowned with an imperial crown of silver, flanked by two *retablos* (retables) depicting Saint Dominic and Saint Thomas, and three wooden reliquaries. Another ten *retablos* decorated the walls of the chapel, reflecting the private devotions of the household. Five of these were approximately one *vara* (80 centimetres) in height, and depicted the Prayer in Gethsemane, Saint Theresa, Saint Francis Xavier, Saint Louis of France, and Saint Henry II, Holy Roman Emperor. Among the other five, described in the inventory as small, were representations of Saint Catherine and a Nativity scene. As Goldthwaite has suggested, these images reflect the

102 Vuclanus, Adonis and Venus, Banquet of the Gods, Bacchus, Orpheus, Diana and Actaeon. Once more this pattern is interesting as landscapes and classical motives became more popular in the eighteenth century. Mithological painting was also common among the lettered classes of Cusco. See Mesa and Gisbert, *Pintura*, 288–289, 293.

103 From a different perspective, the portrait of bishop Diego de Arce Reinoso (1585–1665), Inquisitor General and Councillor of State could reveal some form of patronage in Spain, as his career had prospered during the reign of Philip IV. For Arce's influence in court see J.H. Elliot, *The Count-Duke of Olivares: The Statesman in an Age of Decline* (New Haven, 1986), 670.

104 AGN, protocolos notariales s.XVIII, protocolo 957, Francisco Sánchez Becerra 1706, f. 1535v.

extent to which the exercise of personal devotion was centered on pictures.[105] The chapel also had three wooden reliquaries, reclinatories, lectern, and missal. The fact that private chapels required a special privilege to conduct liturgical services asserted, no doubt, the special relation of the Medina clan with ecclesiastical authorities through Bishop Feliciano de Vega. On the other hand, the central importance of prayer within the household is also reflected in the portable oratory (*escaparate*) and essential items of the liturgical apparatus owned by Peralta and Barrientos.[106]

In general terms, however, it would appear that the most important room in the houses of protectors and advocates was the study. In the case of Medina, it was large enough to accommodate the 732 volumes of his library (see Chapter 6). Unlike the sparse decoration of his *sala*, the study was more lavishly decorated. Its centrepiece was a Crucifix under a canopy flanked by pictures of Saint Anthony of Padua and Saint Francis of Asisi. The room was filled with two writing cabinets of German manufacture, three tables, two benches, seven chairs, and a wardrobe.[107] Eight religious pictures, eight still lives imported from Flanders, and two maps were hung on the walls.[108]

The probate list of goods of Ibarra also reveals the prominent position of knowledge and letters in his domestic world. Even if notary Pedro Pérez did not produce a room by room inventory, the house would have the space to store and browse in comfort his 440 volume library. On the other hand, the eleven fine-wood writing cabinets (*escritorios*) inlaid with ivory or tortoiseshell, two paper cabinets (*papeleras*), and three desks (*escribanías*)—one of ebony inlaid with ivory and one of walnut manufactured in Salamanca—attest to the predominant place of reading and writing in Ibarra's dwellings.[109] In turn, the study of Lasso de la Vega was furnished with three writing desks, two round tables in the centre, one large leather canapé, another two tables inlaid with mother of pearl, nine English-made velvet upholstered stools, two

105 See Goldthswaite, *Wealth*, 144, 153.

106 Whereas the inventory of Peralta registers a cassock, chalice, misal, lectern, candlesticks, and altar linens, that of Barrientos has a chalice, misal and what was 'necessary to say mass.' See, respectively, AGN, protocolos notariales s.XVIII, protocolo 957, Francisco Sánchez Becerra 1706, f. 1536; and protocolo 1143, Marcos de Useda 1739, f. 239.

107 Symonds notes that "A curious custom of furnishing that was prevalent on the Continent and not in England was the making of escritoires in pairs." This suggests that both were designed to stand in the same room, 59. This pattern is found in Ibarra, where the escritorios are always inventories in pairs, AGN, protocolos notariales s.XVII, protocolo 1461, Pedro Pérez Landero 1675, f. 304.

108 AGN, protocolos notariales s.XVII, protocolo 818, Diego Gutiérrez 1635, fs. 495v–496.

109 AGN, protocolos notariales s.XVII, protocolo 1461, Pedro Pérez Landero 1675, fs. 302–10v.

armchairs, another eleven plain chairs and a small buffet. The area not occupied by his 358 volume library, displayed in four book-stands, was adorned with a bronze crucifix, seven pictures of the Virgin Mary, two silver framed prints, one bronze plate, and a clock.[110]

The importance of the study, along with its books and writing desks, in the domestic world of advocates and protectors, is also evidenced in less handsome dwellings. The 500 book library and cordovan-top desk of Antonio Maldonado de Silva, advocate of Indians in Charcas, held a disproportionate place among his goods inventoried in 1651 composed of his clothes, a gilded bed, two trunks, sixteen paintings (two large and twelve small), and a horse.[111] In turn, protector-*fiscal* Felipe Santiago Barrientos, who appears to have occupied a three room apartment in a house, possessed two old writing cabinets, a large English-made desk, and the library inherited from doctor Tomás de Salazar (†1738), an *oidor* of the audiences of Santa Fe and Lima.[112] On the other hand, even if at the the time of his death the 70 volume library of Juan de Peralta Sanabria was rendered useless by moth and mice, he nonetheless had a large writing cabinet mounted on a table and adorned with an ivory crucifix, as well as writing desk of cocobolo wood, and a small portable writing cabinet.[113]

The furnishings of these studies indicate that these were places designed to make the activity of reading a more comfortable and enjoyable affair. More importantly, however, the cabinets, tables and desks, as well the existence of professional and business documents in these rooms, are testimonies of these being working environments. On the other hand, the assemblage of silver plates, knives and forks, as well as a silver basin and wine bottles in the study of Medina, suggest that the studies were spaces integrated into the ordinary daily life of the household.[114]

Protectors and advocates of Indians lived a comfortable, and at times ostentatious, existence. Besides the ownership of grand houses, the domestic goods found in the inventories reveal a sophisticated consumption pattern. These

110 AGN, protocolos notariales s. XVIII, protocolo 873, Agustín Gerónimo de Potalanza 1770–77, fs. 731v, 733–34v.

111 AGN, protocolos notariales s.XVII, protocolo 1092, Francisco de Medina, 1651 53, fs. 207v–209.

112 AGN, protocolos notariales s. XVIII, protocolo 1143, Marcos de Useda 1739, fs. 232, 239. On 26 April 1738 Tomás de Salazar named Barrientos his ejecutor and granted him powers to undertake his testament (*poder para testar*), AGN, protocolos notariales s. XVIII, protocolo 4, José de Agüero 1736–41, f. 498. On Salazar see Lohmann, *Los ministros*, 125.

113 AGN, protocolos notariales s.XVIII, protocolo 957, Francisco Sánchez Becerra 1706, f. 1535.

114 AGN, protocolos notariales s.XVII, protocolo 818, Diego Gutiérrez 1635, f. 496.

goods were displayed in the public areas of the house and included a range which covered retables, sculptures, and ivory or tortoiseshell inlaid furniture. The rich resources of the Peruvian silver mines, made it possible to adorn homes with all manner of objects wrought in precious metals. Some protectors were models of refinement as evidenced by imported goods such as Asian inlaid furniture, Flemish paintings, or English desks.[115] Their art collections, on the other hand, combined humanistic interests with the doctrinal and practical concern of Counter-Reformation Catholicism. True to their profession, however, the most important room in the house was without doubt the study.

Personal Apparel

The personal appearance of protectors and advocates of Indians was determined by their position as royal officials. The most significant source in this respect are the surviving portraits of four protectors-*fiscales* of Indians: León Pinelo, Ibarra, Bravo de Lagunas and Baquíjano (Plates 1, 2, 3 and 4). These pictures follow a widespread layout in seventeenth and eighteenth century viceregal art, whereby the subject faces straight ahead or is turned three-quarters to the side in the centre of the composition as a full figure.[116] The distinctive element in their appearance is the *garnacha*, an open-fronted ankle-length black gown with open sleeves and lined in taffeta, over a dark suit. Although *letrados* and academics wore similar gowns, the *garnacha* was reserved for those with rank of ministers of the audiences (*oidores* and *fiscales*).[117] The protectors are also represented using the *golilla*, a white starched pointed collar which replaced the ruff as symbol of office after the pragmatic sanction of 1623 was issued aimed to 'repress' luxury.[118] They also wear the *puñetas*, a piece of lace attached to the sleeves, also reserved for doctors and magistrates.

Significantly, the portraits denote the close ties between the protectorship and the University of San Marcos. Bravo de Lagunas (Plate 4), for instance, is depicted standing beside a desk which displays not only an open book, pens

115 Rishel, *Revelaciones*, 253–254, 514. For English exports see R.W. Symonds, "English Eighteenth Century Furniture Exports to Spain and Portugal," *The Burlington Magazine for Connoisseurs* 78 (455) (1941), 57–64.

116 Ricardo Estabridis, "El retrato del siglo XVIII en Lima como símbolo de poder," in Ramón Mujica, ed. *El Barroco Peruano*, vol. 2 (Lima, 2003), 135–71.

117 See Bernardino Bravo Lira, "Símbolos de la función judicial en el Derecho Indiano," 258–263; and Carmen Bernis Madrazo, *El traje y los tipos sociales en el Quijote* (Madrid, 2001), 125–130.

118 Néstor Luján, *La vida cotidiana en el Siglo de Oro español*, 6th ed. (Madrid, 1991), 61–62. As Elliot notes, this change was promoted by the Count-Duke of Olivares as one of the measures of austerity in the Spanish court. See *The Count-Duke of Olivares*, 147.

and inkwell, but his doctoral biretta, and the two *becas* which denote him as a former scholar of the royal colleges of San Martín (red) and San Felipe y San Marcos (light blue). In the same manner, both León and Ibarra rest their right hands respectively on the books of the Digestum Vetus (Plate 1), and Code and Infortiatum (Plate 2), the subjects they taught at San Marcos. The statutes of the university also appear in a prominent position among Baquíjano's books (Plate 3). In this regard, it is also noteworthy that academic insignia appear in the notarial inventories of advocates and protectors. Thus Ibarra, Medina and Maldonado de Silva had among their goods gowns, birettas, doctoral swords and velvet *capirotes*—a piece of cloth round the shoulders used in academic ceremonies to denote the degrees of master and doctor.[119]

The paintings also allude to the subject's social rank, interests and personal taste. All portraits display the coat of arms of the protectors in the traditional Spanish form. In the case of Baquíjano, however, his shield is surmounted by the coronet of count (referring to his title of Vistaflorida), and placed over a Maltese cross; on the other hand, his condition of supernumerary knight of the Royal Order of Charles III, a dignity he achieved in 1792, is reflected by the badge attached to his suit.[120] Similarly, Ibarra places his arms over the cross of the Order of Alcántara.

The protector's interests are alluded mainly by the book shelves that appear as background for their portraits. These were mainly law books, but also denoted interest in theological and scientific issues. Personal taste and consumption patterns are reflected by the use of rings (León Pinelo), wigs (Bravo de Lagunas), monocles (Baquíjano), gold-buckled shoes (Bravo de Lagunas and Baquíjano), and inkwells (Bravo de Lagunas and Baquíjano). Time pieces (Bravo de Lagunas), however, could also be regarded as representing professional occupation as they represent the need for keeping a schedule.[121]

---

119 In the case of Medina "Un escaparate en que hay lo siguiente: una bolsa con capirote y borla, una fuentecilla y jarro de plata que pesa," AGN, protocolos notariales s.XVII, protocolo 818, Diego Gutiérrez 1635, f. 496. For Ibarra and Maldonado de Silva see, protocolo 1461, Pedro Pérez Landero 1675, f.310; and protocolo 1092, Francisco de Medina, 1651–53, f. 207v. 209.

120 The badge of the order, established in 1771, is a maltese cross with the image of the Immaculate Conception, surrounded by the motto "Virtuti et Merito" and the inscription of "CIII"; the medal hangs from a blue and white ribbon. Baquíjano was still Protector of Indians when he entered the Order of Charles III in 1792. See Lohmann, *Los americanos en la órdenes nobiliarias*, 2nd ed. (Madrid, 1993), 2: 278–279.

121 See Kelly Donahue-Wallace, *Art and Architecture of Viceregal Latin America, 1521–1821* (Albuquerque, 2008), 207.

It would appear that, in general terms, advocates and protectors favoured dark clothes, which they combined with their gown of office. This would have been Medina's daily attire to judge from the doublet, six black shirts and three pairs of hoses that appear in his inventory of goods.[122] In turn, Lasso de la Vega possessed eight plates (six of silk, one of burato, and one of wool); while Barrientos had no less than six suits to use with *golilla*.[123] All this reflects the importance of office dress as an act of state. As is evidenced in Juan de Solórzano who commented that the *garnacha* not only was the successor of the *infulas* or laticlavius used by the senators and other Roman magistrates, but also the 'appropriate insignia and ornament' that rendered and conveyed honour to those who wore it.[124]

Spending in dress was not only dictated by office alone, but by the requirements of fashion. In this respect, protectors were no exception to the observations of Amadée Frèzier (1682–1773) who stated that the men and women of Lima were prone to show themselves 'magnificent in their clothes.'[125] Once more inventories provide the evidence. Peralta Sanabria, for instance, owned a gold-embroidered blue coat.[126] The wardrobe of Lasso de la Vega contained four robes of silk lined with velvet, as well as gold cufflinks, buckles, and buttons. Although the three moth-eaten wigs indicate that his public appearances were considerably restricted, if non existent, his personal apparel included twenty six gold boxes and three silver boxes. Similarly, Barrientos indulged in conspicuous consumption of clothing as evidenced by his twenty-four shirts of Brittany, two *chupas* or jacket of yellow and red brocade, two sets of velvet coats and matching trousers, two gold embroidered coats, three beaver hats, and brocade nightgown.[127]

Nor were the women at all behind their husbands and fathers in personal ostentation. In this respect, the portrait of Joaquina de Brun Carvajal y Vargas (Plate 5), daughter of protector-*fiscal* Tomás de Brun, is an eloquent example.

---

122 The inventory of Medina included six black shirts and three trousers. AGN, protocolos notariales s.XVII, protocolo 818, Diego Gutiérrez 1635, f. 495.

123 Lasso, f. 733v; AGN, protocolos notariales s. XVIII, protocolo 1143, Marcos de Useda 1739, fs. 233.

124 "[Q]ue esta toga talar, que sucedió en su lugar a las Infulas o Laticlavios que usaban los Senadores y otros magistrados romanos, sea propiamente insignia y ornamento de honor y manifieste el que se le debe dar y guardar a los que las traen." Juan de Solórzano Pereira, *Política Indiana*, 5.4.14, note. 31.

125 "Magníficos en su atavío," Frèzier, *Relación*, 191.

126 AGN, protocolos notariales s.XVIII, protocolo 957, Francisco Sánchez Becerra 1706, f. 1535v.

127 AGN, protocolos notariales s. XVIII, protocolo 1143, Marcos de Useda 1739, f. 233.

The half-figure composition reveals a haughty woman with an elegant oval face, brown eyes and full lips; as was fashionable among eighteenth century ladies, she displays a black taffeta beauty spot on her forehead. Her dark hair is pulled back, tied at the nape with a ribbon, and topped by *piocha* of pearl. Joaquina's embroidered brocade dress has a blue-and-red floral pattern on a silver-gray background. The tightly fitted bodice has three-quarter sleeves, which are completed by a double ruffle that ends above the wrists. The bodice is decorated with white lace. Her sumptuous appearance is enhanced by the lustre of jewels: a pearl necklace-and-earrings set; a diamond, pearl and gemstone brooch in the upper chest; and several strings of pearls on each wrist.[128] On the other hand, women of less well-off protectorship families were not at all behind their aristocratic counterparts. Petronila de Ardiles, widow of protector-*fiscal* Felipe Santiago Barrientos, for example, was the proud owner of a diamond ring, golden reliquary, and a number of brocade gowns.[129]

The possession of jewels was another perceptible manifestation of sophisticated consumption among female members of protectorship families.[130] Once more it corroborates the observation of Frèzier that the women of high society Lima was 'insatiable with the pearls and stones, with the bracelets, earrings, and other accessories.'[131] It appears that the main source for these luxury objects was dowries. In 1691, for example, María Teresa Calvo del Corral y de la Torre, daughter of *oidor* José del Corral y Calvo de la Banda, brought upon her marriage to protector-*fiscal* Francisco de Rojas Acevedo 5,151 pesos in gold objects and jewels. These included a diamond *ahogador* or choker (500 pesos), a diamond and emerald butterfly (450 pesos), a 59 emerald choker (500 pesos); a pair of emerald earrings (500 pesos); a pair of earrings with three 'pumpkin' shaped pearls each (250 pesos); and various diamonds and other precious stone bracelets, rings and earrings.[132] Similarly, María Magdalena de Vargas

128 Her lineage and place in viceregal society is also evidenced by the coat of arms to the left of Joaquina which displays the quarters of Carvajal and Vargas and the coronet of countess. The arms are set against a double headed eagle, a device granted to the first correo mayor Lorenzo Galíndez de Carvajal by Charles v, which holds from its beaks the inscription "Correo Mayor." See Juan Luis Espejo, *Nobiliario de la Capitanía General de Chile* (Santiago, 1967), 228.

129 AGN, protocolos notariales s. XVIII, protocolo 1143, Marcos de Useda 1739, fs. 232–39.

130 On this subject see Priscilla Muller, "Spanish and Spanish Colonial Jewelry," *Art Institute of Chicago Museum Studies* 25 (2) (2000), 35–51, 104–105.

131 "[I]nsaciables con las perlas y las pedrerías, con los brazaletes, zarcillos y otros accesorios." Frèzier also stated that he had seen ladies wearing 60,000 pesos in jewels (i.e. more than 240,000 libras). See *Relación*, 191.

132 AGN, protocolos notariales s. XVIII, protocolo X, Pedro Pérez Landero, 1691, fs. 38–43.

Carvajal, inherited from Catalina Isidora de Vargas Carvajal (Brun's wife), two *aderezos* or sets of necklace, earrings and bracelets, one of diamonds and one of gold.[133]

Diamonds and precious gems are also found in the possession of the women of the family of protector-*fiscal* Pedro de Santiago Concha. His maternal grandfather general Juan Nicolás Roldán Dávila, a prominent landowner in Trujillo, endowed his mother with jewelry valued in 1,650 pesos, consistent of a choker of 'thick' pearls and nine diamonds with a devotional image of Our Lady of Carmen (1000 pesos); a pair of earrings encrusted with coral and three emeralds (200 pesos); a carnation and a jazmin in gold with an emerald (100 pesos each); a *suche* (tree?) in yellow gold (50); and a hyacinth of gold with seven pearls (200 pesos).[134] On the other hand, Pedro's wife, María Teresa de Traslaviña, brought upon their marriage jewels valued at 2,563 pesos, which included two diamond rings (480 pesos); three *tembleques* (articulated head ornament) of diamonds (522 pesos); almond shaped diamonds (1261 pesos); and one *polisón* (pendant) of diamonds (300 pesos).[135]

Perhaps the most conspicuous example of this display of wealth were the jewels of María Francisca de Jáuregui y Aguirre, valued at ten-thousand pesos, married to García José Lasso de la Vega in 1735—that is, six years prior to his appointment as protector-*fiscal*. These were composed of a pair of gold *manillas* or bracelets boasting no less than 706 diamonds (4176 pesos); a gold *polisón* with 64 diamonds and two pearls (589 pesos); two pairs of gold earrings with six pendants and encrusted, respectively, with 54 and 56 diamonds (400 pesos each); a gold cross pendant with 47 diamonds (352 pesos); another pair of bracelets with two strings of pearls of 156 granos and two emeralds (250 pesos); a 18 pearl rosary (300 pesos); a gold *mirame lindo* or adornement with 85 diamonds (484 pesos); a gold *tembleque* with 6 pearls (400 pesos); another pair of earrings of six pendants with a diamond in each (400 pesos); and 'loose diamonds' (331 pesos).[136]

In addition to clothes and jewelry, an important component of personal appareance was the form of transport employed. Advocates and protectors either took horse or rode in a carriage. There is little doubt that the *carroza*,

---

133 AGN, protocolos notariales s. XVIII, protocolo 597, Francisco Luque 1759, f. 1122. In 1764 Marìa Magdalena married Nicolás Próspero Manrique de Lara y Carrillo de Albornoz.

134 AGN, protocolos notariales s. XVIII, protocolo 955, Francisco Sánchez Becerra 1705, fs. 1609–11v.

135 They are refered as "mulatilla," "zambita," "negritas" and "negrito." See f. 547.

136 AGN, protocolos notariales s. XVIII, protocolo 883, Salvador Gerónimo de Portalanza, 1734–1735, ff. 269–271v.

a four wheel carriage with braced suspension, was the status symbol for transport in the seventeenth and eighteenth centuries.[137] These appear in the inventories of Medina, Ibarra, Peralta and Lasso de la Vega. In better times Lasso de la Vega would have displayed two guilded carriages and one calash which, at the time of his death, were moth-eaten and useless.[138] Ibarra also had an upholstered litter with cushions, as befitted his condition of *oidor* of the audience.[139] Other protectors and advocates employed mules for daily use, as revealed in the inventories of Antonio Maldonado de Silva, advocate of Indians for Charcas, and Felipe Santiago Barrientos, who also had six mules used for transporting goods.[140]

Although the personal appearance of advocates and protectors was definied by their office and rank, in many cases they were also conspicuous consumers of clothing and jewellery. In the first case, although wool and rough cotton was locally produced, the lace, silk, embroidery and brocade worn by the protectors and their families would have been imported from Asia or Europe.[141] In the case of jewellery, protectors benefited from living in Lima, a city which was not only a natural market for costly gems, but also an important supplier thereof due to the impressive craftsmanship of Peruvian goldsmiths. Most pieces of diamonds or pearls, however, would have been European imports.

Slaves

The ownership of slaves was perhaps the most distinguishable symbol of anyone who wanted to establish a status in viceregal Peru, and was considered de rigueur for anyone with pretentions of respectability. And although slave labour was important to agriculture and transport, blacks slaves were most conspicuous as retainers and household servants for advocates and

137 See Guillermo Lohmann, "De coches y calesas en Lima en el siglo XVII," *Revista del Archivo General de la Nación* 14 (1996), 111–57.

138 "[M]uy viejo apolillado y maltratado" and "Viejo…falto de muchas piezas desarmado e inservible."

139 309v.

140 AGN, protocolos notariales s.XVII, protocolo 1092, Francisco Medina 1651 53, fs. 207v 209; and protocolos notariales s. XVIII, protocolo 1143, Marcos de Useda 1739, f.239.

141 Elena Phipps, Johanna Hecht, and Cristina Esteras Marín, *The Colonial Andes: Tapestries and Silverwork, 1530–1830* (New Haven and London, 2004), 25–27. The Spanish Crown discouraged the production of luxury textiles in Spanish America to avoid competition with the Metropolis. Whereas lace usually came from Flanders, embroidery was imported either from Spanish factories (such as the Molero de Toledo manufacture, established in 1714), or commissioned to China or the Philippines. See *Revelaciones*, 153–154.

protectors.[142] In Lima, where these officers resided, it is estimated that blacks constituted forty-five percent of the population between 1600 and 1790.[143] As Frederick Bowser observed, blacks were employed in this city on a lavish scale. High civil and ecclesiastical dignataries were accompanied in the street by as many as four armed black lackeys; similarly, the aristocratic ladies of Lima used liveried black servants to carry their sedan chairs, and as coachmen on their carriages.[144] By the end of the eighteenth century Flores Galindo points out that more than eighty percent of the 9,229 registered slaves in Lima were in domestic service.[145]

Information gathered in notarial records reveals that a number of households of protectors and advocates of Indians were served by slaves. In some cases evidence is scant: Alonso Hurtado de Mendoza, for example, is listed as a proprietor of various slaves, but there is no indication of their exact number or duties performed.[146] In turn, Cipriano de Medina, owned eleven domestic slaves: five male, three single female slaves and one mulattoe female slave with two children.[147] a figure close to the number of blacks in attendance in the more aristocratic household of Nicolás de Ribera y Dávalos (*fl.*1620), *alcalde* and *regidor* of Lima, who had a staff of sixteen slaves to serve him at home.[148] Likewise, protector-*fiscal* Francisco de Rojas Acevedo received a twelve year old slave girl as part of the dowry brought by his wife in 1691, and possessed three slaves for domestic service upon his death in 1719.[149]

Black slaves were also part of the households of many eighteenth century protectors. The 1706 inventory of goods of Juan de Peralta Sanabria shows that he was attended by five slaves.[150] Pedro de Santiago Concha, not only grew up in a home served by black servants, but also received six female slaves as part

142 Frederick P. Bowser, *The African Slave in Colonial Peru, 1524–1650* (Stanford,1974); Fernando de Trazegnies, *Ciriaco de Urtecho: Litigante por amor*, 3rd ed. (Lima, 1995); Marcel Velásquez, *Las Máscaras de la representación: El sujeto esclavista y las rutas del racismo en el Perú (1775–1895)* (Lima, 2005). A general overview on the subject is found in Herbet S. Klein, *African Slavery in Latin America and the Caribbean* (Oxford, 1986).

143 The figure is a result of comparing various studies on the subject compiled by Velásquez, *Las Máscaras*, 45.

144 Bowser, *African Slave*, 100.

145 Flores Galindo, *Aristocracia*, 98.

146 Lohmann, *Regidores*, 2: 154–155.

147 AGN, protocolos notariales s.XVII, protocolo 818, Diego Gutiérrez 1635, fs. 494v–96v.

148 Bowser, *African Slave*, 101.

149 AGN, protocolos notariales s.XVII, protocolo 1497, Pedro Pérez Landero 1691, ff. 38–43; and protocolo 1116, Gregorio de Urtazo, 1719, f. 588.

150 AGN, protocolos notariales s.XVIII, protocolo 957, Francisco Sánchez Becerra 1706, f. 1535.

of the dowry brought by his wife, María Teresa de Traslaviña.[151] Lasso de la Vega received one fourteen year old slave girl as part of the dowry of his first wife in 1735, and was attendeded by four slaves at his home in Lima at the time of his death in 1775; although the notary declared one was ill and one astray.[152] In turn, Felipe Santiago Barrientos had three slaves of different castes: a male Creole, a female Guinea and a female Mina.[153] These figures are consistant with the average range of slave ownership in Lima in the second half of the eighteenth century.[154]

The use of domestic slaves in the case of the extended families of protectors is documented in the families of protectors. María Correa de León Pinelo, mother of protector-fiscal Francisco de Rojas, gave two black slaves to her son Alejo, two to her grandchildren, and retained two others for her personal service.[155] Catalina Isidora de Carvajal Vargas, wife of Tomás de Brun, declared one slave for her personal service; whereas her mother left a twenty-three year old female mulattoe and a twenty-five or thirty year old zambo slaves in her testament of 1746.[156] Likewise, the hacienda Castillejo, one of the entailed properties of the Carvajal Vargas clan, possessed seventeen permanent slaves.[157] On the other hand, the childhood home of José de Baquíjano on Calle Gurumendi in Lima had no less than fourteen slaves in attendence.[158]

151 In 1705 José de Santiago Concha Salvatierra received two slaves from Pedro's mother Angela de Roldán Dávila. See AGN, protocolos notariales s.XVIII, protocolo 955, Francisco Sánchez Becerra, 1705, ff. 1609r.–1611v; and protocolo 64, Francisco Cayetano y Arredondo, 1734, ff. 544–547v.

152 AGN, protocolos notariales s.XVIII, protocolo 883, Salvador Gerónimo de Portalanza, 1734–1735, ff. 269–271v.

153 These names refer to the slave's origin. Whereas Creole slaves were born in America, the other two had been imported from Guinea-Bissau and São Jorge da Mina, and Angola, respectively. See Bowser, *African Slave*, 30, 40.

154 In a survey of testaments of eighty-seven slaveowners in Lima in 1770, Flores Galindo found that eighty percent owned between one and five slaves. See Alberto Flores Galindo, *La ciudad sumergida: Aristocracia y plebe en Lima, 1760–1830*, 2nd ed. (Lima, 1991), "Esclavos en Lima, 1770," Table 4, 98.

155 AGN, protocolos notariales s.XVIII, protocolo 1095, Gregorio de Urtazo 1704, fs. 418v, 419.

156 AGN, protocolos notariales s.XVIII, protocolo 597, Francisco Luque 1759, fs. 1118v.–1122; and protocolo 373, Francisco Estacio Meléndez 1746, fs. 102–103.

157 1307r.– 1309v.

158 See Mark A. Burkholder, *Politics of a Colonial Career: José Baquíjano and the Audience of Lima*, 2nd ed. (Wilmington, 1990), 16. There is also evidence that the José Toribio, brother of Pedro José Bravo de Lagunas, was the proprietor of six slaves for domestic service. AGN, protocolos notariales s.XVIII, protocolo 84, Orencio de Azcarrunz, 1769, f. 182v.

Black slaves were indispensable to the operation of these households, and would serve as cooks, laundresses, maids, handymen, coachment and gardeners. As Bianca Premo has recently suggested, the links of slaves with a specific household were often reinforced by the fact that elite families in Lima relied on female slave labour for child care.[159] It was also common for owners to use their skilled or semi-skilled slaves for rental, providing them with a fixed income and transferring their own expenses in maintanence.[160] As a highly adjustable labour force, slaves were means to pursue the private interests of their owners. It would appear, for instance, that Medina used part of his slaves to attend his infirmary, following the model of the hospital of Santa Ana whereby African slaves served as practical nurses, bookkeepers, cooks, laundressess and the like.[161]

From a commercial perspective blacks were also valuable investments. Following the price estimates for 1635 suggested by Bowser, the total number of slaves owned by Medina could have reached the handsome figure of 5,168 pesos.[162] In a similar fashion, the six young slaves received by Santiago Concha as part of his wife's dowry were valued at 1600 pesos;[163] as was the fourteen-year old Creole girl included in the dowry of Lasso de la Vega at 450 pesos. Thus, slaves could be used as collaterals for loans, and objects of speculation to be traded in response to fluctuations in value. The fact that they were not mere pieces of property, is reflected in the costs they implied to the owner in housing, food and wellbeing.[164] This would often involve taking care of them in illness. For example, until his death protector-*fiscal* Peralta retained both Francisco, a Mina slave of over forty years of age described as 'broken,' and

---

159 Bianca Premo, *Children of the Father King: Youth, Authority and Legal Minority in Colonial Lima* (Chapel Hill, 2005), 51.

160 Even if wages were low, rental provided a fixed income for their owners and transferred their own expenses in house and food. See Klein, *African Slavery*, 32–33; Flores Galindo, *Aristocracia y plebe*, 98; Bowser, *African Slave*, 102. the most highly paid domestics commanded as much as thirteen to fifteen pesos a month (p. 104).

161 The infirmary had "Dos estradillos pequeños en que duermen los negros," AGN, protocolos notariales s.XVII, protocolo 818, Diego Gutiérrez 1635, f. 495v. For the role of black slaves in the Santa Ana hospital see Bowser, *African Slave*, 105.

162 Five male slaves at 508 pesos each, four female slaves at 465 each; and two children at 384 if male, or 458 pesos if female. See Bowser, *African Slave*, Tables B.1 and B.3, pp. 345–44.

163 AGN, protocolos notariales s.XVIII, protocolo 64, Francisco Cayetano y Arredondo, 1734, f. 546.

164 Very little is known on this subject, but the daily expenditures of slave trader Manuel Bautista Pérez on individual food and medicines for slaves between 1626 and 1634 is studied in Linda A. Newson and Susie Minchin, "Diets, Food Supplies, and the African Slave Trade in Early Seventeenth-Century Spanish America," *The Americas* 63 (4) (2007), 517–550.

Feliciana who was 'ill with *calenturas*' (fevers) and spate blood.'[165] In the same manner, Lasso de la Vega took care of Jacinto, a male slave who was 'ill of the waist and urinated blood.'[166]

The black slaves of advocates and protectors of Indians were not only objects of luxury and ostentation, but also significant economic assets. To Peninsular-born officials in particular, the ownership of domestic servants implied an altogether significant change in the dynamics of daily life, and in their living standards. In this repect, slaves are perhaps the most important differentiator of economic and social standing in viceregal society.

The revenue of advocates and protectors of Indians was not limited to their salaries as Crown Officials. By far the most frequent source of additional income were the wages they obtained as university lecturers and professors. Other than this, they undertook a number of profitable activities such as legal practice, commerce, and agricultural exploitation. In many cases, their position would have been supported by the productive and symbolic capitals of their family entourage.

As a result of these factors, the material culture of advocates and protectors included precious furniture, works of art, magnificent dress, imposing houses, coaches and their suite of slaves. Therefore, in general terms, the economic situation of advocates and protectors was above that of other legal practioners of the audience of Lima with an Indigenous clientele. That this was the case in respect to procurators goes without saying, as these constituted a class below the university trained professionals. However, it is significant that, although some advocates which worked for Indian plaintiffs such as licenciate Juan Pacheco (*fl.*1689–1716), owned a house, jewelry and paintings, in most cases the income and consumption standards of these letrados did not match those of the protectorship rank.[167]

---

165 "[E]nferma de calenturas y echar sangre por la boca." AGN, protocolos notariales s.XVIII, protocolo 957, Francisco Sánchez Becerra 1706, f. 1535.

166 "[E]nfermo actualmente de la cintura y que arroja sangre por la orina." AGN, protocolos notariales s. XVIII, protocolo 873, Agustín Gerónimo de Potalanza 1770–77, f.735.

167 AGN, protocolos notariales s.XVIII, protocolo 695, Alejo Meléndez de Arce 1719–26, fs. 974–75v. The evidence is sketchy but other testaments of advocates involved in Indian cases include José de Urtaide, advocate and relator of the audience of Lima (protocolo 769, Jacinto de Narvasta 1702–05, fs. 309-309v); Ginés de Bustamante, advocate of the audience of Lima born in Panama (protocolo 777, Jacinto de Narvasta 1712–14, fs. 734–35); and Tomás de Salazar, advocate of the audience of Lima, attorney for prisoners of the Holy Inquisition, and lecturer of Prime of Laws (protocolo 1037, José de Torres Campo 1725, fs. 157–159). Their involvement in Indian cases is found in AGN, Real Audiencia, causas civiles, leg.245, c.917, c.1689 (Pacheco); leg.7, c.40, 1703 (Bustamante); leg.8, c.45, 1704 (Salazar).

The investment in domestic embellishment and personal appearance, not only provided the advocates and protectors with visible signs of wealth and distinction, but also brings forth significant clues of the values held by these officials. The infirmary of Medina, the collection of religious paintings of Ibarra, and the oratories of Peralta and Barrientos, all denote, for example, the role played by piety and charity among these men. More to the point, however, the material culture they created was centered in their role of legal professionals. The predominance of the studies in their housing arrangements, the importance of libraries among their goods, and the insignia with which these men were portrayed are testimonies to their distinctive identity as men of letters and men of law. It is only against this backdrop that we can fully understand the character of this group, and the breadth and extention of their legal culture.

CHAPTER 6

Legal Culture

It was not uncommon for contemporary texts to refer to protectors of Indians as jurists. In the rescript that approved the appointment of Pedro Bravo de Lagunas as interim protector in 1735, the Viceroy Marquis of Castefuerte would make a point of noting not only his zeal and selflessness, but also his 'literature,' that is, his education and culture. In turn, both Cipriano de Medina and Leandro de Larrinaga were referred to by contemporaries as 'Papinians' of Peruvian jurisprudence.[1] This chapter analyses the education and intellectual background of the advocates and protectors-*fiscales*. It examines the university curriculum followed by the University of San Marcos as well as the legal literature found in the holdings of the libraries of Cipriano de Medina, advocate of Indians from 1621 until his death in 1635, and García José Lasso de la Vega, protector-*fiscal* in 1740. The chapter therefore provides an insight into the ideas, categories and doctrine available to the legal practitioner in seventeenth and eighteenth century Lima.

Legal Education

As reviewed earlier in this work, the faculty of civil and canon law ('laws and canons') at the University of San Marcos was, at some stage, the house of studies for virtually all advocates and protectors-*fiscales* between 1589 and 1781. It is well known that this institution held a pre-eminent position in colonial society.[2] The seventeenth-century diaries of Suardo and Mugaburu, for example, evidence the participation of the university corporation in the main events of court life, such as the reception of the viceroy and *Te Deum* liturgies; similarly, the vice-regal household, *oidors* and ecclesiastic authorities took part in the main activities of colleges and faculties of San Marcos. In the same vein, the

1 "[E]n persona de celo, desinterés y literatura," "Libramiento de 711 ps. 6 rs. en comisos al Dr. Dn. Pedro Bravo de Castilla, Fiscal Protector interino..." BNP, mss. C92, f. 3. "[D]e abogado lució con gran fecunda y maravillosa elegancia, con atención a la justicia y verdad...como el jurisconsulto Papiniano." Quoted in Luis Antonio Eguiguren, *La universidad en el siglo XVI*, 1 vol. in 2 books of *Historia de la Universidad* [San Marcos] (Lima, 1951), 1: 546.

2 See, for example, David Brading, *First America: The Spanish Monarchy, Creole Patriots, and the liberal state, 1492–1867* (Cambridge, 1993), 321, 335.

 | DOI 10.1163/9789004305175_008

violent disputes over elections of chairs and the pageantry of doctoral degrees became part of the social landscape of Lima.[3]

The status of the student and academic body of San Marcos was also projected in dress. As their Peninsular counterparts, doctors of law had the right to wear swords and spurs at formal occasions. On the other hand, *pasantes*, as students were called, could be identified by their *becas* ('v' shaped sashes around their neck) which were green for canon law, red for civil law and the royal college of San Martín, and light blue for the royal college of San Felipe y San Marcos. In addition, university education afforded graduates with a number of privileges. Hugo de Celso (*c.*1481–1551), for example, recorded that Castilian Law granted the honour of counts to doctors and José Berní Catalá (1712–87), the Valencian jurist, considered that advocates were the 'priests' of temporal matters and as such deserved treatment of the highest dignity.[4]

Obtaining a university degree, however, was not an easy task. Francisco Bermúdez de Pedraza (1576–1655), a jurist and ecclesiastic, explained that a student required three qualities: 'a bag of gold for the great expenses and many books; a head of iron for the continuous work; and buttocks of lead to sit through the schools.'[5]

Legal education at San Marcos was acquired through a curriculum based on the European *ius commune* of Roman and canon law. As its Iberian and European counterparts, the teaching at the faculty of civil and canon law was aimed at delivering extensive knowledge of the authoritative texts of the discipline, as well as learning how to analyse, frame and make persuasive arguments for cases.[6] Latin was the language of the lecture hall and the texts.

---

3 See José de Mugaburu and Francisco de Mugaburu, *Diario de Lima (1640–1694)*, vol. 2, ed. Carlos A. Romero (Lima, 1935), 18 (procession of Candelaria), 53 (reception of the archbishop), 65 (reception of the viceroy at university), 69 (play at San Martín with viceroy), 58 and 94 (reception of the new viceroy). An example of the disputes during the elections of chairs is found in Juan Antonio Suardo, *Diario de Lima*, ed., Rubén Vargas Ugarte (Lima,1935), 42, 100. For the ceremonies and customs around the doctorate (*paseo*, *yantar* and *vejámen*), see Luis Antonio Eguiguren, *El paseo triunfal y el vejámen del graduado* (Lima, 1949).

4 Hugo de Celso, *Reportorio Vniversal de las todas las leyes destos reynos de Castilla*, fac. ed. (1553; Madrid, 2000), 108v; Joseph Berní Catalá, *Resumen de los privilegios, gracias, y prerrogativas de los abogados españoles*...(Valencia, 1764), 17.

5 "[P]ara ser buen estudiante, auia de tener tres calidades, bolsa de oro para los grandes gastos, y muchos libros, cabeça de hierro para el continuo trabajo, y asiento de plomo por el que auia de tener en las escuelas." Francisco Bermúdez de Pedraza, *Arte legal para estudiar la iurisprudencia* (1612; Madrid, 1992), 16.

6 James A. Brundage, *The Medieval Origins of the Legal Profession; Canonists, Civilians and Courts* (Chicago, 2008), 148.

Although canon law was the predominant subject of study, Roman law was the foundation of legal education. Students thus began their academic work with lectures on the Institutes, which provided a basic introduction to the categories of the law (persons, things and actions). Once past this introductory stage, they dealt with the foundations of either civil or canon law.

In the case of civil law, in addition to the professorship in Institute (1576), the faculty provided a professorship that lectured in the Code (1620), and three chairs for the teaching of the Digest: prime of laws (1571) would lecture on the *Infortiatum* (books 24 to 38 of the Digest); vespers of laws (1571) would deal with the *Digestum Novum* (books 39 to 50 of the Digest); and "Digesto Viejo" (1694) with the *Digestum Vetus* (books 1 to 23 of the Digest). In turn, canon law was taught from the chairs of prime and vespers where the *corpus iuris canonici* was read. The professors of prime and vespers shared the lectures on *Decretales*, the ecclesiastical dispositions issued until 1234 and compiled by Gregory IX (r.1227–41), the *Sextum* which was the legislation for 1234–98 compiled by Boniface VIII (r.1294–1303), and the *Clementinas*, a compilation of decrees after 1298 by Clement VI (r.1342–52). In addition to this, a professorship of Decretum was established in1619 for the specific study of this legal text.[7] At the close of the eighteenth century this structure of professorships remained in place.[8]

The constitutions of the university established that the professorships of prime of canon law and civil law were granted 'in property,' that is, until retirement or death. With the exception of *Digestum Vetus*, who was originally appointed for two years, the rest of the chairs were four year appointments.[9] Professors were elected by the student body and confirmed by the Spanish Crown. Bitter disputes among students and faculty over candidates often resulted in chairs remaining vacant for years.[10] In these cases, the university

7 Luis Antonio Eguiguren, *Catálogo Histórico del Claustro de la Universidad de San Marcos, 1576–1800* (Lima, 1912), 23–43; Francisco Javier Alejo Montes, *La universidad de Salamanca bajo Felipe II: 1575–1598* ([Burgos], 1998), 117–120, 243.

8 See the 1788 report of Rector Nicolás Sarmiento de Sotomayor (†c.1796) on the state of the university to Viceroy Teodoro de Croix (v.1784–90), in Carlos Daniel Valcárcel, *San Marcos: Universidad decana de América*, 2nd ed. (Lima, 2001), appendix III, 158.

9 See the *real cédula* of 7 June 1624 confirming the constitutions of 1578, as well as its additions, in Eguiguren, *Diccionario histórico cronológico de la Real y Pontificia Universidad de San Marcos y sus colegios: Crónica e investigación*, 3 vols. (Lima, 1940–51), 2: 752. For the chair of Digestum Vetus see Antonio de la Calancha, "Historia de la Universidad de San Marcos, hasta el 15 de julio de 1647...," in Ibid., 1: 12 (§26).

10 There are a few testimonies of this phenomenon. A good example of the violent rivalries that followed professorship elections is that of Gregorio de Rojas, one of the candidates to the chair of prime of laws, and his supporters, who were attacked by the opposing group

resorted to appointing substitute professors, who often undertook most of the burden of lectures.

Lectures by the chairs of prime of laws were delivered between 7.00 and 8.30 am, and those of canon law later in the morning, to allow students to attend both; in the case of the lectures of vespers in laws and canons, these were delivered between 3.00 and 4.30 pm in winter, and one hour later in summer (4.00–5.30 pm).[11] Archbishop Feliciano de la Vega recalls that, during his days as a student in San Marcos in the late sixteenth century, mornings were focused on 'grave matters' such as Bartolus' commentaries on the *Digestum Vetus* and *Infortiatum*, while afternoons were dedicated to Baldus's comments on the Code, and nights to Panormitanus' ('Abad') comments to the decretals, as well as the concordant titles of the *Sextum*, *Clementinas* and *Extravagantes* and the Siete Partidas. The fact that Vega declared he studied at least twelve to thirteen hours a day, must be counterbalanced with the feasts and solemnities of the liturgical calendar observed during the Colonial period, not omitting the activities organized around the university itself.[12]

The fact that San Marcos was modelled on the University of Salamanca ensured that lectures were undertaken in the *mos italicus* tradition of the post-glossators. This implied treating the *corpus iuris civilis* as an authoritative text which was used to develop principles that could solve contemporary legal issues.[13] Following in the tradition of their European counterparts, the *mos italicus* method at San Marcos fostered a knowledge that would supplement the lacunae in local law and made its professors natural counsellors in government and courts.[14]

---

aided with black and mulatto slaves with swords, rowels and stones, leaving several injured. See *real cédula* Madrid, 15 August 1675 in Eguiguren, *Diccionario*, 2: 341.

11 Eguiguren, *La universidad*, 1: 335–336.

12 Eguiguren, *Diccionario*, 1: 439; and *La universidad*, 1: 282–323. A similar phenomenon occurred in Italian universities at least until the seventeenth century. See Brundage, *Medieval Origins*, 252, and Paul F. Grendler, *The Universities of the Italian Renaissance* (Baltimore, 2002), 143–144.

13 Reales Cédulas of Charles V, Valladolid, 21 September 1551, and Philip II, Madrid, 17 October 1562. See León Pinelo, *Recopilación*, 1.22.1. Salamanca was influenced by the 1440 reforms of the University of Bologna, and by the presence of the law graduates of the Spanish College of Bologna founded in 1365 by Cardinal Albornoz. Juan Beneyto, "The Science of Law in the Spain of the Catholic Kings," in *Spain in the Fifteenth Century, 1369–1516: Essays and Extracts by Historians of Spain*, ed. J.R.L. Highfield (London, 1972), 278. On the mos italicus see Ernest. Holthöfer, "Literaturtypen des *mos italicus* in der europäischen Rechtsliteratur der frühen Neuzeit (16–18 Jahrhundert)," *Ius Commune* 2 (1969), 131–166; Grendler, *Universities*, 432.

14 David Ibbetson and Andrew Lewis, eds., *The Roman Law Tradition* (Cambridge, 1994), 5. A good introduction to the influence of Roman Law in Spanish American Law is Miguel

Besides formal lectures, faculties organized *repetitiones* or reviews of sessions of the courses for the students, delivered by bachelors or licentiates appointed directly by the rector of the university and supervised by the professorship. It was customary that repetitions were held after dinner.[15] Equally important for legal education were the disputations or formal debates in the presence of an audience, developed out of *quaestiones* or explorations of contested points. This provided students with the capacity for framing legal arguments and provided training in judicial oratory.[16]

In principle, the course of study in civil or canon law took five years to complete.[17] Available documentation suggests, however, that most students entered university colleges at around fifteen, matriculated for some years in the faculty of arts to polish up their Latin, moved to read law and obtained their bachelor degree at around twenty five, that is, ten years after they entered.[18] Following this trend, protector-*fiscal* Francisco Ruiz de Berecedo, for example, stated in his *relación de servicios* that, after perfecting his Latin and studying at the faculty of arts at the Jesuit College in Santiago, he read theology in this same institution for three and a half years, and later transferred to the college of San Martin in Lima where he spent eight more years at the faculty of laws and canons of San Marcos and graduated as a bachelor and licentiate in canon law.[19]

Luque Talaván, *Un Universo de Opiniones: la literatura jurídica Indiana* (Madrid, 2003), 125–146. An excellent study based on the contemporary view of the subject is Alejandro Guzmán Brito. "La vigencia del derecho romano en Indias según el jurista Juan del Corral Calvo de la Torre" *Justicia, sociedad y economía en la América española (siglos XVI, XVII y XVIII)*, VI Congreso del Instituto Internacional de Derecho Indiano (Valladolid: Casa-Museo Colón , 1983). 71–89. The role of professors as counsellors is exemplified in many of the protectors reviewed in this work.

15 *Constituciones y Ordenanzas antiguas, añadidas y modernas de la Real Universidad y Estudio General de San Marcos*...(Lima: Imprenta Real, 1735), Tables C and R; and Eguiguren, *La universidad*, 1: 330.

16 Eguiguren, *La universidad*, 1: 331, Brundage, *Medieval Origins*, 255–257 and Grendler, *Universities*, 152–157. On the link between rhetoric and law see Peter Mack, *A History of Renaissance Rhetoric, 1380–1620* (Oxford, 2011), 278–279.

17 See Alejo Montes, *La universidad de Salamanca*, 1998.

18 See for example, the ages of colegiales of San Martin and the dates of the exams for the degrees of bachelor of licentiate. "Catálogo de los Colegiales," in Eguiguren, *Diccionario*, 2, 135–255; AGN, Grados de Abogados, leg. 1–3; Universidad Nacional Mayor de San Marcos, Secretaría General, Actas de Grados de Licenciado y Doctor, caja 17 (705), 1571–1667.

19 "[D]esde sus tiernos años se aplico á los estudios de Artes, y Theologia; y que en el Colegio de la Compañia de la Ciudad de Santiago se perficionó en la lengua latina, y comenzó a oir de la Facultad de Artes, en la qual se le confirió el grado de Maestro y prosiguió en la de Theologia, por espacio de tres años y medio, sustentando en ellos varios Actos

Degrees in civil or canon law were conferred after public examination. Candidates wishing to take a degree had to provide evidence of proper enrolment at the university and of concluding their course of studies; although in some cases the absence of a specific course could be replaced with a payment to the faculty.[20] Explicit information about the process to obtain the degree of licentiate in canon law is provided in the case of Juan de la Rynaga Salazar (son of advocate of Indians Leandro de la Rynaga) on 14 June 1614.[21] This consisted of an oral examination of six questions, three on decretals and three on the *Decretum*. In addition to the Dean of the Faculty and university examiners, the 1578 constitutions of San Marcos required that ministers of the audience be also present in licentiate exams, but without a vote.[22] Following his approval by the faculty (*omnibus approbantibus nemine discrepante*), Rynaga proceeded to take the oath of loyalty to the crown and a profession of the Catholic Faith.[23] The degree concluded with a meal offered by the graduate to the faculty members.

An overview of the few surviving dossiers of degrees at San Marcos, as well as of eighteenth-century incorporations of advocates to the royal audience of Lima, suggests that, while it took bachelors two to five years to prepare for their licentiate degrees, the doctorate was taken within months, or even days, of the

---

Literarios con general aplauso de sus Maestros, por lo qual se le confirió el Grado de Doctor en la misma Facultad: Que despues el año de mil seiscientos y noventa y dos passó al Colegio Real de San Martin de la Ciudad de Lima, donde estudió la Facultad de Canones y Leyes, por espacio de cerca de ocho años, y defendió en el repetidos Actos presidiendo Conclusiones publicas, y leyendo de Oposicion de veinte y quatro horas para sus examenes, con general aprobacion" (sic). "Relacion de los grados y servicios del Licenciado Don Francisco Ruiz y Berecedo, Protector Fiscal de el distrito de la Audiencia del Reyno de Chile," Manuscrito Medina, vol. 23, pieza 23, f.1.

20 Juan Delgadillo Sotomayor, for example, paid 50 reales in compensation for a missing course prior to his examination as licentiate in canon law in 1669. Universidad Nacional Mayor de San Marcos, Secretaría General, Actas de Grados de Licenciado y Doctor, caja 17 (705), 1571–1667, f. 425.

21 "Cuaderno de Grado de Bachiller, 1571–1664," Universidad Nacional Mayor de San Marcos, Archivo Histórico Domingo Angulo, fs.[47], fs. 37–47.

22 These were *oidores* Alberto de Acuña, Juan Jiménez de Montalvo, Francisco de Alfaro (*c*.1551–*fl*.1628), and Luis Merlo de la Fuente (1558–1638). For the cédulas regarding the number of examiners and the presence of *oidores* see León Pinelo, *Recopilaición*, 1.22.27, 28 (pp. 308–309).

23 León Pinelo, *Recopilación*, 1.22.35; Eguiguren, *La universidad*, 1: 282–293. Hispanic universities placed particular stress in the doctrine of the Immaculate Conception. See, for example, the profession of faith for the university of San Cristóbal de Huamanga (1677), Universidad San Cristóbal de Huamanga, *Constituciones, 1677* (Ayacucho, 1998), 71–75.

licentiate.[24] The latter was the case of advocate of Indians Diego Hurtado de Avendaño, who obtained his doctorate in canon law a few years after he was awarded his licentiate in 1607.[25] In the case of Rynaga, who was awarded his doctorate four months after his licentiate, besides the fact that the *maestre escuela* (school master) pronounced the formula conferring the degree and the Rector Pedro Muñiz y Molina (1545–1616) took the oath to the new graduate, university authorities noted the money handouts (*propinas*) and fees (*derechos*) paid by the candidate.[26]

Interestingly, these payments (approximately 100 pesos each for the rector and *maestre escuela* and 50 per doctor) were understood as 'compensations' for the lecture hours spent on the candidate if a proper course of studies would have been followed. In this context, the ceremony itself became the focal point of attention. This was an elaborate ritual composed of a horseback procession to the cathedral, where the candidate was accompanied by four lackeys, two pages in livery, and a band of musicians (*paseo*); the reading of a satirical piece which 'humiliated' the candidate (*vejámen*); the conferment of the degree in the cathedral before the university corporation, followed by the bestowal of the doctoral emblems (ring, sword and spurs) and the distribution of gloves among academics as presents; and the feast offered to the rector and faculty (*yantar*).[27] In law, as in other faculties, access to funds was crucial for obtaining the doctorate which could cost up to 3,000 pesos, that is, the annual salary of an *oidor*.[28] It would thus appear that, whereas San Marcos held examinations for the degrees of bachelor and licentiate, the doctorate in law was a pageant rather than a rigorous test of the candidate's legal knowledge.

24 See AGN, Grados de Abogados, leg. 1–3 and Universidad Nacional Mayor de San Marcos, Secretaría General, Actas de Grados de Licenciado y Doctor, 705, caja 17 (1571–1667); 704, caja 19 (1660–1676); 702, caja 20 (1747–1759); 703/148, caja 21 (1747–1764).

25 This was on 6 of April 1622. See Universidad Nacional Mayor de San Marcos, Secretaría General, Actas de Grados de Licenciado y Doctor, caja 17 (705), 1571–1667.

26 See "Cuaderno de Grado de Bachiller, 1571–1664," Universidad Nacional Mayor de San Marcos, Archivo Histórico Domingo Angulo, fs. 42–44.

27 Eguiguren, *La universidad*, 1: 282–293; M.C. Mirow, *Latin American Law: A History of Private Law and Institutions in Spanish America* (Austin, 2004), 35.

28 Testimonies of this fact are also found in the degrees of medicine, as evidenced by Juan del Valle y Caviedes: "el doctor don Melchor Vásquez,/científico a tres mil pesos/porque la Universidad/le dio el grado de talego" (Doctor Don Melchor Vásquez/scientist at three thousand pesos/because the university/grave him a degree for [i.e. due to] moneyed). Juan del Valle y Caviedes, *Obra Completa*, Biblioteca Clásicos del Perú vol. 5, eds. Martía Leticia Cáceres, Luis Jaime Cisneros and Guillermo Lohmann (Lima) 349.

Legal education continued after university, when bachelors, licentiates or doctors wishing to become advocates, worked and studied for two or three years in a lawyer's practice before entering the royal audience. Protector-*fiscal* Pedro León Escandón, for example, stated in his dossier of application as an advocate in Lima, that he was an apprentice for three years in the study of Tomás de Salazar, learning 'the matters of practical jurisprudence.'[29] It was during this period, commonly referred to as *prácticas*, that graduates became acquainted with the complex body of royal law.

That would-be lawyers had to study current law outside universities started to change in the eighteenth century with the decision of the Spanish Crown to endow chairs for the study of Spanish Law (1714) and the foundation of the academies of Santa Bárbara (1761) and La Purísima Concepción (1773) for the study of practical jurisprudence and royal law;[30] these academies would, in turn, serve as models for the creation of similar institutions in Chuquisaca (1780), Mexico (1794) and Lima (1804).[31] In this same vein, one of the first dispositions introducing the teaching of applicable law at the University of San Marcos dates from 1782 when Rector José Ignacio Perales, instructed his recently appointed professor of vespers of law 'to accompany his teachings with the national law [derecho patrio] and to warn his disciples, most specially and distinctly, of the unconformity between these and the Roman [Law].'[32] Although interim protector José Baquíjano Carrillo would subscribe to the idea

29 "Expediente seguido ante el Real Acuerdo de Justicia por Dn. Pedro de León y Escandón, alumno del Real Colegio de San Martín," 1734, AGN, Grados de Abogados, leg. 1, cuaderno 2 (1734), f. 5.

30 Hernán Espinosa Quiroga, *La academia de leyes y práctica forense*, Colección de Seminarios e Institutos 4 (Historia del Derecho) (Santiago, [1957?]), 2–3. Canon Law was not exempt from this tendency with the foundation of the Real Academia de Sagrados Cánones, Liturgia, Historia y Disciplina Eclesiástica in 1773.

31 Respectively the Real Academia Carolina de Practicantes Juristas de Chuquisaca, Academica Pública de Jurisprudencia Teórico Practica y Derecho Real Pragmático de Mexico and the Colegio de Abogados de Lima, all of which had been previously established as private organisations. For the Colegio of Lima see Geraldo Arosemena Garland, *El Colegio de Abogados de Lima y sus decanos* (Lima, 1977) and Aníbal Gálvez, *El colegio de abogados de Lima: Historia de su fundación* (Lima, 1915).

32 "Con el preciso cargo de que ha de acompañar en su enseñanza, las [leyes] de derecho patrio advitiéndo a sus discípulos muy especial y señaladamente la disconformidad que interviene entre éstas y las Romanas conforme al nuevo Plan de Estudios que se han meditado con arreglo á lo dispuesto en las universidades de Salamanca y Alcalá." Carlos Daniel Valcárcel, ed., *La Universidad: Libro XIV de claustros (1780–1790)*, book 19, vol. 1 of *Colección Documental de la Independencia del Perú* (Lima, 1971).

of distancing legal education from the authority of Roman Law,[33] all protectorship officials obtained their degrees by studying the medieval texts of the *ius commune* and became acquainted with applicable law during their apprenticeship with practising lawyers. The legal culture created by this structure was characterized by a dual understanding of the law: just as local statutes could not be understood without supranational (monarchical) or universal (Church) jurisdictions, common legal principles were needed to thread practical legal issues. This duality is manifest in the law books of the protectors.

Law Books in the Audience of Lima

Knowledge of the law was also fostered through access to legal literature and books.[34] For Melchor Cabrera de Guzmán, the author of a treatise on the 'perfect' advocate, possessing many books was a necessary condition for the good exercise of jurisprudence. He stated that, although this need had been pointed out by authorities such as Aristotle, Seneca and Paul, the main reason to have law books was the number of matters that could be consulted; they were somewhat 'deities' as they constituted the depository of the legal science. Cabrera de Guzmán therefore advised lawyers to spend 'most'—but not all—their salaries buying books.[35]

True to Cabrera de Guzmán's ideal, documentary sources reveal significant book collections among legal professionals in Lima. In the sixteenth century there are inventories of the private libraries of *oidores* Lisón de Tejada (†1549),

33 José de Baquíjano y Carrillo, *Alegato que en la oposición a la cátedra de prima de leyes de la real Universidad de San Marcos de Lima dixo el Dr. D. Joseph de Baquíjano y Carrillo, catedrático de Vísperas de la misma facultad...el día 29 de abril de 1788* (Lima, 1788), [35–39].

34 See the seminal studies on this subject by Irving Leonard, *Romances of chivalry in the Spanish Indies with some registros of shipments of books to the Spanish colonies* (Berkeley and Los Angeles, 1933) and *The Books of the brave* (Cambridge, Mass., 1949); José Torre Revello, *El libro la imprenta y el periodismo en América durante la dominación española* (Buenos Aires, 1940); and Guillermo Lohmann Villena, "Los libros españoles en Indias," *Arbor* 2 (6) (1944): 221–249.

35 Melchor Cabrera Núnez de Guzmán, *Idea de un abogado perfecto, deducido de reglas, y disposiciones del Derecho, comprobada con la autoridad de sus interpretes* (1679; Madrid, 1693), 210–213, 215–216. The library was found in Medina's working study. There is no evidence, however, that he kept his books 'in good air, adorned with cleanliness, curiosity and good odours' ("á buen aire, y vista, adornados con limpieza, curiosidad y buenos olores") in the way Cabrera recommended. Ibid., 240.

22 volumes; Gregorio González de Cuenca (†1581), 349 volumes; and Juan Bautista de Monzón, 46 volumes.[36] Also, Cristóbal Ferrer de Ayala (†1609), fiscal of the audience and advisor to Viceroy García Hurtado de Mendoza, possessed a collection of more than 260 books, mainly of civil and canon law, acquired in 1590.[37] Seventeenth century inventories include the library of Manuel de Castro y Padilla (1573–1622), *oidor* in Charcas and Lima, who possessed some 153 volumes, mostly on law.[38] Larger collections were those of Doctor Hernando Arias de Ugarte (1561–1638), whose career included the appointments of oidor in Panama (1595) and bishop in Quito (1614), Bogotá (1618) and Lima (1630), with 640 volumes.[39] Equally important was the library of Cristóbal Cacho de Santillana (†1640), an oidor in Lima, with 524 books.[40]

By contrast there are no studies of the libraries of eighteenth century magistrates of the audience of Lima. Notarial sources, however, reveal important book collections in the cases of *oidores* Manuel de Gorena y Beiria (†1774) and Pedro José Bravo del Ribero y Correa Padilla (1701–86). In the case of Gorena, the post-mortem inventory of 12 January 1775 gives a detailed account of his 475 volume library, part of which was brought from Spain.[41] In turn, the inventory of the library of Bravo del Ribero, one of the most influential magistrates in the second half of the eighteenth century, consists of 916 entries; thereby constituting one of the largest book collections of the vice-royalty of Peru.[42]

---

36 Teodoro Hampe Martínez, *Bibliotecas privadas en el mundo colonial: La difusión de libros e ideas en el virreinato del Perú (siglos XVI–XVII)* (Frankfurt, 1996).

37 Eguiguren, *Diccionario*, 2: 288–289.

38 AGN, protocolos notariales s. XVII, protocolo 182, Cristóbal de Barrantes, 1617–25, fs. 573v–75.

39 Teodoro Hampe Martínez, "La biblioteca del arzobispo Hernando Arias de Ugarte: Bagaje intelectual de un prelado criollo (1614)," *Thesaurus* 42 (1987): 337–361.

40 Cacho de Santillana is among the 138 book owners studied by Carlos Alberto González Sánchez, "Los libros de los españoles en el virreinato del Perú. Siglos XVI y XVII," *Revista de Indias* 56 (206) (1996), 7–47.

41 AGN, protocolos notariales s. XVIII, protocolo 169, escribano Tomás Ignacio Camargo 1771–1776, fs.595v–600; AGI, Contratación, 5489, N.1, R.23, f.8; available in http://pares.mcu.es/. Details of his life are found in the aforementioned notarial protocol and in Lohmann, *Los ministros*, 52–53.

42 AGN, protocolos notariales s. XVIII, protocolo 649, escribano Francisco Luque, 1786, fs. 428v–449. In spite of his importance, there is no complete study of the life and career of Bravo del Ribero. Brief biographical details are found in Manuel de Mendiburu, *Diccionario Histórico Biográfico del Perú*, 2nd. ed, 11 vols. (Lima, 1932–34), 3: 124; Lohmann, *Los ministros*, 18–19; Tauro, *Enciclopedia*, 1: 335; and José Nicolás Flores Arroyo, "El virrey y la oposición. Una historia política de la admniotración de justicia," in *El virrey Amat y su tiempo*, eds. Carlos Pardo-Figueroa Thays and Joseph Dager Alva (Lima, 2004), 252–255.

Other sources such as sale notes or travel inventories also evidence important collections. An example of the first is a manuscript with a list of 434 texts—including details of place and year of publication—owned by *oidor* Cristóbal Messía y Munive (*c.*1717–97).[43] Similarly, there are two sale documents that list, respectively, 67 and 89 volumes sold by *oidor* Pedro Antonio de Tagle Bracho y Sánchez de Tagle (1722–1802) between 27 July and 22 August 1776 in La Plata.[44]

Outside Peru, studies on the legal culture of the audiences of Mexico, Charcas, Chile and Buenos Aires also reveal important book collections among their jurists in the seventeenth and eighteenth centuries.[45] Particular attention, however, has been given to eighteenth century audiencia magistrates as evidenced in the studies of the libraries of Francisco Tomás de Ansótegui (1756–1822), regent of Buenos Aires, José Manuel Messía de la Cerda y Vargas (1695–1760), *alcalde del crimen* in Mexico and Sebastían Calvo de la Puerta (1717–67) *oidor* in Guatemala.[46]

---

43 BNP, ms Z 765 (1774). On Messía see his *relación de méritos* in BNP, Archivo Astete Concha, Z 1180 (1755) and law degree, BNP, Archivo Astete Concha, mss. Z 390 (1753). Biographical references are found in Mendiburu, *Diccionario*, 7: 384; Lohmann, *Los ministros*, 70–71; and Alberto Tauro del Pino, *Enciclopedia Ilustrada del Perú* (Lima, 1988), vol. 4: 1331. A brief genealogical study of his family is found in Juan Luis Espejo, *Nobiliario de la Capitanía General de Chile* (Santiago, 1967), 572–574.

44 BNP, ms Z 550/1776 y BNP, ms. Z 612. On Tagle Bracho see "Juvilación con goce de medio sueldo de oydor de la Aud. De Lima a Dn. Pedro de Tagle y Bracho…," Lilly Library, Latin American mss. Peru, 1792, Jan. 21; "Titulo de Ministro Honorario del Consejo de Indias á dn. Pedro de Tagle y Bracho…," Lilly Library, Latin American mss. Peru, 1791, Dec. 22; and AHN, Ordenes Militares, expedientillos, N.12134, fs.1–1v; facsimile available at http://pares.mcu.es/. A brief biography is found in Lohmann, *Los ministros*, 135–136. The Tagle Bracho family has been studied by Carlos Escudero Ortiz de Zevallos, "La familia Tagle Bracho en el Perú: Apuntes genealógicos," *Revista del Instituto Peruano de Investigaciones Genealógicas* 20 (1994), 79–93; and Susy Sánchez, "Familia, comercio y poder: Los Tagle y su vinculación con los Torre Velarde (1730–1825)," in *Los comerciantes limeños a fines del siglo XVIII: Capacidad y cohesión de una elite, 1750–1825*, ed. Cristina Mazzeo de Vivó (Lima, 1999).

45 For Mexico, Guatemala and Chile see the works by Javier Barrientos Grandón, *La cultura jurídica en la Nueva España (sobre la recepción de la tradición jurídica europea en el virreinato)* (Mexico, 1993); and *La cultura en el reino de Chile: bibliotecas de ministros de la real audiencia de Santiago (s. XVII–XVIII)* (Santiago, 1992). For Charcas see Daisy Rípodas Ardanaz, "Bibliotecas privadas de funcionarios de la real audiencia de Charcas," *Memoria del Segundo Congreso Venezolano de Historia* (Caracas, 1975), vol. 2.

46 See José María Mariluz Urquijo, "La biblioteca de un oidor de la real audiencia de Buenos Aires," *Revista del Instituto de Historia del Derecho* (Buenos Aires) 7 (1955–56), 140–146; Javier Barrienton Grandon, "La librería de don José Manuel Messía de la Cerda y Vargas

Notarial records also reveal that jurists involved in the protection of Indians possessed significant book collections. An analysis of the available post-mortem inventories between the sixteenth and eighteenth centuries reveal the existence of four book collections among advocates or protector of Indians. Two of these, however, are merely referential and do not give a detailed account of the library holdings. Thus, Antonio Maldonado de Silva, Advocate of Indians in Charcas (1608–10), declared in his testament of 1651 that he possessed a library of 'more than 500 books.'[47] Similarly, the executors of Juan Peralta y Sanabria, protector-*fiscal* of Indians (1692) and *oidor* in Lima (1704) declared the existence of a library of more than 70 books, rendered useless by moths and mice.[48]

A detailed inventory of books is found in the cases of advocate Cipriano de Medina (1593–*fl.*1626) and protector-*fiscal* García José Lasso de la Vega e Hijar y Mendoza (1741). In the case of Medina, the inventory was made on 4 January 1635 and contains 478 entries, including manuscripts and working papers, which makes 732 volumes of printed books (see Appendix 2). The Medina library constitutes the only testimony of the legal culture of an advocate or protector of Indians in the sixteenth and seventeenth centuries.[49] In the context of the seventeenth century Spanish Monarchy, its dimension is comparable to provincial university colleges.[50] With some exceptions, such as Justus Lipsius *Politicorum*, the Bible, Cayetano Tomás de Vio's comment to the *Summa*

(1695–1760), alcalde del crimen de la real audiencia de Méjico," *Revista Chilena de Historia del Derecho* 17 (1992–93), 57–85, and *Ibidem*, "Librería de don Sebastían Calvo de la Puerta (1717–1767) oidor de la real audiencia de Guatemala," *Revista de Estudios Históricos Jurídicos* (Valparaíso) 22 (1999), 37–73.

47 Antonio Maldonado de Silva, testament, 2 June 1651, AGN protocolos notariales s.XVII, protocolo 1092, escribano Francisco de Medina 1651–1653, f.208.

48 "Ytten una librería de la qual han salido más de settenta libros comidos de polilla y rattones que no pueden servir. Y otros picados." See AGN protocolos notariales s.XVIII, protocolo 957, escribano Francisco Sánchez Becerra, 1706, f.1534r.

49 Cipriano Medina y Gómez, *inventario de bienes*, 4 January 1635, AGN protocolos notariales, protocolo 818, Escribano Diego Gutierrez, 1635, fols. 496 to 504. Hereafter I shall refer to the entry number in the appendix. A brief reference to the library was published by Teodoro Hampe Martínez, *El Comercio*, Lima, 26 January 1988, A2.

50 The 1641 list for the College of Sigüenza, for example, contained 480 titles. See Isidoro Montiel, *Historia de la Universidad de Sigüenza*, vol. 2 ([Zulia?], [1963]), 271–285. This seems to have been a respectable figure for newly founded colleges, for in 1638 John Harvard, MA, bequeathed some 400 books to the "Little School of Clergymen of New England," he founded two years earlier, Anthony Robert Jobson, *Great libraries* (London, 1970), 196.

Theologica and the Cantar del Mio Cid, the library of Cipriano de Medina was composed entirely of law books.[51]

In turn, the collection of Lasso de la Vega, which includes 170 titles, was inventoried on 29 March 1775.[52] Although the inventory was performed at a time when, for all intents and purposes, protectorship appointments had ceased, the library constitutes a valuable testimony of the legal culture of protectors during the eighteenth century. Unlike the case of Medina, however, almost one quarter of his titles correspond to non-legal texts and varied from classics to poetry and royal funerals.

The study of book collections, however, is constrained by methodological considerations that should be considered before presenting the analysis of the libraries of Medina and Lasso de la Vega.[53] The first is the lack of precision of the notes taken by notaries, who made the inventories of goods shortly after the death of the testator and under the supervision of the executor (*albacea*). The need to finish the task swiftly, often led to brief references to the goods. In the case of books this results in unintelligible entries. This is observed in many of Medina's holdings such as 'Practica interrogatorum' [9] or 'Practica de exsaminar proceso' [23]. Although both entries clearly refer to procedural law, it is impossible to determine their authorship or precise title. Similarly, even when the entry refers to a particular author, the absence of detail in the notes makes its identification merely speculative. Thus the entry 'Covarrubias,' [L-75] in the library of Lasso de la Vega, even within a juridical context could refer to Diego de Covarrubias y Leiva (1512–77), the eminent jurist of the second scholastic, or José de Covarrubias (*fl.*1786), a regalist author. Similar problems might arise with more precise references such as Mariano Socini (1401–67) and his grandson Mariano Socini (1482–1556), both distinguished jurists from Siena.

The second consideration refers to the fact that book inventories might not include all the books possessed by the owner. Information on the books possessed by Pedro Antonio de Tagle Bracho for example, is only available through two sale receipts signed in La Plata in 1776. However, his travel documents prior to his departure from Cádiz to Lima in 1749 point out that his luggage included a number of boxes containing books.[54] As the number or

---

51 See, respectively, items 110, 143, 301 and 342 in appendix 2.

52 García José Lasso de la Vega Híjar y Mendoza, *Inventario de bienes*, 29 March 1775, AGN protocolos notariales s.XVIII, protocolo 873, escribano Antonio Jerónimo de Portalanza 1770–1775, fs. 730–735.

53 Maxine Chevalier, *Lectura y lectores en la España de los siglos XVI y XVII* (Madrid, 1976), 41–43, and Luis Miguel Enciso, *Barroco e ilustración en las bibliotecas privadas españolas del siglo XVIII* (Madrid, 2002), 19–21.

54 AGI, Contratación, 5490, N.1, R.49, f.3, available in http://pares.mcu.es/.

contents of these boxes were not specified, it is impossible to assess what proportion of his library is represented in lists drafted in La Plata. This case evidences that the existence or absence of books in a library does not necessarily imply either readership or ignorance of certain texts. On one hand, notaries could have expressly excluded certain texts from inventories by fear of the Inquisition. On the other hand, practical experience suggests that not all books in a library are read by their owners, that many books would have escaped the notarial list by being held elsewhere, and that that access to the texts absent in the list could have been obtained outside private libraries (as it would have been the case of those with access to libraries such as that of San Marcos and its colleges).

The Library of Cipriano de Medina

Castilian Law

As was pointed out earlier, Castilian Law constituted the largest and possibly most important portion of both libraries studies in this chapter. At the start of the seventeenth century, Castilian law was constituted by the Siete Partidas (1265–1348); the Ordenanzas Reales de Castilla (1484), a collection of laws enacted by the successors of Alfonso X, the Laws of Toro (1505) which dealt with the order of preference on the application of laws, and the Nueva Recopilación (1567) which compiled the legislation after 1505. The vast collection of books dealing with various aspects of this legislation in the Medina library reflects, therefore, the vital important place of Castilian Law in the Indies. The preoccupation of the rescripts, decrees and ordinances issued for Spanish possessions in the New World with the organisation of government and Church, placed Castilian law in the unique position of regulating most aspects of private, procedural and criminal law.

Medina possessed the *Siete Partidas* with Gregorio López's gloss [61], and works on particular aspects of the Partidas such as Bartolomé Humala on the first two partidas [245] and Diego de Villalpando on P.7.1.22 [292]. On the *Ordenanzas Reales de Castilla* [290], a selection of laws enacted between 1284 and 1484, the library had the edition of Alfonso Díaz de Montalvo (1405–99) [299]. A number of comments on this body of law are also found. Diego Pérez de Salamanca (†*c.*1574), a lecturer in Liber sextus at the University of Salamanca, on books I–IV [293]; Rodrigo Suárez (1440/60–1500/20) [67]; and the *additiones* on Suarez' work by Diego de Valdés [68].

Possibly the single most extensive collection in the library is that dedicated to the Laws of Toro (1505), which assigned the proper place, on the scale of priorities, both to new and old laws. Comments on these dispositions included Marcos Salón de Paz (*c.*1500–68/76) [50]; Juan Guillén de Cervantes (b.1509), a doctor and professor in Canon Law at the University of Seville [51]; Luis Velásquez de Avendaño [53]; Diego del Castillo de Villasante (*c.*1500–*c.*60) [54]; Tello Fernández Messia (†1595), a lawyer in Granada [56]; López de Palacios Rubios [57]; Fernando Gómez Arias de Talavera (†*c.*1550) [296]; and two copies of Antonio Gómez (1512–62/72), a professor in Lérida, highly successful comment [19, 350]. Due to its place in the library, Medina may have also possessed a copy of the gloss on the Laws of Toro by Miguel de Cifuentes (c.1500–60) [58].[55]

The holdings on the Nueva Recopilación (1567) [262] were equally large. The Medina library possessed the two general comments on this body of law: Alfonso de Azevedo (1518–98), *Commentariorum iuris civilis in Hispaniae* [267], and Juan Gutiérrez (1530–1618) *Practicarum Quaestionum circa Leges Regias Hispanicae* [233]. More specific matters were treated in other works. Diverse aspects of Book v were commented on by Andrés Angulo (1545–c.1600), on title 6 [206], García de Gironda on tributes [283], and possibly Juan de Matienzo, an oidor in Lima [35]. Alfonso Narbona (1594–1611), professor of the Institute, wrote a comment on the third part of the Nueva Recopilación [14], and Francisco de Aviles on its chapter on corregidores [439].

Treatises on various statutes of Castilian law are also found in the Medina library. Pedro Nuñes de Avendaño on the mandates of corregidores [438], Luis Mejía Ponce de León (1524–c.1590) on the income of municipalities or *Leyes de Toledo* [72], Ignacio de Lasarte Molina on sale duties or *alcabala* [281], and Jaime Collantes de Avellaneda (c.1550–98) on pragmatic dealing with agricultural material [196].

The library of Medina has few absences in Castilian Law. In the case of the *Ordenanzas*, the library lacks the *Additamenta* to Pérez de Salamanca by Antonio Ramírez de Mendona (Salamanca, 1586) and the treatise on appeals by Pedro Nuñez de Avendaño (Salamanca, 1569). Similarly absent in the case of the Laws of Toro are the glosses of Diego Castillo (Salamanca, 1544) and Diego Espino de Cáceres (Salamanca, 1559), as well as the additions to Antonio Gómez by Diego Gómez Cornejo (Salamanca, 1598). Neither did the library possess the comments by Velásquez de Avendaño (Madrid, 1593). These absences, however, by no mean undermine the comprehensive holdings of the library in Castilian law. The only surprise being the widely known repertoire by Celse Hugue Descousu [Hugo de Celso] (*c.*1480–1540) (Alcalá, 1540) and the *Sumarios de la Recopilación* (Madrid, 1628) by Rodrigo de Aguiar Acuña (*c.*1560–1629).

55 This could also be his comment on the *Ordenamiento* (Medina del Campo, 1555).

Ius Commune

Among the medieval commentators of Roman law the library possessed the works of Cino da Pistoia (1270–1336/7) [418], Bartolus of Sassoferrato (1313–57) [359], Baldo degli Ubaldi (*c.*1327–1400) [324, 362], Andrea d'Isernia (†*c.*1353) [453], Alberico da Rosate (1290–1360) [461, 467], Angelo degli Ubaldi (1328–*c.*1407) [387, 442–444] da Saliceto (†1411) [419], Paolo di Castro (1360–1441) [360, 397], Alessandro Tartagni de Imola (1424–77) [372, 420] and Giasone dal Maino (1435–1519) [383, 421]. A legal manual for students used in Salamanca in the seventeenth century considered that, among these authors, Baldus was the 'prince of interpreters' with Bartolus and Accursius.[56] The library also possessed a number of later commentators of the Roman sources such as Giovanni Francesco Porporato (1485–1544) [456] and Gerolamo Cagnolo (1491–1551) on various titles of the Digest [139]; Niccolò Belloni (†1552) [89] and Antonio Pichardo Vinuesa (1565–1631) [320] on the Institute; and Franceschino Corti (†1553) [426] and Carlos de Tapia (1567–1644) [208] on the Code. Other jurists who wrote on diverse aspects of Roman law but who are mentioned by unidentified works are Alberico da Rosate (†1354) [461, 467], Bartolomeo di Saliceto (c.1363–1412) [419] and Gianfrancesco Riva de San Nazarro (*c.* 1480–1535) [371].

The academic reception of Roman law in the Spanish Monarchy was not only reflected in the appearances of *collationes*, such as that of Juan Martínez de Olano (*c.*1550–1600) [416] but also in lectures on Roman law. *Repetitiones* on various sections of the Digest appear in the Medina library, such as López de Palacios Rubios [13],[57] Diego Segura [266][58] and Juan de Orozco (†1558) [61], either a comment on the first books of the Digest or a scholarly work of palangenesis. The holdings also included the comments on the Institutes by Antonio Pichardo Vinuesa (1565–1631), a professor of the Institute in Salamanca (1594–1612) [307]. A general reference is made to jurists such as Diego de Covarrubias (1512–77) [127, 128],[59] Manuel Costa (d.c.1564) [275][60] and Antonio de Padilla y Meneses (†1565) [259][61] authors of various commentaries but mentioned in the book list by unspecified works.

---

56 Francisco Bermúdez de Pedraza, *Arte para estudiar la jurisprudencia* (Madrid, 1612), 56. For a bibliography of these authors see Helmut Coing, ed. *Handbuch der Quellen und Literatur der neueren europäischen Privatrechtsgeschichte*, 2 vols. in 3, Max-Planck-Institut für Europäische Rechtsgeschichte (München, 1973–77) 1: 271–276.

57 *Repetitio rubricæ et capitulis per vestras de donationibus inter virum et uxorem* (D.24.1).

58 D.28.2.3.6; 28.2.?; 30.126; 31.67.5; 36.1.?; 41.2.1.4; 45.1.23; 31.28; 9.10.

59 *In varios civilis ac pontificii iuris titulos* (vol. 1, Lyon, 1568); and *Variarum Resolutionum quas libris quatuor complexi sumus Tomus secundus* (Lyon, 1568).

60 *Commentaria et Repetitiones* (Lyon, 1564).

61 *In quœdam imperatorum rescripta & nonnulla iurisconsultorum responsa commentaria* (Salamanca, 1563).

In the case of canon law there was Dino de Mugello (1253–98), possibly the only member of the school of glossators in the library. Medina possessed a copy of his *consilia* [96] and his comment on the title *De regulis iuris* [129] originally included in an edition of the *Sextum*, a compilation of ecclesiastical law between 1234–98 edited by Pope Boniface VIII (*r.*1294–1303). Equally important is the presence of Niccolò Tedeschi's Panormitano (1383–1453) commentaries in the Medina library, possibly, the most frequently quoted authority of the *corpus iuris canonici* in the sixteenth century [364]. Other authorities in canon law in Medina's library were Pope Innocent IV (*r.*1243–54) [450], Giovanni d'Andrea. (*c.*1270–1348) [468], Pietro d'Ancarano (*c.*1330–1416) [389, 447], Philipp Decio (1454–1534) [369] and Riva de San Nazarro [371]. Medina also possessed a number of comments on specific aspects of ecclesiastical law such as Luis Gómez (1484–1543), colegial of San Clemente in Bologna, lecturer in Padua and judge of the Rota, *In regule denontolendis jure questionum* [146] and *De constitutionibus* [170]; Guillermo Cassador's (1477–1527) decisions of the Roman Chancery [94]; and Manuel Rodrigues, OFM (1545–1619) *Questiones regulares* [346]. It is perhaps worthy of note that Medina did not have the works of his brother-in-law, the eminent Feliciano de Vega.[62]

Tractati

One of the particular aspects of legal literature from 1540 onwards was the apparition of specialised treatises. As the *Tractatus universi iuris* (Lyon, 1549) [462] proves, this type of literature would arrange works around particular laws or specific matters. Although most of these works were steeped in the *mos italicus* tradition, they pointed more towards future developments than the bulk of commentaries and consilia because they were usually concentrated more firmly on specific matters, than did the commentaries which followed the *ordo legum* of the *corpus iuris civilis*. The popularity of this literature is demonstrated by the publication of a further *Tractatus universi iuris*, 25 volumes (Venice, 1584–86) ordered by Pope Gregory XIII (*r.*1572–85). Unlike the collection published in Lyon, this later work is not found in the library. However, a number of individual tracts which composed it have been identified. These are Giovanni Campeggio "De testibus" [122] and Francesco Ercolani "De attentatis appellatione pendente" [101].

The increasing importance of this literature towards the end of the sixteenth century can be seen through the holdings which might concern Indian status and the role of Medina as a lawyer for Indians. In the case of rustics and miserables, to which Indians were often compared, there are two references. The

62 Vega wrote *Quamdiu acquirenda haereditate*, *Tractatus de censuriis*, and a relectio on procedural aspects of canon law (vid.*infra*).

first is Gapar Baeza, *Tractatus de inope debitore* [440], on helpless debtors. The second is an unidentified entry, 'Tractatus de privilegiis pauperum'[29]. This could be either Gabriel Alvarez de Velasco (†1658), an oidor in Santa Fe and Lima, *Tractatus de privilegiis pauperum et miserabilium personarum* (Madrid, 1630–36) or Alfonso de Guzman Genzer, *De privilegiis pauperum* (Madrid, 1630).

Although the legal action of Indians was circumscribed within the framework of a *Republica Christiana*, literature on the rights of infidels in the courts of justice would not be entirely absent. The opinions of Pope Innocent IV cited by Solórzano, and of Henry of Segusio, Hostiensis, for example, were present in the commentaries to the Decretals of Giovanni d'Andrea [468]. Similarly, the jurisdiction of ecclesiastical courts over infidels and the tolerance of the Christian prince to non-Christian peoples had been dealt with by Ancarano [389], Tudeschi [364] and Tartagni di Imola [372].[63]

The library also had important holdings regarding tutorship, an institution which inspired many of the mechanisms designed to protect Indians in law courts. The library possessed the treatises of Gaspar Baeza [440], Borgnino Cavalcano (1530–1607) [198], an unidentified comment around the legislation of Emperor Marcus Aurelius (*r.*161–180) and possibly Juan Gutiérrez, *Tractatus de tutelis et curis minorum* (Salamanca, 1602) among the eleven volumes of his work [233]. No record of the work by Leander Galganetus (*fl.*1609) also used in Indian matters by Solózano,[64] nor Ioannes Paulus Galtieri, *Praxis tutelaris absolutissima* (Naples, 1601) can be traced.

Equally important for Medina was procedural law. Aspects directly related to Indian rights in judicial courts are found, for example, in a treatise on the *restitutio in integrum* [47], a mechanism which relieved Indians of the consequences of a transaction into which they had entered. General works on procedural law were Roberto Maranta (†*c.*1540) *Practica iudiciaria* [225], Jaime Antonio Marta (1559–*c.*1623) [319], Giovanni Battista Piotto [156], Sebastiano Vanzi [157], Juan de Montealegre [78, 316], Suárez de Paz [446], Marcantonio Pellegrini (1530–1616) [240] and Lancellotus [27]. It is possible, however, that the treatises on procedure by Gutiérrez [233] and Prospero Farinacci (1544–1618) [330] were included in the library. Other writers on procedure whose titles remain unidentified are Giulio Claro (1525–72) [305], Fulvio Pacciani (†1613) [43], and Filippo Decio (1454–1553) [369].[65] Medina also had studies in

63 See James Muldoon, *Popes, Lawyers and Infidels* (Liverpool, 1979), 18–28. For Solórzano's use of Pope Innocent IV is found in 2.28.3, 23. See Juan de Solórzano, *Política Indiana*, eds. Francisco Tomás y Valiente and Ana María Barrero (Madrid, 1996).

64 Solórzano, *Política Indiana*, 2.28.51.

65 For a discussion on this area see Coing, *Handbuch*, vol. 2, bk.1: 397–408.

the procedural law of specific jurisdictions. The main focus of interest was no doubt Castilian law, which provided the procedural rules in the Indies. Among the holdings was the notorious 'curia' of Juan Rodríguez de Pisa [207], the practical manual of Alonso de Villadiego Vascuñana [21], and an unidentified "práctica" [23]. For other jurisdictions there was Ottaviano Vestri (†1572) on the Papal states [230], and the *Stilus Curiae Parlementi* for Paris [181]. The most notorious absence is, no doubt, the *Curia Filipica* (Lima, 1603) a vast commentary on procedural law under the Spanish Monarchy signed by Juan de Hevia Bolaños (1570–1623).

Legal Humanism

Legal humanism[66] was not unknown to the rector of San Marcos. The library had some of the works of the chief European representatives of early sixteenth century legal humanism such as Andrea Alciati (1492–1550) [274, 314] and Ulrich Zäzi (Zazius) (1461–1535) [361,417]. Legal humanism, therefore, was a marginal phenomenon in the context of vicerregal Peru in late sixteenth and the seventeenth centuries. This conclusion reiterated the view originally advanced by Douglas Osler regarding the influence of the elegant school in Europe.[67] In part this was due to the fact that the universities of the Hispanic Monarchy maintained the *mos italicus* as its preferred method of teaching and did not use the historical and philological analysis of the Roman sources proposed by the humanists. Moreover, the University of San Marcos would continue to increase the traditional study of the *corpus iuris civilis* during the

66 The bibliography is legion. In general: Hans Erich Troje, "Die Literatur des gemeinen Rechts unter dem Einfluss des Humanismus," in Coing, *Handbuch*, vol. 1, bk.2: 615–795. For an interpretation of the phenomenon see Osler, "The myth of European Legal History," 393–410. Also: José María Lahoz Finestres, *El humanismo jurídico en Europa* (Las Palmas, 2002); Ian Mclean, *Interpretation and meaning in the Renaissance: The case of Law*, (Cambridge, 1992); Donald Kelley, "Civil Science in the Renaissance: the problem of interpretation," Anthony Pagden (ed.), *The Languages of Political Theory in Early-Modern Europe* (Cambridge, 1987); Peter Stein, "Legal humanism and legal science," *Tijdschrift voor Rechtsgeschiedenis* 54 (1986): 297–306; Ibid. "Elegance in Law," *Law Quarterly Review* 77 (1961): 242–256; Alejandro Guzmán Brito, "Mos Italicus y mos Gallicus," *Revista de Derecho de la Universidad Católica de Valparaíso* 2 (1978): 11–40; Francisco Carpintero Benítez, "Mos italicus' 'mos gallicus' y el humanismo racionalista: Una contribución a la historia de la metodología jurídica," *Ius Commune* 6 (1977): 108–177; Guido Kisch, *Erasmus und die Jurisprudenz seiner zeit: Studien zum humanistischen Rechtsdenken* (Basel, 1960); Dominico Maffei, *Gli inizi dell'humaneismo giuridico* (Milan, 1956); H.F. Jolowicz, "Utility and elegance in civil law studies," *Law Quarterly Review* 65 (1949): 322–336.

67 See Osler, "Myth," 393–405.

seventeenth century by establishing professorial chairs in Code (1620) and *Digestum Vetus* (1694).[68]

Iura Propria

In contra-position to the lack of interest in the elegant school, Medina had collected a good number of *consilia* and *decisiones* of foreign jurisdictions. The comments and law reports of cities, regions or nations—as opposed to the *ius commune* based on the *corpora iuris* and writings of academic jurists—would show lawyers like Medina how his European counterparts dealt with the plurality of legal authorities. In this sense, it is interesting that a title of "Decisiones peruane" [193], perhaps compiled by Medina himself, is found in the library.

The library's chief interest in this field of legal literature was the universe of the Spanish Monarchy. In first place there is the Iberian peninsula, unified under the Spanish Habsburgs (1581–1668). Medina possessed the decisiones of the Kingdom of Aragon compiled by Martín Monter de Cueva [355], a colegial in San Clemente, Bologna, and councillor of Aragon, and an unidentified volume which could be either the compilation by José de Sessé y Piñol or Juan Cristóbal Vargas Machuca [40].[69] For Catalonia there was the *Decisiones aureae* by Luis de Peguera (1540–1610) [239]. There was also a number of consilia for particular Castilian jurisdictions such as Rodrigo Suarez (1440/60–1500/20), oidor in Valladolid and city councillor in Salamanca [67]; Marcos Salon de Paz [55, 99], a jurist from Valladolid; and Azevedo [289].[70] The library also had two volumes of 'decisions of the Kingdom of Portugal' [213], the compilation of Antonio da Gama (1520–95), a scholar at the college of San Clemente, councillor of State and great chancellor in Portugal [149, 175, 285], and two treatises on diverse aspects of the law of succession in Portugal by Alvaro Vaz [234] and Alessandro de Rho (1548–1632) [84].

In the case of Spanish possessions in Italy, Medina centred his attention in the kingdoms of Naples and Sicily, as no works concerning the Duchy of Milan, incorporated to the Spanish Monarchy in 1535, are found. These possessions were governed, as the Indies, by councils; the Council of Italy being created in 1558 by Philip II.[71] In the case of Naples, incorporated in the crown of Aragon

68 A similar adherence to the mos italicus is also present in Oxford by the decade of 1590. See Alain Wijffels, *Late sixteenth-century lists of law books at Merton College* (Cambridge, 1992).

69 On Spanish decisiones see Coing II,2: 1305–1308.

70 Sobre esto puede verse Santos M. Coronas González, "Alegaciones e Informaciones en Derecho (*porcones*) en la Castilla del Antiguo Régimen," *Anuario de Historia del Derecho Español* 73 (2003): 165–192.

71 An introduction to the Spanish regimes in Italy is found in Gregory Hanlon, *Early Modern Italy, 1550–1800* (London, 2000), Ch. 5.

in 1442, and later to Castile by Charles V in 1516 together with Sardinia and Sicily, there was the *decisiones* compiled by Matteo d'Afflitto (*c.*1450–*c.*1529), professor of laws at the University of Naples [177, 260, 464], with additions by Cesare Ursilli [261]. In addition, the library possessed the *decisiones* for Naples compiled by Vicentius de Franchis [286] and Antonio Capece [Capyseum] (†*c.*1545) [121]. In the case of Sicily there was the *decisiones* of Bartolomeo da Capua [159] and possibly the law reports compiled by Andrea d'Isernia [453].

Outside the Spanish Monarchy the library's attention was centred in the *iura propia* of Catholic Europe and, in particular, the various Italian republics, the Holy See and the Kingdom of France. In the case of France there was an unidentified volume of *decisiones* "forensis galis" [216] and various compilations of particular jurisdictions such as Guy de La Pape (*c.*1402–87) [76, 166] and François Marc [266] for the *parlement* of Dauphiné; Nicolas de Bohier (1469–1539) [325] for the senate of Bordeaux; Barthélemy de Chasseneux (1480–1541) for Burgundy [310]; and the 'Capella Tolosana' [117]. It is possible that the comments on the customs of Poitou by André Tiraqueau (1488–1558) [402] and Anjou by René Choppin (1537–1606) [30] were also in the library. In the case of general Italian *decisiones* there were those compiled by Carrocci [211], Giacomo del Pozzo (1508–63) [306] and Gugliemo Cassador (1477–1527) [94]. Possibly the particular area with more comprehensive holdings was Tuscany. The library possessed the *decisiones* compiled by Antonio Monacho for Florence, Bologna and Lucca [82]; Borgnino Cavalcano (1530–1607) for Fivizzano [258]; and Alessandro de Rho (1548–1632) for Pisa [307]. Additionally, there were the *decisiones* of Antonio Tesauro for Piedmont [347], Ioannes Petrus Surdus (†1592) for Mantua [412], and unidentified volumes dedicated to Treviso [270] and Genova [263].

In general terms, the jurisprudence of kingdoms, provinces or municipalities, constituted an excellent instrument to illustrate to lawyers such as Medina the way in which his European counterparts used the *ius commune* and decided on particular cases. Although the use of comparative law by Latin American jurists remains virtually unexplored, there are a few examples such as a 1616 report on the validity of viceroy dispositions in times of transition by *oidor* Francisco Carrasco del Saz where Afflito and Isernia are used to make his point.[72] Similarly, Afflito is also used by Solórzano to analyse the jurisdictional attributes of the viceroy.[73] In both cases, the use of comparative law provided

72 Francisco Carrasco del Saz, "Initio a domino. Factum. El Rey Nuestro Señor proveyo por su Virrey…" (Lima, 10 January 1616), 1–3. The report concluded that the dispositions of the salient viceroy were valid, but could be revoked by the entrant viceroy.

73 Solórzano, *Política Indiana*, 5.13.41, 43.

magistrates with useful insights in matters of government, administration of justice and conflicts with local custom.[74]

The importance of *iura propria* also reflects the characteristics of book production during Medina's time. As Osler has pointed out, the last two decades of the sixteenth century were characterised by the emergence of a bilingual legal literature centred on individual legal systems, of which the *consilia* and *decisiones* of the territorial tribunals are the chief expression. In this period, the most significant boundary was confessional, therefore limiting the phenomenon of "borrowing" between different legal systems was limited to Catholic countries, as demonstrated with the extensive collection of Italian or French works among Medina's books.[75] Moreover, it is completely significant that even the authors that could have been observed by the Inquisition in Lima came from this sphere of influence. This is the case of Charles du Moulin (1500–66), a French jurist who made annotations to Gaspare Cavalino [105]. Du Moulin converted to Calvinism (1542) and Lutheranism (1556), and in 1566 published the *Grand Coustumier* an annotated version of the Customs of Paris.[76] This behaviour, no doubt, is the reason why Du Moulin's name was struck off from his edition of Decio's *Concilia* (Lyon, 1556) in the Zauli Naldi library, and shows the hostility towards this author in Catholic, Counter-reformation Europe.[77]

The Library of Lasso de la Vega

Castilian and Spanish American Law

Lasso de la Vega possessed an unidentified edition of the chief medieval source of Castilian Law, the Siete Partidas as well as a copy of the Ordenanzas Reales de Castilla. More attention, however, was given to the *Nueva Recopilación*

74 For Afflito's work in the matter of conflicts between royal law and local jurisprudence see Giancarlo Vallone, *Iurisdictio Domini: Introduzione a Matteo d'Afflito ed alla cultura giuridica meridionales tra Quattro e Cinquecento* (Lecce, 1985). Two thirds of the communities of the Kingdom of Sicily, for example, lay under the jurisdiction of Baronial judges; in Naples there were only 76 royal jurisdictions, usually the largest towns, as opposed to 1974 feudal ones. See Hanlon, *Italy*, 67–68.

75 Douglas Osler, "The myth of European Legal History," *Rechtshistorisches Journal* 27 (1997), 406–408.

76 Clarence Smith, 113–114.

77 Andrea Padovani, "La biblioteca Zauli Naldi: Uno specchio della civilità europea a metà Seicento," in *La Repubblica dei Giuristi: Edizioni giuridiche del '500 della librería Zauli Naldi*, ed. Anna Rosa Gentili (Faenza, 1994).

(1567). His library included fifteenth and seventeenth century commentaries to different titles of this law code by Juan de Matienzo, Pedro de González de Salcedo, Alfonso Narbona, and—possibly—Juan de Gutiérrez. Eighteenth century titles on this law code was included the comments of Manuel Arredondo Carmona (*fl.*1729–58), councillor of Granada and Castile on the *autos acordados* or legal decisions.

Castilian Law was complemented by the basic texts of Spanish American Law, such as Juan de Solórzano Pereira, *Política Indiana*; Gaspar de Escalona y Agüero, *Gazofilacio*; and Antonio de León Pinelo, *Tratado de confirmaciones reales* on confirmation of offices. Not limited to, but widely used in, Spanish America was the treatise by Hermegildo de Rojas Jordán de Tortosa regarding incompatibility of offices. In addition to these works, Lasso de la Vega possessed a number of works on Indians such as Alfonso de la Peña Montenegro (1596–1687) *Itinerario para párrocos* (1668) and Juan de Acosta (1540–1600), *De procuranda indorum salute*. The library also included the 1754 edition of the vocabulary of Quechua written by Jesuit Diego de Torres Rubio (1547–1638) with additions by Juan de Figueredo.

Ius Commune

The holdings of the Lasso de la Vega library reveal knowledge of the main sources of the *ius commune* and a number of sixteenth and seventeenth century commentaries thereon.[78] Thus, in the case of Canon Law, he possessed a copy of the Corpus Iuris Canonici, as well as the works of Giovanni Battista, Cardinal de Luca, the *consultationes* of Giacomo Pignatelli (1625–98), the comments on the second books of the decretals by Archbishop Feliciano de la Vega. These works were complimented by the treatise of Alonso Pérez de Lara on *capellanías* or chaplaincies, an institution which permitted that property be charged with a perpetual sum for the provision of pious works. In the case of Roman Law, the inventory reveals an edition of the Corpus Iuris Civilis and two comments on different titles of the Digest: Philippo Decio, *De regulis iuris* and Pedro Barbosa (†c.1608) *De iudicis*. These were complimented with the *consiliationes* by Nicolo Passeri (1585–1615).

The library of Lasso de la Vega, however, also evidences two distinctive changes in the approach towards Roman and Canon Law which characterised the eighteenth century. The first is the literature concerning the *Real Patronato*, a privilege granted by the Holy See that allowed Spanish Monarchs to present candidates for ecclesiastical dignities and offices. Royal patronage

78 AGN protocolos notariales s.XVIII, protocolo 873, escribano Antonio Jerónimo de Portalanza 1770–1775, fs. 730–735

acquired a significant importance in the eighteenth century following the decision of Charles III to further limit ecclesiastical jurisdiction in the Spanish Monarchy. In fact, during the time of Lasso de la Vega an intense academic and judicial dispute occurred in Lima (1749–50) between Jesuit Antonio de la Cueva Ponce de León (*fl.*1724–61), who defended the independence of the Church, and former protector-fiscal of Indians Pedro José Bravo de Lagunas (1703–62), who defended the rights of the crown.[79] Its importance in the legal sphere would explain the various studies of this privilege in the Indies in libraries such as Antonio Alvarez de Abreu (1683–1775), the Marquis of Regalía, Pedro Frasso (1630–93), the *oido*r in Quito and Lima, and Gaspar de Villarroel (1587–1665) and the Bishop of Chile. These works, which reflected both the regalist and ecclesiastical positions, were complemented by the work of Tommaso del Bene on the immunity of the Church regarding civil jurisdiction.

In the case of Roman Law, the library of Lasso de la Vega would reflect the increasing interest for the Institutes in eighteenth century Europe.[80] At least three editions of this text have been identified. This was partly a consequence of the disposition of the Marquis of Ensenada (1702–81) given in 1752 to limited the study of Roman Law to this text. Thus, all of Lasso's colleagues in the audience (Gorena, Messía and Tagle) possessed at least one copy of the comments of the Institutes by Johan Georg Kees, Arnold Vinnen (1588–1657), or Francisco de Amaya (1580–1640), an *oidor* in Valladolid.[81]

Lasso de la Vega, as Medina, possessed only a scant interest in antiquarian studies of law. The only volume found in his library was the work of José Berní Catalá on the historical privileges of the crown of Castile.

79 Antonio de la Cueva Ponce de León, *Concordia de la discordia* (Lima: Imprenta de la Calle de Palacio, 1749) y Pedro José Bravo de Lagunas y Castilla, *Discordia de la concordia* (1750) en *Colección legal de cartas y dictámenes, y otros Papeles en Derecho* (Lima: Oficina de los Huérfanos, 1761).

80 On the influence of this text in modern Europe see Klaus Luig, "The Institutes of National Law in the Seventeenth and Eighteenth Centuries," *Juridical Review* 17 (1972), 193–226.

81 The Institute appears in the book inventories of Tagle Bracho (§20, 26), Francisco de Amaya's comment in that of Gorena (§25), and Vinnen's comment in both Gorena (§72) and Messía Munive. The library of Cristóbal Messía y Munive, inventoried *c.* 1774 is found in BNP mss. Z765/1774. For the libraries of Tagle and Gorena see Mauricio Novoa, "La cultura política de una audiencia sitiada: los libros de Manuel de Gorena y Pedro Antonio de Tagle Bracho (1774–1776)" in *Homenaje a José Antonio del Busto Duthurburu*, eds. Margarita Guerra and Rafael Sánchez Concha, vol. 2 (Lima, 2012), 653–686.

Tractati

Procedural law was one of Lasso de la Vega's chief fields of interest in the sphere of practical law. Holdings in this respect were mainly the sixteenth and seventeenth century classical works of Suárez de Paz, Pedro Barbosa (†1606) and Alonso Villadiego Vascuñana on civil procedure; Jerónimo Fernández de Herrera Villarroel on criminal procedure; and possibly general works by Giulio Claro and Juan de Gutiérrez. The library also had the eighteenth century comments of the *Curia Filipica* by José Vicente Domíguez.

In the case of civil law, Lasso de la Vega, like most Hispanic magistrates, had a great interest in family law and inheritance, and possessed the treatises of Juan de la Ripia on testaments, Pedro Barbosa on marriage, and Giovanni Battista Lupi on legitimacy. Complementary to this subject was the law of nobility and primogeniture of which Lasso de la Vega possessed a copy of Luis de Molina Morales's *Tractatus de hispanorum primogenitorum*. The law of obligations also occupied a prominent place in the library as it featured Alfonso de Olea's work on cession of rights, Matías Lagúnez's treatise on fruits, and the works of Manuel Román Valerón's (*fl.*1665) and Pedro de Singüenza on contracts. As for the law of persons, unlike those of his fellow magistrates Gorena and Messía,[82] the inventory of Lasso de la Vega did not include the *Tractatus de privilegiis pauperum et miserabilium personarum* by Gabriel Alvarez de Velasco (†1658), *oidor* in Santa Fe y Lima, one of the chief sources in Indian status.

Iura Propria

Lasso de la Vega centred his *consilia* and *desiciones* in the territories of the Spanish Monarchy. These included general works such as the *allegationes* written by Pedro Díaz de Ribadeneyra Noguerol (†*c.*1640) and Juan Bautista Valenzuela Velásquez. In particular, however, the protector-*fiscal* centred his attention on the crown of Aragon and included in his book collection the *desiciones* edited by Cristóbal Crespí de Valldaura (1621–81), a knight of Montesa and vice-chancellor of the Council of Aragon, and also the compilations of jurisprudence of the audiences of Catalonia edited by its regent Miguel de Cortiada (†1691), and Valencia edited by Llorens Mateu y Sanz (1618–80). These were followed in number by the jurisprudence edited for Castile which included the *resolutionum* compiled by Antonio Gómez and possibly the *consilia* by Juan de Gutiérrez. Lasso de la Vega also possessed a copy of the judicial decisions of the audiences of Granada and Seville compiled by José Vela de Oreña (1588–1643).

82 See, respectively, AGN, Protocolos Notariales s. XVIII, protocolo 169, escribano Tomás Ignacio Camargo 1771–1776, fs.595v–600; and BNP, mss. Z765/1774.

As in the case of Medina, Lasso's foreign holdings were basically centred on sixteenth and seventeenth century Italian and Portuguese jurisprudence. In the case of Italy, these included the *disceptationes* of Stefano Graziani for Naples; the decisiones of the Roman Rota compiled by Mattéo Buratti (1553–1627); and possibly the collection of *decisiones* by Giovanni Luigi Riccio (†1643). In the case of Portugal, there was the compilation of jurisprudence edited by Antonio da Gama (1520–95) and its comments by Blas Flórez Díaz de Mena, a Castilian lawyer; Gabriel Pereira de Castro (1571–1632), knight of the Order of Christ and judicial councillor in Lisbon; and Jorge de Cabedo (*c.*†1677), a professor of Law in Lisbon and member of the Royal Council of Portugal.

The university studies of advocates and protectors of Indians were characterized by the systematic study of the medieval texts that formed the *ius commune*. Although *arbitristas* such as Pedro Simon Abril referred to Roman Law as a 'foreign' influence,[83] the traditional approach of the *mos italicus* prevailed in San Marcos until the early eighteenth century. Besides enhancing social status, the hours spent reading a complex array of material, attending lectures and facing examinations provided graduates with a particular method for solving legal issues and a capacity to present arguments in a logical manner. Knowledge of the applicable law was obtained after concluding university studies, by means of an apprenticeship at a legal practice.

The libraries of Medina and Lasso de la Vega provide an insight into the legal culture of the protectors together with their professional careers, as well as of the interests of the upper echelons of the legal elite. Their main focus was Castilian Law, followed by Roman and Canon Law, treatises on specific subjects, and jurisprudence of Catholic Europe. The significant holdings of *mos italicus* authorities, gives an account for the influence of academic law in seventeenth and eighteenth century legal practice. Although book production, historical context, and contemporary legal doctrine varied its approach, the libraries of Medina and Lasso de la Vega have a striking similarity in their structure and content.

In both libraries Castilian Law was the most important feature, as it constituted the main source of private, criminal and procedural law in Spanish America. Unless modified by a specific law, legal transactions and lawsuits were conducted under these rules. University studies and legal literature, however, influenced the manner in which Castilian Law should be interpreted. Using the *Odia restringi* rule as a doctrinal basis, Hispanic jurists made restrictive interpretations of norms that contradicted the *ius commune*. However,

83 Pelorson, *Los letrados*, 324–326; Diego de Saavedra Fajardo, *República Literaria* (1612; Madrid, 1922), 115–116.

when they found that dispositions of Castilian Law observed the principles of *ius commune*, their interpretation was extensive.[84] The interrelation of royal law and civil law fostered the idea that common legal principles were needed to thread practical legal principles, and that law possessed a dual nature—common and local, statutory and supranational. Even if the Castilian norms prohibited the application of Roman Law in its domains, its influence found its way to judicial courts.

84 See, for example, Barrientos Grandon, *Historia del Derecho*, 132–145 and Luque, *Universo de opiniones*, 232.

CHAPTER 7

Litigation at the Royal Audience of Lima

The fact that university-trained protectorship officials spent at least part of their time pleading Indian lawsuits before of the audience of Lima could be a contradiction in terms. As established by the 1575 ordinances, one of chief purposes of the institution of the Defensor General, Advocates and Procurators of Indians, as well as *corregimiento* protectors, was to 'remove the vexation and distress' caused by lawsuits.[1] Part of the role of protectors needed to be focused on preventing Indians from wasting their time and energies in legal battles before the royal audience and, by doing so, enabling them to remain in their towns imbued with police and doctrine. In reality, however, protectors proved to be able litigants. This chapter traces the role of advocates and fiscal-protectors in Indian lawsuits before the royal audience. It traces the importance of legal doctrine in the new developments of Spanish American Law, and the contribution of the protectors to these efforts. In the course of describing the lawsuits, the chapter presents an outline of Indian procedure in the audience of Lima, as well as the remedies and strategies used by the protectors. It also discusses the use of remedies and its influence in the general legal doctrine of the time.

Judicial Business of the Royal Audience

The legal defence of Indian plaintiffs by the advocates and protector-*fiscales* of Indians, as established in the 1575 ordinances, was undertaken within the framework of the royal audience of Lima. This court of appeals was established in 1542 but acquired its definitive jurisdiction in the decade of 1570 after the creation of the high courts in Santa Fe de Bogotá (1549), Charcas (1549), Quito (1563), Panamá (restored in 1564) and Chile (Concepción, 1565–75; Santiago 1609). Presided by the Viceroy of Peru and, as from 1776, by a regent, the royal audience had executive, legislative and judicial functions.[2] Upon the death of

1 Francisco de Toledo, *Disposiciones gubernativas para el virreinato del Perú*, ed. Maria Justina Sarabia Viejo (Sevilla, 1986–89), 2: 107 (§ix).

2 Although dated, a good introduction to the sources and bibliography of the royal audiences is found in Santiago Gerardo Suárez, *Las Reales Audiencias Indianas: Fuentes y Bibliografía* (Caracas: Academia Nacional de la Historia, 1989); for a more recent work see Norberto

 | DOI 10.1163/9789004305175_009

a viceroy it assumed political and military powers. The audience was originally staffed by four university-trained *oidors*, but by the end of the sixteenth century, and possibly due to the steady increase of lawsuits since the 1580s, Viceroy Marquis of Cañete (*v*.1590–96) increased the number of magistrates to six thus allowing the possibility of creating a second *sala* or chamber.[3] This number was maintained at least until the decade of 1660s;[4] by the end of the decade of 1770s, the royal audience of Lima had almost doubled its number to eleven magistrates.[5]

The royal audience served as an appellate court for sentences issued by provincial, local or specific tribunals and magistrates—in many cases with conflicting or even overlapping jurisdictions.[6] An overview of the existing dossiers of appeals reviewed by the audience of Lima in the sixteenth and seventeenth centuries reveals that the vast majority of cases originated from provincial *corregimientos* (or the magistrate with equivalent functions in the vice-regal capital), followed by the *alcalde ordinario* or city magistrate of Lima, and an array of special tribunals such as those undertaken by the officials of the royal treasury.[7] The fact that New World audiences were granted the royal seal allowed them to dispatch all lawsuits, provisions and executors' letters with the formalities of the royal chanceries of Valladolid. In some cases, following the

---

Dagrossa, "Bibliografía de Historia del Derecho Indiano" (2011), 283–99; available at http://www.larramendi.es.

3 See Francisco López de Caravantes, *Noticia general del Perú*, 6 vols., BAE 292–93, 295–98 (Madrid, 1986–89), 2: 29 ff. In theory, however, the Laws of the Indies established the number in eight *oidors* and four alcaldes del crimen; the lack of magistrates prompted the enactment of dispositions such as the one authorizing the audience to hear lawsuits even with one oidore. See Antonio de León Pinelo, *Recopilación de las Indias* (1635), 3 vols. ed. Ismael Sánchez Bella (México, 1992), 5.1.3; 5.1.22.

4 José de Mugaburu and Francisco de Mugaburu, *Chronicle of Colonial Lima: The Diary of Josephe and Francisco Mugaburu, 1640–1697*, ed. Robert Ryal Miller (Norman, 1975), 43.

5 Leon Campbell, "A Colonial Establishment: Creole Domination of the Audiencia of Lima during the Late Eighteenth Century," HAHR 52 (1) (1972), 3.

6 For the various jurisdictional courts and tribunals in the colonial period see José Soberanes, "La administración superior de justicia en la Nueva España," Boletín Mexicano de Derecho Comparado 13 (37) (1980), 143–200; and M.C. Mirow, *Latin American Law: A History of Private Law and Institutions in Spanish America* (Austin, 2004), 19–33. In the case of criminal justice see Charles Cutter, *The Legal Culture of Northern Spain, 1700–1810* (Albuquerque, 2001) and Tamar Herzog, *Upholding Justice: Society, State, and the Penal System in Quito (1650–1750)* (Ann Arbor, 2004). I have also profited from the valuable information on this subject provided by Dr. Renzo Honores.

7 See AGN, Real Audiencia, causas civiles (1543–1700); Recop. 5.12.23, 14, 15; Guillermo Lohmann, "El corregidor de Lima," *Anuario de Estudios Americanos* 9 (1952), 131–71.

medieval doctrine of the *casos de corte*, audiences could directly dispense justice to paupers, *miserables*, widows or orphans, as well as caciques in their disputes over governorship succession (as seen in this chapter).[8] Its rulings were normally appealed by a means of a "supplication"; it was not unusual that, by means of a second supplication, the case could be appealed to the Council of the Indies.[9]

Below the audience, a number of authorities, tribunals and magistrates were specifically created for Indian disputes, following the existence of two juridical estates or 'republics' during the colonial period—the *república de indios* and the *república de españoles*.[10] In principle, minor cases could be brought to the local *cabildo* (town council) or to the Indian corregidors (*corregidores de naturales* created in 1565) established in the main indigenous urban centres to impart justice over a group of *repartimientos*.[11] The situation was different for Indians living in important cities. In Lima, for example, the Juzgado General de Indios provided first instance criminal and civil jurisdiction for lawsuits involving Indians litigating against each other. Established in 1603, the *juzgado* was presided over by a viceroy-appointed official, who conducted oral trials; a permanent notary (*escribanía*) was established in 1688 to keep a record of the court's dealings.[12] A similar situation occurred in Cuzco, where a *juez de naturales* was appointed from the ranks of the Spanish *regidores* to act as a first instance judge for Indians living in the area covered by

---

8 Juan de Hevia, *Primera y segunda parte de la Curia Filipica*, 2 vols. in 1, (1603; reprint, Madrid, 1644), 35–6.

9 See Víctor Tau Anzoátegui, "La 'ley se obedece pero no se cumple': En torno a la suplicación de las leyes del derecho indiano," *Anuario Histórico-Jurídico Ecuatoriano* 4 (1980), 53–110; and Mirow, *Latin American Law*, 20. Appeals to sentences issued by the royal audiences to the Council of the Indies are still to be studied as a phenomenon, but examples are found in studies by David Brading *Miners an Merchants in Bourbon Mexico*, 1763–1810 (Cambridge: Cambridge University Press, 1971), 117–18; Bianca Premo, *Children of the Father King: Youth, Authority and Legal Minority in Colonial Lima* (Chapel Hill, 2005), 185–86; Sophie Mathis, "Vicente Mora Chimo, de 'Indio principal' a 'Procurador General de los Indios del Perú': cambio de legitimidad del poder autóctono a principios del siglo XVIII," *Bulletin de l'Institut Français d'Etudes Andines* 37 (1) (2008), 204–206.

10 Rafael Sánchez-Concha, "El Cuerpo de República en el pensamiento político colonial," *Humanitas* 21 (1992), 60–73; Alejandro Cañeque, *The King's Living Image: The Culture and Politics of Viceregal Power in Colonial Mexico* (New York and London, 2004), 214–22.

11 Juan de Matienzo, *Gobierno del Perú (1567)*, ed. Guilllermo Lohmann Villena (Paris, 1967), 51–52; Ballesteros 1945, 620; Guillermo Lohmann Villena, *El corregidor de indios en el Perú bajo los Austrias* (Madrid, 1957), 259–260.

12 BNP mss. C 3396, Lima, June 1791 – Feb. 1793, fs.1–2.

FIGURE 6
Indian Alcalde, highlands (sierra). Watercolour by Baltazar Martínez de Compañón, Trujillo del Perú. *18th century.*
IMAGE COURTESY OF BIBLIOTECA NACIONAL DEL PERÚ

FIGURE 7
Indian Alcalde, valleys. Watercolour by Baltazar Martínez de Compañón, Trujillo del Perú. *18th century.*
IMAGE COURTESY OF BIBLIOTECA NACIONAL DEL PERÚ

Local justice, 18th century. The officials in figures 6 to 8 have the staff of office (vara) *which denotes them as judicial authorities of the* corregimiento, *and from 1784 intendencia, of Trujillo. Note the difference in dress between the Indian* alcalde *for the highlands (6), the 'valleys,' presumably larger urban areas or even an Indian* corregimientos (7), *and the* alcalde ordinario *of the city of Trujillo (8, in the following page).*

FIGURE 8
Alcalde Ordinario. Watercolour by Baltazar Martínez de Compañón, Trujillo del Perú. *18th century.*
IMAGE COURTESY OF BIBLIOTECA NACIONAL DEL PERÚ

that city and a radius of five leagues.[13] There evidence that a *corregidor de naturales* was established in the late sixteenth century to impart justice for the Indians living within the city of Arequipa.[14]

There is evidence that Indians also brought suits outside the circuit of magistrates appointed to hear their cases. Visitation judges, for example, provided an alternative source to settle disputes. An overview of the cases resolved by the Spanish corregidor residing in the provincial seats shows that Indian plaintiffs were not an unusual feature of this tribunal.[15] There are also a handful of

13 Jean-Jacques Decoster, "El rol del Cabildo en la administración colonial," in *Ylustre Consejo, Justicia y Regimiento: Catálogo del Fondo Cabildo del Cuzco (causas civiles)*, eds. Jean-Jacques Decoster and José Luis Mendoza (Cusco, 2001), 16. An excellent account of the various forms of local litigation in the city of Cuzco, from a notarial perspective, is found in Katheryn Burns, *Into the Archive: Writing and Power in Colonial Peru* (Durham, 2010), 50, 88–96, 114–22.

14 Alejandro Málaga Medina, "Los corregimientos de Arequipa, siglo XVI," *Historia* (Universidad Nacional de San Agustín, Arequipa) 1 (1975), 59.

15 Examples of the few catalogues of corregimiento lawsuits are Helard Fuentes Rueda, *Corregimiento de Arequipa: Catálogo de Causas Civiles y Penales (1550–1784)* (Arequipa: n.e., 1988) or Jean-Jacques Decoster and Brian S. Bauer, *Justicia y Poder: Cuzco, siglos XVI–XVIII, Catálogo del Fondo Corregimiento Archivo Departamental del Cuzco* (Cuzco, 1997).

dossiers which evidence the participation of the *alcaldes ordinarios* of Cuzco in seventeenth and eighteenth century indigenous disputes.[16] Traces of this phenomenon are visible also in Lima where a cacique family living in Nazca, a city 450 km south of Lima, initiated legal actions before its *alcalde ordinario*.[17] Outside jurisdictional courts, the *cacique* (ethnic lord and community governor) adjudicated most conflicts in Indian communities.[18]

Another aspect that should be taken into account before reviewing the cases is that, although the trials were written, Castilian Law expressly prohibited the citation of juristic authors or the motivation of sentences. As Carlos Garriga has pointed out, magistrates of the Spanish Monarchy could only be motivated by their own consciences.[19] This is explains why laws and legal dispositions are only seldom referred to in writs or judicial sentences; and why if they are, these were normally referred to in a general manner. In the suit of Melchor and Salvador Ataurimachi to maintain their rights as descendants of Inca lineage, for example, protector-*fiscal* Francisco de Valenzuela claimed in 1644 that the nullity presented by the Crown procurator did not affect the substance of the case in conformity with 'one of the compiled laws' (possibly referring to the Recopilación of Castile of 1567).[20] In turn, procurator general of

16 Decoster and Mendoza, *Ylustre Consejo*, cases 110, 369, 391, 451, 455, 471.

17 "Testimonio de los autos que se seguían por ante el alcalde ordinario de la ciudad de los Reyes, D. Francisco de Zárate, sobre la apertura del testamento que otorgó don García Nazca, principal del valle de Nazca...," AGN, Derecho Indígena, leg. 31, c. 161 (1569).

18 See the seminal studies of Ella Dunbar Temple, "Los caciques Apoalaya," *Revista del Museo Nacional* 11 (2), 147–78 and Carlos Díaz Rementería, *El cacique en el Perú: Estudio histórico-jurídico* (Sevilla: Universidad de Sevilla, 1977), as well as more recent works of Susan E. Ramírez, "Amores Prohibidos: The Consequences of the Clash of Juridical Norms n Sixteenth Century Peru," *The Americas* 62 (1) (2005), 47–63; and Juan Carlos de la Puente Luna, *Los curacas hechiceros de Jauja: Batallas mágicas y legales en el Perú colonial*, Colección Estudios Andinos 1 (Lima, 2007), 108–123 (which includes a comprehensive bibliography on the subject).

19 Carlos Garriga, "La recusación judicial: del derecho indiano al derecho mexicano," in *La supervivencia del derecho español en Hispanoamérica durante la época independiente*, Cuadernos del Instituto de Investigaciones Jurídicas (México: Universidad Nacional Autónoma de México, Instituto de Estudios Jurídicos, 1998), 207–208.

20 "Autos que siguieron don Melchor y don Salvador Ataurimachi, indios principales del pueblo de San Juan de Huamanguilla, jurisdicción de la ciudad de Huamanga, sobre que se les guardasen los privilegios y excepciones a que tenían derecho por ser del linaje de los incas, e hijos de don Fernando Ataurimachi, quien lo fue a su vez de don Fernando Rucana, que por línea recta descendía de Guaina Cápac, según afirma," AGN, Derecho Indígena, leg. 8 c. 109 (1643), f.57.

Indians Melchor de Carvajal stated in a writ of 1704 that the contract between Indians Juan Guamán and Lorenzo Tataje did not observe 'the solemnities provided in the Royal Law of the Indies regarding the sale of real estate of Indians' (*Recopilación de Indias* 6.1.17).[21] Lastly, protector-*fiscal* Pedro José Bravo de Lagunas, claimed in his defence writ of 1 July 1736, that the 'laws and ordinances of the kingdom' specified that *corregidores* could not send Indian prisoners to *obrajes* or mills (*Recopilación de Indias* 6.13.8).[22]

Evidence of specific citation is found when referring to royal *cédulas*, as when the *coadjutor* of Indians of Santiago pleaded in favour of four Indians claiming that no encomiendas could be established in the reduction by virtue of 'various royal cédulas dispatched for this reason [and] specially by that of 26 April 1703.'[23] In general terms, precise citation seems to have been a later phenomenon, as in the 1793 report to governor general of Chile Ambrosio O'Higgins (1716–1801), by Pérez de Uriondo where reference is made to laws 20, 24, 22, title 3, book 6 of the 'municipal [laws],' that is the Laws of the Indies, stating that no Spaniards could live in Indian pueblos.[24] There are also cases of precise references to juristic authors, as the one found in a writ by a plaintiff in Moquegua, Peru, who cited 'the great practical Febrero,' that is José Febrero (1733–1790), to plead a case before the sub-delegate in 1810.[25]

Advocates and protectors-*fiscales* undertook their obligation when Indian cases had reached the royal audience. Some lawsuits, such as those involving disputes over *cacicazgos* were heard at first instance by the audience of Lima, following the doctrine that Indians were entitled to the *caso de corte*.[26] In other cases, protector intervened in appeals from lower courts. Either way, the cases reviewed in this chapter represent Indian litigation involving *letrado* justice, that is, cases pleaded and settled by university-trained professionals.

21 "Autos seguidos por Don Juan y Don Pedro Huamán, indios principales de la ciudad de Ica, contra Doña Josefa de Aquije, sobre nulidad de la venta de una viña," AGN, Real Audiencia, Causas Civiles, leg.8, c.45, 1704, f. 53v.

22 AGN, Real Audiencia, Causas Civiles, leg. 22, c. 124, 1736, f. 33.

23 "Juan de Novoa, coadjutor de indios sobre libertad de los indios Pedro Anteleb y hermanos," Archivo Nacional de Chile, Real Audiencia, vol. 2797, f. 45v.

24 "Juicio que siguen con Simón Salgado y otros sobre el deslinde de las tierras del pueblo antiguo de Tagua Tagua," Archivo Nacional de Chile, Real Audiencia, vol. 1589, pz. 3, fs. 229v–230.

25 "[A]l gran práctico Febrero." AGN, Real Audiencia, causas eclesiásticas, recursos de fuerza, leg. 5, c.1, f. 208v.

26 Solórzano, *Política Indiana*, 2.28.25.

Advocates of Indians

Litigation Strategies

Evidence is scarce, but it would appear that advocates of Indians undertook the defence of Indians at the royal audience of Lima mainly in land disputes and cacicazgo successions. A good example of the first is the 1605–10 dispute between the cacique and Indians of Laupaca and Gonzalo López over 100 fanegadas of land. The case was brought to the audience of Lima by advocate of Indians Leandro de la Rynaga, who invoked the doctrine of the *caso de corte* to initiate actions (f.1–1v). Following the pleads of both parties, the audience ordered the local corregidor to undertake *provanzas* or testimonials of witnesses in the towns or villages where the disputes. It was only after this that the *oidors* issued a sentence; in this case ordering López to reinstate the lands and its fruits to the Indians. Even if procedural law discouraged this practice, López's widow, Doña Isabel de Monsalve and her lawyer presented a *recurso de suplicación*, or second appeal, to the audience (6v).

The audience not only admitted the suplicación, but also allowed Monsalve's lawyer, Juan Bautista de Quiaza, to present new evidence in the form of copies of the books of the Royal Treasury—which documented that the land was the property of the Crown and that, in consequence, the transfer to López had been lawful. In his writ he argued that the original proprietor of the lands was Antonio Payco, cacique of Laupaca. As the line of Payco ended with no legal successor, the lands were then transferred to the Royal Treasury (7–7v). Faced with such proof, Rynaga replied that the lands should be given to an administrator of *censos* until the conclusion of the lawsuit; this strategy would guarantee that the Indians did not lose possession of the land, nor its produce until the conclusion of the trial. The audience agreed with this petition and on 15 February 1610 granted the administration of the lands to the administrator of *censos* Diego de Otazu (12–12v). The end result of the lawsuit, however, is unknown.[27]

Perhaps a more detailed insight into the work of advocates of Indians is found in the prolonged *cacicazgo* disputes that were settled in the audience of Lima. In 1601, for example, Leandro de la Rynaga Salazar initiated proceedings on behalf of Juan Felipe Paucar Guacra in his claim for the *cacicazgo* of Luringuanca, Jauja,

---

27 "Ejecutoria de las sentencias de vista y revista y autos pronunciados por esta Real Audiencia en la causa que en ella han tratado el cacique é indios de Laupaca reducidos en Huarmey, etc.." BNP ms. b 1289 (1605), f. 6v. The sentence was given by *oidors* Boan, Juan Fernández de Recalde, Juan Ximénez de Montalvo, Juan de Villela, Hernando Arias de Ugarte, and Juan Paez de Laguna.

in the central Andes.[28] On 23 January 1601, he presented the testimonials undertaken before the corregidor of Jauja, Francisco de Alderete Maldonado, in 1596. For Rynaga, the provision of Viceroy Luis de Velasco, granting the *cacicazgo* to Juan Felipe (1600) was sufficient proof of his claim and opposition to it was merely to 'bother' his party (40–40v). His actions proved successful, and in March of that year, *oidors* Avendaño and Boan ratified the provision and declared his defendant, Juan Felipe, the cacique of Luringuanca (42).

Unlike other cases, in which protectors litigated against private attorneys, on this occasion Rynaga opposed the *fiscal* of the royal audience, Antonio de Ibarra. Shortly after the sentence, Ibarra appealed, using a *recurso de suplicación* in which he argued that Diego Mango Guala, Juan Felipe's father, was an illegitimate son and could not have lawfully succeeded to the cacicazgo (43–43v). Three days later Rynaga and his procurator protested against Ibarra's accusations because they were a re-statement of previous arguments against the appointment of Juan Felipe, already discarded when the viceroy saw the case (44). Despite these claims, however, the audience accepted the appeal from *fiscal* Ibarra, incidentally a former *abogado de indios*, and ordered a new *averiguación* to be carried out in Jauja. The parties were notified of this on 23 and 29 August 1601 (44v–45).

In this case, Rynaga's strategy was focused on undermining the new testimonies. On 26 October 1601, for example, he attempted to overrule the presentation of the testimonies undertaken by Ibarra himself in Jauja (26–27 September) on the grounds that Juan Felipe was absent at the time of the notification (46). Rynaga managed not only to obtain authorization to undertake a new testimonial in Jauja (23 November), but also delayed the presentation of Ibarra's *provanza* until 11 December (46v–52). Although there is no record of the result of the lawsuit, the case brings into light not only Rynaga's influence with the *oidors*, but also his close connection with the court's daily work. The same day Ibarra filed his petition to present the provanza, for example, he had signed and presented a reply (46).

Another example of litigation strategies is found in the dispute over the *cacicazgo* of the Guaranga of San Lorenzo de Quinti, a town of considerable importance which had political authority over neighbouring pueblos, where Juan del Campo and Cipriano de Medina, respectively first and second advocates of Indians measured forces against each other.[29]

---

28 "Juan Felipe Guacra Paucar y Francisco Guacra Paucar sobre el cacicazgo de segunda persona de Luringuanca," 1600 Nov. 18 – 1602 Jan 22, Lilly, Latin American mss. Peru.

29 "Causas sobre el cacicazgo del Pueblo de Quinti. Huaman Chata, Miguel et al," Lilly Latin American mss. Peru. 1596, Aug. 23 – 1626, Mar. 13.

The proceedings began on 20 August 1621, when Cipriano de Medina and procurator Alonso de Torres Romero (*fl.*1626) requested the audience for ratification of the *cacicazgo* in favour of Miguel de Guamanchata (73). Doctor Medina presented copies of the proceedings undertaken by Antonio Barreto, corregidor of Huarochirí. After the *cacicazgo* vacated, Matín Vilcayauri and Migual de Guamanchata had disputed the property. Their claim was supported with the testimonials of at least six witnesses (76–76v, 79–81). The witnesses were examined by corregidor Barreto on 13–15 May 1621 (77–77v, 82–82v). Using evidence composed of alleged pedigrees from previous caciques, private opinions of the candidates, and testimonies of the neighbouring *principales*, on 14 July 1621 Barreto recommended to the audience the appointment of Guamanchata. He argued that Guamanchata was the candidate who was most 'benemerit, and of greater rason and capacity for the government of the said cacicazgo'(86). Copies of the proceedings undertaken by Barreto in Huarochirí were then sent to Lima for the opinion of Gerónimo de Samanez, Protector General of Indians. On 15 August 1621 the protector ratified the opinion of corregidor Barreto, and recommended to the Real Audiencia the appointment of Guamanchata for the post of cacique. He did not add new light to the argument, but stated that the corregidor had been diligent in his actions (86–86v).

Doctor Juan del Campo, first advocate of Indians, and his procurator Juan Ortiz de Mena (*fl.*1612–22), questioned the position of Guamanchata in a writ of 31 August 1621. To do so, he would embark on the reconstruction of the succession of the *cacicazgo* in the last 50 years. In his writ, Del Campo argued that it was testimonies of the visitation by Pedro de Herrasti, not the views of *indios principales* or notable Indians, that constituted the most accurate evidence to determine the rights to the cacicazgo (fs.87–88). The rightful candidate was not Guamanchata, but Martín Vilcayauri a great-nephew of cacique Fernando Llacsavilca (fs.87–88).

On 6 September 1621, Medina's procurator replied with the line of argument established by the corregidor in Huarochirí (fs.82v–85): the legitimate line of the cacicazgo was that of Pedro Llaxachari, and that Miguel Guamanchata, his only grandson, was the rightful heir. The procurator argued that Guamanchata's family had been caciques 'at the time the Spanish had entered in this kingdom,' and his uncle had been confirmed in the post by Viceroy Toledo. Lastly, although he did not dispute the validity of the revisita of Herrasti, the Procurator General of Indians argued that the appointment of Llacsavilca to the cacicazgo was only interim, since Guamanchata was a minor at the time of his father's death, and possibly the visitator was ill informed when he added Llacsavilca's name to the list of caciques (fs.89–89v).

On 17 September, *oidors* Diego Nuñez de Morquecho and Alberto de Acuña—the former advocate of Indians—ordered that further proof was needed and the parties were given 20 days to undertake new testimonies in Huarochirí (f.90). These were duly carried out in the town of Santa María de Jesús de Huarochirí between 21 October and 15 November 1621 before the corregidor Antonio Barreto, who reported interviewing a total of 21 Indian witnesses presented by Guamanchata (fs.101–11), but no witnesses on the side of Vilcayauri (f.119). The corregidor thus reported that Vilcayauri 'had not proven anything'(f.121v).[30] The Real Audiencia reviewed the evidence and declared the cacicazgo in favour of Miguel Guamanchata (fs.124, 126v).

Despite his defeat in court Juan del Campo continued to contest Guamanchata's right. On 13 September 1622, he and his procurator, Ortiz de Mena, presented a further candidate for the cacicazgo, Martín Chuquisapiente (f.129). After some judicial infighting over the legality of adding this new action to the procedure initiated a year before, the audience agreed to review new testimonials on the case (fs.172–76v; 150–71). Their validity was bitterly disputed. For his part, Medina opposed the presentation of new proof on the grounds that it changed the demand, thus undermining the original request to accumulate the procedure (f.147). Having reviewed the testimonials, on 7 February 1625, the audience ruled in favour of Guamanchata once more, arguing that Chuquisapiente was unable to prove his claim (f.215).

Despite a second adverse sentence, del Campo petitioned that new testimonials be undertaken on behalf of his defendant. In a writ of 15 April 1625, he petitioned to the audience a *restitutio in integrum* on the grounds that Chuquisapiente, as an Indian, was not liable to the terms of prescription, and could therefore present proof at any time during the procedure (f.226). Despite the fact that the audience had granted del Campo three consecutive extensions to present new testimonials, the audience granted the petitions (fs.226v, 229, 230v). The testimonials were finally presented on 26 May 1625, but the final result of the lawsuit is unknown (f.231).

In addition to his successful defence of cacique Guamanchata, there is evidence that Medina obtained other legal victories for his Indian plaintiffs. In 1625, for example, he secured for Gerónimo Polan the important *cacicazgo* of San Juan de Begueta, in Chancay.[31] Similarly, in 1626 he was able to persuade the audience to admit a third appeal by Francisco Carlos Melipi, a principal

30 "[N]o aber Probado cossa alguna." Ibid, 121v.

31 "Causa de don Geronimo Polan, indio con Francisco Chancoy sobre el cacicazgo del pueblo de Begueta del distrito de la villa de Chancay," Lilly Latin American mss. Peru, 1621, Oct. 26 – 1625, May 16.

Indian, to the sentences by the corregidor and the audience absolving Juan Temoche, the cacique of Naringuala, Piura, of abuses of his subordinates (fs.2–2v, 108v, 111, 113).[32]

Litigating for the Inca Heiress

Perhaps the most important lawsuit entrusted to an advocate of Indians was the defence of Ana María de Loyola Coya (1594–1630), the great-granddaughter of the XVI Inca Diego Sayri Túpac, and her husband Juan Enríquez de Borja (1573–1634)—marquises of Oropesa since 1614.[33] The legal claim was published in a tract 1616. In the absence of any records in the National Archive of Peru, this constitutes the only source for this case which was heard in the audience around 1614. Although the defence was by a team of five counsellors, which included Diego Messía de Zúñiga (†1636), a professor of Institute and rector of San Marcos, the head of the defence appears to have been, by the order in which they appear in the tract, Leandro de la Rynaga Salazar, at the time *first* advocate of Indians.[34]

The Marquises of Oropesa demanded from the Spanish Crown the payment of 340,000 pesos. The basis of the claim was the infringement of the agreement (or *asiento*) signed between Inca Sayri Túpac and Viceroy Andrés Hurtado de Mendoza, first Marquis of Cañete, as representative of King Philip II in 1558, which created an entail (or *mayorazgo*) for the Inca's legitimate descendants. It stipulated that the holder of the mayorazgo would receive a perpetual income of 10,000 ducats per annum drawn from the tributaries of four pueblos in Yucay, Cusco. In the event that the tribute did not amount to 10,000 ducats, the Crown would be liable to top-up this amount, either directly from the

32 "Francisco Carlos Melipis indio contra Dn. Juan Temocho sobre los capítulos que le puso," Los Reyes, 1 September 1606–13–April 1627, BNP ms. b 994.

33 Ana María was the daughter of Beatriz Clara Coya and Martín García Oñaz de Loyola, governor general of Chile and lord of the House of Loyola. Her marriage in 1611 to Juan Enríquez de Borja (1573–1634), grandson of St. Francis of Borgia, made the Marquises of Oropesa the foremost family in the Peruvian viceroyalty. The couple, who had ten children in all, spent their time between Lima and Cusco. See Guillermo Lohmann Villena "El señorío de los Marqueses de Santiago de Oropesa," *Anuario de Historia del Derecho Español* 19 (1948–49): 347–458 and Javier Gómez de Olea, "Los marqueses de Santiago de Oropesa," *Revista del Instituto Peruano de Investigaciones Genealógicas* 20 (1994), 129–39.

34 Leandro de la Reynaga [sic] Salazar, et. al., *Por el marqués de Oropesa, como marido de dona Maria de Loyola Coya. Sobre la satisfacion que pretende le haga su Majestad por los derechos y pretensiones en que viene informado por la Real Audiencia de Lima*... (Lima?, [1616]), 2. The other counsellors were doctors Melchor de Urbina, Lorenzo Pardo del Castillo and Francisco Ramos Galván.

Royal Chest or by the grant of new encomiendas. Due to the fact that since 1588 the tributes of Yucay had not yielded the annual sum of 10,000 pesos, Rynaga, on behalf of the Marquises, petitioned a compensatory payment of 340,000 pesos. This amount, he argued, was the sum of the income the Coya had failed to receive (2, 18v).

In the first part of the tract, Rynaga would state his case, presumably rebuking the Crown's defence. First he argued that there could be no question about the benefits of the contract between Sayri Túpac and Philip II: The Crown of Castile had gained a new kingdom, and the vice-royalty of Peru was pacified. Any doubt regarding the legitimacy of the contract would be nothing short of returning to the previous state of things (15–15v).[35] Secondly, he pointed out the legitimacy of Coya's succession to the entail, citing a disposition in Castilian law which validated female succession to a *mayorazgo* when the male line had ended (9).[36]

In third place, Rynaga replied to the argument that Manco Inca had lost all *dominium* due to his rebelliousness in Vilcabamba. Citing Bartolomé de las Casas' *Brevísima relación de la destrucción de las Indias* (1542), Rynaga argued that Manco Inca's uprising was a direct consequence of the ill treatment of Indians (11v). Rynaga, however, observed that two *cédulas* of 1552 and 1557 ratified this view, and that Manco Inca received official pardon from the King. In addition to this, rescripts of 1552 and 1554 had restored the property of Manco's son, Sayri Túpac, and the rebellious caciques of Vilcabamba. In sum, Rynaga stated that crimes should not be held against the successors of those who perpetrated them, and neither could their private property be affected (12).

For Rynaga, although the contract between Sayri Túpac and Philip II resulted in a formal transfer of sovereignty of the former Inca Empire to the King of Castile, this did not include property held in private *dominium*. Neither did it imply, he argued, that private *dominium* disappeared after the transfer of political sovereignty (15). In fact, the bulls that secured papal endorsement of Spanish sovereignty over the lands Columbus had claimed for the Catholic Kings, only affected 'public and universal *dominium*,' but not private *dominium* (9v–10). Therefore, Pope Alexander VI (*r.*1492–1502) had transferred the public and universal *dominium* of the cities and towns of the New World, but not the private property of its inhabitants (11). In view of this principle, Rynaga pointed out that after the conquest the caciques had their properties returned (20v).

35 "[Y] assi pues es tan notorio quan util fue a su magestad lo que capitulo el marques, nulla erit ratio por donde el remedio que pudiéra aver no cumpliéndole, fuera bolver las cosas al primer estado." Ibid., 15v.

36 P 3.18.2; 2.15.2.

Despite the importance of the lawsuit in political terms, Rynaga did not hesitate to point out that Ana María de Loyola Coya, as an Indian woman, 'was a minor' and could thus invoke the *restitutio in integrum* against procedural terms, in case the audience questioned the fact that she was demanding reimbursement of an agreement signed 50 years earlier.[37] The final result of the lawsuit is unknown. However, the fact that the instructions left by the Marquises of Oropesa prior to their departure from Peru in 1626 omit any mention of the lawsuit suggests that it was solved prior to that date.[38] When the fifth marquise, María de la Almudena Enríquez de Cabrera, died in Spain with no issue in 1741, the Oropesas still held the encomienda in Yucay and considerable economic interests in Peru.[39]

The Protector-*fiscal*

Evidence of the intervention of protectors-*fiscales* in Indian lawsuits taken before the audience of Lima between 1643 and 1741 is scarce. The earliest record is a 1643 petition by Melchor and Salvador Ataurimachi, *principales* of San Juan de Huamanguilla, Huamanga, to remain absolved of tribute, *mitas* and personal services due to the fact that they were of Inca lineage. The corregidor of Huamanga had declared the claim null and void, prompting the appeal by the Ataurimachi brothers to the audience of Lima. The suit was received in the audience of Lima in 1644 and was defended by procurator-*fiscal* Francisco de Valenzuela. The argument of both the corregidor and the fiscal of the audience, who defended the interest of the crown regarding taxation, was that the documentary evidence of one of the Indian parties was submitted outside time, thus making the claim null.[40]

37 "[P]or ser menor la marquesa o no ha podido correr contra ella en su tiempo, o si ha corrido tiene restitucion." Rynaga, *Por el marqués de Oropesa*, f.21.

38 "Razón de los papeles que quedaron en Yucay el año de 1626 en que se volvieron a España los señores marqueses de Oropesa" 1626, BNP ms. b239.

39 "Petición que formula el Duque de Medina para que se conduzcan los pleitos…," BNP, Archivo Astete Concha f 94. The marquis of Oropesa was made grandee of Spain in 1651. The fifth marquise was also tenth duchess of Medina de Rioseco; her death signified the end of the foremost Inca legitimate line. See Gómez de Olea, "Los marqueses de Santiago de Oropesa," 135.

40 "Autos que siguieron don Melchor y don Salvador Ataurimachi, indios principales del pueblo de San Juan de Huamanguilla, jurisdicción dela ciudad de Huamanga, sobre que se les guardasen los privilegios y excepciones a que tenían derecho por ser del linaje de los incas, e hijos de don Fernando Ataurimachi, quien lo fue a su vez de don Fernando

FIGURE 9
Royal Audience of Lima. Felipe Gumán Poma de Ayala, El primer nueva corónica y buen gobierno de Felipe Guaman Poma de Ayala. *1616. Ed. John V. Murra and Rolena Adorno (México, 1980). Guamán Poma de Ayala depicts the* oidores, alcaldes del crimen (*criminal high court magistrates*) *and* fiscales *at the* estrado (*bench*). *The presiding judge sat below a canopy bearing the royal arms of Castile (not seen in this image).*

In a writ of 2 September 1644 Valenzuela argued that although the documentary evidence was received out of time, this did not affect the central point of the lawsuit, which was to grant tax exceptions to the Ataurimachi brother, because the nullity only referred to the laws of procedure. Stressing the fact that in this royal audiences 'minutiae of law are not attended,' that 'the royal chest is not wronged in any way' and that claim of the Ataurimachis was 'legitimately substantiated' he requested that no nullity should proceed. The following day, *oidors* agreed, albeit with a discordant vote, to Valenzuela's petition.[41]

Rucana, que por línea recta descendía de Guaina Cápac, según afirma," AGN, Derecho Indígena, leg. 8, c. 109 (1643).

41 "[E]n esta real audiencia a donde no se atiende apices de derecho: por lo qual y a tento a que el real fisco no esta damnificado en via alguna; y estar la causa legitimamente sustanciada: a vuestra alteza pide y suplica declare no aver nulidad intentada." Ibidem, fs.57, 57v. The *oidors* which agreed to the petition were Gabriel Gómez de Sanabria, García Francisco Carrillo de Alderete (†1661) and Luis de Loma Portocarrero (1604–c.1650); the discordant vote was issued by Andrés de Villela (1594–1674).

Judicial dossiers evidence that the intervention of the protector-*fiscal* could also be possible even if Indian interests were not directly affected, as in the 1662 petition submitted by the notable *vecinos* of Cajamarca to Viceroy Count of Santisteban (*v.*1661–66) on whether the Order of St John should be granted the administration of the city's hospital. Consulted on the matter, Diego de León Pinelo, stated that it was not convenient to give the administration of the hospital to the order, as this would increase the Spanish influence over the Indian pueblos in Cajamarca. In his opinion, the petition was a scheme to increase the influence of Spaniards and Creoles in the city of Cajamarca, thus converting it into a Spanish city. His arguments, however, were unconvincing and ultimately the viceroy conceded the licence to the order of San Juan to administer the hospital.[42]

Similarly, in 1744 the Count of Villanueva del Soto earned the cacique and Indians of the pueblos of Sincos, Mito and Orcotuna in Huancayo an important victory against María Cecilia Martínez de la Peña, proprietor of the estate of Yanacocha. The Indians sought the nullity of the sale of pasture land, agreed between Martínez de la Peña and the visitador and land judge, Pedro de Valenzuela y de los Rios. In his writ of 11 September 1744 he argued that the nullity of the sale and composition of the lands was notorious, particularly as it had been established by a rescript of 1725 that 'Indians should not be dispossessed of lands that they have been possessing since time immemorial.'[43]

The protector-*fiscal* also intervened in cases of abuse to Indians, as seen in the case brought in 1733 by the Indians of the mill of Pichuichuro against its proprietor Gaspar de Cedillo, chief officer of the Real Caja of Cusco. The general was accused by the caciques of the neighbouring communities of wrongs and abuses committed against the Indians. In particular, they stated that Indians were taken by force from their ayllus, then put in shackles without being paid their salaries. In the mill, they were subject to innumerable cruelties which had left Ignacio Quispe crippled due to continuous flogging. Also Sebastián Tito Quispe denounced that his eighteen to twenty year old son Melchor threw himself in the boiling cauldron to avoid further flogging (fs.2–3v).[44]

---

42 "[C]iudad o villa de Españoles." AGN, Superior Gobierno, Real Acuerdo, GO RE, leg. 1, c. 3 (1662), fs. 18v–19, 36.

43 "Autos seguidos por Don Domingo de Cordova Huacra Paucar, cacique e indios principal del repartimiento de Luin-Huanca en la provincia de Jauja, a su nombre y en el de las comunidades de los pueblos de Sincos, Mito y Orcotuna, contra Doña Maria Cecilia Martínez de la Peña, vecina del pueblo de Huancayo y propietaria de la estancia Yanacocha…," AGN, Derecho Indígena, l. 15, c. 270 (1743–1748), f. 186.

44 "Autos relativos a las acusaciones que se formularon contra el General Gaspar de Cedillo, por supuestas exacciones y violencias cometidas contra los indios del Obraje denominado

Although the case was initially seen by Viceroy Marquis of Castelfuerte (*v.*1724–36), who had sent Antonio Candioti as visitor to the area, his successor, the Marquis of Villagarcía (*v.*1736–45), established that evidence was inconclusive, that Candioti was tricked by the caciques, and that Tito Quispe had retracted his accusations and his son's death a mere accident. Nonetheless, on 25 June 1736 he submitted the case to the protector-*fiscal* Pedro Bravo de Lagunas for his opinion (f.3v). In his report of 1 July 1736, Bravo de Lagunas stated that 'it appeared to be of justice' that Cedillo be absolved of the charges brought against him (f.32). Nonetheless, in compliance with his obligation as protector he demanded that the price of corn and clothing sold to Indians should be regulated as it was proven that even the scarcity of these goods was less harmful than their excessive price (f.33). In addition, he stated that salaries should be paid 'in silver and in hand' (f.33v). Lastly, he admonished corregidors of the practices of selling goods at excessive prices and of sending Indian prisoners to work in mills as free labour (f.34). The viceroy absolved Cedillo and sent the proceedings to the corregidor of Pichuichuro (fs.171–72).

Evidence suggests, however, that direct involvement of protectors-*fiscales* in Indian lawsuits diminished by the end of the seventeenth century; instead, the participation of the protectorship institution (as created by Toledo in 1575) in indigenous disputes seems have rested increasingly in the Procurator General of Indians. This phenomenon can be traced at least to the decade of 1670, when procurator general of Indians, Jose de Altube, acted without the advice of the protector-*fiscal* in the action undertaken by two Indian sisters for the possession of the hacienda of Guanchac in Huanta (Ayacucho) heard before the royal audience.[45] Similarly, there is evidence of another procurator general, Melchor de Carvajal, pleading in 1715 on behalf of three Indians for unpaid salaries in 1715; first before the *alcalde ordinario* and later appealing to the high court.[46]

José Mejía de Estela (*fl.*1667–1715), an experienced legal operator—recruited during the protectorship of Márquez de Mansilla—whose private activities with Indian clients can be traced to the decade of the 1660s, provides a good example of the activities of the Procurator General of Indians in the late

---

Pichuichuro, cargos de los cuales fue exonerado," AGN, Real Audiencia, causas civiles, leg. 22, c.124 (1736), fs. 101.

45 "Autos seguidos por Doña María Ruiz y Doña Inés de Cerpa, contra Don Luis de Cárdenas sobre el mejor derecho a la posesión de unas tierras conocidas como Guanchac, sitos en la jurisdicción de Huanta," AGN, Real Audiencia, causas civiles, leg. 196, c.745 (1668), fs.223.

46 "Autos seguidos por Felipe Santiago, Fernando Guamán, Bartolomé Alonso y Juan Maldonado, indios de la provincia de Canta, contra Doña Catalina Henriquez, sobre jornales insolutos," AGN, Real Audiencia, causas civiles, leg.28, c.164 (1715), fs.12, 19.

seventeenth and early eighteenth centuries.[47] In 1696, he undertook the defence of Agustín de Saucedo, Indian *principal*, against Martín Limas and two other Indians of Piura in a dispute over property, a house. Mejía de Estela appealed the sentence issued by the corregidor of Piura to the audience, arguing that Saucedo had acquired the house without the intervention of the protector of Indians of Piura because such an intervention was required when one of the parties was a 'Spaniard mestizo or mulatto' but not when it was another Indian (fs.33–33v).[48] Similarly, in 1704 he assumed the case of the widow of Indian Lorenzo Tataje, in a dispute over a vineyard in Ica, without the help of the protector-*fiscal* but with that of a prominent lawyer, Doctor Tomás de Salazar (†1738)—who had agreed to defend the widow by virtue of her condition of 'poor and miserable' (f.55).[49]

One explanation for the apparent distance of protectors-*fiscales* in litigation can be found in the various tasks undertaken by these officials. One of the most important of these was the intervention in *retasas* of Indians, that is the counting of tributaries. In 1661, for example, León Pinelo petitioned a *retasa* or new counting of tributaries, in the name of the caciques and Indians of Zaraos and Chupiquarangas in Tarma. As a result, Domingo de Aroche, the *contador* or comptroller, reported a total of 286 tributary Indians, 30 of which would serve the Church (fs.157v–158). The purpose was to reduce the number of tributaries, and Juan de Astudillo, *justicia mayor* of the province, was then informed of the new number.[50] Similarly there is evidence that this task was undertaken in 1701 by protector-*fiscal* Juan de Peralta who propitiated a new counting of tributaries in Parinacochas.[51]

Less frequent was the involvement of protectors-*fiscal* in events exogenous to their function, although highly relevant in colonial society, such as the

47 "Autos seguidos por Isabel Pascuala contra María Magdalena Llatán y Francisca Clara sobre el mejor derecho a una suerte de tierras en el pago de Chorrillos," AGN, Real Audiencia, causas civiles, leg. 194, c. 737 (1668), fs. 167.

48 "Autos seguidos por Martín Limas, Francisca Isa y Baltasar Chuquimoro, indios de la jurisdicción de Piura, contra Don Agustín de Saucedo, indio principal, sobre el derecho a una casa," AGN, Real Audiencia, causas civiles, leg. 285, c.1083 (1696), fs.22.

49 "Autos seguidos por Don Juan y Don Pedro Huamán, indios principales de la ciudad de Ica, contra Doña Josefa de Aquije, sobre nulidad de la venta de una viña," AGN, Real Audiencia, causas civiles, leg.8, c.45 (1704), fs. 64.

50 "Expediente sobre la petición presentada por el Protector de Naturales en nombre de los caciques e indios del repartimiento de Zaros y Chupiguarangas, para que se efectue una nueva numeración de contribuyentes," BNP, Archivo Astete Concha, ms. z 451 (1661).

51 "Retasa de los indios del repartimiento de Guaynacotas, en la provincia de Parinachochas…," AGN, Derecho Indígena, leg.12, c.185 (1702), fs.2v.

canonization process of Nicolás de Dios—a Chiclayo-born Indian who died in 1677, with 'fame of sanctity, and miracles.' In 1709, protector Isidoro López de Eceiza was requested to interview witnesses to assess the alleged virtues of Nicolás only to find that he had entered into 'illicit friendships.' Although these (and other) findings eventually convinced the Archbishop of Lima to abandon the process in Rome, vice-regal authorities reopened the case in the decade of 1770 and requested the involvement of the protector-*fiscal*.[52]

More to the point, however, a case heard at the audience of Lima in 1689 helps to illustrate the diminished presence of protector-*fiscales* in the direct defence of Indians at courts of justice. That year, Pedro de la Cruz, an Indian, appealed a decision which dispossessed him of the occupation of two fanegas of land in the valley of Surquillo owned by the *cofradía* of Our Lady of Loreto, a lay brotherhood composed of Indians established in the parish of Santa Ana in Lima.[53] The *cofradía* had obtained a favourable first instance judgement at the Juzgado General de Indios in Lima, after proving that Cruz, a tenant of their land, had failed to pay the rent of nine pesos per annum, and was damaging their property by cutting the trees down to use them as firewood.[54] At this point, the defence of Cruz was assumed by procurator general of Indians José Mejía de Estela, who demanded the annulment of the Juzgado's sentence, laconically stating that it was a 'matter of justice.' The next day, the *oidors* ordered that the proceedings should be taken to the protector-*fiscal* Márquez de Mansilla for his opinion (f.44–44v).[55]

In his report, Márquez de Mansilla questioned the *cofradía*'s own property rights regarding the two fanegas. He stated that whilst Cruz was in lawful possession of the land by royal decrees of 17 September 1688 and 15 July 1689, the *cofradía* did not have any proof of a grant by an ecclesiastical judge. The reason for this, Márquez de Mansilla, stated, was that the lands in Surquillo were *tierras de repartición*, or crown land, destined for Indian use only. Therefore, legal transactions undertaken by the *confradía* over these lands were null and void

52 Biblioteca Nacional de Chile, Archivo de la Biblioteca Barros Arana, Documentos Bibliográficos 21 (*c.*1770), fs. 1–3.

53 The *fanega* was equal to a bushel or a bushel and a half. The *cofradía* de *Nuestra Señora de Loreto* is mentioned in the description of Lima by Bernabé Cobo, "Fundación de Lima, escripta por el P. Bernabé Cobo de la Compañía de Jesus. Año de 1639," in *Obras del P. Bernabé Cobo*, BAE 91–92 (Madrid, 1956) 2: 456.

54 "Autos seguidos por Fray José de Sazo Ponce de León contra Pedro de la Cruz, indio, sobre la posesión de tierras en el valle de Surquillo," AGN, Real Audiencia, causas civiles, leg. 261, c.987 (1689), fs. 60.

55 Juan de Peñaloza y Benavides (*c.*1625–1709), Pedro Frasso (*fl.*1660–89), Juan Jiménez de Lobatón (1634–1693) and Carlos de Cahonar and Gaspar de Cuba y Arce (*c.*1633–1715).

(45r). The *cofradía* replied to Márquez de Mansilla's opinion with a writ by Melchor de Carvajal (*fl.*1689–1715), also a procurator general of Indians, reiterating the validity of the Juzgado's decision (f.50). However, as no titles of property were presented by Carvajal to counter the opinion of the protector-*fiscal*, procurator Mejía de Estela insisted on the fact that the lands occupied by Cruz were *tierras de repartición* which had been in possession of his family for at least 40 years (fs.52–52v). Although the sentence issued by the royal audience does not emerge in the dossier, the case illustrates how protectors, without altogether abandoning the defence of Indians at the royal audiences, assumed more consultative functions. It is altogether significant that, despite being *fiscales* only in the honorary sense, the audience sought and recognized the authoritative opinion of protectors in Indian matters, just as they did of crown appointed *fiscales* for matter relating to the royal fisc.

If anything, the available evidence points to the fact that between 1643 and 1744, the protector-*fiscal* was not confined to Indian litigation in the audience. León Pinelo's request for a *retasa* of tributaries or López de Eceiza's role in a canonisation procedure, illustrates the diverse scope of intervention of the protectors-*fiscales* of Indians. On the other hand, evidence suggests that, with the disappearance of the advocate of Indians, crown appointed procurators of Indians undertook the bulk of litigation in the audience. In some cases, the Indian condition of miserable would prompt important advocates such as Tomás de Salazar to offer advice. In most cases, however, the election of a *letrado* seems to be subject to the plaintiff's possibilities or the procurator's connections.

Legal Culture and Judicial Practice

The influence of *ius commune* evidenced in the university training and libraries of protectors and advocates of Indians seen in the previous chapter, did not go unaccounted for in their practice before the audience of Lima. Such influence, however, should be assessed against the backdrop of its formal prohibition in the courts of justice of the Spanish Monarchy by disposition of the Siete Partidas.[56] The prohibition, which dated from the Lex Visigothorum or *Fuero Juzgo* (c.631), stated that in the kingdoms under the crown of Castile, Roman Law could not be, and was not, considered as law. Although the disposition was originally meant to reiterate that the Castilian monarch was not subject to the temporal grasp of the Holy Roman Emperor, it was applied by extension to

56 P. 3.6.1.

Spanish America.[57] Thus, Juan de Hevia Bolaños (1570–1623), the enigmatic author of a procedural treatise written in Lima, warned his readers that '[T]he laws of the civil and common Imperial Law of Romans, are received in this kingdom as natural reason, not as laws, authority, or power [*potestas*].'[58]

In spite of this situation, one of the chief areas in which the influence of *ius commune* is more evident is Indian legal status itself. Although Indian legal status was first discussed in a number of sixteenth century rescripts which referred to Indians as *miserabile personae,* the legal privileges that derived from this status were developed by Juan de Solórzano, a former *oido*r of the audience of Lima and (1610–27), in his *Política Indiana* (1647).[59] Perhaps the most important group of privileges was centred around the procedural remedy of *restitutio in integrum.*[60] Originally instituted in Roman law as a relief of minors who had been entered into a transaction under the influence of fraud or duress, the *restitutio* could set aside the effects of transactions in inheritance, procedural, obligations and contract law.[61] As minors could be liable in certain aspects concerning criminal law, the *restitutio* was applicable only in civil law.[62] For Solórzano, Indians could benefit from the *restitutio* both in lawsuits and legal transactions. In the first case, he stated that Indians were not liable to judicial contumacy and could present witnesses and evidence at any moment of the proceedings.[63] Thus, Indians were exempt to being declared in

57 Gregorio López refers to the fact that Oldrado de Ponte (d. 1335) considered that the use of Roman Law in Spain was was punished by death because the King of Castille did not recognize a superior in temporal matters. The use of Roman Law purely in pro-ratione terms was also suscribed by Juan Lopez de Palacios Rubios (1447–1524). See the gloss to P.3.4.6 (ed. López).

58 "Las leyes del derecho Civil, y comun Imperial de los Romanos, se reciben en el Reyno, en quanto razon natural, y no en quanto a leyes, autoridad y potestad, suya, pues no son, ni la tienen en [estos…] Reynos." Hevia, *Curia Filipica*, 33.

59 This key element in Spanish American Law is not discussed in other works by Solórzano. It is therefore absent in the chapters concerning the rights of the Spanish Crown to retain the Indies in *De Indianorum Iure* (1629–39) and in his comment to the emblem LXV on the King's obligation to defend the poor—one of the *miserabile personae* in the *ius commune*—in *Emblemata Centum* (1651). See, respectively, *De Indianorum Iure* (*Lib. III: De retentione Indianorum*) (Madrid, 1994) and "Pauperum Tutamen," in Juan de Solórzano *Emblemata Centum Regio Politica* (Madrid, 1779), 533–40.

60 *Política Indiana*, 2.28.25.

61 G.4.57; D.4.4.16.1. Originally granted by the praetor, the *restitutio* gave form to the *actiones populares* presented in virtue of the *lex Plaetoria.* See Alan Watson, *The Law of Persons in the Later Roman Republic* (Oxford, 1967), 157.

62 D.4.4.37 f.

63 Solórzano, *Política Indiana*, 2.28.25; D.4.4.7.11–12.

absentia in a lawsuit. In the case of legal transactions, Solórzano stated that Indians could invoke the *restitutio in integrum* when they sold real estate or 'other things of price and estimation' without the intervention of the protector general of Indians.[64]

Litigation dossiers point out the use of this remedy by advocates of Indians in the late sixteenth and early seventeenth centuries. As seen in Section II, advocate of Indians Juan del Campo Godoy and his procurator petitioned, by means of the *restitutio in integrum*, the right of one of the claimants to a *cacicazgo* to present testimonials before the royal audience even if the legal deadline had long expired.[65] In another case concerning the dispute over a *cacicazgo*, both Solórzano himself and former advocate of Indians Alberto de Acuña, were among the *oidor*s who agreed to grant an extension to undertake testimonials eleven months after a sentence was issued by the very same court, on the grounds that the defendant,

> Could and did not make any *provanza*, and had thus remained without defence and was entitled to the benefit of the *restitutio in integrum* against the passing of time and omission of [presenting] evidence due to his being fragile Indian and miserable person.[66]

As in the case of terms in legal proceedings, the right to invoke a *restitutio in integrum* in the absence of intervention by royal officials in Indian legal transactions is found in a case pleaded by Leandro de la Rynaga on behalf of Indian plaintiff Juana Sánchez. Doctor Rynaga argued that the sale of a house undertaken by his client was null and void because no royal official had intervened in the contract. Therefore, to avoid being damaged by this sale, Sánchez had the right to invoke "the benefit of the restitution.... Due to the fact that Indians are reputed as minors" (f. 69). By virtue of this remedy, the *oidors* of the audience revoked the first sentence, annulled the contract and returned the

64 Solórzano, *Política Indiana*, 2.28.25, 38, 42–43.

65 "Causas sobre el cacicazgo del Pueblo de Quinti. Huaman Chata, Miguel et al." 1596, Aug. 23 – 1626, Mar. 13, Latin American mss. Peru, fs. 226–226v, 229, 230 230v.

66 "[N]o avia podido ni avia hecho provanza alguna por lo cual avia quedado yndefenso y le competia el beneficio de la restituycion yn yntegrum contra el lapso del tiempo y omissa provanza por ser como hera yndio fraxil y persona miserable" [sic] (f.57). "Causa de don Geronimo Polan, indio con Francisco Chancoy sobre el cacicazgo del pueblo de Begueta del distrito de la villa de Chancay," 1621, Oct. 26 – 1625, May 16, Latin American mss. Peru. *Oidors* were Solórzano, Alberto de Acuña, Juan Jiménez de Montalvo (1561–1629) and Diego Nuñez de Morquecho.

property to Sánchez, and ordered that the defendant be given his money back, including the 30 pesos paid for *alcabala* or sales tax (f. 86).[67]

In the first half of the eighteenth century, the influence of Roman Law within the ranks of the protectorate of Indians was no longer confined to university trained protectors-*fiscales*. In the case of María Solano, an Indian minor of Lambayeque, procurator general of Indians José María de Estela cited both the Law of Soria (1380), which favoured women in testaments, and the "edicto del divo Adriano"; that is, the *senatus consultus Velleianum* (*c.*46 A.D.), a norm in Roman Law which could be invoked to protect women from certain transactions.[68] More significant, however, is the 1739 case of the protector of Indians of Huamanga, José Enríquez de Borja, who intervened in a sale of land between Indians Andrea Huacharima and Gerónimo Cahuana. To secure the transaction, the protector made sure that both plaintiffs renounced their respective rights to a possible *restitutio in integrum*, but also that the women involved in the transaction relinquished their rights as defined in the *senatus consultus Velleianum*. Thus, the agreement between the Indians stipulated that,

> the said Andrea Huachrima, due to being a woman, renounced the laws and epistles of the Divo Adriano Senatus Consultu Beleyano which talks in favour of women so as to not profit from it (f.539) in any way, and also I the said Gerónimo Cahuana renounce in form all the privileges and laws that could exist and be exercised by the said Petrona Maldonado. (f.539v)[69]

---

67 "Y ansi le compete el veneficio de la restitucion por la clausula general e por ser reputados los yndios por menores y conpeteles el mesmo veneficio la qual rrestitucion pido contra el dho contrato para aquello que mas su d[erecho] convenga." "Expediente de la causa seguida entre Juana Sánchez, india, y Antonio de Bobadilla sobre el engaño en la venta de unas casas," Los Reyes, enero 1596, BNP ms. a 149, 89 fs. *Oidors* were Alonso Criado de Castilla (†1608) and Diego Nuñez de Avendaño (†1606).

68 "Autos referidos al cumplimiento del testamento de Francisca Juliana, india; y fundación de una Memoria y Aniversario por Don Bernardino Pascual, nombrando por capellán a Don Antonio de Melo," AGN, Real Audiencia, causas civiles, leg.7, c.40 (1703), fs. 14.

69 "[R]enunciamos a todas las leyes fueros y derechos de nuestro fabor y la general renunciasion que los prohive y con la dha Andrea Hucharima por ser mujer renunsio las leyes y Espístolas del Divo Adriano Senatus Consultu Beleyano que hablan a fabor de las mujeres para no aprobecharme de (f.539) ellas en manera alguna y asi mismo yo el dho Gerónimo Cahuana asimismo renunsio a la forma dha todos los privilexios y leyes que pueda haver y gozar la dha Petrona Maldonado" (f.539v). "Expediente sobre la petición presentada por Gerónimo Cahuana, indio, para que se le de licencia a fin de que pueda vender un pedazo de tierra de Totorilla." Huamanga, 3 December 1739 – 10 December 1739. BNP Archivo Astete Concha, ms. z 134.

A few decades later, however, the first—if tenuous—notions of criticism of the use of Roman Law would come precisely from within the protectorship ranks.[70] In a letter to protector-*fiscal* Bravo de Lagunas, José Antonio de Borda Orosco y Peralta (†1784), a former *alcalde ordinario* of Lima who settled in Spain, pointed out the 'defects and insufficiencies of Roman Law and other laws, after the formation of nations.' Although the main purpose of the letter was to propose to Bravo de Lagunas a new compilation of Spanish American Law following the 'natural order' which reduced Roman Law to its general principles, Borda also argued that Solórzano's work was dated and stated that if he would be living today he would surely 're-cast his *Política* [*Indiana*].'[71] There is also evidence that, through other correspondents, Bravo de Lagunas possessed contacts with fierce critics of the use of Roman Law in law courts such as the eminent Gregorio Mayans y Síscar (1699–1781).[72] Similarly, protector-*fiscal* José de Baquíjano Carrillo would offer a critical view of the influence of Roman Law in university teaching in his in his 1787 *relectio* to obtain the chair of prime of Laws at the university of San Marcos.[73]

The work of advocates and protectors-*fiscales* of Indians was linked with the consolidation of Lima as the seat of the royal audience, but also as the apex of a host of tribunals and courts that made up the vice-regal judicial system.[74] In this context, advocates and Protectors-*Fiscales* of Indians proved to be able and effective litigants for their indigenous defendants. Not only did they use their influence in court, but also the juristic tools provided by an extensive legal culture. In fact, evidence of the *restitutio in integrum* by advocates of Indians at the time Solórzano was an *oidor* in the audience of Lima could provide certain clues to the influence of the legal practices and culture in the

---

70 In the case of Spain see, for example, José Berní Catalá, Berní, Josef. 1738. *El abogado instruido en la práctica civil de España*, 2 vols in 1 (Valencia, 1738), 32ff; Vicente Vizcaíno Pérez, *Compendio del Derecho Público y Común de España o de las Siete Partidas colocadas en orden natural*, 4 vols (Madrid, 1784), 1: xviii–iv.

71 "Carta de don Joseph Antonio de Borda Orozco y Peralta, Doctor en ambos Derechos en la Real Universidad de S. Marcos de Lima," 23 June 1761, in Joseph Bravo de Lagunas y Castilla, *Colección legal de cartas y dictámenes, y otros Papeles en Derecho* (Lima, 1761), [5, 2v, 8–8v].

72 Josef Eugenio Llano y Zapata to Pedro Josef Bravo de Castilla, c.1758, Lilly Library, Peruvian Mss., f. 2v.

73 José de Baquíjano Carrillo, *Relectio extemporanea ad explicationem legis Pamphilio XXXIX d. De Legatis et Fideicomissis III*...(Lima, 1787).

74 James S. Amelang uses the term "legal city" to describe the similar role of Barcelona. See "Barristers and Judges in Early Modern Barcelona: The Rise of a Legal Elite," *The American Historical Review* 89 (5) (1984), 1266.

construction of Indian status in *Política Indiana*—particularly when dealing with Indian judicial rights. That this doctrine would remain unquestioned until the mid-eighteenth century is, in itself, a compelling example of the impact of Spanish American juristic practice.[75]

As a whole, the evidence examined points out that protectors were successful attorneys at the royal audience. In many cases, however, the plaintiffs were *caciques*; which implies that the business of litigating at the audience was a matter for those who could afford travelling and lodging in Lima. At the close of the seventeenth century, the involvement of university trained protectors in the direct defence of Indian plaintiffs appears to have diminished in favour of a more preponderant role of the procurator general of Indians. Within the audience, the protectors assumed a similar role to the *fiscal* or crown attorney, acting as a counsellor of the *oidors* in Indian matters; outside the audience, they assumed a variety of roles. Although the protectorship of Indians was, in general terms, an initial step in many careers, their influence both at court and in contributing to doctrinal development stemming from the *ius commune* (as in the use of the *restitutio in integrum*) was significant.

---

75 See, for example, Juan de Paz, *Consultas y resoluciones varias, theologicas, Juridicas, Regulares, y Morales* (1687; Amberes, 1754), 30–1.

Conclusion

In 1868 Miguel Zavala, a former army colonel, published a tract in reaction to the causes, repercussions and violent repression of an indigenous upheaval that occurred in Huancané, Puno, two years earlier. The colonel concluded that republican governments had done very little to improve the life conditions, education and legal protection of Indians; this situation had, in practice, barred Indians from the full exercise of their civil and political rights. In this context, he proposed to re-establish a Protectorship of Indians in Peru, convinced that this institution would improve the situation of the indigenous population. The proposal considered the appointment of protectors in each of the Andean departments of Peru with the obligation to undertake annual visits to the towns and villages in their jurisdiction; to guide Indians towards a 'civilised life' in respect of moral, hygiene and domestic life; and to duly record all complaints referred to the mistreatment of Indians. In addition to this, Zavala considered that protectors should also supervise the compliance of laws and decrees enacted in favour of Indians, and bring to court those who had breached them.[1]

The protectorship of Indians thus retained its prestige a century after the Council of the Indies decided it should be dispensed with. By all accounts the institution possessed an impressive history in Peru which begins when the Spanish Crown appointed bishops to act as royal offices with jurisdictional powers over Indian disputes. The ecclesiastics were replaced in 1575 by a troika charged with the obligation of undertaking the defence of Indians both in and outside the courts of justice. However, when this troika became fully operative in the decade of 1590, its core functions increasingly became the defence of Indian lawsuits in court. Protectors delivered their role of attorneys to indigenous plaintiffs even after the 1575 ordinances were incorporated in the *Recopilación de Indias* of 1680. By the time the institution was abolished in the mid-1770s, protectors had continuously enjoyed the rank and pre-eminences of a *fiscal* of the royal audience for at least one century. The Protectorship of Indians is a good example of how colonial authorities established institutions to address the local demands of society (Indian litigation), but also of how these were also modelled by the people who served in them (attaining real and honorary *fiscal* rank).

1 Miguel Zavala, *Protectorado de Indios; o sea, proyecto de ley ofrecido a las consideraciones de los H.H. representantes de la nación en la presente legislatura de 1868, con el fin de mejorar la deprimida condición social del indio, haciendo realizables sus derechos* (Lima, 1868).

 | DOI 10.1163/9789004305175_010

Between 1575 and 1775 the protectorship of Indians was staffed by a prominent group of men, mostly creoles. Either by birth or by marriage, they were part of an urban elite formed of a fusion of *encomenderos*, magistrates, merchants, landowners and old aristocrats. Social mobility was not unusual among protector ranks and, in some cases, they established significant family networks that survived beyond the first generation. Their consumption patterns and material culture suggest, in most cases, a significant economic performance, but only very few reached the very high echelons of wealth.

Although Chandler and Burkholder have suggested that the protectorship of Indians did not offer a reasonable prospect of promotion, the evidence provided by this study suggests otherwise. Both in the cases of non-*letrado* and *letrado* officials, attaining protectorship office usually implied an important first step for obtaining prestigious academic posts or becoming magistrates at the high court of justice.[2] There is also proof that protectors had access to university education based in roman and canon law, and to the relevant scholarly and comparative literature of their time. In general terms, they stood above the average legal professional in the colonial period.

On the other hand, the analysis of the lawsuits provides sufficient evidence to conclude that protectors were instrumental in providing a successful defense of Indian interests in the audience of Lima. It is true that indigenous plaintiffs pursuing justice at the high court of justice were, quite possibly, a small minority within the universe of Indian litigation. However, the ability of advocates such as Rynaga and Medina to allow further testimonials, delay appeals, and overturn previous sentences in favour of Indians indicates how their professional expertise and their networks of power worked in favour of their causes. Similarly, the thoroughness of their legal defence in many Indian disputes (as well as the role played by piety and charity in their material entourage), could denote a genuine sense of duty to the office.

The employment of legal remedies based in Roman Law by early seventeenth century advocates of Indians most likely influenced works such as the *Política Indiana* written by Juan de Solórzano, who served as *oidor* in Lima, and were continuously used throughout the eighteenth century. They became less frequent at the close of the colonial period. However, unlike the plaintiffs advised by advocate Rynaga or protector-*fiscal* Márquez de Mansilla, María Tone Esquiagola, an Indian woman and *cacica* of Yanaguara, did not present herself as *miserable* in her writ before the *intendente* of Arequipa in 1810, nor invoked any of the privileges attached to this status in the proceedings.[3]

2 See Burkholder and Chandler, *From Impotence to Authority*, 72.

3 Archivo Regional de Arequipa, Intendencia, causas ordinarias, leg 58, 1810, 6.IX.1810.

The history of the protectors of Indians presented in this study provides the first social and intellectual group portrait of a relevant section of the colonial legal profession working at the royal audience of Lima. Peru. A more complete understanding of this fascinating institution, however, should be achieved by studies focusing on the *corregimientos* and criminal litigation.

Appendices

APPENDIX 1

Biographical Notes

Biographical notes are provided below for the Defensors General, Advocates and Protectors-*Fiscales*. Entries include the subject's life span, parentage, geographical origins, education, appointment and offices, marital history and wealth. Due to the fact that Defensors General of Indians appointed after 1657 were all granted the honorary rank of *fiscal* (even if the office of Protector Fiscal of the Indians was formally abolished that same year) officials appointed after this date are referred to as protectors-*fiscales*. Men distinguished with a preceding asterisk are covered by entries in Alberto Tauro, *Enciclopedia Ilustrada del Perú*, 2nd ed., 6 vols. (Lima, 1988); information provided there has not been duplicated here, apart from dates of birth and death, and audience career. Sources and secondary works used to document these biographies are in footnotes at the beginning of their biographies; additional information for family members is also provided when relevant.

*Acuña, Alberto de (Jaen, Spain *c.*1565– Lima,1630).[1] Abogado de Indios (1590–1597). Son of licentiate Gabriel Nuñez and Juana de Acuña. He travelled to Peru (1584) as part

1 There are a number of sources to document the life of Acuña. See Manuel Moreyra Paz-Soldán, *Oidores y Virreyes*, vol. 2 of *Estudios Históricos*, ed. Grover Antonio Espinosa Ruiz (1957; Lima, 1994), 137–46; Luis Antonio Eguiguren, *La universidad en el siglo XVI*, book 1 *Narración*, vol. 1 of *Historia de la Universidad* (Lima, 1951), 45; Javier Barrientos Grandon, "La creación de la audiencia de Santiago y sus ministros fundadores," *Revista de Estudios Histórico Jurídicos* 25 (2003), 233–338; and Guillermo Lohmann Villena, *Los ministros de la Audiencia de Lima en el reinado de los borbones (1700–1821)* (Sevilla, 1974), 151–52. For his appointment as viceregal advisor see Buenaventura de Salinas Cordoba, *Memorial de las historias del nvevo mvndo Pirv*, ed. Luis E. Valcárcel and Warren L. Cook. Colección de Clásicos Peruano 1. (1630; Lima, 1957),139. For his early activities as advocate of Indians see "Auto político que el Dr. Alberto de Acuña eleva ante las autoridades correspondientes con recomendaciones para una buena administración de estos dominios del Perú," BNP ms F261, 43ff. The memorial would state that Indians were "miserables" and poor (f.30), that tribute paid for the defensors of Indians (f.30v) and advises that chasquis should be paid by corregidores from the funds of the *caja de comunidad*, administered by the protector of the corregimiento (f.40 40v). Only parts of the manuscript are legible as it was affected by one of the fires that affected the National Library of Peru. A transcription is found in Eguiguren, *Diccionario histórico cronológico de la Real y Pontificia Universidad de San Marcos y sus colegios: Crónica e investigación*, 3 vols. (Lima, 1940–51) 2: 499–506. Reference to his university degrees in Spain are found in AGI, Lima, 210, n.13, f.2; available from http://pares.mcu.es/, cod. es.41091.agi/16403.9.216/Lima, 210, n.13. His appointment as *oidor* of Panama dates from 1595 but evidence contained in the reports of viceroy Luis de Velasco suggests that his departure was not

 | DOI 10.1163/9789004305175_011

of the entourage of viceroy Count of Villar dom Pardo (*v.*1585–90). He became the viceroy's 'lettered advisor' with a salary of 2,000 pesos. Villar dom Pardo appointed Acuña as *abogado general de indios* before his departure (1589–90) and remained in his position until his departure for Panama (1597), where he was appointed *oidor* of the audience. From Panama he moved to Quito, where he was *oidor* for a brief period (1602–3), and returned to Lima as *alcalde del crimen* (1603). He was then appointed *oidor* of Lima, a position he held until his retirement (1607–28). Acuña held a bachelor degree in law from Salamanca, a licentiate from Seville and a doctorate from San Marcos. He was one of the witnesses of the virtues and miracles of St. Francisco Solano. He first married Isabel Ortiz de Arbildo y Bérriz (†1590), the daughter of Francisco Ortiz de Arbildo (1541–93), a perpetual *regidor* of the cabildo of Lima (1562–86), and of Quiteria de Merlo (†1590).[2] He married (1590) Ana Verdugo, daughter of Juan Verdugo, perpetual *regidor* of Lima, and Beatriz Medel de Salazar, *encomendera* of Copacabana (which yielded 700 pesos per annum); their son Gabriel de Acuña y Verdugo was *alcalde ordinario* of Lima (1632) and corregidor of Jauja.[3]

Balaguer de Salcedo, Pedro.[4] Madrid, 1545– Lima, (*c.*1605). Defensor General 1603. Son of Gregorio Balaguer de Salcedo and Madona Flor de Fracasa. He began his career as Secretary of the University of Alcalá, and secretary and accountant for Francisco Zapata y Cisneros (†1594) Count of Barajas and president of the Council of Castile. After his arrival in the vice-royalty of Peru, he was appointed by Viceroy García Hurtado

---

before April 1597. For his judicial career see Juan de la Rynaga Salazar, *Memorial discursivo sobre el oficio de protector General de los Indios del Piru* ([Madrid], [1626]), 2v; and Velasco to Philip II, Callao, April 1557, Roberto Levillier, ed.,*Gobernantes del Perú: Cartas y Papeles, siglo XVI*, 14 vols. (Madrid, 1921–26), 1926, 14: 63. For his participation in the canonization of St. Francisco Solano see Diego de Córdova, *Vida, virtudes y milagros del Apostol del Peru el Venerable P. Fray Francisco Solano*...(Madrid, 1643), 521.

2 Isabel Ortiz de Arbildo sister of Sebastián Sánchez de Merlo, regidor of the cabildo of Lima, an *encomendero* of Huarochirí, and secretary of governor Cristóbal Vaca de Castro. Also, two of his wife's sisters married prominent members of the viceregal government: Angela Ortiz de Arbildo married Alvaro Ortiz de Navamuel y de los Ríos, secretary to viceroy Toledo.

3 Gabriel de Acuña married in 1629 Mariana de Egües y Beaumont.

4 García Hurtado de Mendoza to Philip II, Callao, 1 May 1590, Levillier, *Gobernantes*, 12: 1590; provision of 21 November 1590 by the viceroy Marquis of Cañete. Lilly Latin American mss. Peru, 1590, Nov. 21, f. 1; García Hurtado de Mendoza to secretary Juan de Ibarra, Lima 19 August 1594, Levillier, *Gobernantes*, 13: 188–93; Guillermo Lohmann Villena, *Los americanos en la órdenes nobiliarias*, 2nd ed. 2 vols. (Madrid, 1993), 1: 119; "Testimonio de los autos seguidos por Don Antonio Berzosa, corregidor del cercado de Lima, contra el Alcalde Ordinario, sobre la jurisdicción en el conocimiento de las causas de los indios...,"AGN GO-BI 5, leg. 139, c.100, fs. 9v-12v; and AGI, Indiferente, 2097, N.183, f.1. Available in http://pares.mcu.es. His testament was written on 22 April 1605 and is found in AGN, protocolos notariales s. XVII, Pedro Gonzáles Contreras, protocolo 788, ff. 20371–20375v.

de Mendoza, fourth Marquis of Cañete (*v.*1590–95), to organise the system of *chasquis*, the postal service (1590), and actively participated in military actions against the incursions of Francis Drake in Lima and Valparaíso (1594). He was also appointed *corregidor* of El Cercado, official of Cajas Reales of Lima, and familiar of the Holy Office. As Defensor General, he proposed the establishment of a Juzgado General de Indios or General Indian Court presided over by the viceroy (1603). His appointment as procurator for the Villa Rica de Oropesa in Huancavelica, and a request to the audience of Lima to travel to Spain to pursue commercial transactions (1588) suggests that Balaguer de Salcedo was also active in business. He married María Ruiz and had one daughter, Mariana Balaguer de Salcedo.[5]

*Baquíjano Carrillo, José de.[6] (Lima, 1751-). Protector-*fiscal* 1781–83. Son of the first count of Vistaflorida, Juan Bautista de Baquíjano y Urigüen (1701–59), a merchant from Biscay and María Ignacia Carrillo de Córdoba y Garcés de Marcilla, a *limeña*. He entered the college of Santo Toribio at the University of San Marcos (1762), where he graduated as bachelor and doctor in canon law (1765). After being received as advocate by the audience of Lima (1769), he became personal secretary to Bishop Agustín de Gorrichátegui (1771). Two years later he was appointed legal advisor to both the *cabildo* and *consulado* of Lima. After returning to Spain, where he lobbied for further advancement, he was appointed professor of Institute (1778) and vespers of laws (1780) at San Marcos and incorporated to the audience of Lima as interim *fiscal* for criminal matters (1780) and interim protector of Indians (1781–83). Following the reforms of the he returned to university and was elected as vice-rector of the university (1791) and professor of vespers in canon law (1792). He embarked for Spain after requesting an

5 Mariana Balaguer de Salcedo married Francisco de la Cueva (not to be confused with Francisco de la Cueva Guzmán [b.1626], first marquis of Santa María de Conchán). Captain De la Cueva was born in Jerez de la Frontera, and began his military career at the service of the Duke of Osuna in Naples, after which he was transferred to Peru where he was appointed corregidor and *alcalde ordinario* of Lima. Their son, Pedro de la Cueva y Balaguer (*c.*1598–63), returned to Spain in 1618 where he married his cousin Marina de la Cueva, succeded in the mayorazgo of Cueva, and was appointed knight of Santiago (1628). Balaguer's great-grandson, Cristóbal de la Cueva (b.1623), was alférez mayor of Jerez de la Frontera and returned to Lima where he was appointed *alcalde ordinario* and *regidor* of the ayuntamiento of Lima. Cristóbal married Brianda de Guzmán, daughter of maestre de campo Juan de Guzmán, *alguacil perpetuo* of the audience of Lima; their son, Pedro José de la Cueva Guzmán (b.1648) was knight of Santiago (1674). Lohmann, *Los americanos*, 1: 119–20.

6 The biblography on Baquíjano is significant. Sources on his writings are found in books 2 and 3 of *Los ideólogos*, vol. 1 of *Colección Documental de la Independencia del Perú* (Lima, 1972). For a biography see José de la Riva Agüero "José Baquíjano y Carrillo," in *Obras completas*, vol. 7 (Lima, 1971); Mark Burkholder and D.S. Chandler, *Politics of a Colonial Career: José Baquíjano and the Audiencia of Lima* (Albuquerque, 1980); and José de la Puente Brunke, *José Baquíjano y Carrillo* (Lima, 1995).

early retirement from the university (1795). He obtained an honorary (1795) and later full *alcalde del crimen* (1800), a position he assumed two years later (1802). He then obtained the post of *oidor* in the audience of Lima (1806; assumed 1807). During the regency during the Napoleonic wars he was councillor of State (1812). Baquíjano was a knight of the order of Charles III and third Count of Vistaflorida. He did not marry, nor have issue.

*Barrientos y Díaz, Felipe Santiago de (Santiago c.1678–Lima 1739).[7] Protector-*fiscal* 1730. Sixth son of Joseph de Barrientos and Melchora Días. He received his legal education at the college of San Martín in Lima (1695), where he also obtained a doctorate in Law. Although he was admitted as an advocate in the audience of Lima and represented plaintiffs before the Inquisition, his career was centered in the university. At San Marcos he became professor of Institute (1720), vespers in law (1722) and prime of canon law (1731). He was advisor (*asesor letrado*) to the city of Lima and to Viceroy Marquis of Villagarcía (*v.*1736–45). He married Petronila de Ardiles y Mundaca (1703) and had four children Juan Antonio, Joseph, Melchora and Francisco de Barrientos y Ardiles.

*Bravo de Lagunas, Pedro (Lima 1703–62).[8] Protector-*fiscal* Sept.1735–July 1763. Son of maestre de campo Pedro Bravo de Lagunas y Bedoya (†1724) and Mariana de Castilla y Loaisa. At thirteen years of age he obtained a scholarship for the royal college of San Martín (1717), and then matriculated in the college of San Felipe y San Marcos (1727), where he was graduated as doctor *utrusque ius*. He was elected as rector of San Marcos (1728) and later to four consecutive professorships: *Digestum Vetus* (1729), Code (1735), vespers of canon law (1740), and prime of laws (1742). He was advisor (*asesor letrado*) to Viceroy Marquis of Villagarcía (*v.*1737–45). After holding an interim position as protector-fiscal (Sept.1735–July 1763) he obtained a position of supernumerary *oidor* in Lima (1746) and assumed the magistracy one year later (1747). He was later appointed honorary councillor of the Indies (1751). Bravo de Lagunas was a staunch supporter of the *regio patronato* or royal prerogatives regarding ecclesiastical appointments in the

7 Details of his career are found in Lohmann, *Los ministros*, 10. An inventory of his goods is found in AGN, protocolos notariales s.XVIII, protocolo 1143, Marcos de Uceda 1739, f.232. In this same notarial book there are two powers of attorney 17 February (f. 236r.) and 16 March 1739 (f. 233r) appointing his wife executor and granting her capacity to draft his last will and testament.

8 José Antonio de Lavalle, "Pedro José Bravo de Lagunas y Castilla (Apuntes sobre su vida y obras)," in *Estudios Históricos* (Lima, 1935); Lohmann, *Los ministros*, 17–18. For his academic career see Luis Antonio Eguiguren, *Catálogo Histórico del Claustro de la Universidad de San Marcos, 1576–1800* (Lima, 1912), 27–28, 30, 36, 42; and "Catálogo Colegio de San Martín," in Eguiguren, *Diccionario*, 2: 227. Evidence of his appointment as protector and judicial career is found, respectively in BNP ms. c92 and c3698. His testament of 27 August 1751 is found in AGN, protocolos notariales s.XVIII, protocolo 83, Orencio de Azcarrunz, 1764–68, fs.476–78v.

vice-royalty of Peru. He published *Discordia de la concordia* (Lima, 1750) in reply to *Concordia de la* discordia (Lima, 1749) written by Antonio de la Cueva y Ponce de León, a Jesuit priest, who disputed these rights. He also authored the *Voto consultivo* (Lima, 1755), a tract which defended the position of the audience of Lima regarding the wheat trade with Chile. After his retirement from the judiciary (1757) he took Holy Orders and entered the Congregation of the Oratory (1759). A year before his death his collected writings were published as *Colección legal de cartas, dictámenes y otros papeles de derecho* (Lima, 1761). He died unmarried and without issue.

*Brun, Tomás de (Bolea, Spain 1680–Lima1728).[9] Protector-*fiscal* 1720–23. Son of Domingo de Brun y Marraco and Tomasa Normante y Agramonte. After an education at the University of Huesca, he obtained a post as protector-*fiscal* in Lima (1720–23) later to be promoted to *alcalde del crimen* (1723). He married Catalina Isidora de Vargas Carvajal y Hurtado de Quesada, III Countess of Castillejo, VI Countess Del Puerto, and hereditary Correo Mayor de Indias (1724). Although the couple had three children, only Joaquina María Brun de Carvajal y Vargas (later the wife of her relative Fermín de Carvajal-Vargas y Alarcón, first Duke of San Carlos 1722–97) survived to adulthood.

*Campo Godoy, Juan del Campo (Osorno, Chile 1591–Charcas *fl.*1653).[10] Advocate of Indians (1624–47). His father was Francisco del Campo, a military officer with a distinguished service record in the wars of Sicily, Flanders, and Italy, who arrived in Chile as part of the entourage of Governor Alonso de Sotomayor (1545–1610) and was appointed governor of Arica and Osorno. His mother was Isabel Rosa Godoy, a creole *encomendera*,

9 Lohmann, *Los ministros*, 21–22. See AGN, protocolos notariales s.XVIII, protocolo 1041, José de Torres Campo 20-1-1728, f. 65; protocolo 1759, Francisco Luque, fs.1120.

10 Accounts of the academic career of Juan del Campo are found in the *relación de servicios* of his son Nicolás Matías, *Memorial…nobleza y servicio de sus padres*, 27v-28, and Pedro López de Echaburu, *Relación de los servicios del doctor Don Nicolás Matías del Campo y de la Rinaga, abogado que ha sido de la Audiencia de Lima* (Madrid?, 1666?), [2v]. Details of his career as magistrate are found in *Autos Acordados de la Real Audiencia de Quito, 1578–1722*, Anuario Histórico Jurídico Ecuatoriano 2 (Guayaquil, 1971), 53–60, 63; Joseph de Aguilar, *Bachiller don Joseph de Aguilar, Bilicia y Godoy, Cura de San Christoval de los Guachos en el obispado de Guamanga…* (Madrid, [1664]), [1v-2]; Nicolás Matías del Campo y de la Rynaga, *Memorial historico y ivridico, que refiere: El origen del Oficio de Protector general de los Indios del Perú* (Madrid, 1671), 5; Buenaventura de Salinas Córdova, *Memorial de las historias del nvevo mvndo Pirv*, eds. Luis E. Valcárcel and Warren L. Cook (1630; Lima, 1957), 293. In his memorial Aguilar, an ecclesiastical judge in Huamanga and first cousin of Campo, describes the ceremonial and procedure of Campo's resignation as president of the audience of Quito. There is also a poem in honour of Campo in Rodrigo de Carvajal y Robles, *Fiestas que celebró la ciudad de los Reyes del Perú, al nacimiento del Serenísimo Príncipe don Baltazar Carlos de Austria* (1632; Sevilla, 1950). The verses were reproduced in Nicolás Matías del Campo y La Rynaga, *Memorial…nobleza y servicio de sus padres*, 28v.

in Osorno. Campo moved to Lima where he studied in San Marcos and, according to his son, applied eleven times for professorships in law; of these, three were obtained: Institute (1620), prime of canon law (1632) and vespers in canon law (1636). He was also elected rector of the university (1630), where he presided over the celebrations of the birth of Prince Baltazar Carlos (1629–46). He served as advocate of Indians for '38 years.' He was also advisor under three consecutive viceroys: the Marquis of Guadalcázar (*v.*1622–29), Count of Chinchón (*v.*1629–39) and Marquis of Mancera (*v.*1639–48). Del Campo gained considerable influence under the Count of Chinchón due to his appointment as "hacedor" or administrator of the viceroy's estate. He was appointed as *alcalde de corte* of Quito (1646) but took office three years later (1649–52). He then obtained the position of oidor of the audience of Charcas (1653), following the death of Francisco de Sosa. He married María de la Rynaga Salazar (sister of Leandro de la Rynaga) and had seven children: Francisco (1622), Teresa (1625), Nicolás Matías (1630–*fl.*1671), Lorenzo (1633), María Martina (1637), Constancia (1639) and Juana (1642). Nicolás, who became a knight of Santiago and *oidor* in Charcas and Panama, wrote a memorial on the protectorship of Indians.[11]

Carrasco del Saz, Francisco (Spain-Lima? †1639)[12] (Defensor General of Indians 1635). He arrived in the Indies in 1606 as part of the entourage of Juan de Loayza

11 The family achieved its social pinnacle when the daughter of Nicolás Matías, Rosa del Campo y Zárate (†*c.*1776), married Antonio Sarmiento de Sotomayor y de los Ríos (*fl.*1733), third count of Portillo in 1715. It is significant that their second son Nicolás Cayetano Sarmiento de Sotomayor y Haro (†*c.*1796), fifth count of Portillo and sergeant major of the noble regiment of cavalry in Lima, requested to be buried in the monastery of St Rose of Lima—not in the convent of St. Augustine where his paternal family had burial rights—perhaps as a homage to his grandfather Nicolás Matías, who was a commisary of the feasts and celebrations in Madrid that followed the canonization of St. Rose in 1668. Details of the family life, posts and connections are found in the testamentary dispositions of Rosa del Campo y Zárate, countess of Portillo: AGN, Protocolos Notariales s.XVIII, protocolo 882, escribano Salvador Gerónimo de Portalanza 1733–34, 30 October 1733, f.469v-70v; protocolo 196, escribano Alejandro de Cueto 1760, 31 January 1760, f.267ss; protocolo 632, escribano Francisco Luque 1776, 1 February 1776, f.137v–38v. See also the last will of Luisa del Campo y Zárate, another daugher of the oidor Nicolás Matías del Campo: AGN Protocolos Notariales s.XVIII, protocolo 882, escribano Salvador Gerónimo de Portalanza 1733–34, 12 May 1734, f.619, and protocolo 196, escribano Alejandro de Cueto 1760, 31 January 1760, 266v–67. For the role of Nicolás Matías in the feasts of St. Rose see Ramón Mujica Pinilla, *Rosa limensis: Mística, política e iconografía en torno a la patrona de América* (Lima, 2001), 299–300. Sarmiento de Sotomayor's testament is found in AGN, Protocolos Notariales s.XVIII, protocolo 90, escribano Ignacio Ayllón Salazar, 1796, 2 January 1796, f.330–31v.

12 The few biographical details on Carrasco del Saz are found in the work about his distinguished relative and namesake, Guillermo Lohmann, "Francisco Carrasco del Saz,

Calderón, oidor of Charcas and Lima (1625), and was appointed protector general of Indies of Charcas prior to his appointment in Lima. He married Juana María de Taboada, a native of La Plata.

Cruz de Aspeitia, Baltazar de la. (Spain-Lima?) (Defensor General 1575–82).[13] First Defensor General of Indians. Corregidor of Canta (1589) and was considered as a candidate for the post of defensor by Hurtado de Mendoza—Villar's successor—when the office was reinstated (*c.*1590). He was later appointed appointed corregidor for Tarma and Chincha (1594). There is evidence that he acted as the viceroy-appointed administrator of the religious foundation (*obra pía*) instituted by encomendero Lorenzo de Aldana.

Heredia, Antonio (Defensor General of Indians 1590).[14] Secretary to Viceroy García Hurtado de Mendoza (*v.*1589–1596).

Hurtado de Avendaño, Diego (Advocate of Indians 1608).[15] He was educated at the royal colleges of San Martín (matriculated 1596), and of San Felipe y San Marcos (matriculated 1599) at the University of San Marcos. He obtained both his licentiate and doctorate in canon law (1607) under the patronage of Leandro de la Rynaga Salazar, professor and dean of the faculty at the time. Although he does not appear in the lists of law professors in San Marcos, the testimony of Rynaga Salazar gives faith to

---

jurisconsulto y tratadista," *Revista Histórica* 39 (1996–98), 168; this jurist was advisor of viceroy Count of Monterrey (1604–6), fiscal of the Tribunal of Santa Cruzada (1608), advisor of the cabildo of Lima (1610) and oidor of the audience of Panama (1616); he wrote a commentary of the Laws of the Indies, *Interpretatio ad aliquas leges Recopilationis Regno Castellae* (Madrid, 1620).

13 See Ruigómez, *Protector de Indios*, 70. The appointments of Cruz as corregidor are found in *Libros de Cabildos de Lima*, ed. Juan Bromley (Lima, 1935–67) 11: 95–100; 12: 89–99. His role in the Obra Pía of Aldana is found in Margot Beyersdorff, *Historia y Drama Ritual en los Andes Bolivianos (siglos XVI–XX)*, 2nd ed. (La Paz: Plural, 2003), 84.

14 Levillier, *Gobernantes*, 14: 63, 164, 234.

15 For his education at San Marcos see "Catálogo de los Colegiales que hubo en el Real Colegio de San Martín," Eguiguren, *Diccionario*, 2: 139; and "Catálogo de los Colegiales que tuvo el Real y mayor de San Felipe y San Marcos," Eguiguren, *Diccionario*, 1: 524. There is also a request to Feliciano de Vega, dean of the faculty of canon law at San Marcos, to extend a copy of his degrees at Universidad Nacional Mayor de San Marcos, Archivo Histórico Domingo Angulo, Cuaderno de Grado de Bachiller, 1571 1664, fs. 105 9. Eduardo Torres Arancibia, *Corte de Virreyes: El entorno del poder en el Perú del siglo XVII* (Lima:, 2006), 197. For his appointment as corregidor of Otavalo see Raúl Hernández Asensio, *La frontera occidental de la Audiencia de Quito: Viajeros y relatos de viajes (1595–1630)* (Lima, 2004), 176; Christiana Borchart de Moreno, *El corregimiento de Otavalo: Territorio, población y producción textil (1535–1808)* (Quito, 2007), ; Javier Ortiz de la Tabla Ducasse, *Los encomenderos de Quito, 1534–1660: Origen y evolución de una élite colonial* (Madrid, 1993), 106.

some link with the university after graduation. He was appointed advocate of Indians (1608). He was sent as procurator to Spain to represent the personal interests of Captain Fernando de Andrade (1611). He was appointed Corregidor of Otavalo in the audience of Quito (1617). He married Isabel Ossorio de Villagra who, as a widow, was granted the *repartimiento* of San Miguel de Chimbo (Otavalo) as encomienda with a rent of 1,800 pesos per annum. The couple had three children: Ana María (Lima, 1611), María Isabel (Lima, 1616) and Gabriel, who possessed the encomienda until the mid-seventeenth century.

*Hurtado de Mendoza, Alonso (Tarazona, Spain *c.*1610–Lima 1692).[16] Protector-*fiscal* 1680. Born in Tarazona (Zaragoza, Spain) to Jurado Jerónimo Hurtado de Mendoza (†1647), treasurer of the Reales Cajas de Santiago de Chile (1618–29), and Leonor de Cosgaya Antillón Beaumont y Navarra. He arrived in Chile in 1618, was appointed *relator* of the audience of Santiago in 1639. He was *regidor* perpetuo of the city of Lima between 1661 and 1695. He married (1643) Isabel de Jaraquemada, a native of Santiago and daughter of *maestre de campo* Diego Solórzano del Hoyo y Jaraquemada, corregidor of Santiago (1626–31) and María Isabel Gómez de Silva. In his last will (1692) he declared one daughter outside wedlock, Josefa Hurtado de Mendoza. He had six children with his wife: Diego, Ana María, Clara, Leonor, Isabel and María Hurtado de Mendoza y Jaraquemada.[17]

*Ibarra, Alvaro de (Lima 1621–75).[18] Protector-*fiscal* 1655–57. Son of Captain Gregorio de Ibarra y Ruiz de Loyoza, a native of Vizcaya, and Isabel de Merodio y

16 See Guillermo Lohmann Villena, *Los regidores perpetuos del cabildo de Lima (1535–1821): Crónica y estudio de un grupo de gestión*, 2 vols. (Sevilla, 1983), 2: 154–55; and Juan Luis Espejo, *Nobiliario*, 471–72. For his role as protector see "Autos que sigue Juan de Campos Villacataparaco sobre el cacicazgo…" 1680, Apr. 20—1695, Apr. 14, Lilly, Latin American mss, fol. 29v. For his role as advisor to the *cabildo*, see AGN, GO-BI 5, leg. 139, c.100, f. 3. His testament is found AGN, Protocolos Notariales s.XVII, protocolo 496, escribano Diego Fernández Montaño (26.02.1692), f. 915.

17 At the time of her last will in 1705, Isabel Jaraquemada declared the following situation for her children: Clara Hurtado de Mendoza was married captain Manuel de Silva; Leonor was married maestre de campo José Ortega Luján, knight of Santiago; María had died as wife of José de Espejo and had a daughter Isabel de Espejo (wife of Antonio Diez Jordan and later of Diego Pérez Lascano, with a son of the same name); captain Diego Hurtado de Mendoza y Jaraquemada married Catalina Iturrizarra, daughter of oidor Bernardo de Iturrizarra, their son Diego Hurtado de Mendoza y Jaraquemada (1695–1742) was a profesor and rector of San Marcos. See AGN, Protocolos Notariales s.XVII, protocolo 835, escribano Pedro Pérez Cabañas (20.07.1705), ff. 1559–1562v. As for her out of wedlock daughter Josefa, Hurtado de Mendoza bequeathed a dowry of 12,000 pesos (see his testament above).

18 For a general accout of his life see Lohmann Villena, *El Conde de Lemos: Virrey del Perú* (Madrid, 1946), 133–49; Lohmann, *Los ministros*, 172–73; Eguiguren, *Diccionario*, 1: 820, and

Alcocer, a *limeña*. He was matriculated in the royal college of San Martín (1633), where he studied law. After receiving his doctorate he became professor of Code (1647) and prime of laws (1650) at San Marcos; the latter contended with Antonio Maldonado de Silva, professor of decretals and former advocate of Indians in Charcas (1608–10). Among his most distinguished pupils was advocate of Indians Juan del Campo Godoy. He was appointed protector-*fiscal* by Viceroy Count of Alva de Aliste (*v*.1655–61) in 1655. That same year, however, he was commissioned to investigate the deposition of the governor of Chile, Antonio de Acuña y Cabrera (1597–1662). Despite his short period as *fiscal*, the memorial written by Campo claims that Ibarra, who 'had occupied his superior talent only in the good of Indians,' maintained his appointment as protector-*fiscal* of Lima until 1 February 1657, when a *real cedula* was issued ordering the elimination of the protectors-*fiscales* in Peru. He was oidor of Chile (1655), Quito (1664) and Lima (1669). In Lima, his condition of senior *oidor* made him regent of the vice-royalty following the death of Viceroy Count of Lemos (*v*.1667–72) in office on 6 December 1672. He held the post until September 1674 when Viceroy Count of Castellar (*v*.1674–78) made his entry into the city of Lima. That same year he was appointed as Bishop of Trujillo but died childless without entering into this ecclesiastical dignity.

Ibarra, Antonio de (Durango, Biscay c.1570).[19] Abogado de Indios 1599–1600. Son of Martín de Ibáñez de Ibarra and María de Murueta. He was the nephew of Francisco de Ibarra (1539–75), the famous explorer and conqueror of New Biscay. Ibarra was a *vecino* of Mexico City who arrived in Peru as part of the entourage of Viceroy Luis de Velasco (*v*.1596–1604), the former viceroy of Mexico. He obtained a bachelor degree in canon law from the University of Mexico (*c*.1586) and later appears as a doctor in Peruvian official documentation (1601)—although there is no trace of where he obtained this last degree. He served as protector of Indians and vice-regal advisor in Mexico. In Peru he was appointed *fiscal* of Lima (April 1600–Dec.1601), corregidor of Parinacochas,

---

Catálogo Claustro, 27. There are many references in Campo, *Memorial*, 5v, 12; Lilly, Latin American mss. Peru, 1673, Sep.18.

19 Details of his career are found in Javier Barrientos Grandon, "La creación de la audiencia de Santiago y sus ministros fundadores," *Revista de Estudios Histórico Jurídicos* 25 (2003), 233–338. See AGI, Mexico, 220, N.20, fs.1–20; a facsimilie is available from http://pares.mcu.es/, cod. es.41091.agi/16403.13.22/ Mexico, 220, N.20 and "Causas sobre el cacicazgo del Pueblo de Quinti. Huaman Chata, Miguel et al.," Lilly Latin American mss. Peru, 1596, Aug.23—1626, Mar.13, fs. 43–43v. Details of his appointments are found in Levillier, ed., *Gobernates*, 14: 202, 249; Lilly Latin American mss. Peru,1600, Nov. 18-1602, Jan. 22. f48; Rynaga, *Memorial*, 3; Heredia, *Consultas*, 1: 219; *Libros de Cabildos de Lima*, 14: 804, 746–49; Heredia, *Consultas*, 2: 343; Tristan Platt,Thérése Bouysse-Cassagne and Olivia Harris, *Qaraqara-Charka: Mallku, Inka y Rey en la provincial de Charcas (siglos XV–XVII)* (La Paz, 2006), 222, 226.

Cajamarca (1602–4) and Jauja (1604–7). After a first unsuccessful attempt (1602), Ibarra was appointed *fiscal* of Charcas (1607–13) where he eventually became *oidor* (Jan.1613). He married (1605) Ana María de Zárate, daughter of Pedro de Zárate, captain of the arquebus regiment of the Royal Guard of Lima, and Isabel Dávalos de Solier, daughter of Nicolás de Rivera (1487–1563), *el viejo*, first *alcalde* of Lima.

*Lasso de la Vega Híjar, García José (Lima, 1705–75).[20] Protector-fiscal 1741–*fl.*1745. Son of *regidor* José Lasso de la Vega and Leonor Rosa de Híjar y Mendoza. He entered the college of San Martín (1721) and obtained a doctorate in canon law. He was the third Count of Villanueva del Soto. He married María de Jaúregui (1735); their daughter, Micaela, became a professed nun in the monastery of Our Lady of Prado. After his first wife's death (*c.*1764), he married Francisca Zamudio de las Infantas del Solar (1766).

León Escandón, Pedro de. (Madrid, *c.*1708–1770).[21] Protector-*fiscal* 1736–39? Son of Joseph de León y Espinoza (knight of Santiago) and María Luisa de Escandón, he moved to the vice-royalty of Peru as page of his uncle Francisco Antonio de Escandón (†1739), Archbishop of Concepción (1723) and Lima (1732–39). He matriculated at San Martin (1723) and San Felipe y San Marcos (1736) and obtained the degrees of bachelor and doctor of canon law. He was received as advocate of the audience of Lima (1734). There is evidence to suggest that Viceroy Castefuerte's friendship with Archbishop Escandón was instrumental in León's appointment as protector of Indians. He sailed back to Spain (*c.*1739) where he pursued a fruitful career in Court: From a position as *oidor* in the chancery of Valladolid, he was promoted as councillor of the Indies (1752) and Castile (1766); and later to that of War and the Holy Inquisition.

*León Pinelo, Diego de. (Córdoba, Argentina1608–Lima 1671).[22] Protector 1655–71. The youngest son of Captain Diego López de Lisboa y León and Catalina de Esperanza

---

20 Lohmann, *Los ministros*, ; AGN, Real Audiencia, causas civiles, leg. 15, ca.257 (1736–44), f. 65.

21 Joseph Antonio Alvarez y Baena, *Hijos de Madrid, ilustres en santidad, dignidades, armas, ciencias y artes de Madrid*...vol. 4 (Madrid, 1791), 258–59; Alfredo Moreno Cebrián, *El virreinato del Marqués de Castelfuerte, 1724–1736* (Madrid, 2000), 104, 261; "Expediente seguido ante el Real Acuerdo de Justicia por Dn. Pedro de León y Escandón, alumno del Real Colegio de San Martín,"; AGN, grados de abogados, leg. 1, c.2 (1734), fs.1–1v; ES.41091. AGI/1.16404.42.3.267//CONTRATACION,5474,N.1,R.20, available in http://pares.mcu.es; and AGN, protocolos notariales s.XVIII, protocolo 506, Gregorio González de Mendoza, 1749–52, fs.140–141.

22 The bibliography on the Leon bothers is legion. A guide to the various writings on this family is found in Juan E. Morón Orellana, *Antonio de León Pinelo* (Lima, 1993), 18–20. For Diego see "Méritos y cargos del Dr. Diego de León Pinelo y de su hijo Diego de León Gutiérrez" (1648), in Ernesto de la Torre Villar, *Los pareceres de Juan de Padilla y Diego de León Pinelo, acerca de la enseñanza y buen tratamiento de los indios* (Mexico, 1979), 65 79. Contemporary testimonies are also found in Francisco and José Mugaburu,. *Chronicle of Colonial Lima: The*

Pinelo. Bachelor in canon law (1632) from Salamanca, and licentiate and doctor in canon law from San Marcos (1636). Substitute lecturer in Code (1633), and substitute in the chairs of vespers and prime of canon law, and rector in two successive periods (1656–58). He married Mariana Gutiérrez de Paredes (†1703). They had three children: Diego de León Pinelo Gutiérrez (1636–*fl.*1687), a doctor of theology and rector of the university of Lima; Catalina de León (*b.*1638) and Beatriz de León (*b.*1639).

López de Eceiza, Isidoro (Villfranca de Oría?—Lima, 1739).[23] Protector-*fiscal* 1708–20. Son of Nicolas del Pozo y Silva, and Domingo López de Eceiza (†1699), a Basque from Villafranca de Oria and knight of Santiago, who died in the voyage to Quito, where he had been elected president of the audience. He obtained a scholarship for the college of San Martín (1697). Transferred to Guatemala as *fiscal* of the audience (1721) and appointed honorary councillor of the Indies before he died (1739). He married (1712) María de Saavedra y de la Cueva, daughter of the Marquis of Rivas de Saavedra.[24]

Luna, Domingo de (*fl.*1595–33).[25] Defensor General of Indians 1630. He was part of the entourage of viceroy Count of Monterrey and his advisor both in Mexico (1595–1603) and Peru (1604–6), as well as a witness in his testament of 1608. He was appointed *corregidor de naturales* and treasurer thereof in Lima (1606); visitation judge (*juez visitador*) in 16 *corregimientos* in Cusco, Arequipa and Arica; and *visitador* of Indian reducciones (1608); and judge of land (*composición de tierras*) in the valley of Carabayllo in Lima and administrator of *censos* of Indians (1621). It would also appear, as evidenced in his participation as witness to the life of St. Francisco Solano, that he acquired the military rank of captain. Prior to his appointment as Defensor General of Indians, he was also protector of Indians in Huancavelica; in this position, Buenaventura de Salinas testifies that Luna was the author of a memorial requesting that the caciques of Huancavelica pay the cost of mercury extracted in Peru in view of

---

Diary of Josephe and Francisco Mugaburu, 1640–1697, ed. Robert Ryal Miller (Norman, Okla., 1975), 88; Campo, *Memorial*, 20; and Torre Villar, *Pareceres*, 83. An account of his writings is found also found in Torre Villar, *Pareceres*, 37–53.

23 See AGN, protocolos notariales s. XVIII, protocolo 323, Francisco Estacio Meléndez 1720; Eguiguren, *Diccionario*, 2: 212; and Lohmann Villena, *Los ministros*, 39–40; Burkholder and Chandler, 39.

24 Maria was daughter of Francisco José Ramírez de Saavedra (widower of Mariana de Luna y Sarmiento) and Brianda de la Cueva y Guzmán. See Rosas, *La nobleza*, 202–205.

25 Details of his career are found in Eguiguren, *Diccionario*, 1: 389.; Real Cédula of 4 Februrary 1606 by Count of Monterrey in *Libros de Cabildos de Lima*, 15: 29–33; Luis Miguel Glave, *De rosa y espinas: Economía, sociedad y mentalidades andinas, siglo XVII* (Lima, 1998), 37–41; and Eguiguren, Diccionario, 2: 960. For his involvement in Huancavelica see Salinas, *Memorial*, 293–94, 300. His name as witness for the life of Solano is found in Diego de Córdova, *Vida, virtudes y milagros del Apostol del Peru el Venerable P. Fray Francisco Solano*...(Madrid, 1643), 523.

the impossibility of complying with the mita demands due to the rigorous labour laws covering Indians.

Márquez de Mansilla, Esteban (Lima 1645–*c.*1700).[26] Protector-*fiscal* 1689. Son of Captain José Márquez de Mansilla and Luisa Vásquez de Acuña, a member of the extended family of the future counts of Vega del Ren (1686). He was a scholar and rector of San Felipe y San Marcos and obtained an appointment as *oidor* in Panama. He married Lucía Francisca de Colmenares y Vega (b.1669), daughter of Sebastián de Colmenares Avilés (1634–1709), secretary to Viceroy Count of Lemos, inspector (*veedor*) of the Spanish Armada in the South Seas (1683), and Agustina María de Vega y La Rynaga (1647–86)—herself grand-niece of Leando de la Rynaga; the couple was childless.

Martínez de España, José. Protector-*fiscal* 14 April 1728.[27]

*Medina Gómez, Cipriano de (Seville, *c.*1559–Lima,1635).[28] Advocate of Indians 1593–*fl.*1626. Son of Salvador de Medina and Isabel Gomez Adalid. He obtained a licentiate in law and practiced as lawyer in the audience of Seville until he arrived in Lima (1584). He was incorporated to San Marcos (1598) as lecturer and substitute professor of Institute, under Francisco de León Garavito (1541–1612), prime of laws, under Jerónimo López Guarnido (1525–96), and vespers of canons under Fernán Vásquez de Fajardo (1534–97). He was elected vice-rector (1592) and rector (1604) of San Felipe y San Marcos, as well as rector of the University of San Marcos on two occasions (1605, 1617). He would remain part of the university at least until 1619. He refused an appointment as professor of vespers of canon law by Viceroy Velasco, arguing that it had not been provided by *oposición*, as established by the ordinances of the university (1599). He married (1586) Sebastiana de Vega y Feria, daughter of Francisco de Vega and

26 See Eguiguren, *Diccionario*, 1: 530; Lohmann Villena, *Los ministros*, 180; Rizo Patrón, *Linaje*, 17, 74, 256.

27 Lohmann, *Los ministros*, 66.

28 Traces of his life are found in Luis Antonio Eguiguren, *Diccionario histórico cronológico de la Real y Pontificia Universidad de San Marcos y sus colegios: Crónica e investigación* (Lima, 1940–51), 1: 385–90; Alberto García Carraffa and Antonio García Carraffa, *Enciclopedia Heráldica y Genealógica Hispano Americana* (Madrid, 1919–63), 55: 170. Evidence of his practice in Seville is found in the inventory of his library which lists a small book of manuscript notes 'as advocate of the audience of Seville' ("Ittem otro pequeño de apuntamientos siendo abogado de la Audiencia de Cevilla manuscript.") appendix 1, § 475. In the case of university his library also lists a copybook of his lectures ("Ittem un quaderno de las lecturas antiguas que izo el Sr. Doctor"), appendix 1, §476. For his career in San Marcos see Eguiguren, *Catálogo Histórico del Claustro de la Universidad de San Marcos, 1576–1800* (Lima, 1912), 21–43; *La universidad*, 1: 608–12; and *Diccionario*, 1: 385–86, 328, 442. For the testament of Fray Cipriano de Medina, 3 September 1652, see AGN, Protocolos Notariales s.XVII, protocolo 612, Marcelo Antonio de Figueroa 1652, f.2396–2404v.

Feliciana Padilla Celis, and sister of Feliciano de Vega (1580–1640), a professor of canon law, rector of the university of San Marcos, and bishop of Popayán and La Paz. The couple had two sons: Cipriano de Medina y Vega OP (1594–1664), professor of moral theology and bishop of Huamanga, and Agustín de Medina y Vega (1604–47), knight of Santiago and fiscal of the audience of Lima. Cipriano de Medina y Vega was the first beneficiary of the *capellanía* founded by his uncle Feliciano in 1631. As the *capellanía*, which provided an annual income of 200 pesos, was founded to benefit those descendants of Doctor Medina who took the holy orders, the second beneficiary was his grandson, Cipriano de Medina y Agüero, professor of moral theology at San Marcos—a chair instituted in 1635 by his uncle, Bishop Vega—and bishop of Huamanga, Doctor Medina himself would have influenced he appointment of his younger son. Agustín de Medina y Vega married María de Agüero, a member of an old encomendero family.

Peralta Sanabria, Juan de. (Lima, 1648–1706).[29] Protector-*fiscal* 1692–93. Son of Captain Juan de Peralta y Yegros and Juana Ramírez de Sanabria. He entered the college of San Martín (1664) to study canon law and obtained a doctorate. Evidence suggests that his appointment as protector-*fiscal* was interim. He was professor of Code and Institute, and appointed as *oidor* of Lima (1704). He died unmarried and childless.

*Rojas Acevedo, Francisco de (Lima, 1652–1716).[30] Protector-*fiscal* 1693–1701. Son of Gregorio de Rojas y Acevedo (1621–*c*.1680), a professor of Institute, prime of canon law, and vespers of laws at the University San Marcos, later appointed *fiscal* at the audience of Charcas (1678). He was a scholar at San Martín (1667) and doctor in laws from San Marcos. His mother was María Andrea Correa de León Pinelo (†*c*.1704), sister of protector-*fiscal* Diego de León Pinelo. He was appointed as advisor for Indian matters (1697) by Viceroy Count of Monclova (*v*.1689–1705) He acquired for 2,867 pesos and 3 reales the *futurario* right of being elected *alcalde del crimen* in Lima (1699), but was merely in office just over a year (09.06.1701–31.08.1702). He moved to Santiago as *oidor* (1703–10) and later returned to Lima once again as *alcalde del crimen* (1710). He would become honorary councillor of the Indies (1716). He lived in a house in calle de los Estudios de la Concepción de Jesús. He married (1691) María Teresa Calvo del Corral y de la Torre, daughter of José del Corral y Calvo de la Banda (*c*.1625–86), *oidor* of Lima (1679), and Francisca Antonia de la Torre y Cegarra—but she died ten months later. He died childless and, as part of his last will, released his slave Ignacia de Rojas.

---

29 See Lohmann, *Los ministros*, 99; AGN, protocolos notariales s. XVIII, protocolo 957, Francisco Sánchez Becerra (01.10.1706), ff. 1535–1537v.

30 See AGN, protocolos notariales s. XVIII, protocolo 1116, Gregorio de Urtazo 1719, fs. 588v–92; Eguiguren, *Diccionario*, 2: 194. His record of public service and other personal details are found in Lohmann Villena, *Los ministros*, 99, 121–22.

Ruiz de Berecedo, Francisco (Santiago *c.*1674–1752).[31] Protector-*fiscal* 1723–78. Son of Juan Alonso Ruiz de Berecedo (Burgos) and Juana Alemán y Pozo y Silva (Concepción). He graduated from the Jesuit college of Santiago where he obtained the degrees of Master of Arts and Doctor of Theology, and later matriculated in the royal college of San Martín in Lima to study law (1692). He obtained the degrees of bachelor and licentiate of canon law at San Marcos. He became substitute lecturer in prime of laws under the supervision of professor Diego Gonzalez Montero. He returned to Chile (1699) and was received as advocate in the audience of Chile; and later appointed advocate of the poor (1701) and advisor in Indian matters (1709) under Governor Francisco Ibáñez de Peralta (1644–1712). He was elected *alcalde ordinario* of Santiago (1713). He served as protector in the audiences of Santiago (1707–13), New Granada (1720–23) and Lima (1723–28) before joining the audience of Santiago as *oidor* (1730). He was appointed protector-*fiscal* by viceroy Diego Morcillo Rubio de Auñón, Archbishop of Lima (*v.*1720–24). He had an important library. He first married Jerónima del Castillo y Ureta; and secondly (1743) Bernarda de Aldunate, daughter of José de Aldunate and Rosa Garcés de Mansilla.

*Rynaga (or Larrinaga or Reynaga), Leandro de la (Osorno, Chile, 1563–Lima, 1624).[32] Advocate of Indias 1601–*c.*1624. Son of Juan de la Rynaga Salazar (1505/11–1600) and Francisca Medel de la Mina, both peninsular. Captain Rynaga was an *infanzón*, or

31 See "Relacion de los grados y servicios del Licenciado Don Francisco Ruiz y Berecedo, Protector Fiscal de el distrito de la Audiencia del Reyno de Chile" (1716), BNCH, Medina mss. vol. 23, pieza 23, n/f; Espejo, *Nobiliario*, 158; and Lohmann, *Los ministros*, 123; Jaime Eyzaguirre, *Historia del Derecho* (Santiago, 200), 196.

32 The best account for the history of this family until the mid seventeenth century is Nicolás Matías del Campo y de la Rinaga, *Memorial y discurso informativo...Representa los estudios, y ocupaciones propias en servicio de su Magestad; y las del Doctor Iuan Bautista del Campo y de la Rinaga, su hermano, cura rector de la Villa de Huancabelica...Informa la nobleza, y servicio de sus padres* (Madrid, 1668). Other sources include Roberto Levillier, ed.,*Gobernantes del Perú: Cartas y Papeles* (Buenos Aires, 1926), 14: 63, 234; Rynaga Salazar, *Memorial Protector General*, 4v; Eguiguren, *Diccionario*, 1: 385–86 and *La universidad*, 542–55; AGN, Cabildo Justicia Ordinaria, causas civiles, CA JO 1, caja 36, doc. 40 (1622), f.5v; Eguiguren 1951, 545. Juan de la Rynaga claimed that his father was advocate of Indians for 24 years, see his *Memorial*, 3. For a genealogical study of the Rynaga Salazar family in the XVI and XVII centuries see Guillermo Lohmann Villena, *Amarilis Indiana: Identificación y semblanza* (Lima, 1993), § 5, 329–42. Reference to his wedding is found in Rosa Pérez Cánepa, "El primer libro de matrimonios de la parroquia del Sagrario," *Revista del Instituto Peruano de Investigaciones Académicas* 12 (1961), 90. Other secondary references include Guillermo Lohmann, *Los regidores perpetuos del cabildo de Lima (1535–1821): Crónica y estudio de un grupo de gestión*, 2 vols. (Sevilla, 1983), 2: 162–63; Aurelio Miró-Quesada, *El primer virrey poeta en América (Don Juan de Mendoza y Luna, marqués de Montesclaros)* (Madrid, 1962), 174–75.

member of the lower nobility in the Basque country, who arrived in America in 1534 to participate in the conquests of Peru and Chile, and gained a certain notoriety by supporting the royalist cause against the uprising of Gonzalo Pizarro (†1548). These deeds awarded him the appointments as corregidor of Osorno (1563–64) and Chachapoyas (1571–74), *alcalde ordinario* of Lima (1570, 1576), and alcalde of Huánuco (1597), where he possessed two encomiendas. Leandro attended the University of San Marcos where he graduated as bachelor in canon law (1586). He was appointed professor of Institute (1589) and prime of canon law (1596). The consolidation of his academic career came with his election as rector of the college of San Felipe y San Marcos and of the University of San Marcos (1599), where he was re-elected on four occasions (1603, 1609, 1619 and 1620). Viceroy Velasco proposed him for a magistracy at the audience of Lima, since he considered him someone 'proficient in advocacy' (1599). The Council, however, rejected the proposal as he was a native of the audience. He became advisor of Viceroys Count of Monterrey, Marquis of Montesclaros, Prince of Squilace, and Marquis of Guadalcázar. This closeness, no doubt, was instrumental in his appointment as *regidor* of the *cabildo* of Lima even if his bid for the post was 2,000 pesos lower than the highest bid (1611). He was appointed alcalde of the city the following year (1622). He married (1586) Juana Cervera de Rivadeneyra (1568–1653); at the time of her death she declared the following children: Juan (*c.*1588–1635), was first professor of Decretum in San Marcos, alcalde *ordinario* of Lima, *oidor* in Panama and author of the 1626 memorial on the protectorship of Indians; María (1599–1672), married to Juan del Campo Godoy; Bartolomé, married (1616) to Mencía de Santillán Cepeda de la Torre; friars Luis, Bernardo and Cristóbal religious of St. Augustin; and Jacoba (1603) nun at the monastery of La Encarnación.[33]

*Santiago Concha (or Concha) y Roldán, Pedro José de (Lima 1706).[34] Protector-*fiscal* 1730–34. His father was José de Santiago Concha y Salvatierra (1667–1737), *oidor* in Lima (1694–1709; 1718–23) and Santiago (1709–17), interim governor of Chile (1717), and first marquis of Casa Concha (1718). His mother was María Roldán Dávila, daughter of General Juan Nicolás Roldán Dávila, a prominent figure and landowner in Trujillo, Peru. He entered the royal college of San Martín (1718), where collegiate

33 Bartolomé de la Rynaga and Mencía Santillán had Leandro de la Rynaga Santillán (*c.*1620–*c.*1650), knight of Calatrava, as well as Francisca and Juana. See Lohmann, *Los americanos*, 1: 60. The last will of Juana Cervera(19.07.1653) is found in AGN, protocolos notariales s. XVII, protocolo 480, Antonio Fernández de la Cruz, fs 1885–1889.

34 Details of his life and career are found in "Catálogo de los Colegiales en el Real Colegio de San Martín," in Eguiguren, *Diccionario*, 2: 227, Lohmann, *Los ministros*, 34–35; Moreno Cebrián, *Marqués de Castelfuerte,*, 261, 264–65. His destitution and reinstatemet are found, respectively, in Jorge Juan y Antonio de Ulloa, *Noticias secretas de América, sobre el estado Naval, Militar, y Político de los Reynos del Perú y provincias de Quito, costas de Nueva Granada y Chile*, 2 vols. (1826; Bogotá, 1983), 2: 357.

authorities considered him 'much accredited for his good letters.' Santiago Concha's appointment as protector was preceded by a payment to the royal treasury of 20,000 pesos. He faced an accusation by Pedro Prieto de Vargas of ignoring the ill-treatment of Indians on his father's estates (1734). The case was consulted in the Council of Indies which agreed to his destitution (*real cedula* of 4 September 1735). Jorge Juan (1713–73) and Antonio de Ulloa (1716–95) observed that, although the charges against Santiago Concha 'were just,' other officers employed for Indian matters who behaved similarly had not been sanctioned. The order of his destitution, however, was received by Viceroy Marquis of Castelfuerte (*v.*1724–36) after Santiago Concha's death at 29 years of age (24 October 1735). He married (1734) María Teresa de Trasalviña y Oyagüe who appealed the decision of destitution after his death with the purpose of reestablishing his honour a rescript, rescinding it was issued in 1735.

*Sosa Rengifo, Francisco de (Lima, 1577–Charcas? 1653).[35] Advocate of Indians *c.* 1616. He was the son of Captain Diego de Sosa, a peninsular, and María Rengifo y Salazar. His father, a native of Toledo, claimed to be a "conquistador" of Peru. He was elected one of the seventeen founding scholars of the royal college of San Felipe y San Marcos (1592). After obtaining a doctorate in law, he was incorporated as a senior member of the University of San Marcos, where he was lecturer in Institute (1600), professor of prime of canon law (1607) and rector (1611). His public career started with his appointment as *alcalde ordinario* of Lima (1613). As such, he headed the petition of the merchants of Lima to establish the Tribunal del Consulado. Viceroy Prince of Squilace appointed him visitor general of the royal navy and general auditor of war (1619). The Council of the Indies appointed him *oidor* of New Granada (1621–33), and president of the audience of Charcas, a post in which he remained until he died in office. Friar Buenaventura de Salinas y Córdoba (1592–1653), a professor of Latin and rhetoric at San Marcos, claimed that, in the field of jurisprudence, Doctor Sosa had been 'most eminent.'

Torres de la Fresneda, Antonio (Guadalajara, Spain).[36] Defensor General of Indians 1597. He was head valet (*camarero*) to Viceroy García Hurtado de Mendoza (*v.*1589–96)

---

35 See "Razon de la ascendencia del Sr. Dr. Dn Francisco de Sosa y Rengifo..." (c.1625). BNP mss. b 841; "Información de legitimidad y nobleza de Francisco de Sosa, vecino y regidor de Toledo, y del cap. Diego de Sosa, su hermano, conquistador el Perú, hijos legítimos de Francisco de Sosa y de María del Corral, su mujer.," BNP, Archivo Astete Concha, ms. z270; Salinas, *Memorial*, 168.

36 AGN, Protocolos Notariales siglo XVII, protocolo 819, Francisco Hernández 1606–1608, fs. 312–13; Lohmann, *Los americanos*, 1: 119; *Libros de Cabildos de Lima*, 14: 490; *Inventing Lima*, 73. There is reference to an ejecutoria de hidalgía of Torres de la Fresneda in *Memorial genealógico al Rey N.S. por Don Juan Joseph de Cevallos Ribera y Dávalos, conde de las Torres, &c.* (Madrid: Imprenta Real de la Gaceta, 1770), 134. The other candidate in the dispute of the administration of *alcabalas* was the current administrator, Diego Núñez de Figueroa. *Libros de Cabildos de Lima*, 13: 227; 14: 484, 489–90. 4952444.

and later appointed corregidor of Andahuaylas (1599) by Viceroy Luis de Velasco (*v.*1596–1604). He was supported by the councillors of the the *cabildo* of Lima in his disputed appointment as supletory administrator of *alcabalas* of the City of Lima (1603). He married Mariana de Zuñiga, also born in Guadalajara. Their children were Agustina and Juan de Torres y Fresneda; Agustina married Perafán de Ribera, corregidor of Huamalíes.

Valenzuela, Francisco de (†1655).[37] Protector-*fiscal* 1640–55. He was the first protector-*fiscal* of Indians by virtue of his 'letters' and 'great services, inherited and proper.' The same year as this appointment he obtained the office of *fiscal* of the Tribunal de la Santa Cruzada, an office traditionally exercised by a *fiscal* of the audience. He died in office.

---

37 See Ruigómez, *Protector de indios*, 81. The history of the appointment of Velenzuela and the changes in the office between 1640 and 1655 is found in Ernesto de la Torre Villar, *Los pareceres de Juan de Padilla y Diego de León Pinelo acerca de la enseñanza y buen tratamiento de los indios* (Mexico, 1979), 82ss and Real Cédula 28 August 1648, Madrid, in Ruigómez, *Protector de indios*, 216.

APPENDIX 2

The Library of Cipriano de Medina (1635)

The chief guide for the identification of the works in the following book list was Douglas Osler, ed., *Bibliographica iuridica*, 2 vols. (Frankfurt : V. Klostermann, 2000). I also profited from more specific book lists such as Rosa Gentili, ed. *La Repubblica dei Giuristi: Edizioni giuridiche del '500 della librería Zauli Naldi* (Faenza, 1994) and Alain Wijffels, *Late sixteenth-century lists of law books at Merton College* (Cambridge, LP Publications, 1992). For legal texts relating to the Spanish Monarchy until the seventeenth century, Gerardo Ernesto de Frankenau, *Sagrados Misterios de la justicia hispana*, Maria A. Durán Ramas, ed. (1703; Madrid: Centro de Estudios Constitucionales, 1993). A number of electronic catalogues of legal collections were also used. I found the Boalt Law Library Catalog, University of Berkeley, which includes the holdings of the Robbins Collection (http://lawcat.berkeley.edu/) comprehensive and helpful for it included biografical data and futher references to works. The electronic catalogue of the Max-Planck-Institut für europäische Rechtsgeschichte (http://www.rg.mpg.de/library/search) was also most useful.

Identification of the works was complemented with visits to the British Library (http://blpc.bl.uk/) to establish particular characteristics of works. I also profited greatly of the Catálogo Colectivo de Patrimonio Bibliográfico Español (http://gl.www.mcu.es/bibliotecas/MC/CCPB/) which includes 637 public, private and university libraries in Spain. This catalogue helped to establish the use of existence of particular works and editions in the Spanish Monarchy.

Cipriano Medina y Gómez. Inventario de bienes, 4 January 1635. AGN Protocolos Notariales s.XVII, protocolo notarial 818, escribano Diego Gutierrez 1635, fs.496v–504.

1. El Derecho Civil en cinco cuerpos [Corpus Iuris Civilis]
2. Item dos cuerpos de Derecho Canónico el uno del Sexto y Clementinas y el otro del Decreto de letra muy antigua y pequeñas de a más de a quartilla [Sextum, Clementinas, Decretum]
3. Un cuerpo de Antonio Safma diversori juris
4. Silva Responsos un cuerpo
5. Rodriguez De Executionibus [Rodríguez, Amador. *Tractatus de executione sententiae et eorum quae paratam habent exequutionem*. Madrid, 1613.]
6. Paschelio De viribus paleci potestatie un tomo
7. Moral Di Concilia un tomo
8. Observaciones de Macingenio un tomo [Mynsinger von Frundeck, Joachim. *Singularium obseruationum iudicii Imperiales Camerae*. Venice, 1563.]
9. Practica interrogadorum

 | DOI 10.1163/9789004305175_012

10. Carrotio De Remediis un tomo [Carocci, Vincenzo. *Tractatus de remediis contra praeiudiciales sententias, vel damnosas executiones*. Geneva, 1521; Venice, 1620; Cologne, 1621.] (vid.222)
11. Regules de Dueñas otro tomo [Dueñas, Pedro de. *Regularum utriusque iuris cum apliationibus ac limitationibus liber primus*. Salamanca, 1554; Lyon, 1557.]
12. Tractatus de indulgentiis un tomo
13. Repetitiones de Palatio Rubiis un tomo [López de Palacios Rubios, Juan. *Repetitio rubricæ et capitulis per vestras de donationibus inter virum et uxorem*. Valladolid, 1503.][38]
14. Dos cuerpos de Narbona sobre la Recopilación [Narbona, Alfonso de. *Commentaria in tertiam partem novæ recopilationis legum Hispaniæ pars prima*. Toledo, 1623.]
15. Carrança de gentes [?] un tomo
16. Carrotio de locatio un tomo [Carocci, Vincenzo. *Tractatus locati et conducti*. Venice, 1584, 1592, 1597, 1617; Cologne, 1584.] (vid.148)
17. Tractatus de absulutione florenti un tomo
18. Practica de Ferrara un tomo viejo [Ferrariis, Ioannes Petrus de. *Practica Papiensis* Venice, 1549.] (vid.222)
19. Dos cuerpos de Antonio Gómez uno sobre las varias otro sobre las leyes de Toro. [Gómez, Antonio. *Commentariorum variarumque resolutionum Iuris civilis communis et Regii*. Venice, 1535.][39] (vid.52)
    [———. *Opus praeclarum & Commentum super legibus Tauri*. Salamanca, 1552.][40] (vid.350)
20. Decitiones Rote viejo ympergamino
21. Política de Villadiego un tomo [Villadiego Vascuñana y Montoya, Alonso de. *Instrucción política y práctica judicial conforme al estilo de los consejos, audiencias y tribunales de corte y otros ordinarios del reyno*. Madrid, 1612.]
22. Compendio resolutionum un tomo
23. Practica de exsaminar proceso un tomo
24. Peregrino De fideicomitis un tomo [Pellegrini, Marcantonio. *De fideicommissis præsertim universalibus tractatus frequentissimus*. Venice, 1595]
25. Penas y delitos un tomo
26. Feliciano De cencibus en dos tomos [Solís, Feliciano. *Commentarii de censibus: quatuor libris fere omnem materiam de censibus complectentes libris*. 2 vols. Madrid, 1595–1605; 1606–7; Milan, 1614.]

---

38 Also Salamanca, 1523; Lyon, 1524; Valladolid, 1543; Frankfurt, 1573; Lyon, 1576.

39 The complete work: *Commentariorvm variarumque resolutionum Iuris ciuilis communis & Regii*, 3 vols., Salmanca, 1562–63, 1579–77. Separate editions of volumes: Vol. 1, Salamanca, 1555; vol. 3, Tinghi, 1585; Salamanca, 1589; Lyon, 1602, 1609; Cologne, 1631.

40 Salamanca, 1560, 1575, 1582, 1598; Frankfurt, 1591, 1617; Venice, 1591; Lyon, 1602; Geneva, 1616, 1620, 1623, 1628; Antwerp, 1617, 1624. See Coing vol. 2, bk.1: 305.

27. Lanciloto De atentatie un tomo [Lancellottus, Ioannes Paulus or Roberto Lancellotto. *Tractatus de attentatis et innovatis lite & appellatione pendente.* Rome, 1576; Venice, 1598; Frankfurt, 1600.]
28. Gusmán De Vixionibus un tomo [Guzman Genzer, Alonso. *Tractatus de evictionibus*]
29. De privilegis pauperum un tomo [De privilegiis pauperum. Alonso Guzmán Genzer? Gabriel Alvarez de Velasco?]
30. Anguiano De legibus tomo [Anjou. Choppin, René. *De legibus Andium municipalibus libri duo posteriores*]
31. Carrasco In recopilationem un tomo [Carrasco del Saz, Francisco. *Interpretatio ad aliquas leges Recopilationis Regni Castellae.* Sevilla, 1620.]
32. Singuleria Doctorum un cuerpo
33. Robles De representatione un tomo [Robles Salcedo, Blas. *Novus et methodicus tractatus de repraesentatione.* Madrid, 1624; 1632.]
34. Regule utriusque juris un tomo.
35. Matienso un tomo [Matienzo, Juan de.]
36. Tractatus De asecurationibus et pignoribus un tomo [Stracca, Benvenuto. ¿*De Assecurationibus et proxenetis*?]
37. Conncilia Janes Baptista de Valençuela un tomo [Valenzuela Velásquez, Juan Bautista. *Consilia.*]
38. Concilia Antonio de Butrio borien un tomo [Butrio, Antonio de. *Consilia*]
39. Felicio De societate un tomo [Felicio, Ettore. *Tractatus de communione seu societate, deque lucro, ac quaestu damno itidem ac expensis.* Turin, 1610.]
40. Decisioni Regni Aragoni un tomo [Aragon. José de Sesse y Piñol? Juan Vargas Machuca?]
41. Bovadilla en dos cuerpos [Castillo de Bobadilla, Jerónimo. *Política para corregidores y señores de vasallos en tiempos de paz y de guerra.* Madrid, 1597; Barcelona, 1616.]
42. Surdo De alimentis [Surdus, Ioannes Petrus. *Tractatus de alimentis.* Venice, 1594.] (vid.265 & 412)
43. Fulbio Patiano dos cuerpos [Pacciani, Fulvio. *Practicabilis Tractatus…liber primus—secundus.* 2 vols. Venecia, 1594?]
44. Metodus juris avelis un tomo
45. Deciano Tractatus deriminalium dos tomos [Deciani, Tiberio. *Tractatus criminalis.* 2 vols. Turin, 1593]
46. Castillo quatro tomos los tres controversiarum jures y el otro de mayorasgos. [Castillo de Sotomayor, Juan del. *Quotidianarum controuersiarum iuris liber.* 3 vols. Madrid, 1603–11; Darmbstadii, 1613.] (vid.290, 248)[41]

---

41 *Quotidianarum controversiarum iuris.* 6 vols. Madrid, Granada. 1603–27. *Opera Omnia*, 8 vols. Lyon, 1658, 1667; Cologne, 1726–27, 1753.

47. Tractatus de in integrum restitutione en un tomo grande [Tractatus de in integrum restitutionibus][42]
48. Mascardo tres tomos de pranatio rubis [Mascardi, Giuseppe. *Conclvsiones probationvm omnivm : quae in vtroqve foro quotidie versantur*. 3 vols. Venice, 1583–88, 1593; Frankfurt, 1607; Turin, 1614–15.]
49. Estefano Graciano Diceptatione forentiun cinco tomos [Gratianus, Stephanus. *Disceptationes forensium iudiciorum*. 5 vols. Rome, 1609–1625.]
50. Burgos De paz in legibus tauri un tomo [Salon de Paz, Marcos. *Ad Leges Taurinas insignes*. Valladolid, 1568.] (vid.55, 99)
51. Guillén Servantes un tomo De legibus tauri [Guillén de Cervantes, Juan. *Commentariorum in leges Tauri*. Mantuaecarpentanae, 1594.]
52. Antonio Gomez un tomo Bariarum [Gómez, Antonio. *Commentariorum variarumque resolutionum Iuris civilis communis et Regii*] (vid.19)
53. Avendaño In legibus tauri un tomo [Velásquez de Avendaño, Luis. *Legum Taurinarum…vtilissima glosa sequitur*. Toledo, 1588]
54. Castillo In legibus tauri un tomo [Castillo de Villasante, Diego del. *Las leyes de Toro glosadas*. Medina del Campo, 1553, 1563.]
55. Consejos de Burgos de Paz un cuerpo [Salon de Paz, Marcos. *Consiliorum*. Medina del Campo, 1576.] (vid.50, 99)
56. Pedro Ferdinandis In legibus tauri un tomo [Fernández Messia, Tello. *Prima pars commentariorum in constitutiones taurinas*. Granada, 1566; Madrid, 1595.]
57. Palacios Rubios Inlegibus tauri un tomo [López de Palacios Rubios, Juan. *Glossemata legum tauri quas vulgus* de Toro *appellat*. Salamanca, 1542; Lyon, 1576.]
58. Sifuentes un tomo [Cifuentes, Miguel de.]
59. Colutancia de Pedro de Cenedo un tomo [Cenedo, Pedro Jerónimo. *Collectanea ad ius canonicum*. Venice, 1596]
60. Choronica del emperador despaña don Alfonso esptimo en romançe un tomo
61. Las partidas de Gregorio Lopez en quatro tomos [López, Gregorio. *Las Siete Partidas del Sabio Rey don Alonso el nono*. Salamanca, 1555.][43]
62. Orosco *supra* digestus vetus un tomo [Orozco, Juan. *Ad responsa prudentum commentarij : duo hi Tomi, in priores integrosque Digestorum duos libros sunt*. Salmanca, 1558.]
63. Mantica De conyeturis un tomo mas otro tomo [Mantica, Franciscus. *Tractatus de coniecturis ultimarum voluntatum*. Frankfurt, 1580.]
64. Simón de Pretis De interpretatione volontatum un tomo [Praetis, Simon de. *De ultimarum voluntatum interpretatione tractatus amplissimus*. Frankfurt, 1583.]

---

42 For a list of treatises on the restitutio see Coing, *Handbuch*, vol. 2 bk. 1: 329.

43 Salamanca 1565, 1576,1580; Valladolid, 1587/88; Madrid, 1587/98, 1609/11.

65. Sarmienti opera un tomo. [Sarmiento de Mendoza?]
66. Reduan de rebus ecclesie non alienandis un tomo
67. Rodrigo Xuares dos cuerpos el uno de alegaciones el otro de concejos [Suárez, Rodrigo. *Lectura legum aliquarum huius Regni utilem et praticabilem materia continens. Consilia etiam et Allegationes*. Valladolid, 1539.][44]
68. Otro cuerpo intitulado Adiciones a Rodrigo Xuares [Valdés, Diego de. *Ad volumen Repetitionum Roderici Suarez Additiones*. Valladolid, 1590.]
69. Mexía In legibus toleti un tomo [Mejía Ponce de León, Luis. *In legem Regiam Toleti conditam sub titulo tercio de los proprios y Rentas de los concejos.* Sevilla, 1568.]
70. Pinelo en dos tomos [Pinhel, Aires?]
71. Quesada Diversarum questionum un tomo [Quesada, Antonio de. *Diversarum quaestionum iuris liber*. Salamanca, 1571.]
72. Mexía *Supra* tassam panis un tomo [Mejía Ponce de León, Luis. Laconismus, seu Chilonium pro pragmaticae qua panis precium taxatur in interioris foro hominis elucidatione. Sevilla, 1569.]
73. Tres cuerpos de Caldas Pereyra De jure confiteutico [Caldas Pereyra y Castro, Francisco. *De uniuerso iure emphyteutico*.Coimbra, 1604–1605; Frankfurt, 1612–13.]
74. Otro del mismo Receptarum sententiarum [Ibídem. *Receptarum sententiarum, seu quaestionum forensium et controversiarum civilium libri duo*.]
75. Dos cuerpos de Mieres de maioratu [Peláez de Mieres, Melchor. *Tractatus maioratuum et meliorationum Hispaniae*. Madrid, 1620]
76. Deciciones de Guidon Papa un tomo [Pape, Guy la. *Decisiones Grationopolitanae*. Venice, 1558; Lyon, 1607, 1610.] (vid.166)
77. Alexandro trentencinco un tomo Variarum repocusionum un tomo [Trentacinque, Alessandro. *Consiliorum siue responsorum*. 2 vols en 1. Venice, 1610.]
78. Practica de Montealegre un tomo [Montealegre, Juan de. *Praxis civilis de exercitio praticarum actionum tam in communi quam regio iure sancita*. Madrid, 1614.] (vid.316)
79. Practicas de Senedo un tomo [Cenedo, Pedro Jerónimo. *Practicae qvaestiones canonicae et civiles*. Zaragoza, 1614.]
80. Cinco cuerpos de manuscriptus de informaciones en derecho y otros recaudos
81. Decisiones de León Antonio
82. Decisiones ausentes un tomo por Antonio Monacho [Monacho, Antonio. *Decisionum lucensium, florentinarum et bononiensium*. Venice, 1619; Cologne, 1620.]

---

44 Valladolid, 1590; Medina del Campo, 1550, 1600 (?); Lyon, 1559, 1560; Salamanca, 1568 (?), 1588; Frankfurt, 1594.

83. Concilia y politi de Marcilis un tomo muy viejo [Marsili, Ippolito. *Consilia: In quibus fere continentur quæ ad reorum defensionem, hominumque a calumniis innocentiam tuendam necessaria sunt.* Lyon, 1537, 1547; Venice, 1585.]
84. Alexandro Raudense In responso de legítima subcesione un tomo [Rho, Alessandro de. *Responsum secundum de legitima successione in Portugaliae Regnum.* Milan, 1579.] (vid.307)
85. Salutio De alienantis rebus fidei comisii un tomo
86. Contemplasion
87. Cosme Gumier Super pragmatica santione un tomo de letra antigua [Guymier, Cosme. *Pragmatica sanctio.* Toulouse, 1528.][45]
88. Loci comunis juris di civilis un tomo
89. Velono Super instituta otro tomo [Belloni, Niccolò. *Super utraque parte Institutionum lucubrationes.* Basel, 1544.][46]
90. Egidio tomato De muneribus un tomo pequeño [Tomati, Egidio. *Tractatus de muneribus patrimonialibus.* Lyon, 1558.]
91. Bienes confiscados un tomo pequeñito
92. Nicolás Abanto In singullaribur juris un tomo pequeño
93. Francisco Ciculiana de causione et negoturia un tomo [Ercolani, Francesco. *Tractatus de cautione de non offendendo.* Venecia, 1569, 1571.]
94. Desiciones de Casadoro un tomo [Cassador, Guillermo. *Decisiones.* Venecia, 1544; Lyon, 1547.]
95. Andrés Abegea In libro pactorus
96. Concilia de Dino un cuerpecito.
[Dino del Mugello. *Consilia.* Lyon, 1551]
97. Raçón de estado un librito [Botero, Giovanni. *Diez libros de la razón de estado.* Trans. Antonio de Herrera. 1589. Madrid, 1593.]
98. Eberando De locis comunibur un cuerpo viejo [Evert, Nicolaus von Middleburg. *Topicorum seu de locis legalibus liber.* Louvain, 1516; Lyon, 1556; Venecia, 1567.]
99. Questiones de Burgos otro cuerpecito [Salon de Paz, Marcos. *Prima pars Qvaestio Civilivm.* Medina del Campo, 1526.] (vid.50 & 55)
100. Gravete De antiquitate juris otro tomo [Cravetta, Aimone] (vid.136)
101. Francisco de Harcu De atentatie otro cuerpecito [Ercolani, Francesco. "De attentatis appellatione pendente." In *Tractatvs vniversi ivris*, vol. 5. Venice, 1584–86]
102. Francisco Curtio De feudis un tomo [Corti, Franceschino. *Tractatus feudorum.*]
103. Lanfranco Desicionum un tomo [Lanfranco da Oriano]

45 An earlier edition of this work is Paris : P. Pigouchet (impensis J. Parui), 1503. Yet "letra antigua" refers to gothic type which was used in the Toulouse edition and in Lyon, 1538.

46 Also Lyon, 1557,1566, 1568, 1578; Venice, 1563, 1573, 1583, 1621.

104. Rolandis Avari De confectione inventari un tomo [Della Valle, Rolando. *Tractatvs non minvs vtilissimvs qvam necessarius : de inuentarij confectione*. Pisauri, 1574.]
105. Gaspar Cavalino De victionibus un cuerpo [Cavallino, Gaspare. *Tractatus de euictionibus*.] (vid.356)
106. Traquelo in tractatii de mor saysi un tomo [Tiraqueau, André. *Tractatus Le mort saisit le vif, hoc est, De traslationes possessiones ex defuncto in superstitem*. Venice, 1555; Verona, 1588.]
107. Jacobini Georgio De feudis un tomo muy viejo [San Giorgio, Giacomino da. *Tractatus feudalis…Tractatus de homagijs*. Lyon, 1533; Cologne, 1575.] (vid.125)
108. Decisiones de Pedro Genintendo un tomo pequeño
109. Bocabulario utriusqui juris un tomo [Vocabularium utriusque iuris.]
110. Justo Cipsio políticoris un cuerpo [Lipsius, Iustus. *Politicorum libri sex*. (1589). Lyon, 1592.]
111. Concilia Veloni un tomo viejo [Belloni, Niccolò. *Consiliorum*. Basel, 1544; Lyon, 1550.]
112. Tractatus finum segundorum un tomo viejo
113. Codoocodam dan audelio tuteli un cuerpo [Tutela. Marcus Aurelius]
114. Practica Lanfranqui un cuerpo viejo de letra antigua [Lanfranco da Oriano. *Practica Lanfranci*. Lyon, 1515.][47]
115. Practica de Folerio un cuerpo [Follerio, Pietro. *Praxis censualis super pragma de censibus*. Venice, 1569.] (vid.215)
116. Tractatus Sepola un tomo viejo [Cipolla, Bartolomeo.]
117. Capellanes capellato losane un cuerpo [Toulouse. Capella Tolosana.]
118. Tractatus de consortibus un tomo
119. Tractatus de perscriptionibus muy antiguo y pequeño
120. Paris de Puteo De sindicatu un tomo [Pozzo, Paride del. *In materiam syndicatus omnium officialium*. Lyon, 1548.]
121. Decisiones de Capiseo otro tomo viejo [Capysium, Antonium. *Decisiones nouae sacri Regii Concilii Neapolitani*. Venice, 1541.]
122. Juanes Campegio De testibus un cuerpecito [Campeggio, Giovanni. "De testibus." In *Tractatvs vniversi ivris*, vol. 4. Venice, 1584–86.]
123. Angelo Aretineo De maleficis un cuerpo pequeño antiguo [Arentino, Angelo. *De maleficiis*] (vid.182)
124. Tratado de maleficis en un cuerpo [De maleficiis tractatus.]
125. Jacobo de Santo Georgio de feudis un tomo [San Giorgo, Giacomino da. *Tractatus de feudis*.] (vid.107)
126. Concilia de sebilci un tomo pequeño de letra antigua
127. Cagnoro De regulis juris un tomo [Cagnolo, Girolamo. *Commentaria in titulum… de regulis iuris*. Venecia, 1566, 1585.]

---

47 Also Lyon, 1521, 1528, 1550, 1562; Colonia, 1573, 1592.

128. Solorsano De paresidiis un tomo [Solórzano Pereira, Juan de. *De Parricidii Crimine disputatio*. Salamanca, 1605.]
129. Dino De regulis juris un tomo [Dino del Mugello. *De regu. Iur. Commentarius mirabilis super titulo de regu. Iuris*. Lyon, 1543, 1552. 1577; Cologne, 1569.]
130. Practica de Antonio Libano un tomo
131. Cobarrubias dos tomos [Covarrubias Leyva, Diego de. *¿Opera Omnia?*][48]
132. Ittem otros seis cuerpos de Cobarrubias [Ibidem]
133. Dos cuerpos de especuladores pequeños
134. Concilia de Antonio de Butrio un tomo [Antonio da Budrio. Consilia seu Responsa. Venice, 1575.]
135. Tractatus indicatum un tomo
136. Aymon Gravete De antiquitate temporum un tomo [Cravetta, Aimone. *Tractatus de antiquitate temporis*. Venice, 1549.][49]
137. Nicolao Vigelio un tomo digo dos tomos [Vigel, Nikolaus.]
138. Praxis ecclesiastica de viccium un tomo
139. Cagnolo Super pandectas un tomo [Cagnolo, Girolamo. *In constitutiones & leges primi, secundi, quinti, & duodecimi Pandectarum*. Venecia, 1549.]
140. Tractatus juris de sucsesione y otras cosas un tomo [Tractatus iuris de successione]
141. Juan Mileyo Voyo práctica criminal tomo pequeño [Milles de Souvigny, Jean. *Practica criminalis*. Venice, 1549.] (vid.154)
142. Silva nuptialis tomo pequeño [Nevizzano, Giovani. *Sylvae nuptialis libri sex*. Lyon, 1526, 1572; Venice, 1573.]
143. Adfavetum aurium tomo pequeño letra antigua
144. Practica de Ypólito tomo pequeño [Marsili, Ippolito. *Practica causarum criminalium*. 8vo. Lyon, 1542, 1546.]
145. Aparatus doctoris guilleni de monte super clementinas un tomo [Guillaume de Montlauzun. *Apparatus excellentissimi doctoris Guillelmi de Monte Haudino super Clementinas*. Paris, 1517.]
146. Ludovico Gomez In regule denontolendis jure questionum un tomo antiguo de letra antigua. [Gómez, Luis.] (vid.170)
147. Biblia antigua un tomo antiguo de letra antigua
148. Prisentio carrosio dos tomos uno De locatio otro De ascensione [Carocci, Vincenzo. *Tractatus locati et conducti*.] (vid.16)
    [———.Tractatus de Excusione bonorum in civilibus et Criminalitius causis. Venecia, 1594, 1597; Frankfurt, 1597.]

48 Salamanca, 1576–77, 1577–78; Venice, 1567, 1604; Antwerp, 1614–15.

49 Also Venice 1565, 1570, 1576, 1580; Lyon, 1550, 1559, 1562, 1581; Frankfurt, 1572, 1616; Spirae, 1594, 1595; Cologne, 1616.

149. Decisiones de Gama tomo pequeño [Gama, Antonio da. *Decisiones supremi senatus regni Lusitaniæ.*] (vid.175 & 285)
150. Victoria In relectione tomo pequeño [Vitoria, Francisco de. *Relectiones.* 8vo. Salamanca, 1565.]
151. Augustino Veroyo In questionibus tomo pequeño [Bero,' Agostino. *Familiares quaestiones.* 8vo. Bolonia, 1550; Venecia, 1574.]
152. Sebola in titulo de dilicio et dictum tomo pequeño [Cipolla, Bartolomeo. *Commentaria in tit. ff. De ædilitio edicto.* 8vo. Lyon, 1550.]
153. Sebola tres tomos pequeños uno de juramento litis otro de dilicio etdicto otro de depósitos pequeños [Cipolla, Bartolomeo.]
154. Pracsis Juami Miley un tomo [Milles de Souvigny, Jean. *Praxis criminis persequendi, elegantibus aliquot figuris illustrata.* Paris, 1541; Lyon, 1550.] (vid.141)
155. Pudeo In pardestis un tomo [Pozzo?]
156. Ploto in tractatus de incite jurando un tomo [Piotto, Giovanni Battista. *Tractatus de in litem iurando*.Venecia, 1570, 1583.]
157. Bancio De nullitatibus un tomo [Vanzi, Sebastiano. *Tractatus de nullitatibus processuum ac sententiarum.* Venice, 1581; Cologne, 1625.]
158. Sebastiano Mafain Lege sis qui pro entore un tomo [Maffa, Sebastianus. *Commentaria…D.Thom. Simeontii in l. Si qui pro Emptore.* Venecia 1572.]
159. Bartolomeo Capua Super pragmática un tomo [Capua, Bartolomeo da. *Super sacris Constitutionibus, Capitulis, & Pragmaticis Regni Siciliae.* Lyon, 1556, 1560, 1568.]
160. Colectanea juris civilis un tomo pequeño
161. Tractatus de mercatura un cuerpo pequeño [Stracca, Benvenuto. *De mercatura, seu Mercatore tractatus.*]
162. Decisiones Belamere un tomo [Bellamera, Egidio. *Decisiones seu conclusiones, exacte revise & diligenter castigate.* Lyon, 1529.] (vid.459 & 463)
163. Concordancias de Rebufo un tomo [Rebuffi, Pierre. *Concordatorum : inter sanctissimvm dominvm nostrvm Papam Leonem decimvm et Sedem Apostolicam ac Christianissimum dominum nostrum Regem Franciscum.* Paris, 1539.]
164. Andrea Salsieto De prensuntionibus un tomo [Alciati, Andrea. *De presumptionibus.*]
165. Thomas Gramatico Concilia un cuerpo [Grammatico, Tomasso. *Consilia criminalia et fiscalia.* Venice, 1555; Lyon, 1575.] (vid.378)
166. Desición de Guidor papa un tomo [Pape, Guy la. *Decisiones.* Lyon, 1610.] (vid.76).
167. Hipólito Gonacosa un tractatus equarum
168. Bernabé Tractatus de comuni doctorum opinione un tomo
169. Sebastiano de Medicis De fortuitu casu un tomo [Medici, Sebastiano. *De fortvitis casibus.*][50]

50 An abridged version of this work was issued in the *Tractatvs vniversi ivris*, vol. 7. Venice, 1584–86, pp. 195–224.

170. Ludovico Gomez De constitutionibus un tomo pequeño [Gómez, Luis.] (vid.142)
171. Alciato Super decretales un tomo pequeño [Alciati, Andrea. *In Codicis Iustinianei et Decretalium Gregorii IX. titulos aliquot commentaria complectens.*][51]
172. Fontanela De pactis un tomo grande [Fontanella, Juan Pedro. *De pactis nuptialibus sive capitulis matrimonialibus tractatus.*]
173. Mieses de Macoratu un cuerpo
174. Morla In emporium juris un tomo [Morla, Pedro Augustino de. *Emporium utriusque iuris in uso forensis ad modum frequentium.* Valencia, 1599.]
175. Decisiones de Gama un tomo [Gama, Antonio da. *Decisiones supremi senatus regni Lusitaniae.* Valladolid, 1599.] (vid.149 & 285).
176. Consuetidinio Pitueri sondis un tomo
177. Decisiones de Matheo de Aflictis [D'Afflitto, Matteo. *Decisiones sacri regii consilii Neapolitani.* Neapoli, 1499; Lyon 1548, 1574, Venice, 1612.] (vid. 260–61 & 464)
178. Repetitionis in capitulo Reynutius un tomo [Benoit, Guillaume. *Solennis ac perutilis Repetitio c. Raynutius extra de testa.*][52]
179. Philipo Decio De regulis juris [Decio, Filippo. *De regulis iuris.*][53]
180. Navarro In capitulum interbesba un tomo [Azpilcueta, Martin de.]
181. Stilus parlamentis francis un tomo viejo [Francia. Stilius Curiae Parlamenti]
182. Angelus De maleficis un tomo antiguo (vid.123)
183. Navarro De penitencia un tomo [Azpilcueta, Martín de. *Enchiridion Sive Manvale Confessariorvm Et Poenitentivm.* Venecia, 1579; Antwerp, 1601.]
184. Navarro In apología de reditibus ecclesiasticis un tomo.[Ibidem. *Tractatvs de reditibvs beneficiorvm ecclesiasticorvm.* Roma, 1568.]
185. Práctica criminal de Ludovico Carrero un tomo [Carerio, Ludovico. *Practica causarum criminalium.* Venice, 1556; Lyon, 1562.]
186. Andres Gail In practisis di observationibus un tomo [Gail, Andreas von. *Obseruationes practicae Imperialis Camerae.* Turin, 1595.]
187. Juanes Corrasio Miseradarum un tomo [Coras, Jean de. *De Miscellaneorum iuris civilis libri sex.* Cologne, 1581, 1590.]
188. Tractatus de previligio juramenti un tomo
189. Peregrino De previligii fisci un tomo [Pellegrini, Marcantonio. *De iuribus et priuilegiis fisci, libri VII.* Cologne, 1588; Turin, 1589; Montisbeligardi, 1619.] (vid.240 & 327)
190. Alegaciones Lopi un tomo [López de Palacios Rubios, Juan. *Allegatio in materia haeresis.*]
191. Bicentis De juramento un tomo [Carocci, Vicenzo. *Tractatus luculentus de iuramento litis decisorio.* Venice, 1595, Turin, 1596.]

---

51 This comment was issued as vol. 3 of Alciati's *Opera omnia*, 4 vols. in 2 (Basel, 1582).

52 Issued in 2 vols. in 1 (Lyon, 1522) and 5 vols. in 2 (Lyon, 1582).

53 Editions are legion. See Coing, *Handbuch*, vol. 2, bk.1: 211.

192. Carolde De ecepcionibus un tomo
193. Decisiones peruane un tomo
194. Decisiones rote causarus
195. Causarum executibarus un tomo
196. Collante De refrumuntaris un tomo [Collantes Avellaneda, Jacobo de. *Commentariorum pragmaticae in fauorem rei frumentariae & agricolarum & rerum, quae agriculturae destinatae sunt.* Madrid, 1606, 1614.]
197. Josepho Ludovico Decisionis rote un tomo [Ludovicus, Iosephus. *Decisiones causarum rotæ Lucensis.* Venice, 1586.]
198. Cauleano De tutoribus un tomo [Cavalcani, Borgnino. *Tractatus de tutore et curatore.*] (vid.258)
199. Juan Baptista Costa dos cuerpos uno del actio necosiata [Costa, Giovanni Battista.]
200. Otro de retrotractione
201. Parladorio un libro pequeñito [Yáñez Paladorio, José.] (vid.241)
202. Vicita de cárcel un tomo [Cerdán de Tallada, Tomás. *Visita de la cárcel, y de los presos : en la qual se tratan largamente sus cosas, y casos de prisión assi en causas ciuiles como criminales.* Valencia, 1574.]
203. Tractatus De regularitate ecclesiastica de Villadiego [Villadiego, Gonzalo García de. Tractatus contra hereticam prauitatem et etiam tractatus de irrigularitate. Salamanca, 1519]
204. Remigio De inmuniitate ecclesiastica un tomo [Gonni, Remigio de. De immunitate Ecclesiarum, personisque ad eas confugientibus. Tractatus aureus. Casalmaggiore, 1582.]
205. Tractatus de votu un tomo
206. Angulo De meliorationibus [Angulo, Andrés de. *Commentaria ad leges regias meliorationum.* Madrid, 1585, 1592, 1599.]
207. Aria pisana un tomo [Rodriguez de Pisa, Juan. Curia pisana. Medina del Campo, 1548; Salamanca, 1593.]
208. Tapia De constitionibus principiae un tomo [Tapia, Carlos de. *Commentarius in rubricam, et legem finalem ff. de constitutionibus principum.* Naples, 1586.]
209. Praxcis spolidori un tomo
210. Tractatus de hisquevi
211. Carrosio dos cuerpos uno De desiciones otro De practica vilia [Carocci, Vicenzo. *Decisiones casuum.*]
212. Decisiones rote abenions un tomo [Laurentius, Hieronymus. *Decisiones Rotae Avenionis.* Avignon, 1564;Venice, 1591.]
213. Dos cuerpos de decisiones del Reyno de Portugal
214. Repertorium de Nicolai de Milis un tomo [Millis, Nicolaus de. *Repertorium aureum.* Frankfurt, 1581.]

215. Practica criminal de Folerio un tomo [Follerio, Pietro. *Canonica criminalis praxis*. Venice, 1583.] (vid.115)
216. Institutione forenses galis un tomo [France.]
217. Dialogus relatorie un tomo
218. Tractatus del tempore pistis un tomo [Bardi, Marcantonio. *Tractatus de tempore utili et continuo*. Venice, 1573.]
219. Patrocinis juris un tomo
220. Alegaciones del negocio del Conde de Baylen
221. Dilectorum redrum un tomo
222. Practica de Ferrara un tomo [Ferrari, Giampietro. *Practica*. Frankfurt, 1581; Aurea practica, Venice, 1586; *Praxis aurea*, [Geneva], 1594.]
223. Concilia de Ferreto un tomo [Ferretti, Giulio. *Consilia et tractatus*. Venice, 1563.][54]
224. Propius motus un tomo [Iglesia Católica. Rescriptos papales].
225. Practica de Maranta un tomo [Maranta, Roberto. *Practica iudiciaria canonica et civilis*. Cologne, 1598, 1602, 1606, 1614, 1615.][55]
226. Tratos y contratos de mercados en romanse [Mercado, Tomás de. *Tratos y contratos de mercaderes y tratantes*. Salamanca, 1569; Sevilla, 1571, 1587.]
227. Tractatus de susecione per crasum
228. Speculum conyugioorum
229. Castro de anone civilibus [Mendes de Castro, Manoel. *De annonis civilibus libri XI Cod.* Madrid, 1592.]
230. Octaviano Vestri un tomo [Vestri, Ottaviano.]
231. Altamirano Visitatione un tomo [Altamirano, Baltasar. *Tractatus de visitatione, circa Tex. in Capit. 3. Concilij Tridentini Sess. 24. de Reformatione*. Sevilla, 1581.]
232. Navarro De restitutione un tomo [Azpilcueta, Martin de. Martini ab Azpilcueta, *Commentaria aliqvot...de detractione, fama, & eius restitutione*. Venice, 1594.]
233. Juan Gutierres y sus obras onse tomos [Gutiérrez, Juan.]
234. Balasco en tres tomos el uno De jure infiteitico otro De partitionibus otro De consultationes [Vaz, Alvaro. *Tractatus de Iure Emphyteutico*. Cremona, 1591; Lisboa, 1611, 1612.]

   [———. *Praxis partitionum et collationum inter haeredes, secundum jus Regium Lusitani*. Coimbra, 1605.]

   [———. *Consultationum ac rerum iudicatarum in regno Lusitaniæ*. Lisbon, 1593.]

---

54 Giovanni Battista Ferreti, wrote *Consiliorum, siue Responsorum* (Venice, 1572). The title of Giulio Ferreti, however, is closer to the notarial record.

55 This was a corrected version of *Tractatus de ordine judiciorum* (*vulgo speculum aureum, et lumen advocatorum*) (Naples, 1525). See Coing, *Handbuch*, vol. 2, bk.1: 397.

235. Aiora De partitionibus [Ayerve de Ayora, Antonio. *De bonorum partitionibus tractatum*. Madrid, 1596.]
236. Reglas de Graciano un tomo [Graciano.]
237. Bernardo Días in regulis un tomo [Diaz de Lugo, Juan Bernardo. *Regule cum suis ampliationibus et falletijs quingente numero*. Burgos; 1528, Lyon, 1554, 1564.]
238. Peguera De laudemis un tomo [Peguera, Luis de. *Illustrationes feudales et emphyteuticales ad constitutionem Item ne super laudemio*.]
239. Decisiones de Ludovico Peguera un tomo [Peguera, Luis de. *Decisiones aureae… ex variis S. Regii Consilii Cathaloniae*. Barcelona, 1605.][56]
240. Peregrino de citatione reali un tomo [Pellegrini?] (189 & 327)
241. Parladorio dos cuerpos [Yánez Paladorio, José.] (vid.201)
242. Speculum testamentorum un tomo [Spino y Cáceres, Diego. Speculum testamentorum. Salamanca, 1587.]
243. Questiones de Flores un tomo [Flores Diez de Mena, Blas. *Recentiorum practicarum quæstionum iuris canonici, et civilis ad praxim utriusque fore spectantium*. Medina del Campo, 1603.]
244. Templum omvuum judicum
245. Humada In prime et secunda parte un tomo [Humada Mudarra, Bartolomé de. *Scholivm, sev brevis interpretatio, ad glossam (in primam et secvndam Partitarvm partem)*. Madrid, 1588.]
246. Gomez de León In desitionibus un tomo
247. Antonio Amalis desisiones un tomo [Amatis, Antonio].
248. Castillo de usufructu un tomo [Castillo de Sotomayor, Juan del. *Ususfructus singularis et utilis tractatus*.](vid.46 & 281)[57]
249. Obras de Ceballos quatro cuerpos [Ceballos, Jerónimo de].
250. Dos cuerpos de Peralta [Peralta, Antonio de].
251. Palacio Rubio de regri aragono un tomo [López de Palacios Rubios, Juan.]
252. Tractatus del concilio general un cuerpo
253. Fuero Jusgo un cuerpo un tom[…] [Fuero Juzgo.]
254. Esforsia de constitutione otro tomo
255. Ludouicus Lopez de contractibus un tomo
256. Tractatus de elemosina un tomo
257. Barbosa de solutio matrimonio [Barbosa, Pedro. *Commentariorum ad interpretationem tituli. ff. soluto matrimonio*. 2 vols in 1. Madrid, 1595; Frankfurt, 1606, 1625; Venecia, 1609.]
258. Desiciones de Cavalcano tres tomos [Cavalcano, Borgnino. *Decisiones fori Fiuizanensis*.] (vid.198)

---

56 Also Venice, 1608; Frankfurt, 1609, 1614, 1629, Barcelona, 1611; Turin, 1613.

57 Issued as vol. 1 of *Quotidianarum controuersiarum* (Madrid, 1603; 1634; Darmbstadii, 1613.)

259. Decisiones Pra de Montane un tomo
260. Desiciones de Matheo de Aflictis un [D'Afflito, Matteo. *Decisiones*] (vid.177)
261. Adiciones aure a Matheo de Aflictis un [Ursilli, Cesare. *Aureae iurium additiones, annotationes, & quaedam aduertentiae…ad decisiones sacri Consilij D. Matthaei de Afflicto*. Venecia, 1582.]
262. Quatro cuerpos de la nueva recopilación con lo añadido los dos pequeños.

[*Recopilación de las leyes destos reynos*. Alcalá de Henares, 1567, 1569, 1581, 1592, 1598; Granada, 1625. *Quaderno de lo que se añadio al libro de la nueva Recopilación*. Alcalá de Henares, 1581.][58]

263. Desiciones genue un tomo [Genova?]
264. Gaspar Rodríguez De annis Reditibus un tomo [Rodriguez, Gaspar. *Tractatus de annuis et menstruis reditibus*. Medina del Campo, 1604; Lyon, 1605, 1622.]
265. Desiciones de Pedro Sardo un tomo [Surdus, Ioannes Petrus. *Decisiones sacri Mantuanis Senatus*.] (vid.42 & 412)
266. Desiciones de Francisco Marco dos tomos [Marc, François. *Decisiones aureae in sacro Delphinatus Senatu*. 2 vols. Lyon, 1584.]
267. Acevedo siete tomos. [Azevedo, Alfonso de.] (vid.289)
268. Opera de Antonii de Padilla un tomo [Padilla Meneses, Antonio de.]
269. Menchaca dos tomos viejos [Vásquez de Menchaca, Fernando.]
270. Decisiones trivisanni un tomo
271. Ricardo De usufructu un tomo [Ricciardus, Petrus. *Commentaria in subtiles ac illustres materias de usufructu, de usucapionibus*. Venice, 1599.]
272. Angelo Mateasio un tomo
273. Menchaca en tres tomos duplicados [Vásquez de Menchaca, Fernando.]
274. Alciato dos tomos viejos [Alciati, Andrea.] (vid.314)
275. Repeticiones de Segura un tomo [Segura, Diego de. *Repetitiones decem in diuersis materiis*. Salamanca, 1520, 1547.]
276. Dos tomos del índice del Derecho Civil
277. Juan García dos tomos. Uno De novilitate otro De exponsis [García de Saavedra, Juan. *De hispanorum nobilitate et exemption tractatus*. Alcalá de Henares, 1597.] [———. *De expensis et meliorationibus liber unus*. Madrid, 1578, 1622.]
278. Lambertino De vira patronati un tomo
279. Navarro obras quatro tomos [Azpilcueta, Martín de.]
280. Molina De hispanorum primogeneis un tomo [Molina Morales, Luis de. *Tractatus de hispanorum primogenitorum origine et natura, libri quatuor*. Madrid, 1573; Lyon, 1588, 1613; Cologne, 1588, 1601.]

---

58 Also Alcalá, 1592, 1599; Madrid, 1610, 1619, 1620.

281. Lasarte De alcavalas un tomo [Lasarte Molina, Ignacio de. *Tractatus de alcavala seu decima venditionis et permutationis*. Madrid, 1589, 1599.] (vid.288)
282. Vertasola De clausulis un tomo
283. Gironda Gavelis un tomo [Gironda, García de. *Tractatus de gabellis, Regibus Hispaniae debitis omnibus*. Madrid, 1594.]
284. Coste Opera tres tomos [Costa, Manuel de. *Opera Omnia*. Tinghi,1576–84; Salamanca, 1584.]
285. Decisiones de Gama un tomo [Gama, Antonio da. *Decisiones supremi senatus regni Lusitaniæ*] (vid.149 & 175)
286. Decisiones de Franquis un tomo [Franchis, Vicentius de. *Neapolitanæ decissiones Sacri Regii Consilii Neapolitani*. Venecia, 1580.][59]
287. Araclatus clausulari un tomo
288. Adiciones a Lasarte un tomo (vid.281)
289. Concilia acevedi un tomo [Azevedo, Alfonso de. *Consilia*. Valladolid, 1607.] (vid.267)
290. Don Juan del Castillo Controversiarum un tomo [Castillo de Sotomayor, Juan del. *Controversiarum iuris quotidianarum*.] (vid.46 & 248)
291. Plasa De delictis un tomo de tablillas [Plaza Moraga, Pedro. *Epitome delictorum causarumque criminalium ex iure pontificio, regio et cæsareo liber I*. Venecia, 1573.]
292. Villalpando In repeticione legis partitis un tomo de tablilla [Villalpando, Diego de. *Solemmis lectura et repetitio legis vigesime secunde tituli primi septime partite*. Legioni, 1552.]
293. Diego Peres en el Ordenamiento Real dos tomos [Perez de Salamanca, Diego de. *Commentaria in quattuour priores libros Ordinationum Regni Castellæ*. Salamanca, 1560, 1574, 1575, 1609.]
294. Par de tenuta un tomo
295. Corbulo De jure enfiteutico un tomo [Corbulus, Aurelius. *Tractatus de causis ex quibus emphyteuta iure suo privatur*. Urbino, 1586.]
296. Gomes Arias de León In legibus tauri un tomo viejo de tablilla [Gómez Arias, Fernando. *Subtilissima necnon valde utilis glosa ad famosissimas, subtiles, necessarias, ac quotidianas Leges Tauri*. Madrid, 1542, 1546; Zaragoza, 1546.]
297. Otalora De novilitate un tomo [Arce Otárola, Juan de. *Summa nobilitatis hispanicæ et immunitatis regiorum tributorum causas, ius, ordinem, iudicium et excusationem breviter complectens*. Granada, 1553.]
298. Ripa Responsa et Repeticiones en un tomo antiguo pequeño [Riva de San Nazarro, Gianfrancesco. *Responsa*.]

59 Turin, 1584, 1610, 1628; Venice, 1588, 1594, 1626; Barcelona, 1597, Cologne 1609; Milan, 1609; Naples, 1618.

299. Ordenansas Reales un tomo viejo [Díaz de Montalvo, Alfonso. *Ordenanzas reales de Castilla o Libro de las leyes*. Huete, 1484.][60]
300. Baynerio intitulum de regulis jurio un tomo con tablilla [Maynier, Guillaume. *Commentaria in titulum Pandectarum De regulis iuris*. Lyon, 1545.]
301. Secunda secundi de Santo Thomas de Cayetano un tomo con tablilla [Cayetano, Tomás de Vio. Comment to *Summa Theologica*.]
302. Tractatus cautelarum un tomo [Tractatus cautelarum].
303. Cateliano Cota Inmmemoriabilis un tomo viejo [Cotta, Cateliano. *Memorialia ex variis IV Doctoribus collecta*. Ticini, 1511; Basel, 1545; Lyon, 1556, Venice, 1572.]
304. Montalvo super foro regali [Díaz de Montalvo, Alfonso. *Forus legum regni Castelle*. Salamanca, 1501, 1549; n.p., 1543.]
305. Jullio Claro un tomo [Claro Alexandrinus, Julio. *Opera omnia sive practica civilis et criminalis*. Lyon, 1575.]
306. Decisiones de Puteo un tomo [Pozzo, Giacomo del. *Decisiones*. Cologne, 1582.]
307. Desiciones pisanarum un tomo.[Rho, Alessandro de. *Decisionum pisanarum*. Milan, 1601.] (vid.84)
308. Genua de escriptus a pribata un tomo
309. Practica de Paz un tomo [Suárez de Paz, Gonzalo. *Praxis ecclesiastica et secularis, I-III*. Salamanca, 1583.][61] (vid. 465)
310. Cassaneo in consuetudinibus burgundie un tomo [Chasseux, Bathelemy de.]
311. Decisiones rote de barsio un tomo
312. Rolandi Abalia concilia un tomo [Della Valle, Rolando. *Consilia*.] (vid.411)
313. Practica de Simio un tomo
314. Concilia alciati un tomo [Alciati, Andrea. *Consilia*] (vid.274)
315. Ascinio De execusionibus un tomo
316. Montealegre In practica un tomo [Montealegre, Juan de. *Praxis civilis*.](vid.78)
317. Monacho *Supra* sextum decretalium un tomo [Monachus Picardus, Iohannes. *Glossa Aurea nobis priori loco super sexto decretalium*. Paris, 1535.]
318. Resolucionibus criminalibus Cavalino un tomo [Caballo, Pietro. *Resolutionum criminalium*.]
319. Marta De jurisdictione un tomo [Marta, Jaime Antonio. *Tractatus de iurisdictiones per inter iudicem ecclesiasticum et sæcularem exercenda*. Maguntiæ, 1609; Antwerp?, 1616.]
320. Pichardo dos tomos In instituta [Pichardo Vinuesa, Antonio. *Commentaria in quator Institutionum justinianearum libros*. Salamanca, 1620; Valladolid, 1630.]
321. Arismino Tepato dos tomos

60 Also Salamanca, 1514, 1541; Burgos, 1528, 1536; Alcalá de Henares, 1565.

61 Also Samanca, 1586; Olmeti, 1592; Medina del Campo, 1593, 1597; Valladolid, 1609, 1613, 1622; Frankfurt, 1613.

322. Tractatus de clausulis a doctores Marta un tomo [Marta, Jaime Antonio].
323. Balsarano De feudis un tomo
324. Concilia de Valdo dos tomos digo tres tomos [Ubaldi, Angelo degli. *Consilia.* Lyon, 1551.] (vid.362)
325. Decisiones de Boerio un tomo [Bohier [Boerius], Nicolas de. *Decisiones supremi senatus Burdegalenses*....Lyon, 1554 (1544?)]
326. Concilia Moraldi un tomo
327. Concilia peregrini un tomo [Pellegrini, Marcantonio. *Consilia.*][62] (vid.189 & 240)
328. Questiones de Ancarrano un tomo [Ancarano, Pietro Giovanni. *Familiarium iuris quaestionum.* Venice, 1569, 1580.]
329. Concilia Francisco Desi un tomo
330. Farinasio siete cuerpos [Farinacci, Próspero.]
331. García De benefiis dos tomos [García de Ercilla, Fortún.]
332. Concilia de Rugeris un tomo [Johannes Rugerius de Mota?]
333. Concilia de Borreli un tomo[Borrel, Camilo. *Consiliorum centuria prima.* Venice, 1598.]
334. Concilia Flamini de Rubis un tomo [Rossi, Flaminio.]
335. Concilia Juaves bote un tomo
336. Concilia Aldrade un tomo
337. Concilia inmoli otro tomo [Tartagni de Imola, Alessandro. *Consiliorum.*][63] (vid. 372)
338. Paricio de resinatione beneficiorum dos tomos [Parisio, Flaminio. *De resignatione beneficiorum.* 2 vols. Venice, 1619.]
339. Paricio De confidentia un tomo. [Parisio, Flaminio. *De confidentia beneficiali prohibita tractatus* Rome, 1595; Venice, 1619.][64]
340. Cocilia caquerani un tomo [Cacherano d'Osasco, Ottaviano. *Consilia siue Responsa.* Venecia, 1595.]
341. Concilia de Francisco de ponte un tomo
342. Gonçalez In regula canselarie un tomo
343. Desiciones magoni un tomo [Magonius, Hieronymus. *Decisiones causarum tam Rotae Florentinae quam Rotae Lucensis.* Venice, 1588, 1597, 1612.]
344. Ojeda De beneficiorui incompativilitate otro tomo [Hojeda de Mendoza, Alfonso. *De beneficiorum incompatibilitate atque compatibilitate tractatus.* Venice, 1579.]
345. Andrés Faquineo Controversias un tomo [Fachinei, Andrea. *Controversiarum iuris libri decem.* Venice, 1602, 1619, 1620.]

62 *Consilia.* 6 vols (Venice, 1608–23).

63 *Consiliorum volumen primum* [*-septimum*] (Venice? 1536).

64 Both treatises were issued under the title of *Tractatus duo : primus De resignatione beneficiorum...alter De Confidentia beneficiali,* 2 vols. in 1 Toulouse, 1616.

346. Questiones regulares de Manuel Rodríguez un tomo [Rodrigues, Manuel. *Quaestiones regulares et canonicae.*][65]
347. Desisiones antonii thesauri un tomo [Tesauro, Antonio. *Nouae decisiones sacri Senatus Pedemontani.* Venice, 1591, 1595. 1599.]
348. Lara De aniversariis et capellaniis un tomo [Pérez de Lara, Alfonso. *De anniuersariis et capellaniis libri duo.* Madrid, 1608.]
349. Alfaro De oficio fiscalis un tomo [Alfaro, Francisco de. *Tractatus de officio fiscalis.* Valladolid, 1606.]
350. Antonio Gómez in legibus tauri [Gómez, Antonio. *Ad Leges Tavri.*] (vid.19)
351. Bisentio de Franquis un tomo [Franchis, Vicentius de.]
352. Escovar De ratiosiniis un tomo [Muñoz de Escobar, Francisco. *De ratiociniis administratorum et aliis variis computationibus tractatus.* Medina del Campo, 1603, Ursellis, 1606; Frankfurt, 1618; Burgos, 1619; Ursellis et Panormi, 1620.]
353. Roxas De susexionibus un tomo [Rojas, Juan de. *Epitome omnium successionum ex testamento & ab intestato iure communi & regio.* Valencia, 1568; Salamanca, 1581.]
354. Comunis opinionis de grafis un tomo
355. Desisionis causarum civilibus. Autore Martino Montes [Monter de Cueva, Martín. *Decisionum Sacrae Regiae Audientiae causarum civilium Regni Aragonum, discursu theorico et practico.* Zaragoza, 1598; Frankfurt, 1600; Marpurgi, 1601.]
356. Mille loquiorum juris gasparis cavalin otro tomo [Cavallini, Gaspare.]
357. Chrónica del Cid otro tomo
358. Alva De conciliis otro tomo
359. Bartulos en dies tomos [Bartolo da Sassoferrato.][66]
360. Paulo de Castro cinco cuerpos digo siete cuerpos [Paolo da Castro. *Opera Omnia*?] (vid.397)
361. Urbarico Sacio dos tomos [Zasius, Ulrich.] (vid.417)
362. Baldo siete tomos y el uno dellos sobre las decretalías [Ubaldi, Baldo degli.][67] [———. *Ad tres priores libros Decretalium commentaria.* Lyon, 1585.] (vid.324)
363. Decisiones farinasii dos tomos [Farinacci, Próspero. *Decisiones Sacræ Romanæ Rotæ.* vol.1, Lyon, 1610; vol. 2, Antwerp, 1620.]
364. Abades nueve tomos [Tedeschi, Niccolò.][68]

65 *Quaestiones regulares et canonicae : in quibus utriusque iuris & privilegiorum regularium & apostolicarum constitutionum nouae & veteres difficultates dispersae.* 3 vols. Salmanca, 1600–02. In 2 vols. Salamanca, 1604–5; Lyon, 1613.
66 Omnia quae extant opera...Tomus primus [-undecimus], 11 vols. 6th ed. (Venice, 1596).
67 Commentaria in corpus iuris civilis. 10 vols. (Venice, 1586). vol 10 index.
68 Possibly *In quinque Decretalium libros commentaria*, 8 vols (Lyon, 1555).

365. Felinos quatro tomos [Felino, Sandeo.][69]
366. Mariano Socino Decretale un tomo [Socini, Mariano, sr. *Commentaria super prima parte libri quinti Decretalium*. Venice, 1533.]
367. Consejos de Juanes de Ancisis un tomo
368. Omrrico Boxia in decretalibus un tomo
369. Desio en dos tomos [Decio, Filippo.] (vid.396)
370. Inmola cinco tomos.[Tartagni de Imola, Alessandro.] (vid.337, 372 & 420)
371. Ripa tres cuerpos [Gian Francesco Riva de San Nazarro?]
372. Consejos de Alexandro tres tomos digo quatro tomos [Tartagni di Imola, Alessandro. *Consiliorum*] (vid.337)
373. Concilia de Romano un tomo
374. Concilia de Antonio de Rubio un tomo [Rossi, Giovanni Antonio. *Consilia*. Venice, 1581.]
375. Concilia Basandini un tomo
376. Concilia de Ruyno tres tomos digo quatro tomos [Ruini, Carlo. *Responsorum, sive consiliorum tomus primus* [*-quartus*]. Venecia, 1571–79.]
377. Consejos de Barbasia quatro tomos [Barbazza, Andrea. *Consiliorum siue Responsorum*. 4 vols. Venice, 1581.]
378. Consejos de Thomás Grammatico un tomo [Grammatico, Tommaso. *Consilia*.] (vid.165)
379. Consejos de Sosino tres tomos [Socini, Mariano.sr. *Consilia*.] (vid.382)
380. Concejos de Cornio cinco cuerpos [Corneo, Pier Filippo. *Consiliorum, siue Responsorum*. 5 vols. Venice, 1582.]
381. Consejos de Tiberio de Ciano quatro cuerpos
382. Concilia de Mariano Socino dos tomos [Socini, Mariano. sr.] (vid.379)
383. Consejos de Jason [Maino, Giasone. *Consiliorum siue responsorum*. 4 vols. Frankfurt, 1609.]
384. Tractatus varie de dote un tomo
385. Portio sobre la instituta un tomo [Porcio, Cristoforo. *Lectura super prima, secunda et tertia institutionum*. Lyon, 1522; Venecia, 1561, 1564.]
386. Concilia de Gerónimo Grato dos tomos [Grati, Girolamo.]
387. Concejos de Angelo Pelusino un tomo [Ubaldi, Angelo degli. *Consilia*. Lyon, 1551.]
388. Consejos Signorolo un cuerpo
389. Consejos de Ancarrano un tomo [Pietro d' Ancarano. *Consilia siue Iuris responsa*. Venice, 1568.] (vid.447)
390. Consejos de Symón Graveta quatro tomos [Cravetta, Aimone. *Consiliorum siue Responsorum*. 5 vols. Venecia, 1575–81.]

---

69 Possibly *Iuris canonicis interpretatis acutissimi*, 4 vols (Venice, 1601).

391. Concejos de Menochio seis tomos [Menochio, Giacomo. *Consiliorvm sive responsorvm*. 6 vols. Venice, 1577–92; Frankfurt, 1593–94.] (vid.403)
392. Consejos Paulo Puvicio tres tomos
393. Consejos de Sosino Junio tres tomos [Socini, Mariano, jr. *Consiliorum*.][70]
394. Index bartolomei casanei antonio
395. Concilia Ledierici Lenis un tomo
396. Consejos de Decio dos tomos [Decio, Filippo. *Consilia siue Responsa*. 2 vols. Lyon, 1556; Venice, 1570.] (vid.369)
397. Consejos de Paulo de Castro primera y segunda parte un tomo viejo tablilla [Paolo di Castro. *Consiliorum*.][71]
398. Consejos de Francisco de Cursio en un cuerpo digo otro viejos [Corti, Franceschino. *Consiliorum*. 2 vols. Venecia, 1571.][72]
399. Consejos de Alberto Gruno en un cuerpo grande viejo [Bruno, Alberto].
400. Tractatus egidi vocii un tomo.
401. Desisiones de Juan Baptista Ballardo un tomo
402. Traquelos en seis tomos [Tiraqueau, André.][73]
403. Menochio cinco tomos uno pequeño.[Menochio, Giacomo.]
404. Consejos de Zephalo dos tomos [Cefalo, Giovanni. *Consiliorum, liber primus* [*-quintus*]. Frankfurt, 1579–82.]
405. Consejos de Purpurato dos tomos [Porporato, Giovanni Francesco. *Consiliorum*. 2 vols. Venice, 1579.]
406. Consejos de Forsiaoda un tomo
407. Consejos de Laurentii silvani otro tomo [Silvano, Lorenzo. *Consiliourm*. Venice, 1574.]
408. Consejos Landechi un tomo [Laderchi, Giovanni Battista, sr. *Consiliorum siue Responsorum*.Ferrara, 1600 (1594)]
409. Consejos de Gerónimo Gabriel un tomo
410. Consejos de Antonio Nata tres tomos [Natta, Marcantonio. *Consiliorum siue Responsorum*. 3 vols. Venice, 1584.]
411. Consejos de Rolando vali quatro tomos [Della Valle, Rolando. *Consiliorum, seu mauis Responsorum* 0.4 vols. Venice, 1592.] (vid.312)
412. Consejos de Surdo quatro tomos nuebos [Surdus, Ioannes Petrus.] (vid.42 & 265)
413. Consejos de Ludovico Romana un tomo [Pontano, Lodovico. *Consilia*. Venice, 1493; Lyon, 1565; Frankfurt, 1577.]
414. Summa atiensis un tomo [Atienza, Bartolomé de. *Repertorio de la nueva Recopilación de las leyes del Reyno*. Alcalá de Henares, 1571, 81, 92, 98.]

70 *Consiliorum sive malis Responsorum*, 5 vols [vol. 5 by Socini sr.] (Venice, 1571–94).

71 *Consiliorvm*, 3 vols (Venice, 1570, 71–81).

72 A *Consiliorum siue Responsorum...liber tertius* was issued in Venice, 1574.

73 *Opera omnia, quae hactenus extant, septem tomis distincta*. 7 vols. (Frankfurt, 1574).

415. Veltaquino quatro cuerpos
416. Desiciones de Benedicto Capre un tomo [Capra, Benedetto.]
417. Consejos de Uberico Satio un tomo [Zasius, Ulrich. *Responsorum iuris siue Consiliorum.*]
418. Sino sobre el Codigo un tomo [Cino da Pistoia. *Lectura super aureo volumine codice*. Lyon, 1518][74]
419. Salicestos en cinco cuerpos [Saliceto, Bartholomeo da.]
420. Alexandros en cinco tomos [Tartagni di Imola, Alessandro.] (vid.372)
421. Jasones en nueve tomos [Maino, Giasone. [*Omnia commentaria in C.I.C.*]. 9 vols. Venice, 1598.]
422. Arquiriacono sobre el decreto un tomo
423. Ludovico Romana quatro tomos [Pontano, Lodovico].
424. Bartolomeo Socino dos tomos [Socini, Bartolomeo].
425. Aretinos quatro tomos [Accolti, Francesco. [*Commentaria in Corpus iuris civilis*]. 4 vols. Lyon, 1553.]
426. Francisco Cursio sobre el código un tomo [Corti, Franceschino. *In vndetriginta Codicis Iustinianei rubricas*. Lyon, 1552.]
427. Consejos de Juan Calderino un tomo [Calderini, Giovanni. *Consilia*. Lyon, 1550.]
428. Lara De alimentis un tomo [Cordoba de Lara, Antonio. *In legem si quis a liberis Dig. De liberis agnoscendis, sive de re alimentariae*, Sevilla, 1575.][75]
429. Sepola De verborum significatione un tomo [Cipolla, Bartolomeo. *In titulum de verborum et rer. significatione doctissima*. Lyon, 1551]
430. Villalobos In antinoma juris un tomo [Villalobos, Juan Bautista. *Antinomiam Juris Regni Hispaniarum et Civilis.*]
431. Comunes opiniones un tomo.
432. Comunis conclusiones Antonio Grabiel un tomo.
433. Concordia olani un tomo [Martínez de Olano, Juan. *Concordia et nova reductio antinomiarum iuris communis ac Regii Hispaniarum*. Burgos, 1575.]
434. Alvarado De coniecturatamente un tomo [Rodriguez Alvarado, Diego. *De coniecturata mente defuncti ad methodum redigenda*. Sevilla, 1578.]
435. Morquecho De divisione bonosp un tomo
436. Juan Rediri De maiestate principis un tomo [Redin, Johannes. *De maiestate principis*. Venice, 1584–86.]
437. Salazar De usuet consuetudine un tomo
438. Avendaño dos tomos uno De exequiendi otro De responsas [Nuñez de Avendaño, Pedro. *De exequendis mandatis Regum Hispaniae, quae rectoribus civitatum dantur*. Madrid, 1543; Salamanca, 1564, 1573.]

---

74 Could also be *Lectura super Codice*, 2 vols. (Frankfurt, 1578).

75 Could also be *Commentarii in quibus res alimentaria* (Venice, 1580).

439. Aviles In capitulus pretorum otro tomo [Avilés, Francisco de. *Noua diligens ac perutilis expositio capitum seu legum praetorum, ac iudicum syndicatus Regni totius Hispaniae*. Medina del Campo, 1557.]
440. Baesa Non meliorandis dos tomos el otro De inope devitore y otro De decima tutoris [Baeza, Gaspar. *Tractatus de inope debitore.*]
441. Lucas de Peña en los libros delivido un tomo [Penne, Luca da.]
442. Angelo de Perusio en quatro tomos [Ubaldi, Angelo degli.][76]
443. Angelo de Obaldo en tres tomos [Ubaldi, Angelo degli.]
444. Felipe Franco un tomo [Franco, Filippo.] (vid.433)
445. Juanes Antonius de Santo Georgio Presposítus super quartum decretalium un tomo [San Giorgio, Giovanni Antonio da. *Io. In tit. secundi Decretalium, de appellationibus, atque in earundem quartum commentaria.* Venecia, 1578?].
446. Giminiano super sextum decretalium un tomo
447. Pedro de Ancarrano sobre el sexto de las decretales un tomo [Pietro d' Ancarano. *Super Sexto Decretalium...Commentaria.*] (vid.389)
448. Juan Platea sobre los tres libros del Código un tomo [Platea, Ioannes de. *Super tribus vltimis libris Codicis*. Lyon, 1528.]
449. Cardenalis Abarela Super crementinas un tomo [Zabarella, Francesco. *Commentaria in Clementinarum volumen*. Lyon, 1543.]
450. Inosensio sobre las decretales un tomo [Inocencio IV. Decretales]
451. Ananias sobre el quinto de las decretales un tomo
452. Felipe Franco sobre el sexto de los decretales un tomo [Franco, Filippo. *In sextum Decretalium volumen commentaria*. Venice, 1579.]
453. Andreas Sesernia un tomo [Isernia, Andrea d.']
454. Juan Sabro sobre el Código un tomo [Faure, Jean. *Loculenta commentaria super Codice*. Lyon, 1537.]
455. Albiarotus super feudis un tomo [Alvarotti, Jacopo. *Super feudis*. Lyon, 1478.]
456. Purpurato en la Real Parte del digesto viejo dos cuerpos [Porporato, Giovanni Francesco. *In primam Digesti veteris parte commentaria*. Turin, 1588.]
457. Floriano sobre el digesto viejo un tomo [Floriano da San Pietro. *In primam, & secundam ff. vet. partem...commentaria*. Bologna, 1576.]
458. Juan Sabro sobre la Instituta un tomo [Faure, Jean. In quatuor Institutionum libros commentaria. Venice, 1582.]
459. Egidio Velamera sobre los decretales tres tomos [Bellamera, Egidio.] (vid.162 & 463)
460. Veiuga In speculo principis otro tomo
461. Alverico en cinco tomos [Alberico da Rosate] (vid.467)

76 [Commentaria in Corpus iuris civilis]. 6 vols. (Venice, 1579–80); vol. 5 was the index.

462. Los tratados de los doctores dieciseis tomos de letra antigua [*Primum* [*-decimum septimum*] *Volumen Tractatuum ex variis iuris interpretibus collectorum*. 18 vols. Lugduni, 1549.][77]
463. Ittem mas seis tomos de Egidio Velamera [Bellamera, Egidio.]
464. Matheo de Aflictis In constitutione neapolitane dos tomos [D'Afflito, Matteo. *Neapolique sanctiones, et constitutiones nouissima praelectio*. Venice, 1562.] (vid.177 & 260–61)
465. Practica de paz un tomo [Suárez de Paz, Gonzalo.] (vid.309)
466. Inmola sobre las Clementinas un tomo [Imola, Johannes de. *Constitutiones Clementis Qvinti qvas Clementinas vocant : diligenter et accvrate recognitae, atqve emendatae, cum epitomis, casibus*. Venecia, 1567.]
467. Alverico seis tomos [Alberico da Rosate.] (vid.461)
468. Juanes Andreas sobre el sexto de los decretales un tomo [Giovanni d'Andrea. *Sextus Decretalium liber*. Venecia, 1514.]
469. Ittem tres cuerpos de informaciones en Derecho escritos de mano [ms]
470. Ittem una información en Derecho impresa
471. Ittem un libro de apuntamientos manuscriptos del Sr. Doctor en trecientos y quatro foxas [ms]
472. Item otro libro que tiene por título Alegacionis Juris manuscripto [ms]
473. Ittem otro libro donde están manuscriptas unas cédulas de su magestad [ms. Reales Cédulas]
474. Ittem un libro de a quartilla intitulado Alegationis Juris
475. Ittem otro pequeño de apuntamientos siendo abogado de la Audiencia de Cevilla manuscripto [ms]
476. Ittem un quaderno de las lecturas antiguas que izo el Sr. Doctor [ms]
477. Ittem otras tres informaciones impresas
478. Ittem otro libro de las decretales que estava suelto grande [Decretales.]

---

77 In the copy of the British Library (ref. L.50/172) vols. 16 and 17 (index) are bound together; this could have been the usual practice with this collection.

APPENDIX 3

The Library of García José Lasso de Vega (1775)

García José Lasso de Vega e Hijar y Mendoza. Inventario de bienes, 29 March 1775. AGN Protocolos Notariales s. XVIII, protocolo notarial 873, escribano Agustín Gerónimo de Portalanza 1770–77, fs. 732–33.

1. Primeram[en]te dos tomos de Jimenez, concordatie Juris [Jiménez, Sebastían. *Concordantiae utriusque juris civilis et cononici.*]
2. Ytem dos tomos de Calepino Pasierasio [Calepino, Ambrogio da.]
3. Ytem quatro tomos de las Leyes de Partidas [Siete Partidas]
4. Ytem diez tomos del Derecho Civil, y canonico [Corpus Iuris Civilis, Corpus Iuris Canonici]
5. Ytem dos tomos de Castef(j?)on.
6. Ytem cinco tomos de Salgado [Salgado de Somoza, .]
7. Ytem seis tomos de Gavelis [Gironda, García de. *Tractatus de gabellis, Regibus Hispaniae debitis omnibus*. Madrid, 1594.]
8. Ytem diez y seis tomos de Menochio [Menochio, Giacomo. *Opera ominia.*]
9. Ytem dos tomos de Faxardo [Antonio Fajardo Acevedo? Diego de Saavedra Fajardo?]
10. Ytem nuebe tomos de Torrecilla [Torrecilla, Martín de.]
11. Ytem 17 tomos del Cardenal de Luca [Luca, Giovanni Battista de, cardinal.]
12. Ytem un Arte de Lengua Francesa.
13. Ytem un tomito en octabo historia de Barclayo [Barclay, John. *La prodigiosa historia de los amantes Argenis y Poliarco.*]
14. Ytem un tomito en octabo obras de Lucano [Lucan. *Opera.*]
15. Ytem un tomito de obras de oracio Paco [Horacius Quintus Flacus?]
16. Ytem un tomito en octabo vieira Historia de los futuro [Vieira, Antonio de, S.I. Historia de lo futuro. 8vo. Madrid, 1726, 1738.]
17. Ytem un tomito en octabo Poemata Triumbirorura,
18. Ytem quatro tomitos en octabo compendio annual
19. Ytem un tomito en octabo ordenanzas Reales [Ordenanzas Reales de Castilla. 1484.]
20. Ytem un tomito en octabo tablas cronologicas
21. Ytem un tomito en octabo historia eclesiastica
22. Ytem cinco tomos en cuarto de exequias Rs.
23. Ytem un tomito en cuatro Discurso Historico Juridico
24. Ytem un tomo vida del Padre orozco [*Vida del venerables padre Fr. Alonso de Orozco*. Madrid, n.d.]

 | DOI 10.1163/9789004305175_013

25. Ytem un tomo Memoria genial
26. Ytem un tomo Arte de Artilleria [Isla, Lázaro de la. *Breve tratado del arte de la artillería*. Madrid, 1595.]
27. Ytem un en quarto Gozofilasio divine dilectionis
28. Ytem un tomos de Matienzo [Matienzo, Juan de.]
29. Ytem un tomo de Alfaro de oficio Fiscalis [Alfaro, Francisco de. *Tractatus de officio fiscalis*. Valladolid, 1606; Madrid, 1639]
30. Ytem dos tomos del ordenam[ien]to Real.
31. Ytem un tomo Politica de Villa Diego [Villadiego Vascuñana, Alonso de. *Instrucción política y práctica judicial*. Madrid: Luis Sánchez, 1612.]
32. Ytem dos tomos Politica de Bobadilla [Castillo de Bobadilla, Jerónimo. *Política para corregidores*. Madrid, 1597; Barcelona; 1616; Amberes; 1750; Madrid, 1775.]
33. Ytem un tomo de Gaciofilacio Regio [Escalona y Agüero, Gaspar. *Gazophilacium Regium Perubicum*. Madrid, 1647, 1755, 1775.]
34. Ytem un tomo compendio de torrecilla [Torrecilla, Martín de.]
35. Ytem un tomo de Berni antigüedad de los titulos [Berní Catalá, José. *Creación, antigüedad y privilegios de los títulos de Castilla*. Valencia, 1769.]
36. Ytem quatro tomos de la Real[e]s [Nueva Recopilación. 1567.]
37. Ytem un tomo de Rojas de incompativilitate [Hermenegildo de Rojas Jordán de Tortosa?[78] Fernando Alfonso del Aguila y Rojas?[79] José Manuel Rojas y Almanza?[80] *Tractatus de incompatibilitate*.]
38. Ytem dos tomos de Cavalo resoliciones Grales
39. Ytem un tomo Paz practica eclesiastica [Suarez de Paz, Gonzalo. *Practica eclesiastica y civil*. Salamanca, 1583; Medina del Campo, 1593; Valladolid, 1609; Frankfurt, 1613, 1661.]
40. Ytem un tomo de valeron de transacion [Valerón, Manuel Román. *Tractatus de transactionibus*. Lyon, 1665; Antwerp, 1681; Cologne, 1757.]
41. Ytem un tomo oliba de foro eclesies.
42. Ytem cinco tomos de Mostajo de causis Piis
43. Ytem quatro tomos recopilacion de Leyes de Yndias [Recopilación de Leyes de Indias. 4 vols. Madrid, 1681, 1744, 1756.]
44. Ytem cinco tomos Politica Yndiana de Solorzano, y jure Yndiarum [Solórzano Pereyra, Juan de. *Política Indiana*. Madrid, 1648; Antwerp, 1703; 2. vols. Madrid, 1736–39.]

---

78 *Tractatus de incompatibilitate regnorum, ac majoratuum*. Lyon, 1669, 1745; Cologne, 1727.

79 *Additae quaestiones de incompatibilitate regnorum et maioratuum ad tractatii D. Hermenegildo de Roxas*. Lisboa, 1688, 1718.

80 *Tractatus unicus de incompatibilitate et repugnantia possidendi plures Maioratus…tomus primus* [*-secundus*]. Madrid, 1755.

[———. *De Indianorum iure*. Madrid, 1629, 1639, (2 vols.) 1653; Rome, 1641; 2 vols. Lyon, 1672]

45. Ytem dos tomos de Molina de Primogenitis [Molina Morales, Luis de. *Tractatus de hispanorum primogenitorum*. Madrid, 1573.][81]
46. Ytem cinco tomos de Gonzalez [Jerónimo González? José González Flórez?]
47. Ytem dos tomos de Dlvene de inmunitate [Del Bene, Tommaso. *De inmunitate et iurisdictione eclesiastica*. Lyon, 1650–75.]
48. Ytem un tomo opera Julii Clario [Claro, Julio.]
49. Ytem dos tomos Dominguez de Ilustratione Curie Philip [Hevia Bolaños, Juan de. *Curia Philipica*.]
50. Ytem un tomo Castro de diseptaciones Juridicas [Castro y Araujo, José. *Miscellanea disceptationum, canonicorum, civillium et criminalium*. Madrid, 1727.]
51. Ytem un tomo de carmona Autos acordados [Arredondo Carmona, Manuel. *Senatus consulta hispaniae illustrata, sive commentaria ad novissimas recopilationis leges*. Valladolid, 1732.]
52. Ytem un tomo Perez de Lara de Aniversaris A capellanis [Pérez de Lara, Alfonso. *De anniversariis et capellaniis*. Madrid, 1608, 1621; Maguncia, 1610. In *Opera omnia*, 3 vols., Lyon, 1733–57]
53. Ytem un tomo Escovar de Rasiosinis [Muñoz de Escobar, Francisco. *De ratiociniis administratorum et aliis variis computationibus tractatus*. Medina del Campo, 1603.][82]
54. Ytem un tomo carlebal de judicis [Carleval, Tomás. *Disputationes iuris variae: De judicis*. Cologne, 1729; Lyon, 1745; Valencia, 1768.]
55. Ytem un tomo Lima Limata [Archdiocese of Lima. *Lima limata conciliis, constitutionibus synodalibus, et aliis monumentis*. Rome, 1673.]
56. Ytem un tomo de las sinodales de este Arzobispado [Archdiocese of Lima. Synods.]
57. Ytem un Quaderno ordenanzas de consulado [Tribunal del Consulado of Lima. Ordinances.]
58. Ytem un tomo Practica de Adm.cn. de Rentas Rs. pr. Juan Pipa [Ripia, Juan de la. *Practica de la administración y cobranza de rentas reales*. Madrid, 1676, 1715, 1723, 1736; Barcelona, 1694.]
59. Ytem un tomo examen de la verdad por salcedo [González de Salcedo, Pedro. *Examen de la verdad en respuesta a los tratados de los derechos de la Reyna christianissima sobre varios estados de la monarquía de España*. n.p., (c.1666).]

---

81 Also Lyon, 1588; Cologne, 1588. More.

82 Also Ursellis, 1606; Frankfurt, 1618; Burgos, 1619; Ursellis et Panormi, 1620; Noriembergae, 1682; Lyon, 1733, 1737.

60. Ytem un tomo Suarez de jure adherendi [Suárez de Figueroa, José. *De iure adherendi alterius appellatione*. Madrid, 1666.]
61. Ytem dos tomos calderon del sano consejo [Calderón de la Barca, Fernando. *Del sano consejo y eficaz auxilio con que todo vasallo, para ser leal, debe servir a su Rey*. 3pts. in 2 vols. Madrid, 1715.]
62. Ytem un tomito Solorzano de Parricidiis [Solórzano Pereyra, Juan de. *De Parricidii Crimine disputatio*. Salmanca, 1605.]
63. Ytem un tomito sinodales de Guamanga [Diocese of Huamanga, synods.]
64. Ytem un tomo m[...]inoezo sbre la instituta
65. Ytem un tomito el Scielo en el Parnaso.
66. Ytem un tomo de Montenegro Ytinerario de Parrochos [Peña Montenegro, Alfonso de. *Itinerario para párrocos de indios*. Madrid, 1668.][83]
67. Ytem un tomo reglas y constituciones de la Merced [Order of Mercy]
68. Ytem un tomo tapia de Privielgiis
69. Ytem un tomo Hiranso de protestaciones [Iranzo, Juan Jerónimo. *De protestatione et pro haerede gestione tractatus*. Valencia, 1650; Rome, 1673.][84]
70. Ytem un tomo concha de oficio annones [Santiago Concha, Pablo de. *De officio praefecti militaris annonae. Del oficio de proveedor general de las reales armadas del Mar del Sur y presidio del Callao*. Madrid, 1704.]
71. Ytem un tomito Losae de Jure universitatum [Lassaeu, Niccolò. *Tractatus de iure universitatum*. Lyon, 1627.]
72. Ytem veinte tomos de Barbosa
73. Ytem once tomos de Pignateli con Pascucis
74. Ytem dos tomos de Lagunes de fructibus [Lagunez, Matías. Tratatus de fructibus pars prima [-secunda]. Madrid, 1686.][85]
75. Ytem cinco tomos Cobarrubias con Faria
76. Ytem dos tomos de Fraso [Frasso, Pedro. *De Regio Patronatu*. 2 vols. Madrid, 1677–79.]
77. Ytem dos tomos de Montalva [Juan Pérez de Montalbán.]
78. Ytem tres tomos Antonio Gomez, con Ayllon [Ayllón Lainez, Juan de. *Illustrationes sive additiones ad varias resolutiones Antonii Gomez*. Antwerp, 1718]
79. Ytem dos tomos de Antunez [Antunez Portugal, Domingo. *Tractatus de donationibus jurium et bonorum regiae coronae tomus primus* [*-secundus*]. Lyon, 1699, 1726, 1757?]
80. Ytem tomo castro alegaciones, y dicisiones [Pereira de Castro, Gabriel. *Decisiones novissimae supremi senatus Portugalliae*. Lisbon, 1621, 1626.]

---

83 Antwerp, 1678, 1726, 1737, 1754; Madrid, 1771.

84 Also issued as *Praxis protestationum*, Valencia, 1667.

85 Also Venice, 1701; Lyon, 1702, 1727; Geneva 1727, 1757.

81. Ytem quatro tomos Cortiada [Cortiada, Miguel de. *Decisiones cancellarii et sacri regnii senatus Cathaloniae*. 4 vols. Barcelona, 1661–89; Lyon, 1677, 1699, 1714.]
82. Ytem siete tomos Graciano Diseptaciones [Gratianus, Stephanus. *Diceptacionum forensium iudicorum*. Rome, 1609–25; Cologne, 1622; Lyon, 1673; Venetus, 1699; Venice, 1743.]
83. Ytem un tomo Matheo de Regimine Valentie [Mateu y Sanz, Llorens. *Tractatus de regimine urbis ac Regni Valantiae*. Valencia, 1654, 1656.]
84. Ytem diez tomos Gutierrez [Gutierrez, Juan de.]
85. Ytem dos tomos Villarroel gov.no. eclesiastico [Villarroel, Gaspar de.*Gobierno eclesiástico pacífico*. 2 vols. Madrid, 1656–67.]
86. Ytem un tomo cantera Questiones criminales [Cantera, Diego de la. *Quaestiones criminales*. Salamanca, 1589; Frankfurt, 1715.]
87. Ytem un tomo Abreu de vacantes [Alvarez de Abreu, Antonio José. *Discuso jurídico-histórico sobre que las vacantes…de las Iglesias de Indias pertenecen a la Corona de Castilla y León*. Madrid, 1726, 1769.]
88. Ytem un tomo Salcedo de contrabando
89. Ytem un tomo Gama de Lecciones
90. Ytem un tomo Salcedo sobre la recopilacion [González de Salcedo, Pedro de. *Colectánea y comentarios a las leyes españolas*. Madrid, 1643.]
91. Ytem un tomo Memorial ajustrado a las pruebas de la canonicazn de sto.Toribio
92. Ytem un tomo en quarto siguenza declausuliis [Siguenza, Pedro de. *Tratado de clausulas instrumentales*. Madrid, 1627.][86]
93. Ytem un tomo practica de Maranta [Maranta, Roberto. *Tractatus de ordine judiciorum,* Lyon, 1554.][87]
94. Ytem un tomo flores Deciciones [Flórez Díaz de Mena, Blas. *Decisiones in supremo lusitaniae Senatu*. Valladolid, 1599; Lisbon, 1601; Antwerp, 1622.]
95. Ytem un tomo de Cepola de servitutibus [Cipolla, Bartolomeo. *Tractatus de servitutibus*. Cologne, 1616; Lyon, 1688; Lausanne, 1737.]
96. Ytem un tomo Leon Pinelo pro Academia Limensi [León Pinelo, Diego de. *Hypomnema apologeticum pro Regali Academia Limensi*. 1643.]
97. Ytem un tomito Mercado de contractibus [Mercado, Tomás de. *Tratos y contratos de mercaderes y tratantes*. Salamanca, 1569; Sevilla, 1571, 1587.]
98. Ytem un tomito Decis de regulis iuris [Decio, Philippo. *In tit. ff. De regulis iuris*. 8vo. Lyon, 1534.][88]
99. Ytem un tomito Melchor clingio super institutam

86 Also Madrid, 1646, 1663, 1673, 1705, 1754, 1767.

87 Also Lyon, 1573, 1584, 1593; Venice, 1605; Cologne, 1614.

88 Also in 8vo. Lyon, 1556, 1568, 1570, 1578, 1588, 1591, 1610.

100. Ytem un tomito Genmia concilyacion de Leyes [Genua de Passeribus, Nicolás. *Conciliationes cunctarum legum quae sibi contrariantur in toto corpore Iuris Civilis*. Venice, 1615.]
101. Ytem un tomo en quarto Hurtado de Justicia jure [Hurtado, Gaspar de. *Tratactus de iustitia et iure*. Madrid, 1637.]
102. Ytem un tomito vocabularium juris [Vocabularium Iuris.]
103. Ytem un tomito leyes penales
104. Ytem un tomito Leandro de residencia
105. Ytem un tomito Acosta de procuranda indiorum salute [Acosta, José de. *De procuranda indorum salute*. Salamanca, 1588; Cologne, 1596; Lyon, 1670.]
106. Ytem un tomito en cuarto confirmaciones Reales [León Pinelo, Antonio de. *Tratado de las confirmaciones reales*. Madrid, 1630.]
107. Ytem un tomito en cuatro Rodrigz. De Privilegis clericorum [Rodrigues, Manuel.]
108. Ytem un tomo consultas de paz [Salon de Paz, Marcos. *Consiliorum*. Medina del Campo, 1576.]
109. Ytem un tomo Merlo defensa legali [Merlo de la Fuente, José. *Alegaciones*?]
110. Ytem un tomo Medina de Maleficis
111. Ytem un tomo en quarto Andres valencia super Decretales
112. Ytem un tomo Repertorium Ynquisitorum
113. Ytem un tomo Gira de regimine Reguliarum
114. Ytem un tomo Ripia de testamentis
115. Ytem un tomo confirmaciones Reales [Antonio de León Pinelo? Vid. 106]
116. Ytem un tomo Mauro de fidejusoribus [Mauro, Pirro. *Tratatus de fidemissoribus*. Venice, 1620; Frankfurt, 1631; Norimbergae, 1640.]
117. Ytem un tomo Arte de Figueredo [Tomás Rubio, Diego de. *Arte y vocabulario del a lengua quichua general de los indios del Peru*. With additions by Juan de Figueredo. Lima, 1754.]
118. Ytem un tomito selectas de ciceron [Cicero. Epístolas? Oraciones? Selectas.]
119. Ytem un tomito Matheo desecione bonorum [Buratti, Mateo. *Decisiones*. Lyon, 1650, 1660.]
120. Ytem quatro tomos Molina de Justicia e Jure [Molina, Luis de. *De iustitia et iure*.]
121. Ytem un tomo de Ceballos comunes contra comunes [Ceballos, Jerónimo de. *Speculum practicarum et variarum quaestionum communium contra communes*.]
122. Ytem un tomo Ceballos opera [Ceballos, Jerónimo de.]
123. Ytem un tomo Guasino defentione Reorun [Guazzini, Sebastiano. *Tractatus ad defensam Inquisitorum carceratorum, reorum, et condemnatorum*. Lyon, 1672.]
124. Ytem dos tomos valencuela [Juan Bautista Valenzuela Velásquez?]
125. Ytem un tomo Bocabularium de Antonio Nebrija [Nebrija, Antonio de.]
126. Ytem un tomo de Gomez Bauro [Gómez, Antonio de. *Variarum resolutionum iuris civilis communis et regii*. Salamanca, 1552.]

127. Ytem once tomos Diana resoluciones con la suma [Diana, Antonio. *Summa Diana.*]
[———. *Resolutionum moralium.*]
128. Ytem un tomo Lupo de Ylegitimis [Lupo, Juan Bautista. *Commentarii de illegitimis et de natalibus restitutis liberis.* Venice, 1611.]
129. Ytem un tomo Feliciano relaciones canonicas [Vega, Feliciano de. *Recolecciones canonicas sobre el segundo libro de las Decretales.*]
130. Ytem un tomo Flores de Mena varias Questiones [Flores Diez de Mena, Blas. *Practicarum quæstionum iuris canonici, et civilis ad praxim utriusque fore spectantium.* Medina del Campo, 1603.]
131. Ytem un tomo Herrera practica criminal [Fernández de Herrera Villarroel, Jerónimo. *Practica criminal.* Madrid, 1672, 1719, 1724, 1733, 1756.]
132. Ytem un tomo Salcedo practica criminal [López Salcedo, Ignacio. *Practica criminalis canonica.* Madrid, 1565.]
133. Ytem dos tomos vela desertaciones
134. Ytem un tomo crespi de valdaura [Crespi de Valldaura, Cristóbal.]
135. Ytem olea desesione jurium [Olea, Alfonso de. *Tractatus de cessione iurium et actionum.* Valladolid, 1652.][89]
136. Ytem un tomo en quarto Barbosa de Judiciis [Barbosa, Pedro. *Commentarii ad intrepretationem tituli ff. De iudiciis.* Lisbon, 1613; Lyon, 1622; Frankfurt, 1650.]
137. Ytem quatro tomos Historia del Ynga [Inca Garcilaso de la Vega?]
138. Ytem un tomo origen de Yndios añadido
139. Ytem un tomo Barbosa de etate [?]
140. Ytem un tomo Narbona sobre la recopilacion [Narbona, Alfonso. *Commentaria in tertiam partem novæ recopilationis legum Hispaniæ pars prima.*Toledo, 1623.]
141. Ytem un tomo Barbosa de Matrimonis [Barbosa, Pedro de. *Commentaria ad interpretationem tituli ff. Soluto matrimonio.* 2 vols. Madrid, 1594–95.]
142. Ytem tres tomos de Iurba Decisioes Civiles [Mario Giurba?]
143. Ytem Manual de Prelados
144. Ytem un tomo tesoro lengua castellana
145. Ytem un tomo origen del orn de Santiago
146. Ytem un tomo Noguerol Alegaciones Juris [Díaz de Ribadeneira Noguerol, Pedro. *Allegationum iuris.* Madrid, 1641.]
147. Ytem nuebe tomos Ricio [Riccio, Giovanni Luigi.]
148. Ytem un tomo Libros eloquentes [*Varios eloquentes libros reunidos en uno.* Valencia, 1700.][90]

89 Geneva, 1665, 1681, 1683, 1723; Lyon, 1669, 1673, 1683, 1689, 1702, 1720, 1723, 1735, 1740; Madrid, 1682; Venice, 1735, 1752.

90 Valencia, 1711, 1714; Madrid, 1726, 1729; 1755.

149. Ytem dos tomos de Paz historia de las misas[?]
150. Ytem un tomo Gradus a Parnasum [*Gradus ad parnasum.*]
151. Ytem un tomo concilis tridentino
152. Ytem un tomo obras de graciano [Gratian.]
153. Ytem dos tomos defensorio Politico Legal pr. Dn. Luis Fernz de Cordoba [Fernández de Córdoba, Luis.]
154. Ytem un tomo compendio Historial de la Roja
155. Ytem dos tomitos del nuevo Heroe de la Fama
156. Ytem un tomo exequias de Dn. Phelipe Quinto
157. Ytem un tomo el dia de Lima
158. Ytem un tomo el theatro de los Dioses
159. Ytem un tomo exequias de Don Juan V.
160. Ytem un tomo exequias del señor Casteñeda
161. Ytem un tomo Legenda Aurea Santorum
162. Ytem un tomo Poema Heroico Hispano latino
163. Ytem un tomo Florilegio Medicinal [Esteyneffer, Juan de. *Florilegio medicinal.* Madrid, n.d.]
164. Ytem un tomo selva militar y Politica [Rebolledo, Bernardo, count of. *Selva militar y política.* Cologne, 1652; Antwerp, 1661; Copenhagen, 1661.]
165. Ytem un tomo advertencia para reyes y Principes
166. Ytem un tomito Enquiridion instituciones imperiales
167. Ytem un tomito tituli juris
168. Ytem un tomo de Dn. Franco.Candamo obras Poeticas [Bances Candamo, Francisco Antonio de. *Obras lyricas*. Madrid, n.d.]
169. Ytem un tomo del theatro critico [Feijoo Montenegro, Benito Jerónimo. *Theatro crítico*?]
170. Ytem un tomo exequias de Dn. Luis I.

APPENDIX 4

Procurators of Indians in the Real Audiencia of Lima, 1552–1789

Year	Name	Advocate	Plaintiffs	Sources
1552	Francisco López		Francisco Velasco (La Gasca entourage)(1552) Cacique Iliacuxiguaman (1552)	AGN, Derecho Indígena, leg.1, c.1 (1552)
1552–60	Francisco de la Torre	Lic. López	Juan Bendrel (Merchant of Panama) (1552) Domingo de Dextre (1554) Yanaconas of Hernando Pizarro (1560) Indian *Principal* of Canta (1562)	"Autos seguidos en grado de apelación, nulidad y agravio por el capitán Juan Bendrel, vecino de la ciudad de Panamá…," AGN, Real Audiencia, causas civiles, leg. 3, c.13 (1552) "Expediente sobre la causa judicial que siguen Dr. Fco. de la Torre en nombre de los yanaconas del Marques Don. Fco. Pizarro y Don Gonzalo Taulichusco, sobre la propiedad de unas tierras y solares" (1560), BNP ms. a 16, fs.145–48
1559–60	Juan de Bilbao		Cacique Mayentopa (1559) Royal Treasury (1560)	AGN, Derecho Indígena, leg. 31, c. 614 (1559–60).BNP ms. a 183 (1560)
1560	Juan de Arrondolaza		Pedro Portocarrero (landowner in Cusco) (1552) Order of Mercy (Cusco) (1559) Gonzalo Taulichusco (cacique of Lima) (1560) Antonio Vaca de Castro (1572)	AGN, Derecho Indígena, leg.1, c.1 (1552)

 | DOI 10.1163/9789004305175_014

Year	Name	Advocate	Plaintiffs	Sources
1560–66	Francisco de Somorrostro		Indians of Chupachos (1561) Indians & Cacique of Manchay (1562) Cacique of Pomarca (Cajamarca) (1566)	AGN, Derecho Indígena, leg. 1, c. 4 (1561); leg.31, c.615 (1562); leg. 1, c.7 (1566)
1571	Alonso Moreno	Lic. López	Indians and encomendero of Trujillo (1571)	"Expediente sobre la causa seguida entre Alonso Moreno, en nombre de Diego de Mora encomendero del valle de Trujillo y sus indios, contra el Lic. Salido de Ortega, por censos," (1571), BNP ms. a 453, 73fs.
1571–80	Alonso de Lucio		Cabildo of Lima (1565–81) Indians of Chicha (1568) Beatriz de Isásaga (Trujillo) (1571) Luisa Merino, widow of Lic. Salido de Ortega (Trujillo) (1571) Pablo Curas, Cacique of Ichocchonta (1574) Indians of Vegueta (1576) Caciques of Ica, Arica & Tarapacá (1580)	"Expediente sobre la causa seguida entre Alonso Moreno, en nombre de Diego de Mora encomendero del valle de Trujillo y sus indios, contra el Lic. Salido de Ortega, por censos, " (1571), BNP ms. a 453, 73fs "Autos seguidos por Alonso de Luzio, en nombre de Beatriz de Isásaga, vecina de la ciudad de Trujillo…contra Luis Rodríguez quien reclamaba sus salarios por los servicios prestados a doña Beatriz," AGN, Real Audiencia, causas civiles, leg.11, c.59 (1571) AGN, Derecho Indígena, leg.2, c.10 (1568); y AGN, Derecho Indígena, leg.3, c.19 (1574)
1574	Juan Sánchez de Aguirre		Cacique of Tique (1574)	
1585	Francisco Falcón (1521–87)		Indians of Laraos and Mangos (1585)	"Carta de pago de los doscientos pesos que se dieron a los indios Mangos y Laraos para el repartimiento de los pobres," Los Reyes 18 January 1587, BNP ms. a 261

Year	Name	Advocate	Plaintiffs	Sources
1594–96	Juan de Santelices	Rynaga	Juana Sánchez (Indian) (1596)	"Expediente de la causa seguida entre Juana Sánchez, india, y Antonio de Bobadilla sobre el engaño en la venta de unas casas," (1596) BNP ms. a 149
1596	Diego Gil de Avís (c.1544–1600)		Indians of Tarma & Canta (1596)	AGN, Derecho Indígena, leg. 39, c. 793 (1596)
1599	Antonio de Neyra	Dr. Sotomayor	University of San Marcos Indians of San Juan de los Reyes (Junín) Bárbola Carachumbi (Chiclayo)(1599)	"Juan Narváez, indio, como marido de Dña. Barbola Charachumbi, contra Juan González Cornejo y Cristóbal de Palacios, sobre las tierras de que fueren despojadas y rematadas en los susodichos." Los Reyes, 4 December 1596—3 August 1599. BNP ms. a 353.
1601	Jacome Carlos	Rynaga	Cacique of Lurinhuanca (1601)	"Don Fernando Marca Poma…," 1599 Feb. 13—1600, Aug. 21, Lilly, Latin American mss. Peru; "Juan Felipe Guacra Paucar y Francisco Guacra Paucar sobre el cacicazgo de segunda persona de Luringuanca," 1600 Nov. 18—1602 Jan. 22, Lilly, Latin American mss. Peru.
1604–07	Francisco de Avendaño	Rynaga	Indianas of Laupaca (1604–07)	"Ejecutoria de las sentencias de vista y revista y autos pronunciados por esta Real Audiencia en la causa que en ella han tratado el cacique é indios de Laupaca reducidos en Huarmey, etc." (1605), BNP ms. b 1289; "Los indios de Yanayco con los del pueblo de Vizcacha sobre las estancias y pastos llamados Ura Puquiy Mullqui Urco" (1604), BNP ms. b 993

Year	Name	Advocate	Plaintiffs	Sources
1606	Andrés de Mena	Medina	Diego Pérez de Arauz (1606)	
1606–27	Simón de Sosa	Medina	Francisco Carlos Melipi (1606) Indians of Catacaos	
1610	Francisco de Montalvo			
1611	Lucas Jiménez	Rynaga	Indians of encomienda of Sebastían Núnez del Prado (Huánuco) (1611)	"Expediente sobre la petición presentada por Lucas Jiménez, Procurador General de Indios de San Pedro de Guacaybamba para que se expida título de posesión de sus tierras usurpadas por el Pbro. Manuel Cabral," (1611) BNP ms. b 1363
1621	Juan Ortiz de Mena	Del Campo	Cacique of Quinti (1621)	"Causas sobre el cacicazgo del Pueblo de Quinti. Huaman Chata, Miguel et al," Lilly Latin American mss. Peru. 1596, Aug. 23–1626, Mar. 13
1625	Francisco de Arriola	Del Campo	Cacique of Quinti (1625)	"Causas sobre el cacicazgo del Pueblo de Quinti. Huaman Chata, Miguel et al," Lilly Latin American mss. Peru. 1596, Aug. 23–1626, Mar. 13
1612–26	Alonso de Torres Romero	Medina (1621) Del Campo (1626)	Juana Carrillo & Juana Chanchulla (Chincha) (1612) Cacique of Quinti (1621) Cacique of Catacaos (1626)	"Causas sobre el cacicazgo del Pueblo de Quinti. Huaman Chata, Miguel et al," Lilly Latin American mss. Peru. 1596, Aug. 23–1626, Mar. 13
1667	Bernardo de Acuña		Francisca Clara, et al. (Lima) (1667)	"Autos seguidos por Isabel Pascuala contra María Magdalena Llatán y Francisca Clara sobre el mejor derecho a una suerte de tierras en el pago de Chorrillos," AGN, Real Audiencia, causas civiles, leg. 194, c. 737, 1668, fjs. 167

Year	Name	Advocate	Plaintiffs	Sources
1672–77	José de Altube	Dr. Rojas	María Ruiz & Inés Cerpa (Huanta) (1672–77)	Testament AGN, PN 1103, Gregorio de Urtazo 1709, fs. 363–64v. "Autos seguidos por Doña María Ruiz y Doña Inés de Cerpa, contra Don Luis de Cárdenas sobre el mejor derecho a la posesión de unas tierras conocidas como Guanchac, sitos en la jurisdicción de Huanta," AGN, Real Audiencia, causas civiles, leg. 196, c.745, 1668, fjs.223
1667–1715	José Mexia de Estela	Dr. RojasLic. MonteroLic. José Urdaide Dr. Tomás de Salazar	Isabel Pascuala (Lima) (1667) Pedro de la Cruz (Valle Miraflores) (1689) Alférez Francisco Camahuana (1689) Agustín de Salcedo (principal) (Piura) (1696) María Solano (minor) (Lambayeque) (1703) Josefa Anquixe (Ica) (1704)	"Autos seguidos por Don Juan y Don Pedro Huamán, indios principales de la ciudad de Ica, contra Doña Josefa de Aquije, sobre nulidad de la venta de una viña," AGN, Real Audiencia, causas civiles, leg.8, c.45, 1704, fs. 64 "Autos seguidos por Fray José de Sazo Ponce de León contra Pedro de la Cruz, indio, sobre la posesión de tierras en el valle de Surquillo," AGN, Real Audiencia, causas civiles, leg. 261, c.987, 1689, fs. 60 "Autos seguidos por Isabel Pascuala contra María Magdalena Llatán y Francisca Clara sobre el mejor derecho a una suerte de tierras en el pago de Chorrillos," AGN, Real Audiencia, causas civiles, leg. 194, c. 737, 1668, fjs. 167
1685–87	Melchor Pacheco	Lic. Pacheco Lic. Ginés de Bustamante	Francisco Llacsahuana (Tarma) (1685–87)	

Year	Name	Advocate	Plaintiffs	Sources
1704–15	Melchor de Carvajal	Dr. Zárate	Juan & Pedro Huamán (Ica) (1704) Felipe Santiago et al. (Canta) (1715)	"Autos seguidos por Don Juan y Don Pedro Huamán, indios principales de la ciudad de Ica, contra Doña Josefa de Aquije, sobre nulidad de la venta de una viña," AGN, Real Audiencia, causas civiles, leg.8, c.45, 1704, fs. 64
1705	Juan Antonio Dávila y Saavedra		José Calderón (Cacique of Tarma) (1705)	
1789	Alberto Chosop			

SOURCES: AGN, BNP, LIBRO DE CABILDOS DE LIMA, LILLY, LOHMANN 1983.

Bibliography

1 Dictionaries, Guides and Bibliographies

Bastús, Joaquin. *Suplemento al diccionario histórico enciclopédico*. Barcelona: Imprenta de Roca, 1833.

Bautz, Friedrich Wilhem, and Traugott Bautz, eds. *Biographisch-Bibliographisches Kirchenlexicon*, 21 vols. to date. Hamm, Herzberg, Nordhausen: Verlag Traugott Bautz, 1975–.

Burkholder, Mark A., and D.S. Chandler. *Biographical Dictionary of Audiencia Ministers in the Americas, 1687–1821*. Westport and London: Greenwood Press, 1982.

Coing, Helmut, ed. *Handbuch der Quellen und Literatur der neueren europäischen Privatrechtsgeschichte*, 2 vols. in 3. Max-Planck-Institut für Europäische Rechtsgeschichte. München: C.H. Beck'sche Verlagsbuchhandlung, 1973–77.

Craddock, Jerry R. *The Legislative Works of Alfonso X, el Sabio: A Critical Bibliography*. Research Bibliographies and Checklists 45. London: Grant and Cutler, 1986.

Decoster, Jean-Jacques, and Brian S. Bauer, eds. *Justicia y Poder: Cuzco, siglos XVI–XVIII, Catálogo del Fondo Corregimiento Archivo Departamental del Cuzco*. Cuzco: Centro Bartolomé de las Casas, 1997.

Dragossa, Norberto. "Bibliografía de Historia del Derecho Indiano" (2011), 283–299; available at http://www.larramendi.es.

Decoster, Jean-Jacques, and José Luis Mendoza, eds. *Ylustre Consejo, Jvsticia y Regimiento: Catálogo del Fondo Cabildo del Cvzco (causas civiles)*. Cusco, Centro Bartolomé de las Casas, 2001.

Fuentes Rueda, Helard. *Corregimiento de Arequipa: Catálogo de Causas Civiles y Penales (1550–1784)*. Arequipa: n.e., 1988.

Gómez Rivas, León. "Don Francisco de Toledo, comendador de Alcántara, virrey del Peru: Guía de Fuentes." Parts 1 and 2. *Anuario de Estudios Americanos* 49, suplement 1 (1992): 123–171; suplement 2 (1992): 95–152.

Heredia Herrera, Antonia, ed. *Catálogo de las consultas del Consejo de Indias*, 11 vols. to date. Madrid, Sevilla: Dirección General de Bellas Artes y Archivos, 1972–1994.

León Pinelo, Antonio de. *Epitome de la Biblioteca Oriental i Occidental, Nautica y Geográfica*. 1629. Edited by Agustín Millares Carlo. Facsimile edition. Washington: Unión Panamericana, 1958.

———. *Epitome de la Biblioteca Oriental i Occidental, Nautica y Geográfica: Añadido y enmendado nuevamente*. Compiled by Andrés González Barcia, 3 vols. Madrid: Francisco Martínez Abad, 1737–38.

Mendiburu, Manuel de. *Diccionario Histórico Biográfico del Perú*, 2nd ed., 11 vols. Lima: Libería e Imprenta Gil, 1932–34.

Milla Batres, Carlos, ed. *Diccionario Histórico y biográfico del Perú: Siglos XV–XX*, 9 vols. Lima: Milla Batres, 1986.

Pérez Martín, Antonio, and Johannes-Michael Scholtz. *Legislación y jurisprudencia en la España del Antiguo Régimen*. Valencia: Universidad de Valencia, Secretariado de Publicaciones, 1978.

Tauro del Pino, Alberto. *Enciclopedia Ilustrada del Perú*, 6 vols. Lima: Peisa, 1988.

Vargas Ugarte, Rubén, S.J. *Historia General del Perú*, vol. 3 *Virreinato (1596–1689)*. Lima: Carlos Milla Batres, 1966.

Vilar y Pascual, Luis. *Diccionario histórico, genealógico y heráldico de las familias ilustres de la monarquía española*, vol. 2. Madrid: Imprenta de F. Sanchez á cargo de A Espinosa, 1839.

Yanguas y Miranda, José. *Adiciones al diccionario de antigüedades de Navarra*. Pamplona: Imprenta de Javier Goyeneche, 1845.

2 Archival Sources

Archivo General de la Nación (Lima, Peru). Real Audiencia (causas civiles) and Derecho Indígena.

Archivo Histórico Nacional (Madrid, Spain). Códices.

Archivo Nacional (Santiago, Chile). Real Audiencia.

Archivo Nacional del Ecuador (Quito). Real Audiencia and Gobierno.

Biblioteca del Banco Central del Ecuador. Archivo Histórico, fondo Jacinto Jijón y Caamaño.

Biblioteca Nacional de Chile. Manuscrito Medina and Archivo de la Biblioteca Barros Arana.

Biblioteca Nacional del Perú. Manuscritos siglos XVI–XVIII.

Lilly Library, Latin American Mss. Peru and Mexico.

3 Primary Sources

Agia, Miguel. *Tres pareceres graves en derecho*. 1604. Edited by Javier de Ayala. Sevilla: Escuela de Estudios Hispano Americanos, 1946.

Aguilar, Joseph de. *Bachiller don Joseph de Aguilar, Bilicia y Godoy, Cura de San Christoval de los Guachos en el obispado de Guamanga….* Madrid: n.e. [1664].

Alamos de Barrientos, *Discurso político al rey Felipe III al comienzo de su reinado*. Edited by Modesto Santos. Clásicos del Pensamiento y de las Ciencias 7. Madrid: Ministerio de Educación y Ciencias; Barcelona: Anthropos, 1990.

Alfaro, Francisco de. *Tractatus de officio fiscalis*. Vallesoleti: Ludouicum Sánchez, 1606.

Altoaguirre y Duvale, Angel de, and Adolfo Bonilla y San Martín. *Indice General de los Papeles del Consejo de Indias*, 4 vols. CDIU 2nd ser. 14–18. Madrid: Tip. de la Revista de Archivos, Bibliotecas y Museos, 1924–25?

Alvarez, José María. *Instituciones de Derecho Real de Castilla y de Indias*, 2 vols. 1827. Mexico: UNAM. 1982.

Alvarez de Velasco, Gabriel. *Tractatus de privilegiis pauperum et miserabilium personarum*, 3 pts in 2 vols. Matriti: Apud Viudam Ildephonsi Matin, 1630–36.

Alvarez y Baena, Joseph Antonio. *Hijos de Madrid Hijos de Madrid, ilustres en santidad, dignidades, armas, ciencias y artes: diccionario histórico por el orden alfabético de sus nombres…*, vol. 4. Madrid: Oficina de Benito Cano, 1791.

Arévalo, Rodrigo de. "Suma de la Política." In *Prosistas castellanos del siglo XV*, edited by Mario Penna. BAE 116. Madrid: Atlas, 1959.

Asso, Ignacio y Miguel de Manuel. *Instituciones del Derecho Civil de Castilla*. 1771, 5th ed. Madrid: Imprenta de Ramón Ruiz, 1792.

Autos Acordados de la Real Audiencia de Quito, 1578–1722. Anuario Histórico Jurídico Ecuatoriano 2. Guayaquil: Corporación de Estudios y Publicaciones, 1971.

Ayala, Manuel de. *Notas a la Recopilación de Indias: Origen e historia ilustrada de las leyes de Indias*, 2 vols. Edited by Juan Manzano Manzano. Madrid: 1945–1946.

Balzo, Bertrando del. "Familias nobles y destacadas del Perú en los informes secretos de un virrey napolitano (1715–1725)." *Revista del Instituto Peruano de Investigaciones Genealógicas* 14 (1965): 107–133.

Baquíjano Carrillo José de. *Relectio extemporanea ad explicationem legis Pamphilio XXXIX D. De Legatis et Fideicomissis III. quam, in publico certamine pro primaria legum cathedra….* Lima: Typographia Orphanotrophi Ioanes de Deo Correa, 1787.

———. *Alegato que en la oposición a la cátedra de prima de leyes de la real Universidad de San Marcos de Lima dixo el Dr. D. Joseph de Baquíjano y Carrillo, catedrático de Vísperas de la misma facultad…el día 29 de abril de 1788*. Lima: n.e., 1788.

Bennet Stevenson, William. "Memorias sobre las campañas de San Martín y Cochrane en el Perú." In Estuardo Núñez, editor. *Relaciones de viajeros*, book 1, vol. 27 of *Colección Documental de la Independencia del Perú*. Lima, 1975.

Berceo, Gonzalo de. *Vida de Santo Domingo de Silos*. Edited by José Antonio Fernández Flórez. Burgos: Universidad de Burgos, 2000.

Bermúdez de Pedraza, Francisco. *Arte legal para estudiar la iurisprudencia*. 1612. Madrid: Civitas, 1992.

Berní Catalá, Joseph. *El abogado instruido en la práctica civil de España*, 2 vols. in 1. Valencia: Cosme Grancha, 1738.

———. *Resumen de los privilegios, gracias, y prerrogativas de los abogados españoles, que escribió el Dr. D. Joseph Berní y Catalá, abogado de los Reales Consejos*. Valencia: Joseph Th. Lucas, 1764.

Bravo de Lagunas y Castilla, Joseph de. *Colección legal de cartas y dictámenes, y otros Papeles en Derecho*. Lima: Oficina de los Huérfanos, 1761.

Cabrera Núnez de Guzmán, Melchor. *Idea de un abogado perfecto, deducido de reglas, y disposiciones del Derecho, comprobada con la autoridad de sus interpretes*. 1679. Madrid: Oficina de Eugenio Rodriguez, 1693.

Calancha, Antonio de la. *Coronica moralizadora del Orden de San Augustin en el Peru, con sucesos egemplares en esta monárquia*, vol. 1. Barcelona: Pedro Lacavalleria, 1638.

Calvete de Estrella, Juan Cristóbal. "Rebelión de Pizarro en el Perú y Vida de Don Pedro Gasca." In *Crónicas del Perú*, vols. 4–5. BAE 167–168. Madrid: Atlas, 1964–65.

Campo y de la Rynaga, Nicolás Matías del. *Memorial historico y ivridico, que refiere: El origen del Oficio de Protector general de los Indios del Perú en su gentilidad, causas y vtilidades de su continuacion por nuestros gloriosos Reyes de Castilla, nuevo lustre y autoridad que le comunicaron, haziendole vno de sus Magistrados con Toga, y motivos qe persuaden su conservacion*. Madrid: Mateo de Espinosa y Arteaga, 1671.

———. *Memorial y discurso informativo… Representa los estudios, y ocupaciones propias en servicio de su Magestad; y las del Doctor Iuan Bautista del Campo y de la Rinaga, su hermano, cura rector de la Villa de Huancabelica… Informa la nobleza, y servicio de sus padres*. Madrid: Mateo de Espinoza y Arteaga, 1668.

Cárdenas, Bernardino de. *Memorial y relacion verdadera para el Rei N.S. y su Real Consejo de las Indias, de cosas del Reino del Perù, mui importantes à su Real Servicio, y conciencia*. Madrid: Francisco Martínez, 1634.

Carvajal y Robles, Rodrigo de. *Fiestas que celebró la ciudad de los Reyes del Perú, al nacimiento del Serenísimo Príncipe don Baltazar Carlos de Austria*. 1632; Sevilla, 1950.

Casas, Bartolomé de las. *Obras Completas*, 14 vols. in 15. Edited by Isacio Pérez Fernández. Madrid: Alianza Editorial. 1988–1998.

Castillo de Bobadilla, Jerónimo. *Política para corregidores y señores de vasallos, en tiempo de paz, y de guerra, y para prelados en lo espiritual, y temporal entre legos, Iuezes de Comission, Regidores, Abogados, y otros oficiales publicos: y de las Juridiciones, Preeminencias, Residencias, y salarios dellos, y de lo tocante a las ordenes, y cavalleros dellas*. Madrid: Luis Sánchez, 1597.

Castro, Juan Francisco. *Discursos críticos sobre las leyes y sus intérpretes*, 3 vols. Madrid: Joaquín Ibarra, 1765–70.

Carrera, Mariano. *Ensayo acerca del estado de la jurisprudencia en Alemania hasta el año de 1824*…. Lima: Imprenta de J. Masías, 1842.

"Cedula en que su Magestad declara por instrumento publico los conocimientos de los pleitos que se hazen por los Procuradores, Abogados, y Agentes, y otras personas…" Real Cédula, Madrid 16 May 1637. Madrid, 1637.

Celso, Hugo de. *Repertorio universal de las leyes destos reynos de Castilla, abreviado y reduzido en forma de repertorio decisivo, por el doctor Hugo de Celso*…. Medina del Campo: Juan Maria de Terranova y Iacome de Liarcari, 1553. Facisimile edition. Madrid: Centro de Estudios Políticos y Constitucionales, BOE, 2000.

Cobo, Bernabé. "Fundación de Lima, escripta por el P. Bernabé Cobo de la Compañía de Jesus. Ano de 1639." In *Obras del P. Bernabé Cobo de la Compañía de Jesús*. Edited by Francisco Mateos, vol. 2. BAE 91–92. Madrid: Atlas, 1956.

Colección de documentos inéditos relativos al descubrimiento, conquista y organización de las posesiones españolas de América y Oceanía. Primera Serie, 42 vols. Madrid: 1864–84.

Concolorcorvo. *El lazarillo de ciegos caminantes desde Buenos Aires hasta Lima, 1773.* 1773. Buenos Aires: Ediciones Argentina Solar, 1942.

Constituciones y Ordenanzas antiguas, añadidas y modernas de la Real Universidad y Estudio General de San Marcos… Lima: Imprenta Real, 1735.

Cueva Ponce de León, Antonio de la. *Concordia de la discordia* (Lima: Imprenta de la Calle de Palacio, 1749).

Dunbar Temple, Ella, ed. *La universidad. Libros de posesiones de cátedras y actos académicos 1789–1826. Grados de bachilleres en cánones y leyes. Grados de Abogados,* tomo 19, vols. 1–3, de Colección Documental de la Independencia del Perú, Lima: Comisión Nacional del Sesquicentenario de la Independencia del Perú, 1972–74.

———. "Los caciques Apoalaya." *Revista del Museo Nacional* 11 (2).

Eguiguren, Luis Antonio. *Diccionario histórico cronológico de la Real y Ponitifica Universidad Mayor de San Marcos y sus colegios: Crónica e Investigación*, 3 vols. Lima: 1940–1951.

Encinas, Diego de. *Cedulario Indiano*, 4 vol. Edited by Alfonso García Gallo. Facsimile edition. 1596. Madrid: Cultura Hispánica, 1945.

Escalante, Antonio de. *Discurso breve a la Magestad Católica del Rey nuestro señor don Felipe quarto el gran rey de las Españas. Dividise en dos partes. En la primera se trata del auxilio y proteccion real a favor de los pobres y miserables personas. Y hazense alguna provisiones para que su Magestad mande por su Real Prematica, y ley se les guarden sus privilegios y favores. En la segunda se trata de la obligacion correspectiva de todos los vasallos al socorro de las necessidades del Patrimonio y Magestad Real…* Madrid: Viuda de Juan Sanchez [1638].

Fernández de Ayala, Manuel. *Práctica, y formulario de la Chancillería de Valladolid. Dirigido a la Real Chancilleria, Presidente y Iuezes della.* Valladolid: Imprenta de Ioseph de Rueda, 1667.

Fernández de Mesa, Tomás M. *Oración que exhorta a estudiar las leyes de España por ellas mismas.* Valencia: Oficina de Thomàs Lucas, 1752.

Fernández de Navarrete, Pedro. *Conservación de monarchias y discursos politicos sobre la gran consulta que el consejo hizo al señor rey don Felipe Tercero….* Madrid: Imprenta Real, 1626.

Frèzier, Amadeo. *Relación del viaje por el Mar del Sur.* Trans. Miguel Guerin. 1716. Caracas: Biblioteca Ayacucho, 1982.

Fuero Juzgo o Libro de los Jueces. Edited by Real Academia de la Historia. Madrid: Ibarra, Impresor de Cámara de S.M., 1815.

Fuero Juzgo. In *Los Códigos Españoles: Concordados y anotados*, vol. 1. Madrid: Imprenta de la Publicidad, 1849.

Fuero Viejo de Castilla. Edited by Ignacio Jordán de Asso and Miguel de Manuel. Madrid: Joachim Ibarra, 1771.

Fueros de Salamanca, Ledesma, Zamora, Alba de Tormes. Edited by Pilar e Inés Carrasco. Granada: Universidad de Granada, 1997.

Gaius. *The Institutes of Gaius and Rules of Ulpian*. 1895. Translation and notes by James Muirhead. Edinburgh: T.&T. Clark.

Gaceta de Lima de 1756–1762: De Superunda a Amat. Edited by José Durand. Lima: Cofide, 1982.

Gehe, Daniele. *Tractatus de Juribus et Privilegiis miserabilium personarum, tam generalibus, quam specialibus, ad forum nostrum Sax. Maxime accomodatus....* Martisburgi: apud Christianum Forbergerum Halæ Saxon Literis Salfeldianis, 1673.

Gracián, Jerónimo. "Diez lamentaciones del miserable estado de los ateístas de nuestros tiempos." In *Beatus vir: carne de hoguera*. Edited by Emilia Navarro de Kelley. Madrid: Editora Nacional, 1977.

Gumán Poma de Ayala, Felipe. *El primer nueva corónica y buen gobierno de Felipe Guaman Poma de Ayala*. Edited by John V. Murra and Rolena Adorno, 3 vols. México: Siglo XXI Editores, 1980.

Hanke, Lewis, ed. *Los virreyes españoles en América durante el gobierno de la Casa de* Austria; *Perú*, 6 vols. BAE 280–286. Madrid: Atlas, 1978–1980.

Heredia Herrera, Antonia, ed. *Catálogo de las consultas del Consejo de Indias*, 11 vols. to date. Madrid-Sevilla: Dirección General de Archivos y Bibliotecas, 1972?–1994.

Hevia, Juan de. *Primera y segunda parte de la Curia Filipica*, 2 vols. in 1. 1603. Madrid: Imprenta de Carlos Sánchez, 1644.

Infante Juan Manuel. "Libro de los Estados." In *Escritores en prosa anteriores al siglo XV*, edited by Pascual de Gayangos. BAE 51. Madrid: M. Rivadeneyra, 1884.

Juan, Jorge, and Antonio de Ulloa. *Noticias secretas de América*, 2 vols. 1826. Bogotá: Editorial Carrera 7a, 1983.

Koneztke, Richard, ed. *Colección de documentos para la historia de la formación social de Hispanoamérica, 1493–1810*, 4 vols. Madrid: Consejo Superior de Investigaciones Científicas, 1953–1958.

La Universidad: Libro XIV de claustros (*1780–1790*). Edited by Carlos Daniel Valcárcel. Book 19, vol. 1. of *Colección Documental de la Independencia del Perú. Lima: Comisión Nacional del Sesquicentenario de la Independencia del Perú*. Lima: n.e., 1971.

León Pinelo, Antonio de. *Tratado de confirmaciones reales*. Madrid: Iuan Gonzalez, 1630.

——— *Recopilación de las Indias*, 3 vols. Edited by Ismael Sánchez Bella. 1635. México: Miguel Angel Porrúa, 1992.

León Pinelo, Diego de. *Mandó que se imprimiesse este escrito el excelent(mo) señor Conde de Alva de Alista, y de Villaflor…la ivnta, que se ha formado…para conferir las materias y puntos de la Carta, que con la Cedula referida se remite, cerca de la enseñanza y buen tratamiento de los Indios*. [Lima?]: n.e., 1660.

———. *Semblanza de la Universidad de San Marcos*. Translated by Luis Antonio Eguiguren. Biblioteca del IV Centenario de la Fundación de la Universidad Nacional Mayor de San Marcos (1551–1951). 1648. Lima: n.e., 1951.

Levillier, Roberto, ed. *Gobernantes del Perú: Cartas y oapeles siglo XVI*, 14 vols. Madrid: Sucesores de Rivadeneyra, 1921–26.

———. *La Audiencia de Lima: Correspondencia de Presidentes y Oidores, 1549–1564*. Foreword by José de la Riva Agüero, vol. 1. Madrid: Juan Puello, 1922.

Leyes de Estilo. In *Los Códigos Españoles: Concordados y anotados*, vol. 1. Madrid: Imprenta de la Publicidad, 1849.

Libro de acuerdos de la Audiencia Real del Nuevo Reino de Granada. Edited by Enrique Ortega Ricaurte, vols. 1 & 2. Bogotá: Archivo Nacional de Colombia, Editorial Antena, 1947.

Libros de Cabildos de Lima. Edited by Bertram T. Lee and Juan Bromley, 23 vols. Lima: Imprenta Torres Aguirre – Sanmartí y Cía., 1935–67.

Llamas y Molina, Sancho. *Comentario crítico-jurídico-literal á las ochenta y tres leyes de Toro*, 2 vols. in 1. Madrid: Imprenta de Repullés, 1827.

López de Caravantes, Francisco. *Noticia general del Perú*. Edited by Guillermo Lohmann Villena and Marie Helmer, 6 vols. BAE 292–293, 295–298. Madrid: Atlas, 1985–89.

López de Echaburu, *Relación de los servicios del doctor Don Nicolás Matías del Campo y de la Rinaga, abogado que ha sido de la Audiencia de Lima*. Madrid? 1666.

Marroquín, Francisco. *Cartas y testamento*. Biblioteca Guatemalteca de Cultura Popular 61. Guatemala: Editorial de José de Pineda Ibarra, 1963.

Matienzo, Juan de. *Gobierno del Perú*. Edited by Guillermo Lohmann Villena. Travaux de l'Institut Français d'Etudes Andines 11. Paris, Lima: Institut Français d'Etudes Andines, Ministère des Affaires Etrangères, 1967.

Memorial al Rey N.S. Don Felipe IIII. A favor de los indios del Piru. Sobre el oficio de Protector General en la ciudad de Lima, corte y cabeza del Piru. Madrid: Imprenta de Tomás Iunti, 1622.

"Memorial para el buen asiento y gobierno del Perú." In *Colección de documentos inéditos para la historia de España*, vol. 94, edited by Marqués de la Fuentesanta del Valle. Madrid: M. Ginesta Hermanos, Impresores de la Real Casa, 1889 (pp. 164–225).

Memorias de los virreyes que han gobernado el Perú durante el tiempo del coloniaje español, vol. 2. Lima: Librería Central de Felipe Bailly, 1859.

Mendieta, Gerónimo de. *Historia eclesiástica indiana*. Edited by Joaquín García Icazbalceta. 1870. Mexico: Editorial Porrúa, 1971.

Mendoza, Antonio de. "Memorial para el buen asiento y gobierno del Perú." In *Corpus Documental de Carlos V*, vol. 3. Edited by Manuel Fernández Alvarez. 1551. Salamanca: Ediciones Universidad de Salamanca, 1977.

Mikhailovitch Golovnin, Vasili. "Lima y Callao en 1818." In Estuardo Núñez, editor. *Relaciones de viajeros*, book 1, vol. 27 of *Colección Documental de la Independencia del Perú*. Lima, 1975.

Migne, J.P. *Patrologia Latina*, vol. 38. Paris, 1844–64.

Montesinos, Fernando de. *Anales del Perú*, 2 vols. Madrid: Imp. de Gabriel L y del Horno, 1906.

Motolinia, Toribio de Benavente. *Memoriales o libro de las cosas de la Nueva España y de los naturales de ella*. Edited by Edmundo O'Gorman. México: Universidad Nacional Autónoma de México, Instituto de Investigaciones Jurídicas, 1971.

Mugaburu, José, and Francisco de Mugaburu. *Chronicle of Colonial Lima: The Diary of Josephe and Francisco Mugaburu, 1640–1697*. Edited by Robert Ryal Miller. Norman: University of Oklahoma Press, 1975.

Mugaburu, José de y Francisco de. *Diario de Lima (1640–1694)*, vol. 2. Edited by Carlos A Romero. Lima: Imprenta C. Vásquez L., 1935.

Novario, Giovanni Maria. *Praxis aurea priviligiorum miserabilium personarum*. Neapoli: Ex typographia & expensis Dominici de Ferdinando Maccarani, 1623.

Novísima Recopilación. Los Códigos Españoles: Concordados y anotados, vols. 7–10. Madrid: Imprenta de la Publicidad, 1849.

Ortiz de la Tabla Ducasse, Javier, María Jesus Mejías Alvarez, and Agueda Rivera Garrido. Eds. *Cartas de cabildos hispanoamericanos: Audiencia de Lima*, vol. 1. Edited by Sevilla: Consejo Superior de Investigaciones Científicas, Escuela Superior de Estudios Hispano Americanos, Instituto Riva Agüero, 1999.

Palafox y Mendoza, Juan de. "Memorial al Rey por don Juan de Palafox y Mendoza, de la naturaleza y virtudes del indio." In *Memoriales civiles y espístolas-tratados*, vol. 2 of *Tratados mejicanos*, edited by Francisco Sánchez Castañer. BAE 218. Madrid: Atlas, 1968.

Paso y Troncoso, Francisco del, ed. *Epistolario de la Nueva España, 1505–1818*, vol. 1 (1505–1529). Mexico: Antigua Librería Robredo de José Porrúa e Hijos, 1939.

Paz, Juan de. *Consultas y resoluciones varias, theologicas, Juridicas, Regulares, y Morales...nueva edición emendada; en la qual se han añadido quince Pareceres, ó cosas Miscelaneas y postumas del Autor sobre diferentes Materias*. 1687. Amberes: Hermanos de Tournes, 1745.

Pérez, Vicente Vizcaino. *Compendio del Derecho Público y Común de España o de las Siete Partidas colocadas en orden natural*, 4 vols. Madrid: Joachim Ibarra, 1784.

Pérez de Herrera, Cristóbal. *Amparo de Pobres*. Edited by Michel Cavillac. Clásicos Castellanos Madrid: Espasa Calpe, 1975.

Porras Barrenechea, Raúl, ed. *Cartas del Peru (1524–43)*, vol. 3 of *Colección de documentos inéditos para la historia del Perú*. Lima: Sociedad de Bibliófilos Peruanos, 1959.

———, ed. *Cedulario del Perú (siglos XVI, XVII y XVIII)*, 3 vols. Lima: Departamento de Relaciones del Ministerio de Relaciones Exteriores del Perú, 1944–1948.

Puga, Vasco de. *Provisiones cedulas instrucciones de su Magestad....* Mexico: Pedro Ocharte, 1543.

Quiroga, Vasco de. *Don Vasco de Quiroga: Documentos.* Edited by Rafael Aguayo Spencer. Mexico: n.p., 1939.

Real Colegio de San Martín, *El parnaso del real colegio de San Martín.* Lima: Imprenta de Joseph de Contreras, 1694.

Recopilación de las Ordenanzas de la Real Audiencia y Chancillería de Su Magestad, que reside en la villa de Valladolid. Valladolid: Francisco Fernández de Córdova, 1566.

Recopilación de leyes de los reynos de Indias, 4 vols. 1681. Facsimile edition. Madrid: Consejo de la Hispanidad, 1943.

Recopilación de leyes de estos reynos... [Nueva Recopilación 1567], 3 vols. 1640. Facsimile edition. Valladolid: Lex Nova, 1982.

Recopilación del Derecho de Mallorca 1622 por los doctores Pere Joan Canet, Antonio Mesquida y Jordi Zaforteza. Edited by Antonio Planas Roselló. Mallorca: Miquel Font Editor, 1996.

[Reynaga y Salazar, Leandro de, et al.]. *Por el marqués de Oropesa, como marido de dona Ana Maria de Loyola Coya. Sobre la satisfacion que pretende le haga su magestad por los derechos y pretensiones en que viene informado por la Real Audiencia de Lima....* [Lima]: n.e., [1616].

Rezabal y Ugarte, *Tratado del real derecho de las medidas anatas seculares y del servicio de lanzas á que están obligados los Títulos de Castilla. Origen de este juzgado en el Reino del Perú.* Madrid: Oficina de Benito Cano, 1792.

Rynaga Salazar, Juan de la. *Memorial discursivo sobre el oficio de protector General de los Indios del Piru.* [Madrid]: n.p., [1626].

Salinas Córdova, Buenaventura de. *Memorial de las historias del nvevo mvndo Pirv.* 1630. Edited by Luis E. Valcárcel and Warren L. Cook. Colección de Clásicos Peruanos 1. Lima: Universidad Nacional Mayor de San Marcos, 1957.

Sánchez-Arcilla Bernal, José, ed. *Las ordenanzas de las audiencias de Indias (1511–1821).* Madrid: Dykinson, 1992.

Siete Partidas, 5 vols. Edited by Robert I. Burns and translated by Samuel Parsons Scott. Philadelphia, 2001.

Solano, Francisco de, ed. *Normas y leyes de la ciudad hispanoamericana*, 2 vols., vol. 1 (1492–1600), vol. 2 (1601–1821). Madrid: Consejo Superior de Investigaciones Científicas, Centro de Estudios Históricos, 1996.

Solórzano Pereira, Juan de. *Emblemata Centum Regio Politica.* Madrid: Tipografía Regia, 1779.

———. *De Indianorum Iure (Lib. III: De retentione Indianorum).* Madrid: Consejo Superior de Investigaciones Científicas, 1994.

———. *Política Indiana*, 3 vols. Edited by Francisco Tomás y Valiente and Ana María Barrero. 1647. Madrid: Biblioteca Castro, 1996.

Soto, Domingo de. *Al muy alto y muy poderoso señor elPríncipe de España don Philippe... Deliberación en la causa de los pobres del maestro fray Domingo de Soto cathedrático de theología en Salamanca y prior del Covento de Santistevan de la orden de los predicadores*. Salamanca: Officina de Juan de Junta, 1545.

Suardo, Juan Antonio. *Diario de Lima*. Edited by Rubén Vargas Ugarte. Lima: Imp. C. Vásquez L., 1935.

Suárez de Figueroa, Christoval. *Hechos de don García Hurtado de Mendoza, Quarto Marqués de Cañete*. Madrid: Imprenta Real, 1613.

Suárez, Santiago Gerardo. *Las Reales Audiencias Indianas: Fuentes y Bibliografía*. Caracas: Academia Nacional de la Historia, 1989.

Symcox, Geoffrey, ed. *Italian Reports on America, 1493–1522: Letters, Dispatches and Papal Bulls*. Repertorium Columbianum 10. Turnhout: Brepols, 2001.

Toledo, Francisco de. *Disposiciones gubernativas para el virreinato del Perú*, 2 vols. Edited by Maria Justina Sarabia Viejo. Sevilla: Escuela de Estudios Hispano-Americanos de Sevilla, 1986–89.

Torre Villar, Ernesto de la. *Los pareceres de Juan de Padilla y Diego de León Pinelo, acerca de la enseñanza y buen tratamiento de los indios*. Mexico: Universidad Nacional Autónoma de México, 1979.

Universidad Nacional de San Cristóbal de Huamanga. *Constituciones, 1677*. Ayacucho: Universidad Nacional de San Cristóbal de Huamanga, 1998.

Valcarce Velasco, Manuel Antonio. "Señor. La muy Noble, y leal ciudad de Santiago de Chile, y su Reyno...se aliena y conmueve à recordar à V. Mag que entre las Regias virtudes, la mas preheminente y superior...es el asiduo cuidado de los Estudios, y Universidades...." [Madrid]: n.e, [1724?].

Valle y Cavieses, Juan del. *Obra Completa*, Biblioteca Clásicos del Perú, vol. 5, eds. Martía Leticia Cáceres, Luis Jaime Cisneros and Guillermo Lohmann. Lima: Banco de Crédito del Perú.

Vargas Ugarte, Rubén. *Concilios Limenses (1551–1772)*, vol. 1. Lima: n.p., 1551.

Varias relaciones de los Estados de Flandes, 1631 á 1656, vol. 14 of *colección de Libros españoles. Raros ó curiosos*. Madrid: Imprenta de Miguel Ginesta, 1880.

Velasquez de Avendaño, Luis. *Legum Tavrinarvm a Ferdinando & Ioana Hispanorum regibus...glosa sequitur*. Toledo: Ioan & Petrum Rodriguez, 1588.

Villadiego Vascuñana y Montoya, Alfonso. *Instrucción política y práctica judicial*. 1612. Madrid: Francisco Martínez, 1641.

Villarroel, Gaspar de. *Gobierno Eclesiastico-pacifico, y union de los dos Cuchillos Pontifio, y Regio...*, 2 vols. 1656–7. Madrid: Antonio Marin, 1738.

Vives, Juan Luis. "De subventione pauperum." 1532, vol. 6 of *Opera Omnia...Ludovici Valentini Vives...*, edited by Gregorio Mayans. Valentiæ: Officina Benedicti Monfort, 1783.

Vives y Cebriá, Pedro Nolasco. Trans. *Traducción al castellano de los Usages y demas derechos de Cataluña que no están derogados o no son notoriamente inútiles con indicación del contenido de éstos y de las disposiciones por las que han venido a serlo, ilustrada con notas sacadas del los mas clásicos autores del principado*, 4 vols. in 2. Fac. ed., 2nd ed. 1861–63. Edited by Joan Egea y Fernández. Barcelona: Generalitat de Catalunya, Departament de Justicia, 1989.

Zavala, Miguel. *Protectorado de Indios; o sea, proyecto de ley ofrecido a las consideraciones de los H.H. representantes de la nación en la presente legislatura de 1868, con el fin de mejorar la deprimida condición social del indio, haciendo realizables sus derecho*. Lima: Imprenta de J.M. Masías, 1868.

4 Secondary Sources

Acevedo, Edberto Óscar. "El protector de indios en el Perú: (hacia fines del régimen español)." In *Congreso del Instituto Internacional de Historia del Derecho Indiano. IX. 1990. Madrid. Actas y estudios*, vol. 2. Madrid: Editorial de la Universidad Complutense, 1991.

Acosta Rodríguez, Antonio. *La Casa de Contratación y la navegación entre España y las Indias*. Sevilla: Universidad de Sevilla, 2003.

Alejo Montes, Francisco Javier. *La universidad de Salamanca bajo Felipe II: 1575–1598*. [Burgos]: Junta de Castilla y León, Consejería de Educación y Cultura, 1998.

Altman, Ida. *Emigrants and Society: Extremadura and America in the Sixteenth Century*. Berkeley: University of California Press, 1989.

Amelang, James S. "Barristers and Judges in Early Modern Barcelona: The Rise of a Legal Elite." *The American Historical Review* 89 (5) (1984): 1264–1284.

Amézaga, Jorge. "El conquistador don Diego de Agüero y los mayorazgos de su casa." *Revista del Instituto Peruano de investigaciones Genealógicas* 15 (1970): 165–178.

Arco, Ricardo del. "Una notable institución social: El padre de huérfanos." In *Estudios de Historia Social de España*, vol. 3. Edited by Carmelo Viñas y Mey. Madrid: CSIC, Departameno de Historia Social de España del Instituto "Balmes" de Sociología, 1955.

Arosemena Garland, Geraldo. *El Colegio de Abogados de Lima y sus decanos*. Lima: Ilustre Colegio de Abogados de Lima, 1977.

Arrarte, Eduardo, ed. *La casa solariega de Aliaga*. Lima, G. de Aliaga Acenzo, 2004.

Arrizabalaga, Jon. "Poor Relief in Counter Reformation Castile: An Overview." In *Healthcare and Relief in Counter-Reformation Europe*. Edited by Peter Grell and Andrew Cunningham. London: Routledge, 1999.

Ayala, Francisco. *Ideas políticas de Juan de Solórzano*. Sevilla: Escuela de Estudios Hispanoamericanos, 1946.

Aznar Vallejo, Eduardo. *La integración de las Islas Canarias en la Corona de Castilla (1478–1526): Aspectos administrativos, sociales y económicos*. Colección Viera y Clavijo. Sevilla: Universidad de Sevilla; La Laguna: Universidad de La Laguna [1982].

Baeza Martín, Ascensión Baeza. "Presión e intereses en torno al cargo de protector general de indios del Nuevo Reino de León: el caso de Nicolás de Villalobos, 1714–1734." *Anuario de Estudios Americanos* 67 (1) (2010): 209–237.

Ballesteros, Pío. "Los indios y sus litigios, según la Recopilación de 1680." *Revista de Indias* 4 (1945): 607–633.

Baskes, Jeremy. *Indians, Merchants, and Markets: A Reinterpretation of the Repartimento and Spanish-Indian Economic Relations in Colonial Oaxaca, 1750–1821*. Stanford: Stanford University Press, 2000.

Barrera y Acedo-Rico. *Viejas familias de Alcalá de Henares*. Madrid: Editorial Complutense, 2003.

Barrera y Laos, Felipe. *Vida intelectual de la Colonia (Educación, filosofía y ciencias): Ensayo histórico crítico*. 1909, 3rd ed. Lima: Universidad Nacional de San Marcos, [1964].

Barrientos Grandon, Javier. "El mos italicus en un jurista indiano: Francisco Carrasco del Saz (15?–1625)." *Ivs Fvgit* 2 (1993): 43–61.

———. *"Ius Commune" – "Ius Proprium" en las Indias Occidentales*, vol. 1, *Historia del Derecho Indiano del Descubrimiento a la Codificación*. Collana I Libri di Erice 26. Roma: Il cigno Galileo Galilei, 2000.

———. *La cultura jurídica en el reino de Chile: bibliotecas de ministros de la real audiencia de Santiago (s. XVII–XVIII)*. Santiago: Universidad Diego Portales, 1992.

———. *La cultura jurídica en la Nueva España (sobre la recepción de la tradición jurídica europea en el virreinato)*. Mexico: Universidad Nacional Autónoma de México, 1993.

———. "La creación de la audiencia de Santiago y sus miembros fundadores." *Revista de Estudios Históricos Jurídicos* 25 (2003).

———. "La librería de don José Manuel Messía de la Cerda y Vargas (1695–1760), alcalde del crimen de la real audiencia de Méjico." *Revista Chilena de Historia del Derecho* 17 (1992–93): 57–85.

———. "Librería de don Sebastían Calvo de la Puerta (1717–1767) oidor de la real audiencia de Guatemala." *Revista de Estudios Históricos Jurídicos* (Valparaíso) 22 (1999): 37–73.

Bayle, Constantino. *El protector de Indios*. Sevilla: Escuela de Estudios Hispano-Americanos de la Universidad de Sevilla, 1945.

Baudot, Georges. "Le 'complot' franciscain contre la première audience de Mexico." *Caravelle: Cahiers du Monde Hispanique et Luso Brésilien* 2 (1964): 15–34.

Becker, Marvin B. *Civility and society in western Europe, 1300–1600*. Bloomington: Indiana University Press, c.1988.

Bell, H.E. *An Introduction to the History and Records of the Court of Wards & Liveries*. 953, reprint. Cambridge: Cambridge University Press, 2011.

Bellomo, Manlio. *The Common Legal Past of Europe: 1000–1800*. 1988. Washington: The Catholic University of America Press, 1995.

Beltrán de Heredia, Vicente. *Domingo de Soto: Estudio biográfico documentado* (Madrid, 1961).

Beneyto, Juan. "The Science of Law in the Spain of the Catholic Kings." In *Spain in the Fifteenth Century, 1369–1516: Essays and Extracts by Historians of Spain*. Edited by J.R.L. Highfield. London: Macmillan, 1972.

Benito Rodríguez, José Antonio. *La bula de la Cruzada en Indias*. Madrid: Fundación Universitaria Española, 2002.

Berlanstein, Lenard. *The Barristers of Toulouse in the Eighteenth Century*. Baltimore: Johns Hopkins University Press, 1975.

Bernis Madrazo, Carmen. *El traje y los tipos sociales en el Quijote*. Madrid: Visor, 2001.

Beyersdorff, Margot. *Historia y Drama Ritual en los Andes Bolivianos (siglos XVI–XX)*, 2nd ed. La Paz: Plural, 2003.

Bonnett, Diana. *El Protector de Naturales en la Audiencia de Quito, siglos XVII y XVIII*. Quito: Facultad Latinoamericana de Ciencias Sociales, sede Ecuador, 1992.

Borah, Woodrow. "El status jurídico de los indios en Nueva España." *América Indígena* 45 (2) (1985): 257–276.

———. *Justice by Insurance: The General Indian Court of Colonial Mexico and the Legal Aides of the Half-Real*. Berkeley and Los Angeles: University of California Press, 1983.

———. "Juzgado general de indios del Perú o juzgado particular de indios de el cercado de Lima." *Revista chilena de Historia del Derecho* 6 (1970): 129–142.

Borchart de Moreno, Christiana. *El corregimiento de Otavalo: Territorio, población y producción textil (1535–1808)*. Quito: Centro de Investigaciones de la Univesidad de Otavalo, 2007.

Bowser, Frederick P. *The African Slave in Colonial Peru, 1524–1650*. Stanford: Stanford University Press, 1974.

Bouwsma, William J. "Lawyers and Early Modern Culture." *The American Historial Review* 78 (2) (1973): 303–327.

Brading, D.A. *The First America: The Spanish Monarchy, Creole Patriots, and the Liberal State 1492–1867*. Cambridge: Cambridge University Press, 1991.

———. *Mines and Merchants in Bourbon México, 1763–1810*. Cambridge: Cambridge University Press, 1971.

Bravo Lira, Bernardino. *Derecho común y derecho propio en el Nuevo Mundo*. Santiago: Editorial Jurídica de Chile, 1989.

———. "Símbolos de la función judicial en el Derecho Indiano." Santiago: Editorial Jurídica de Chile, 1989.

Brewer, John, and Roy Porter, eds. *Consumption and the World of Goods*. London: Routledge, 1993.

Brooks, C.W. *Pettyfogers and Vipers of the Commonwealth: The 'Lower Branch' of the Legal Profession in Early Modern England*. Cambridge: Cambridge University Press, 1986.

Bronner, Fred. "Elite Formation in Seventeenth Century Peru." *Boletín de Estudios Latinoamericanos y del Caribe* 24 (1978): 3–26.

Brown Jonathan, and Richard Kagan, "The Duke of Alcalá: His Collection and Its Evolution." *The Art Bulletin* 69 (2) (1987): 231–55.

Brundage, James A. *The Medieval Origins of the Legal Profession; Canonists, Civilians and Courts*. Chicago and London: University of Chicago Press, 2008.

Buckland, William. *A Text-Book of Roman Law from Augustus to Justinian*, 3rd ed. revised by Peter Stein. Cambridge: Cambridge University Press, 1975.

Burkholder, Mark A. "From Creole to Peninsular: The Transformation of the Audiencia of Lima." *Hispanic American Historical Review* 52 (1972): 395–415.

———. *Politics of a Colonial Career: José Baquíjano and the Audiencia of Lima*. Albuquerque: University of New Mexico Press, 1980.

———. *Politics of a Colonial Career: José Baquíjano and the Audiencia of Lima*, 2nd ed. Willimgton, 1990.

Burkholder, Mark A., and D.S. Chandler. *From Impotence to Authority: The Spanish Crown and the American Audiencias, 1687–1808*. Columbia: University of Missouri Press, 1977.

Burns, Katheryn. *Into the Archive: Writing and Power in Colonial Peru*. Durham and London: Duke University Press, 2010.

Bushman, Richard L. *The Refinement of America: Persons, Houses, Cities*. New York: Vintage Books, 1993.

Caenegem, R.C. van. *Judges, Legislator & Professors*. Chapters in European Legal History. Goodhart Lectures 1984–85. 1987. Cambridge: Cambridge University Press, 2002.

Caldcleugh, Alexander. "El Perú en las vísperas de la Jura de la Independencia (1821)." In Estuardo Núñez, editor. *Relaciones de viajeros*, book 1, vol. 27 of *Colección Documental de la Independencia del Perú*. Lima, 1975.

Campbell, Leon G. "A Colonial Establishment: Creole Domination of the Audiencia of Lima during the Late Eighteenth Century." *Hispanic American Historical Review* 52 (1972).

Cañeque, Alejandro. *The King's Living Image: The Culture and Politics of Viceregal Power in Colonial Mexico*. New York and London, 2004.

Carpintero Benítez, Francisco. "Mos italicus' 'mos gallicus' y el humanismo racionalista: Una contribución a la historia de la metodología jurídica." *Ius Commune* 6 (1977): 108–177.

Castañeda, Paulino. "La condición de miserable del indio y sus privilegios." *Anuario de Estudios Americanos* 28 (1971): 245–335.

———. "Hernandez Aparicio, Pilar." *La Inquisición de Lima: 1570–1635*, vol. 1. Madrid: Deimos, 1989–1998.

Chauvet, Fidel de. "Fray Juan de Zumárraga, Protector of the Indians." *The Americas* 5 (1948–49): 283–310.

Chevalier, Maxine. *Lectura y lectores en la España de los siglos XVI y XVII*. Madrid: Turner, 1976.

Cid Cebrian Miguel. *La Justicia Gratuita: Realidad y perspectivas de un Derecho Constitucional*. Pamplona: Aranzadi, 1995.

Cisneros, Luis Jaime, and Pedro Guibovich. "Una biblioteca cuzqueña del siglo XVII." *Histórica* 6 (1982): 141–171.

Clarence Smith, J.A. *Medieval Law Teachers and Writers: Civilian and Canonist*. Collection des Travaus de la Faculté de Droit de l'Université d'Ottawa, Monographies juridiques 9. Ottawa: University of Ottawa Press, 1975.

Cook, Noble David. *Demographic Collapse, Indian Peru, 1520–1620*. Cambridge: Cambridge University Press, 1981.

———. "Population Data for Indian Peru: Sixteenth and Seventeenth Centuries." *Hispanic American Historical Review* 62 (1) (1982).

Coronas González, Santos M. "Alegaciones e Informaciones en Derecho (*porcones*) en la Castilla del Antiguo Régimen." *Anuario de Historia del Derecho Español* 73 (2003): 165–192.

Couturier, Edith. "Una viuda aristocrática en la Nueva España del siglo XVIII: La Condesa de Miaravalle." *Historia Mexicana* 41 (1992): 327–363.

———. "Micaela Angela Carrillo: Widow and Pulque Dealer." In *Struggle and Survival in Colonial America*. Edited by David Sweet and Gary Nash. Berkeley: University of California Press, 1981.

———. "Women in a Noble Family The Mexican Counts of Regla, 1750–1830." In *Latin American Women: Historical Perspectives*. Edited by Asunción Lavrin. Westport: Greenwood Press, 1978.

Crook, John.A. *Law and Life of Rome*. London: Thames and Hudson, 1967.

Cuena Boy, Francisco. "El *Defensor Civitatis* y el Protector de Indios: Breve ilustración en paralelo." *Ivs Fvgit* 7 (1998): 179–195.

———. "El ejemplo de los romanos." *Revista Chilena de Historia del Derecho* 22 (2010), 103–124.

———. "Utilización pragmática del derecho romano en dos memoriales indianos del siglo XVII sobre el protector de indios." *Revista de Estudios Histórico Jurídicos* 20 (Valparaíso) (1998): 107–142.

Cuevas, Mariano. *Historia general de la Iglesia en Mexico*, 6th ed. Edited by Jose Gutierres Casillas, 5 vol. Biblioteca Porrua 104–108. Mexico: Editorial Porrua, 1992.

Cutter, Charles R. *The protector de indios in colonial New Mexico, 1659–1821*. Albuquerque: University of New Mexico Press, 1986.

———. *The Legal Culture of Northern Spain, 1700–1810*. Albuquerque: University of New Mexico Press, 2001.

Decoster, Jean-Jacques. "El rol del Cabildo en la administración colonial." In *Ylustre Consejo, Jvsticia y Regimiento: Catálogo del Fondo Cabildo del Cvzco (causas civiles)*. Edited by Jean-Jacques Decoster and José Luis Mendoza. Cusco: Centro Bartolomé de las Casas, 2001.

Descola, Jean. *La vida cotidiana en el Perú en tiempos de los españoles, 1710–1820*. Buenos Aires, Hachette, 1962.

Dewald, Jonathan, *The European Nobility, 1400–1800*. Cambridge: Cambridge University Press, 1996.

Díaz-Plaja, Fernando. *Historia de España en sus documentos: Siglo XVII*. Madrid: Cátedra, Historia, 1987.

Díaz Rementería, Carlos. *El cacique en el Perú: Estudio histórico-jurídico*. Sevilla: Universidad de Sevilla, 1977.

Díaz-Trechuelo López-Spinola, Lourdes. *La vida universitaria en Indias. Siglos XVI y XVI*. Universidad de Córdoba Monografías 1. Córdoba: Servicio de Publicaciones de la Universidad de Córdoba, 1982.

Dougnac Rodríguez, Antonio. "El humanismo jurídico a través de dos relecciones en la universidad de San Marcos de Lima." *Revista de Estudios Histórico-Jurídicos* 15 (Valparaíso) (1992–93): 179–223.

Donahue-Wallace, Kelly. *Art and Architecture of Viceregal Latin Americal 1521–1821*. Albuquerque: University of New Mexico, 2008.

Durán Montero, María Antonia. *Lima en el siglo XVII: Arquitectura, Urbanismo y Vida Cotidiana*. Sevilla: Diputación Provincial de Sevilla, 1994.

Durand, José. *La transformación social del conquistador*, 2 vols. México: Porrúa y Orbegón, 1953.

Dussel, Enrique. *El espicopado latinoamericano y la liberación de los pobres, 1504–1620*. Mexico: Centro de Reflexión Teológica, 1979.

Duve, Thomas. *Sonderrecht in der Frühen Neuzeit: Studien sum ius singlare und den privilegia miserabilium personarum, senum und indorum in Alter und Neuer Welt*. Frankfurt am Main: Vittorio Klostermann, 2008.

Echeverri, Marcela."Los derechos de indios y esclavos realistas y la transformación política en Popayán, Nueva Granada (1808–1820)." *Revista de Indias* 69 (246) (2009), 45–72.

Eguiguren, Luis Antonio. *Catálogo Histórico del Claustro de la Universidad de San Marcos, 1576–1800*. Lima: Imprenta El Progreso Editorial, 1912.

———. *Diccionario histórico cronológico de la Real y Pontificia Universidad de San Marcos y sus colegios: Crónica e investigación*, 3 vols. Lima, Imprenta Torres Aguirre, 1940–51.

———. *La universidad en el siglo XVI*, book 1 *Narración*, vol. 1 of *Historia de la Universidad*. Lima: Universidad Nacional Mayor de San Marcos, 1951.

———. *El paseo triunfal y el vejámen del graduado* Lima: T. Scheuch, 1949.

Elliot, John H. *The Count-Duke of Olivares: The Statesman in an Age of Decline*. New Haven: Yale University Press, 1986.

Enciso, Luis Miguel. *Barroco e ilustración en las bibliotecas privadas españolas del siglo XVIII*. Madrid: Real Academia de la Historia, 2002.

Escudero Ortiz de Zevallos. "La familia Tagle Bracho en el Perú: Apuntes genealógicos." *Revista del Instituto Peruano de Investigaciones Genealógicas* 20 (1994): 79–93.

Espejo, Juan Luis. *Nobiliario de la Capitanía General de Chile*. Santiago: Editorial Andrés Bello, 1967.

Espinosa Quiroga, Hernán. *La academia de leyes y práctica forense*, Colección de Seminarios e Institutos 4 (Historia del Derecho). Santiago: Jurídica de Chile [1957?].

Esquivel y Navia, Diego de. *Noticias cronológicas de la gran ciudad del Cuzco*. Edited by Feliz Denegri Luna, vol. 2. Lima: Fundación Augusto N. Wiese, 1980.

Estabridis, Ricardo. "El retrato del siglo XVIII en Lima como símbolo de poder." In *El Barroco Peruano*, vol. 2. Edited by Ramón Mujica. Lima, 2003.

Fisher, John. *El Perú borbónico, 1750–1824*. Lima: IEP, 2000.

Flores Arroyo, José Nicolás. "El virrey y la oposición. Una historia política de la admnistración de justicia." In *El virrey Amat y su tiempo*. Edited by Carlos Pardo-Figueroa Thays and Joseph Dager Alva. Lima: Pontificia Universidad Católica del Perú, Instituto Riva Agüero, 2004.

Flores Galindo, Alberto. *La ciudad sumergida: Aristocracia y plebe en Lima, 1760–1830*, 2nd ed. Lima: Horizonte, 1991.

Flores-Zúñiga, Fernando. *Haciendas y pueblos de Lima: Historia del Valle del Rímac*, vol. 1, *Valle de Huatica, La Victoria, Lince y San Isidro*. Lima: Fondo Editorial del Congreso del Perú, 2008.

Friede, Juan, and Benjamin Keen, eds. *Bartolomé de las Casas in History: Toward an Understanding of the Man and His Work*. DeKalb: Northern Illinois University Press, 1971.

Fuentes Rueda, Helard. *Corregimiento de Arequipa: Catálogo de Causas Civiles y Penales (1550–1784)*. Arequipa: n.e., 1988.

Gálvez, Aníbal. *El colegio de abogados de Lima: Historia de su fundación*. Lima: Ilustre Colegio de Abogados, 1915.

Gávez, José. "Lima colonial." In *Lima en el IV Centenario de su fundación: Monografía del Departamento de Lima*. Lima: Editorial Minerva, 1935.

García Añoveros, Jesús María. "La idea, 'status' y función del Indio en Juan de Solórzano y Pereyra." En *De Indiarum Iure (Liber III: De retentione Indiarum)* por Juan de Solórzano. Corpus Hispanorum de Pace, 2da. ser., vol. 1. Madrid: Consejo Superior de Investigaciones Científicas, 1994.

Garnsey, Peter. *Social status and legal privilege in the Roman Empire*. Oxford: The Clarendon Press, 1970.

Garriga, Carlos. "La recusación judicial: del derecho indiano al derecho mexicano." In *La supervivencia del derecho español en Hispanoamérica durante la época independiente*, Cuadernos del Instituto de Investigaciones Jurídicas. México: Universidad Nacional Autónoma de México, Instituto de Estudios Jurídicos, 1998.

Gaudamet, Jean. Review of *Studi vari sulla restitutio in integrum* by Giuliano Cervenca. *Revue Historique de Droit Français et Etranger*, 4th. ser., 43 (1965): 660–663.

Geremek, Bronislaw. *La potence et la pitié: L'Europe et les pauvres du Moyen Age a nos jours*. Trans. Joanna Arnold-Moricet. 1978. Paris: Gallimard, 1987.

———. *Les fils de Caïn: L'image des pauvres et vagabonds dans la litérature europeéne du XV au XVII siècle*. 1980. Paris: Flammarion, 1991.

———. *Poverty: A History*. Trans. Agnieszka Kolakowska. Oxford: Blackwell, 1994.

Gil, Fernando. *Primeras "Doctrinas" del Nuevo Mundo: Estudio histórico-teológico de las obras de fray Juan de Zumárraga (†1548)*. Buenos Aires: Ediciones de la Facultad de Teología de la Universidad Católica Argentina, 1993.

Gimenez López, Enrique. "Caballeros y Letrados. La aportación civilistica a la administración corregimental valenciana durante los reinados de Carlos III y Carlos IV." *Anales de la Universidad de Alicante* 8–9 (1988–90).

Glave, Luis Miguel. *De rosa y espinas: Economía, sociedad y mentalidades andinas, siglo XVII*. Lima, 1998.

Goglin, Jean Louis. *Les misérables dans l'Occident Médieval*. Paris: Editions de Seuil, 1976.

Goldthwaite, Richard A. *Wealth and Demand for Art in Italy, 1300–1600*. Baltimore and London: The Johns Hopkins University Press, 1993.

Gómez de Olea, Javier. "Los marqueses de Santiago de Oropesa." *Revista del Instituto Peruano de Investigaciones Genealógicas* 20 (1994): 129–139.

González Calzada, Manuel. *Las Casas, el Procurador de los Indios*. Mexico: Consejo Editorial del Gobierno del Estado de Tabasco, 1981.

González de San Segundo, Miguel Angel. *Un mestizaje jurídico: El Derecho Indiano de los indígenas (Estudios de Historia del Derecho)*. Madrid: Universidad Complutense de Madrid, Facultad de Derecho, 1995.

González Echenique, Javier. "Los obispos de Indias como funcionarios de la corona." *Revista Chilena de Historia del Derecho* 6 (1970): 143–151.

González Mantilla, Gorki. "La consideración del indio como persona: El Derecho Romano, factor de resistencia en el siglo XVI." In *La tradición clásica en el Perú virreinal*. Edited by Teodoro Hampe. Lima: Universidad Nacional Mayor de San Marcos, Fondo Editorial, 1999.

González Sánchez, Carlos Alberto. "Los libros de los españoles en el virreinato del Perú. Siglos XVI y XVII." *Revista de Indias* 56 (206) (1996): 7–47.

Grendler, Paul F. *The Universities of the Italian Renaissance*. Baltimore: John Hopkins University Press, 2002.

Guzmán Brito, Alejandro. "Mos Italicus y mos Gallicus." *Revista de Derecho de la Universidad Católica de Valparaíso* 2 (1978): 11–40.

———."La vigencia del derecho romano en Indias según el jurista Juan del Corral Calvo de la Torre" *Justicia, sociedad y economía en la América española (siglos XVI, XVII y XVIII)*, VI Congreso del Instituto Internacional de Derecho Indiano. Valladolid: Casa-Museo Colón, 1983.

Hampe Martínez, Teodoro. *Bibliotecas privadas en el mundo colonial: La difusión de libros e ideas en el virreinato del Perú (siglos XVI–XVII)*. Frankfurt: Vervuert, 1996.

———. *Don Pedro de la Gasca, 1493–1567: Su obra política en España y América*. Lima: Pontificia Universidad Católica del Perú, 1989.

———. "Continuidad en el mundo andino: Los indígenas del Perú frente a la legislación colonial (siglo XVI)." *América Indígena* 45 (2) (1985): 369–371.

———. "La división gubernativa, hacendística y judicial en el virreinato del Perú (siglos XVI–XVII)." *Revista de Indias* 48 (182–183): 59–85.

Hanlon, Gregory. *Early Modern Italy, 1550–1800*. London: Macmillan, 2000.

Harth-terré, Emilio. *Cómo eran las casas en Lima del siglo XVI*. Lima: n.e., n.d.

Harth-terré, Emilio, and Alberto Márquez Abanto. "Historia de la casa urbana virreinal en Lima." *Revista del Archivo Nacional del Perú* 26 (1962): 15–21.

Hernández Asensio, Raúl. *La frontera occidental de la Audiencia de Quito: Viajeros y relatos de viajes (1595–1630)*. Lima: Instituto de Estudios Peruanos, 2004.

Herzog, Tamar. *Defining nations: Inmigrants and Citizens in Early Modern Spain and Spanish America*. New Heaven and London: Yale University Press, 2003.

———. "¿Letrado o teólogo? Sobre el oficio de la Justicia a principios del siglo XVIII." In *Fallstudien zur spanischen und portugiesischen Jutiz 15.bis 20. Jahrhundert*. Edited by Johannes Michael Scholz. Rechtsprechung Materielen und Studien Veröffentlichungen des Max Planck Instituts für Europäische Rechtsgeschichte Frankfurt am Main 8. Frankfurt am Main: Vittorio Klostermann, 1994.

———. *Los ministros de la audiencia de Quito (1650–1750)*. Quito: Libri Mundi, 1995.

———. *Upholding Justice: Society, State, and the Penal System in Quito (1650–1750)*. Ann Arbor: The University of Michigan Press, 2004.

Holguín Callo, Oswaldo. "El doctor Diego Salinas (1558–1595): Primeros lances de un limeño ambicioso." *Boletín del Instituto Riva Agüero* 14 (1986–87): 9–63.

Holthöfer, Ernest. "Literaturtypen des *mos italicus* in der europäischen Rechtsliteratur der frühen Neuzeit (16–18 Jahrhundert)." *Ius Commune* 2 (1969): 131–166.

Honores, Renzo. "Litigios indígenas ante la Real Audiencia de Lima; 1522–1598." Licenciate's thesis, Pontificia Universidad Católica del Perú, 1993.

———. 2010 "Colonial Legal Polyphony: Caciques and the Construction of Legal Arguments in the Andes, 1550–1640." Paper presented at the International Seminar on the History of the Atlantic World, 1500–1825, Justice: Europe in America 1500–1830. Harvard University, Cambridge, Massachusetts, August 2–10, 2010.

Honores, Renzo, and Hampe Martínez, Teodoro. "Los abogados de Lima colonial, 1550–1650: (Formación, vinculaciones y carrera profesional)." *Revista del Foro*, no. 2 (2002): 365–386.

Huertas Vallejos, Lorenzo. *Ecología e historia: Probanzas de indios y españoles referentes a las catastróficas lluvias de 1578 en los corregimientos de Trujillo y Saña*. Chiclayo: Centro de Estudios de Estudios Sociales Solidaridad, 1987.

Ibbetson, David, and Andrew Lewis, eds. *The Roman Law Tradition*. Cambridge: Cambridge University Press, 1994.

Jacobson, Stephen. *Catalonia's Advocates: Lawyers, Society, and Politics in Barcelona, 1759–1900*. Chapel Hill: University of North Carolina Press, 2009.

Jaeguer Requejo, Rafael. "Notas para la biografía del jurista peruano don García Francisco Carrillo Alderete." *Revista del Archivo General de la Nación* (Lima) 8 (1985): 237–268.

Jobson, Anthony Robert. *Great libraries*. London: Weidenfel and Nicolson, 1970.

Kagan, Richard L. *Lawsuits and Litigants in Castile, 1500–1700*. Chapell Hill: University of North Carolina Press, 1981.

———. "Lawyers and Litigation in Castile, 1500–1750." In *Lawyers in Early Modern Europe and America*. Edited by Wilfrid Prest. London: Croom Helm London, 1981.

———. *Students and society in early modern Spain*. Baltimore: The Johns Hopkins University Press, 1974.

Kawashima, Yasu. "Jurisdiction of the Colonial Courts over the Indians in Massachusetts, 1689–1763." *New England Quarterly* 42 (1969): 532–550.

Keith, Henry H. "New world Interlopers: The Portuguese in the Spanish West Indies, from the discovery to 1640." *The Americas* 25 (4) (1969), 361–362.

Kelley, Donald. "Civil Science in the Renaissance: the problem of interpretation." In *The Languages of Political Theory in Early-Modern Europe*, Edited by Anthony Pagden. Cambridge, Cambridge University Press, 1987.

———. "Jurisconsultus Perfectus: The Lawyer as Renaissance Man" *Journal of the Warburg and Courtland Institutes* 51 (1998), 84–104.

Kenneth J. Andrien, *Crisis and Decline: The Viceroyalty of Peru in the Seventeenth Century*. Albuquerque, 1985.

King, P.D. *Law and Society in the Visigothic Kingdom*. Cambridge Studies in Medieval Life and Thought 5. Cambridge: Cambridge University Press, 1972.

Kisch, Guido. *Erasmus und die Jurisprudenz seiner zeit: Studien zum humanistischen Rechtsdenken*. Basel: Helbing und Lichtenhahn, 1960.

Koneztke, Richard. "La formaciòn de la nobleza en Indias." *Anuario de Estudios Americanos* 3 (10) (1951), 329–357.

Klein, Herbet S. *African Slavery in Latin America and the Caribbean*. Oxford: Oxford University Press, 1986.

Kross, Jessica. "Mansions, Men, Women and the creation of Multiple Publics in Eighteen-Century British North America." *Journal of Social History* 33 (2) (1999): 305–408.

Lavrin, Asunción, and Edith Couturier. "Dowries and Wills: A View of Women's Socioeconomic Role in Colonial Guadalajara and Puebla, 1640–1790." *Hispanic American Historical Review* 59 (2) (1979): 280–304.

Leonard, Irving A. *Romances of Chivalry in the Spanish Indies with Some Registros of Shipments of Books to the Spanish Colonies*. Berkeley and Los Angeles: University of California Press, 1933.

———. *The Books of the Brave*. Cambridge: Harvard University Press, 1949.

Jolowicz, H.F."Utility and Elegance in Civil Law Studies." *Law Quarterly Review* 65 (1949): 322–336.

Lupher, David A. *Romans in a New World: Classical Models in Sixteenth-Century Spanish America*. Ann Abor: University of Michigan Press, 2003.

Luig, Klaus."The Institutes of National Law in the Seventeenth and Eighteenth Centuries." *Juridical Review* 17 (1972): 193–226.

Lavallé, Bernard. "Presión colonial y reivindicación indígena en Cajamarca (1785–1820), según el archivo del protector de naturales." *Allpanchis 12* (35–36) (Cuzco, 1990): 105–137.

Lavalle, José Antonio de. "Pedro José Bravo de Lagunas y Castilla (Apuntes sobre su vida y obras)." In *Estudios Históricos*. Lima: Librería e Imprenta Gil, 1935.

Lahoz Finestres, José María. *El humanismo jurídico en Europa*. Las Palmas: Universidad de las Palmas de Gran Canaria, 2002.

Lavrin, Asunción, and Edith Couturier. "Dowries and Wills: A View of Women's Socioeconomic Role in Colonial Guadalajara and Puebla, 1640–1790." *Hispanic American Historical Review* 59 (2) (1979): 280–304.

Lira Montt, Luis. "Los Beneméritos de Indias y la gestación de la nobleza en América" *Hidalguía* 268–269. (1998).

"El estatuto de limpieza de sangre en Indias" *Boletín de la Academia Chilena de la Historia* 108–109 (2000).

Lohmann Villena, Guillermo. *Amarilis Indiana: Identificacón y semblanza*. Lima: Fondo Editorial de la Pontificia Universidad Católica del Perú, 1993.

———. "De coches y calesas en Lima en el siglo XVII." *Revista del Archivo General de la Nación* 14 (1996).

———. *El Conde de Lemos: Virrey del Perú*. Madrid: Escuela de Estudios Hispano-Americanos, 1946.

———. *El Corregidor de indios en el Perú bajo los Austrias*. Madrid: Ediciones Cultura Hispánica, 1957.

———. "El corregidor de Lima." *Anuario de Estudios Americanos* 9 (1952): 131–171.

———. "El jurista Francisco Carrasco del Saz." *Anuario Mexicano de Historia del Derecho* 11–12 (1999–2000): 339–359.

———. "El licenciado Francisco Falcón (1521–1587): Vida, escritos y actuación en el Perú de un procurador de indios." *Anuario de Estudios Americanos* 27 (1970): 131–194.

———. "El señorío de los Marqueses de Santiago de Oropesa." *Anuario de Historia del Derecho Español* 19 (1948–49): 347–458.

———. "Informaciones genealógicas de peruanos seguidas ante el Santo Oficio." Parts 1 and 2. *Revista del Instituto Peruano de Investigaciones Genealógicas* 8 (1955), 7–110; 9 (1956), 115–252.

———. "Los libros españoles en Indias." *Arbor* 2 (6) (1944): 221–249.

———. *Los ministros de la Audiencia de Lima en el reinado de los borbones (1700–1821)*. Sevilla: Escuela de Estudios Hispano Americanos de Sevilla, 1974.

———. *Los regidores perpetuos del cabildo de Lima (1535–1821): Crónica y estudio de un grupo de gestión*, 2 vols. V Centenario del Descubrimiento de America 1. Sevilla: Publicaciones de la Exma. Diputación Provincial de Sevilla, 1983.

———. *Un tríptico del Perú Virreinal: El virrey Amat, el marqués de Soto Florido y la Perricholi. El drama de dos palanganas y su circunstancia*. Chapell Hill: University of North Carolina departamento of Romance languages, 1976.

López, Carlos. "El romanismo en la 'Política Indiana'." *Anuario de Estudios Americanos* 6 (1949): 715–754.

López Alonso, Carmen. *La pobreza en la España Medieval: Estudio histórico social*. Madrid: Centro de Publicaciones, Ministerio de Trabajo y Seguridad Social, 1986.

López Beltrán, Clara. "La buena vecindad: Las mujeres de élite en la sociedad colonial del siglo XVII." *Colonial Latin American Review* 5 (1996): 219–236.

Luján, Néstor. *La vida cotidiana en el SIglo de Oro español*, 6th ed. Madrid: Planeta, 1991.

Luque Talaván, Miguel. *Bibliografía Española de Genealogía, Heráldica, Nobiliaria y Derecho Nobiliario en Iberoamérica y Filipinas (1900–1997)*. Madrid: Fundación Histórica Tavera, 1999.

———. *Un Universo de Opiniones: la literatura jurídica Indiana*. Madrid: Consejo Superior de Investigaciones Científicas, 2003.

Madero, Marta. "Façons de croire: Les témoins et le juge dans l'œvre juridique d'Alphonse X le Sage, roi de Castille." *Annales HSS* 1 (1999): 197–218.

Macera, Pablo. *Precios del Perú: XVI–XIX Fuentes*, 3 vols. Lima: Banco Central de Reserva del Perú, n.d.

Mack, Peter. *A History of Renaissance Rhetoric, 1380–1620*. Oxford: Oxford University Press, 2011.

Maffei, Dominico. *Gli inizi dell'humaneismo giuridico*. Milan: A. Giuffré, 1956.

Magariños, Sebastián. "La formación intelectual de don Juan de Solórzano Pereyra." *Revista de Indias* 1 (1940): 89–106.

Málaga Medina, Alejandro. "Los corregimientos de Arequipa, siglo XVI." *Historia* (Universidad Nacional de San Agustín, Arequipa) 1 (1975).

Malagón Barceló, Javier. *Historia menor*. Mexico: Secretaría de Educación Pública, 1976.

———. "The Role of the 'letrado' in the Colonization of America." *The Americas* 18 (1) (1968): 1–17.

Malachowski, Richard, et al *Casa Peruana*. Lima, 2000.

Maravall, José Antonio. *Utopía y reformismo en la España de los Austrias*. Madrid: Siglo veintiuno, 1982.

Mariluz Urquijo, José María. "La biblioteca de un oidor de la real audiencia de Buenos Aires." *Revista del Instituto de Historia del Derecho* (Buenos Aires) 7 (1955–56): 140–146.

Martín, Luis. *La conquista intelectual del Perú: El Colegio Jesuita de San Pablo, 1568–1767*. Barcelona: Editorial Casiopea, 2001.

Martín Hernández, Francisco. *Don Vasco de Quiroga (Protector de Indios)*. Salamanca: Universidad Pontificia de Salamanca, 1993.

Martínez, Jóse Luis. *Pasajeros de Indias*. Madrid: Alianza Editorial, 1983.

Martínez de Arzans y Vela, Nicolás. *Historia de la Villa Imperial de Potosí.* 1705.

Martiré, Eduardo. "Algo más sobre Derecho Indiano (entre el ius commune medieval y la modernidad)." *Anuario de Historia del Derecho Español* 73 (2003): 231–263.

Martz, Linda. *Poverty and Welfare in Habsburg Spain: The Example of Toledo*. Cambridge: Cambridge University Press, 1983.

Mathis, Sophie. "Vicente Mora Chimo, de 'Indio principal' a 'Procurador General de los Indios del Perú': cambio de legitimidad del poder autóctono a principios del siglo XVIII." *Bulletin de l'Institut Français d'Etudes Andines* 37 (1) (2008).

McKendrick, Neil, Brewer John, and J.H. Plumb. *The Birth of Consumer Society: The Commercialization of Eighteenth-Century England.* Bloomington: University of Indiana Press, 1982.

Mclean, Ian. *Interpretation and meaning in the Renaissance: The case of Law*. Cambridge: Cambridge University Press, 1992.

Mesa, José de, and Gisbert, Teresa. *Historia de la pintura cuzqueña*, 2nd ed. Lima: Fundación Augusto N. Wiese, 1982.

Miró-Quesada S. Aurelio. *El primer virrey-poeta en América (Don Juan de Mendoza y Luna, marqués de Montesclaros)*. Madrid: Gredos; Lima: Studium, 1962.

Mirow, M.C. *Latin American Law: A History of Private Law and Institutions in Spanish America*. Austin: University of Texas Press, 2004.

Mollat, Michel. *The Poor in the Middle Ages: An Essay in Social History*. Translated by Arthur Goldhammer. 1978. New Haven: Yale University Press, 1986.

Montiel, Isidoro. *Historia de la Universidad de Sigüenza*, vol. 2. [Zulia?]: Universidad de Zulia, Facultad de Humanidades y Educación, [1963].

Moreno Cebrián, Alfredo. *El Corregidor de Indios y la economía peruana en el siglo XVIII.* Madrid: Consejo Superior de Investigaciones Científicas, 1977.

———. *El virreinato del marqués de Castelfuerte, 1724–1736: El primer intento borbónico por reformar el Perú*. Madrid: Catriel, 2000.

Moreyra Paz Soldán, Manuel. *Oidores y Virreyes*, vol. 2. *Estudios Históricos*. Edited by Grover Antonio Espinosa Ruiz. 1957. Lima: Pontificia Universidad Católica del Perú, Instituto Riva Agüero, 1994.

Mörner, Magnus, "Factors and Stratification in Colonial Spanish America with Special Regard to Elites" *The Hispanic Amercian historical Review* 63 (2) (1983): 335–369.

Morón Orellana, Juan E. *Antonio de León Pinelo*. Lima: Universidad Nacional Mayor de San Marcos, 1993.

Mujica Pinilla, Ramón. *Rosa limensis: Mística, política e iconografía en torno a la patrona de América*. Lima: Fondo de Cultura Económica, 2001.

Muldoon, James. *Popes, Lawyers and Infidels*. Liverpool: Liverpool University Press, 1979.

Muller, Priscilla. "Spanish and Spanish Colonial Jewelry." *Art Institute of Chicago Museum Studies* 25 (2) (2000): 35–51, 104–105.

Muro Orejón, Antonio. "El Real y Supremo Consejo de las Indias." *Anuario de Estudios Americanos* 27 (1970): 195–218.

Nader, Helen. *The Mendoza Family in the Spanish Renaissance, 1350–1550*. New Brunswick: Rutgers University Press, 1979.

Newson, Linda, and Susie Minchin. "Diets, Food Supplies, and the African Slave Trade in Early Seventeenth-Century Spanish America." *The Americas* 63 (4) (2007): 517–550.

Nieto Soria, José Manuel. *Iglesia y Poder real en Castilla: Los Episcopados, 1250–1350*. Madrid: Departamento de Historia Medieval, 1988.

Novoa, Mauricio. "El Indio Americano Derecho Romano en Solórzano." *Boletín del Instituto Riva-Agüero* 26 (1999), 253–72.

———. "La cultura política de una audiencia sitiada: los libros de Manuel de Gorena y Pedro Antonio de Tagle Bracho (1774–1776)." In *Homenaje a José Antonio del Busto Duthurburu*, eds. Margarita Guerra and Rafael Sánchez Concha, vol. 2. Lima: Fondo Editorial Pontificia Universidad Católica del Perú, 2012.

Oliveros, Martha Norma. "Construcción del régimen tutelar del indio." *Revista del Instituto de Historia del Derecho Ricardo Levene* 13 (1967): 105–126.

Olmedo Jiménez, Manuel. *Jerónimo de Loayza, O.P.: Pacificador de españoles y protector de indios*. Los Dominicos y América 7. Granada: Universidad de Granda, 1990.

Ortiz de la Tabla Ducasse, Javier. *Los encomenderos de Quito, 1534–1660: Origen y evolución de una élite colonial*. Madrid: Escuela de Estudios Hispano Americanos – CSIC, 1993.

Osler, Douglas. "The Myth of European Legal History." *Rechtshistorisches Journal* 27 (1997): 393–410.

Ots Capdequí, José María. *El Estado Español en las Indias*, 3rd ed. México: Fondo de Cultura Económica, 1957.

Ovalle, Ana Inés. "La Audientia Episcopalis." *Revista Chilena de Historia del Derecho* 9 (1983): 41–47.

Ortega López, Margarita. "El Consejo Supremo de Aragón y la supervisión de la justicia del reino aragonés durante el siglo XVIII." *Manuscrits* 8 (1990), 139–162.

Padovani, Andrea. "La biblioteca Zauli Naldi: Uno specchio della civilità europea a metà Seicento." In *La Repubblica dei Giuristi: Edizioni giuridiche del '500 della librería Zauli Naldi*. Edited by Anna Rosa Gentili (Faenza, 1994).

Papy, Jan. "Lipsius and His Dogs: Humanist Tradition, Iconography and Rubens's Four Philosophers." *Journal of the Warburg and Courtauld Institutes* 62 (1999): 167–198.

Patrucco, Sandro. *Presencia italiana en la Lima borbónica: 1701–1800*. New York: Hobbel, 2006.

Péligry, Christian. "Les éditeurs Lyonnais et le marché Espagnol aux XVI et XVII siècles." In *Livre et lecture en Espagne et en France sous l'ancien régime*. Colloque de la Casa de Velazquez. Paris: Editions A.D.P.F, 1981.

Pereña, Luciano. "Defensor oficial de la corona." In *De Indiarum Iure* (*Liber III: De retentione Indiarum*) by Juan de Solórzano. Corpus Hispanorum de Pace, 2nd. ser., vol. 1. Madrid: Consejo Superior de Investigaciones Científicas, 1994.

Perloson, Jean-Marc. *Les letrados: Juristes castillians sous Philippe III*. [Poitiers]: n.e., 1980.

———. *Pobreza e a assistancia aos pobres na Peninsula Iberica durante media*. Actas de las primeras jornadas Luso-Españolas de historia medieval (IX–1972), 2 vols. Lisboa, 1973.

Phipps, Elena, Hechy, Johanna and Esteras Marín, Cristina. *The Colonial Andes: Tapestries and Silverwork, 1530–1830*. New Haven and London: Yale University Press, 2004.

Platt, Tristan, Thérése Bouysse-Cassagne and Olivia Harris. *Qaraqara-Charka: Mallku, Inka y Rey en la provincial de Charcas (siglos XV–XVII)*. La Paz: Plural, 2006.

Ponce Lozada, Julio césar. *Las comunicaciones en el Virreynato del Perú: siglos XVI, XVII y XVIII*. N.p, n.e., 2004.

Porras Muñoz, Guillermo, "Diego de Ibarra y la Nueva España." *Estudios de Historia novohispana* 2 (1968).

Premo, Bianca. *Children of the Father King: Yourh, Authority and Legal Minority in colonial Lima*. Chapel Hill, 2005.

Prest, Wilfrid. *The Rise of the Barristers: A Social History of the English Bar 1590–1640*. Oxford: Clarendon Press, 1986.

Puente Brunke, José de la *Encomienda y encomenderos en el Perú: Estudio Social y político de una institución colonial*. Sevilla: Publicación de la Excma. Diputación de Sevilla, 1992.

———. *José Baquíjano y Carrillo*. Lima: Brasa, 1995.

———. "La burocracia en el virreinato del Perú: (Apuntes sobre los siglos XVI y XVII)." *Mercurio Peruano* no. 501 (1991): 49–62.

———. "Los jueces en la vida limeña del siglo XVII." *Derecho y Sociedad* 12 (1997–98): 196–202.

Puente Luna, José Carlos, de la. *Los curacas hechiceros de Jauja: Batallas mágicas y legales en el Perú colonial*, Colección Estudios Andinos 1. Lima: Fondo Editorial Pontificia Universidad Católica del Perú, 2007.

Ramírez, Ramon. *Gil Gonzalez de S. Nicolas, Dominico: el primer defensor de los indios en Chile*. Coleccion Cuarto Centenario Dominico 1. Santiago: Orden Dominicana de Chile, 1986.

Ramírez, Susan. *Provincial Patriarchs: Land tenure and the economics of power in colonial Peru*. Albuquerque: University of New Mexico Press, 1986.

———. "Amores Prohibidos: The Consequences of the Clash of Juridical Norms in Sixteenth Century Peru." *The Americas* 62 (1) (2005): 47–63.

Restrepo Manrique, Daniel. *La iglesia en Trujillo (Perú) bajo el episcopado de Baltasar Jaime Martínez de Compañon (1780–1790)*, 2 vols. Vitoria: Servicio Central de Publicaciones del Gobierno Vasco, 1992.

Rípodas Ardanaz, Daisy. "Bibliotecas privadas de funcionarios de la real audiencia de Charcas." *Memoria del Segundo Congreso Venezolano de Historia* (Caracas: Academia Nacional de la Historia, 1975), vol. 2.

Rishel, Joseph J. Comp. *Revelaciones: Las artes en América Latina, 1492–1820*. México: Fondo de Cultura Económica, Antiguo Colegio de San Ildefonso, 2007.

Riu, Manuel, ed. *Pobreza y asistencia a los pobres en la Cataluña medieval*, 2 vols. *Anuario de Estudios Medievales*, anejo 9–11. Barcelona: Consejo Superior de Investigaciones Científicas, 1980–82.

Rizo-Patrón Boylan, Paul. *Linaje, dote y poder: La nobleza de Lima de 1700 a 1850*. Lima: Fondo Editorial de la Pontificia Universidad Católica del Perú, 2001.

Robinson, O.F. *The Criminal Law of Ancient Rome*. London: Duckworth, 1995.

Rock, Rosalind. "Pido y suplico': Women and the Law in Spanish New Mexico." *New Mexican Historical Review* 65 (1990): 137–144.

Rosas-Siles, Alberto. "La nobleza Titulada del Virreinato del Perú." *Revista del Instituto Peruano de Investigaciones Genealógicas* 21 (1995).

Ruigómez Gómez, Carmen. *Una política indigenista de los Habsburgo: el Protector de Indios en el Perú*. Madrid: Ediciones de Cultura Hispánica, 1988.

Shama, Simon. *The Embarrasment of Riches: An Interpretation of Dutch Culture in the Golden Age*. New York: Vintage Books, 1997.

Salomon, Frank. "Indians women of early Colonial Quito as seen through their Testaments." *The Americas* 44 (1988): 325–341.

San Cristóbal, Antonio. *La casa virreinal limeña de 1570 a 1687*, 2 vols. Lima: Fondo Editorial del Congreso del Perú, 2003.

Sánchez, Luis Alberto. "Don Antonio de León Pinelo: Primer bibliografo americano." *Boletín Bibliográfico, Biblioteca de la Universidad Nacional de San Marcos* 3 (5) (1928): 212–222.

———. *La literatura Peruana: Derrotero para una historial cultural del Perú.* Lima: P.L. Villanueva, 1973.

Sánchez, Susy. "Familia, comercio y poder: Los Tagle y su vinculación con los Torre Velarde (1730–1825)." In *Los comerciantes limeños a fines del siglo XVIII: Capacidad y cohesión de una elite, 1750–1825*. Edited by Cristina Mazzeo de Vivó. Lima: Pontificia Universidad Católica del Perú, 1999.

Sánchez-Concha Barrios, Rafael. "De la miserable condición de los indios en las reducciones." *Revista Teológica Limense* 30 (1996): 95–104.

———. "El Cuerpo de República en el pensamiento político colonial." *Humanitas* 21 (1992): 60–73.

Saravia, Javier Iván. "Los Miserables y el Protector. Evolución de la protectoría de indios en el Virreinato peruano. Siglos XVI–XVIII." Licentiate thesis, Universidad Nacional Mayor de San Marco, 2012.

———. "El fiscal protector de indios en el siglo XVII: Espacios de poder y arbitrismo." *Nueva Crónica* 1 (2013), 1–22.

Schwaller, John Frederick. "The Cathedral Chapter of Mexico in the Sixteenth Century." *Hispanic American Historical Review* 61 (4) (1981): 651–674.

Seed, Patricia. 1988. "Marriage, Promises and the Value of a Woman's Testimony in Colonial Mexico." *Signs* 13 (1988): 252–276.

Silverblatt, Irene. "The Universe Has Turned Inside Out…There is No Justice for Us Here': Andean women under Spanish rule." In *Women and Colonization: Anthropological Perspectives*. Edited by Mona Etienne and Eleonore Leacock. New York: Praeger, 1980.

———. "New Christians and New World Fears in Seventeenth Century-Peru." *Comparative Studies in Society and History* 42 (3) (2000), 524–546.

Sobranes, José. "La administración superior de justicia en la Nueva España." Boletín Mexicano de Derecho Comparado 13 (37) (1980).

Socolow, Susan Migden. *The Women of Colonial Latin America*. Cambridge: Cambridge University Press, 2000.

———. "Marriage, Birth, and Inheritance: The Merchants of Eighteenth Century Buenos Aires." *Hispanic American Historical Review* 60 (1980): 387–406.

———. "Women and Crime: Buenos Aires, 1757–1797." *Journal of Latin American Studies* 12 (1980): 39–54.

Stein, Peter. "Elegance in Law." *Law Quarterly Review* 77 (1961): 242–256.

———. "Judge and Jurist in the Civil Law: A Historical Interpretation." In *The Character and Influence of the Roman Civil Law: Historical Essays*. London: The Hambledon Press, 1988.

———. "Legal Humanism and Legal Science." *Tijdschrift voor Rechtsgeschiedenis* 54 (1986): 297–306.

———. "Medieval Rediscovery of the Roman Civil Law." In *The Civilian Tradition and Scots Law: Aberdeen Quincentenary Essays*. Edited by David Carey Miller and Reinhard

Zimmermann. Schriften zur Europäischen Rechts und Verfassungsgeschichte 20. Berlin: Dunker & Humblot, 1997.

Stern, Steve J. *Peru's Indian Peoples and the Challenge of Spanish Conquest: Huamanga to 1640*, 2nd ed. Madison: University of Wisconsin Press, 1993.

Stone, Lawrence. *The Family, Sex and Marriage in England, 1500–1800*. London: Penguin Books, 1990.

———. "Prosopography." *Daedalus, Journal of the American Academy of Arts and Sciences* 100 (1) (1970), 46–79.

Suñe Blanco, Beatriz. "Evolución de la figura del protctor de indios e la frontera norte de Nueva España." In *Estudios sobre América: Siglos XVI–XX*. Edited by Antonio Gutierrez Escudero and María Luisa Laviana Cuetos. Sevilla: Instituto de Estudios Americanos. 2005.

Symonds, R.W. "English Eighteenth Century Furniture Exports to Spain and Portugal." *The Burlington Magazine for Connoisseurs* 78 (455) (1941).

Swayne y Mendoza, Guillermo. *Mis antepasados (Genealogía de las familias Swayne, Mariátegui, Mendoza y Barreda)*. Lima: Tipografía Peruana, 1951.

Tandeter, Enrique. *Coacción y mercado: La minería de la plata en el Potosí colonial, 1692–1826*. Madrid: Siglo Veintiuno de España Editores.

Tau Anzoátegui, Víctor. "La 'ley se obedece pero no se cumple': En torno a la suplicación de las leyes del derecho indiano." *Anuario Histórico-Jurídico Ecuatoriano* 4 (1980).

———. *¿Qué fue el derecho indiano?* 2nd ed. Buenos Aires: Abeledo-Perrot 1982.

Tierney, Brian. *Medieval Poor Law: A Sketch of Canonical Theory and Its Application in England*. Berkeley and Los Angeles: University of California Press, 1959.

———. "The Decretists and the 'Deserving Poor'." *Comparative Studies in Society and History* 1 (4) (1959): 360–373.

Torre Revello, José. *El libro, la imprenta y el periodismo en América durante la dominación española*. Buenos Aires: Casa Jacobo Peuser, 1940.

Torre Villar, Ernesto de la. *Los pareceres de Juan de Padilla y Diego de León Pinelo acerca de la enseñanza y buen tratamiento de los indios*. Mexico: UNAM, 1979.

Torres Arancibia, Eduardo. *Corte de Virreyes: El entorno del poder en el Perú del siglo XVII*. Lima: Pontificia Universidad Católica del Perú, 2006.

Trazegnies, Ferdinand de. "Los Vásquez de Velasco: Historia genealógica de una noble e ilustre familia española del Perú." *Histórica* 16 (1945): 7–41.

Trazegnies Granda, Fernando de. *Ciriaco de Urtecho: Litigante por amor*, 3rd ed. Lima, 1995.

Valcárcel, Carlos Daniel. *San Marcos: Universidad decana de América*, 2nd ed. Lima: Universidad Nacional Mayor de San Marcos, Fondo Editorial, 2001.

Vallejo García-Hevia, José María. "La asesoría general del juzgado de la renta de correos (1755–1762): Campomanes, precursor de la moderna administración del servicio postal." *Revista de Administración Pública* 146 (1998): 51–83.

Vallone, Giancarlo. *Iurisdictio Domini: Introduzione a Matteo d'Afflito ed alla cultura giuridica meridionales tra Quattro e Cinquecento*. Lecce: Milela, 1985.

Vaughan, Alden. *New England Frontier: Puritans and Indians, 1620–1675*. Boston: Little, Brown, 1965.

Velarde, Héctor. *Arquitectura Peruana*, 3rd ed. Lima: Librería Studium Editores 1978.

Velásquez, Marcel. *Las Máscaras de la representación: El sujeto esclavista y las rutas del racismo en el Perú (1775–1895)*. Lima: Fondo Editorial de la Universidad Nacional Mayor de San Marcos, 2005.

Villarán, Manuel Vicente. *Apuntes sobre la realidad social de los indígenas del Perú ante las leyes de Indias*. Lima: Gráfs P.L. Villanueva, 1964.

Viñas Mey, Carmelo. *Estatuto del obrero indígena en la colonización española*. Madrid: 1929.

———. *Notas sobre la asistencia social en España de los siglos XVI y XVII*. Madrid, 1971.

Wachtel, Nathan. "El cielo cara a cara: Francisco Maldonado de Silva y la Inquisición." In *El hombre y los Andes: Homenaje a Franklin Pease G.Y.*, vol. 2. Edited by Javier Flores Espinoza and Rafael Varón Gerbi. Lima: Fondo Editorial de la Pontificia Universidad Católica del Perú, 2002.

Wagner, Henry Raup, and Helen Rand Parish. *The Life and Writings of Bartolomé de las Casas*. Albuquerque, NM, 1967.

Watson, Alan. *The Evolution of Western Private Law*. Baltimore: The Johns Hopkins University Press, 2000.

———. *The Law of Persons in the Later Roman Republic*. Oxford: Clarendon Press, 1967.

Watson, Ellis. *Aristocracy and the Modern World*. London: Palgrave, 2006.

Wijffels, Alain. *Late Sixteenth-Century Lists of Law Books at Merton College*. Cambridge: LP Publications, 1992.

Wölfel, Dominik Joseph. "La Curia Romana y la corona de España en la defensa de los aborígenes canarios." *Anthropos* 25 (1930): 1011–1083.

Zavala, Silvio. "La 'Utopía' de Tomás Moro en la Nueva España." 1937. In *La utopía mexicana del siglo XVI: Lo bello, lo verdadero y lo bueno*. Edited by Octavio Paz. Mexico: Grupo Azabache, 1992.

Zevallos Quiñones, Jorge. "Los Lisperguer en el Perú" *Revista del Instituto Peruano de Investigaciones Genealógicas* 7 (1954).

Zorraquín Becu, Ricardo. "Hacia una definición del Derecho Indiano." *Revista de Historia del Derecho* (Buenos Aires) 22 (1994): 401–417.

Index

www.ingramcontent.com/pod-product-compliance
Lightning Source LLC
LaVergne TN
LVHW010543300926
849162LV00002B/220